Firebase Essentials

Android Edition

Firebase Essentials – Android Edition

Second Edition

ISBN-13: 978-1979961608

Rev 1.0

Table of Contents

1. Introduction 1
    1.1 Downloading the Code Samples 1
    1.2 Download the eBook 1
    1.3 Feedback 2
    1.4 Errata 2

2. Getting Started with Firebase 3
    2.1 Signing into the Firebase Console 3
    2.2 Creating a New Project 4
    2.3 Firebase Projects 5
    2.4 Firebase Pricing Plans 5
    2.5 Summary 5

3. Firebase User Authentication 7
    3.1 An Overview of Firebase Authentication 7
        3.1.1 FirebaseAuth Instance 8
        3.1.2 AuthUI Instance 8
        3.1.3 FirebaseUser Class 8
        3.1.4 AuthCredential Classes 8
        3.1.5 Authentication Provider Classes 9
    3.2 FirebaseUI Auth Authentication 9
    3.3 Firebase SDK Authentication 10
    3.4 Summary 10

4. Email/Password Authentication using FirebaseUI Auth 11
    4.1 Creating the Example Project 11
    4.2 Connecting the Project to Firebase 11
    4.3 Adding the FirebaseUI Project Dependencies 14
    4.4 Enabling Firebase Email/Password Authentication 15
    4.5 Adding the Signed-In Activity 16
    4.6 Designing the SignedInActivity Layout 17
    4.7 Firebase Initialization Steps 17
    4.8 Initiating the Sign-in Process 18
    4.9 Handling the Sign In Activity Result 20
    4.10 Handling the Sign-in 21
    4.11 Signing Out 22
    4.12 User Account Removal 23
    4.13 Summary 24

5. Testing and Customizing FirebaseUI Auth Authentication 25
    5.1 Authentication Testing Environment 25
    5.2 Firebase Console User Management 25
    5.3 Testing the FirebaseAuth App 26
    5.4 Customizing the Password Reset Email Message 28

5.5 Testing the Password Reset 30

5.6 Enabling Smart Lock for Passwords 31

5.7 Color Customization 32

5.8 Specifying a Logo 34

5.9 Deleting the Test Account 35

5.10 Summary 35

6. Google Sign-In Authentication using FirebaseUI Auth 37

6.1 Preparing the Project 37

6.2 Obtaining the SHA-1 Fingerprint 37

6.3 Adding the SHA-1 Key to the Firebase Project 38

6.4 Enabling the Google Sign-In Method 39

6.5 Adding the Google Sign-In Provider within the App 40

6.6 Testing Google Sign-In 41

6.7 Displaying the User's Profile Photo 43

6.8 Summary 47

7. Facebook Login Authentication using FirebaseUI Auth 49

7.1 Preparing the Project 49

7.2 Obtaining the Facebook App ID and App Secret 49

7.3 Adding the App ID and Secret to the Firebase Project 51

7.4 Adding the Facebook Login Product to the App 51

7.5 Setting the OAuth Redirect URI 52

7.6 Adding the Debug and Release Key Hash 53

7.7 Modifying the App 54

7.8 Testing Facebook Login Authentication 56

7.9 Summary 59

8. Twitter Sign-In Authentication using FirebaseUI Auth 61

8.1 Preparing the Project 61

8.2 Enabling Twitter Authentication 61

8.3 Creating a Twitter App 62

8.4 Obtaining the Twitter API Keys 62

8.5 Generating the Access Token 63

8.6 Adding the API Keys to the Project 64

8.7 Adding Twitter to the Provider List 64

8.8 Adding the Twitter Library Dependency 65

8.9 Testing Twitter Authentication 65

8.10 Summary 66

9. Phone Number Sign-in Authentication using FirebaseUI Auth 67

9.1 Preparing the Project 67

9.2 Enabling Phone Number Authentication 67

9.3 Adding Phone Verification to the Provider List 68

9.4 Testing Phone Number Authentication 68

9.5 Summary 70

10. Email/Password Authentication using the Firebase SDK 71

10.1 Creating the PasswordAuth Project 71
10.2 Enabling Authentication Providers 71
10.3 Connecting the Project to Firebase 72
10.4 Designing the User Interface Layout 72
10.5 Getting View Object References 76
10.6 Adding a User Notification Method 76
10.7 Accessing the FirebaseAuth Instance 77
10.8 Adding the Authentication State Listener 78
10.9 Adding and Removing the Listener 79
10.10 Creating the User Account 80
10.11 Implementing the Sign-In Method 81
10.12 Signing Out 82
10.13 Implementing the Password Reset Option 82
10.14 Testing the Project 83
10.15 Summary 84

11. Managing User Accounts using the Firebase SDK **85**

11.1 Enhancing the User's Profile Information 85
11.2 Changing a User's Email Address 86
11.3 Changing a User's Password 87
11.4 Deleting a User Account 88
11.5 Verifying the User's Email Address 88
11.6 Understanding Security Sensitive Actions 89
11.7 Summary 89

12. Handling Firebase Authentication Errors and Failures **91**

12.1 Completion Listeners and Basic Failure Detection 91
12.2 The Failure Listener 92
12.3 FirebaseAuth Exception Types 93
12.4 FirebaseAuth Error Codes 95
12.5 Handling Secure Action Exceptions 96
12.6 Summary 99

13. Google Authentication using the Firebase SDK **101**

13.1 Firebase Authentication with the Google Sign-In API 101
13.2 Creating the GoogleAuth Project 101
13.3 Connecting the Project to Firebase 102
13.4 Configuring the SHA-1 Fingerprint Key 102
13.5 Adding the Google Play Authentication Library 103
13.6 Designing the User Interface Layout 103
13.7 Adding a User Notification Method 105
13.8 Accessing the FirebaseAuth Instance 106
13.9 Adding the Authentication State Listener 107
13.10 Adding and Removing the Listener 109
13.11 Initializing the Google API Client 109
13.12 Implementing the Sign In Method 111
13.13 Registering the User with Firebase 113

13.14 Signing Out...113

13.15 Testing the Project..114

13.16 Summary..115

14. Facebook Authentication using the Firebase SDK **117**

14.1 Authentication with the Firebase and Facebook SDKs 117

14.2 Creating the FacebookAuth Project...117

14.3 Connecting the Project to Firebase 118

14.4 Firebase and Facebook Console Configuration 118

14.5 Configuring the Android Studio Project...118

14.6 Adding the Facebook SDK Library 120

14.7 Designing the User Interface Layout 120

14.8 Adding the Facebook LoginButton 122

14.9 Facebook SDK Initialization Steps 123

14.10 Handling Authentication Results and Callbacks...124

14.11 Testing Facebook Authentication 126

14.12 Initializing Firebase 128

14.13 Registering the User in Firebase 131

14.14 Testing the Project 133

14.15 Detecting the Facebook Log Out 133

14.16 Summary..135

15. Twitter Log In Authentication using the Firebase SDK **137**

15.1 Authentication using Firebase and the Twitter SDK 137

15.2 Creating the TwitterAuth Project 137

15.3 Connecting the Project to Firebase 138

15.4 Enabling Twitter Authentication..138

15.5 Adding the Twitter Library Dependency..138

15.6 Designing the User Interface Layout 138

15.7 Adding the Twitter Login Button 140

15.8 Performing Initialization Tasks 141

15.9 Handling Callbacks and Activity Results...142

15.10 Testing the Twitter Authentication..144

15.11 Initializing Firebase 145

15.12 Registering the User in Firebase 148

15.13 Signing Out..150

15.14 Testing the Project 150

15.15 Configuring Privacy and Terms of Service URLs...150

15.16 Enabling Email Address Permission 151

15.17 Requesting the User's Email Address 151

15.18 Testing Email Permission 152

15.19 Summary..153

16. Phone Number Authentication using the Firebase SDK...**155**

16.1 Phone Number Authentication...155

16.2 Creating the Example Project 156

16.3 Connecting the Project to Firebase 156

16.4 Updating the firebase-auth Package 156
16.5 Designing the User Interface 156
16.6 Performing Initialization Tasks 157
16.7 Sending the Verification Code 159
16.8 Adding the Verification Callbacks 159
16.9 Verifying the Code 161
16.10 Signing In with the Credential 161
16.11 Resending the Verification Code 162
16.12 Signing Out 163
16.13 Testing the App.. 163
16.14 Summary 163

17. Anonymous Authentication using the Firebase SDK **165**

17.1 Anonymous Firebase Authentication 165
17.2 Creating the AnonAuth Project 166
17.3 Connecting the Project to Firebase 166
17.4 Enabling Anonymous Authentication... 166
17.5 Designing the User Interface Layout 167
17.6 Accessing the FirebaseAuth Instance 168
17.7 Adding the Authentication State Listener 170
17.8 Performing the Anonymous Authentication 171
17.9 Signing Out 172
17.10 Testing the Project.. 172
17.11 Summary... 173

18. Linking and Unlinking Firebase Authentication Providers **175**

18.1 Firebase Authentication Account Linking... 175
18.2 Limitations of Firebase Account Linking.. 175
18.3 Implementing Email/Password Authentication... 176
18.4 Testing the Project.. 177
18.5 Linking Other Account Types 178
18.6 Unlinking an Authentication Provider 178
18.7 Summary... 180

19. Firebase Realtime Database **181**

19.1 An Overview of the Firebase Realtime Database 181
19.2 How is the Data Stored?... 181
19.3 Nesting Data 182
19.4 Separating User Data.. 183
19.5 Avoiding Deep Nesting 184
19.6 Supported Data Types 185
19.7 Adding Realtime Database Support to Projects 186
19.8 Offline Data Handling 188
19.9 Summary... 188

20. Writing Firebase Realtime Database Data... **189**

20.1 Obtaining the Database Reference 189

20.2 Performing a Basic Write Operation..190
20.3 Accessing Child Nodes...191
20.4 Writing to Multiple Nodes...192
20.5 Storing a Java Object..192
20.6 Deleting Data..193
20.7 Handling Write Errors..194
20.8 Summary...194

21. Reading Firebase Realtime Database Data **195**

21.1 Detecting Value Changes...195
21.2 Working with a DataSnapshot Object...196
21.3 Extracting Data from a DataSnapshot Object..198
21.4 Reading Data into a Java Object..199
21.5 Summary...200

22. Firebase Realtime Database Rules...**201**

22.1 Accessing and Changing the Database Rules..201
22.2 Understanding Database Rule Types...203
22.2.1 Read and Writing Rules..*203*
22.2.2 Data Validation Rules...*203*
22.2.3 Indexing Rules..*203*
22.3 Structuring Database Rules 203
22.4 Securing User Data...206
22.5 $ Variables..207
22.6 Predefined Variables..208
22.7 RuleDataSnapShot Methods...208
22.8 Data Validation Rules...210
22.9 Indexing Rules..211
22.10 Summary...212

23. Working with Firebase Realtime Database Lists **213**

23.1 The push() Method..213
23.2 Listening for Events..215
23.3 Performing List Queries 216
23.4 Querying and Indexes...218
23.5 Summary...218

24. A Basic Firebase Realtime Database Tutorial **219**

24.1 About the Realtime Database Project 219
24.2 Creating the Realtime Database Project..219
24.3 Adding User Authentication 219
24.4 Adding the Second Activity 220
24.5 Designing the SignedInActivity User Interface 221
24.6 Configuring the Project for Realtime Database Access 222
24.7 Performing the Authentication..223
24.8 Accessing the Database 225
24.9 Writing to the Database 227

24.10 Signing Out 228

24.11 Configuring the Database Rules 228

24.12 Testing the App.. 229

24.13 Adding a Validation Rule 230

24.14 Summary.. 231

25. A Firebase Realtime Database List Data Tutorial... 233

25.1 About the Data List App Project 233

25.2 Creating the Data List Project... 233

25.3 Configuring the Project for Realtime Database Access 233

25.4 Designing the User Interface 234

25.5 Performing Initialization Tasks 236

25.6 Implementing the ListView... 237

25.7 Implementing Child Event Listener.. 239

25.8 Adding Items to the List 241

25.9 Deleting List Items 241

25.10 Querying the List 242

25.11 Changing the Database Rules 243

25.12 Testing the App.. 244

25.13 Summary.. 245

26. Firebase Cloud Messaging.. 247

26.1 An Overview of Firebase Cloud Messaging 247

26.2 Creating the Firebase Messaging Project 247

26.3 Adding Firebase Messaging Support to the Project 247

26.4 Designing the User Interface 248

26.5 Obtaining and Monitoring the Registration Token.. 248

26.6 Sending a Notification to the Device 251

26.7 Receiving the Notification 252

26.8 Including Custom Data within the Notification 253

26.9 Foreground App Notification Handling.. 254

26.10 Sending to Apps and User Segments.. 256

26.11 Conversion Events 257

26.12 Summary.. 257

27. Sending Firebase Cloud Messages from a Node.js Server.. 259

27.1 An Introduction to Node.js.. 259

27.2 Installing Node.js on macOS 260

27.3 Installing Node.js on Windows 260

27.4 Installing Node.js on Linux... 260

27.5 Initializing and Configuring Node.js... 260

27.6 Running a Test 261

27.7 Installing the Firebase Admin SDK 261

27.8 Generating the Service Account Credentials 262

27.9 Initializing the Admin SDK.. 263

27.10 Adding the Destination Registration Token... 263

27.11 Understanding Message Payloads 264

27.12 Defining the Payload and Sending the Message.. 265
27.13 Testing the Code 266
27.14 Topics 266
27.15 Using Topic Conditions 269
27.16 Summary.. 269

28. Managing Firebase Cloud Messaging Device Groups with Node.js..**271**
28.1 Understanding Device Groups.. 271
28.2 Requirements for Creating a Device Group... 271
28.3 Creating a Device Group using HTTP 272
28.4 Creating a Device Group using Node.js 273
28.5 Sending a Message to a Device Group 274
28.6 Managing Device Group Members in Node.js 275
28.7 Summary.. 275

29. Managing Firebase Messaging Device Groups from an Android App **277**
29.1 Managing Device Groups from a Client App.. 277
29.2 Generating the Client ID 277
29.3 Creating the Client App Project 279
29.4 Adding the Group Button 279
29.5 Obtaining the ID Token... 279
29.6 Declaring the Sender ID 281
29.7 Creating an Asynchronous Task 281
29.8 Creating the Device Group 282
29.9 Executing the AsyncTask... 284
29.10 Testing the App... 285
29.11 Removing Devices from a Device Group 285
29.12 Summary.. 285

30. Firebase Cloud Upstream Messaging **287**
30.1 Firebase Cloud Upstream Messaging Architecture 287
30.2 Implementing the App Server.. 289
30.3 Sending an Upstream Message from the Client 289
30.4 Summary.. 290

31. A Firebase Cloud Messaging Upstream XMPP App Server **291**
31.1 About the FCM App Server Project... 291
31.2 Project Dependencies... 291
31.3 CcsClient.java 292
31.4 PayloadProcessor.java 292
31.5 RegisterProcessor.java 293
31.6 AccountStore.java... 293
31.7 MessageProcessor.java 293
31.8 Building and Running the Server 293
31.9 Summary.. 295

32. An Example Firebase Upstream Cloud Messaging Client App **297**

32.1 Creating the Project...297
32.2 Adding Firebase Messaging Support to the Project 297
32.3 Designing the User Interface 297
32.4 Obtaining the Registration Token..299
32.5 Handling Incoming Messages 301
32.6 Registering the User 302
32.7 Sending the Upstream Message 303
32.8 Testing the Upstream Project 304
32.9 Summary 304

33. Firebase Cloud Storage **305**

33.1 An Overview of Firebase Cloud Storage 305
33.2 Storage References 305
33.3 Storage Reference Properties...306
33.4 Uploading a File to Firebase Cloud Storage 307
33.5 Uploading a File as a Stream 307
33.6 Uploading a File From Memory Data...307
33.7 Monitoring and Managing the Upload 308
33.8 Accessing Upload Task Snapshot Properties 308
33.9 Reading Metadata from an Uploaded File 309
33.10 Customizing the File Metadata 312
33.11 Updating File Metadata..313
33.12 Deleting an Uploaded File 313
33.13 Resuming an Interrupted Upload 314
33.14 Managing Cloud Storage in the Firebase Console 315
33.15 Summary...316

34. A Guide to Firebase Cloud Storage Security Rules **317**

34.1 Understanding Cloud Storage Security Rules 317
34.2 Security Rules Structure 318
34.3 The match Keyword...319
34.4 The allow Keyword...319
34.5 The if Statement..319
34.6 Wildcard Matching..322
34.7 Protecting User Files...323
34.8 Summary...324

35. A Firebase Cloud Storage Tutorial **325**

35.1 About the Firebase Cloud Storage Example 325
35.2 Creating the Project...325
35.3 Adding Authentication to the Project...325
35.4 Adding the Signed In Activity...327
35.5 Designing the SignedInActivity User Interface 327
35.6 Performing the Authentication 329
35.7 Recording Video 332
35.8 Adding Firebase Cloud Storage Support 333
35.9 Uploading the Video File to the Cloud..333

35.10 Updating the Progress Bar 335
35.11 Downloading the Video File 336
35.12 Setting the Storage Security Rules 337
35.13 Testing the Project 338
35.14 Summary 338

36. Firebase Remote Config 339

36.1 An Overview of Firebase Remote Config 339
36.2 The FirebaseRemoteConfig Object 340
36.3 Declaring and Setting In-App Parameters 340
36.4 Accessing Remote Config Parameters 341
36.5 Setting Server Side Parameters 341
36.6 Fetching the Parameters 342
36.7 Activating Fetched Parameters 343
36.8 Working with Conditions 344
36.9 Parameter Fetching Strategies 347
36.10 Getting Status Information 347
36.11 Summary 348

37. A Firebase Remote Config Tutorial 349

37.1 Creating the Project 349
37.2 Adding Remote Config Support to the Project 349
37.3 Designing the User Interface 349
37.4 Declaring the Default In-App Parameters 351
37.5 Loading the Config Parameters 352
37.6 Adding the Server-side Parameters 354
37.7 Fetching and Activating the Remote Parameters 355
37.8 Handling Changes at Startup 356
37.9 Creating a Conditional Parameter Change 356
37.10 Summary 358

38. Firebase Analytics 359

38.1 An Overview of Firebase Analytics 359
38.2 The FirebaseAnalytics Object 359
38.3 Events 360
38.3.1 Predefined Events Types 360
38.3.2 Suggested Event Types 360
38.3.3 Custom Event Types 360
38.4 Viewing Events in the LogCat Window 361
38.5 User Properties 361
38.6 Audiences 362
38.7 Summary 362

39. A Guided Tour of the Firebase Analytics Dashboard 363

39.1 The Firebase Analytics Dashboard 363
39.2 Filtering the Data 364
39.2.1 Active users 364

39.2.2 Average revenue 365

39.2.3 first_open attribution 365

39.2.4 Retention cohorts 366

39.2.5 User engagement 367

39.2.6 In-app purchases 367

39.2.7 App version 368

39.2.8 Devices 369

39.3 Location 369

39.3.1 Demographics 370

39.3.2 Interests 370

39.4 Summary 371

40. An Overview of the Firebase Analytics Screens **373**

40.1 The Events Screen 373

40.2 The Audiences Screen 374

40.3 The Attribution Screen 375

40.4 The Funnels Screen 376

40.5 The Cohorts Screen 378

40.6 The StreamView Screen 378

40.7 The DebugView Screen 379

40.8 User Properties Screen 382

40.9 Summary 383

41. A Firebase Analytics Tutorial **385**

41.1 Creating the Firebase Analytics Project 385

41.2 Designing the User Interface 385

41.3 Adding Firebase Analytics Support to the Project 387

41.4 Performing the App Initialization 387

41.5 Adding the orderItem() Method 388

41.6 Enabling Debugging Modes 388

41.7 Adding the User Property in the Firebase Console 389

41.8 Testing the App 389

41.9 Creating an Audience 391

41.10 Summary 392

42. Firebase Test Lab **393**

42.1 An Overview of Firebase Test Lab 393

42.2 Robo Testing 393

42.3 Instrumentation Testing 394

42.4 Game Loop Testing 394

42.5 Test Lab Pricing 394

42.6 Summary 394

43. A Firebase Test Lab Robo Testing Example **395**

43.1 Getting the Test App 395

43.2 Running a Robo Test 395

43.3 Reviewing Robo Test Results 398

43.4 Introducing a Bug 400
43.5 Summary 401

44. A Firebase Test Lab Instrumentation Testing Example **403**

44.1 Getting the Test App 403
44.2 An Overview of Espresso 403
44.3 Enabling Test Lab in the Project 404
44.4 Creating the Espresso Test Class 404
44.5 Recording the Test 405
44.6 Reviewing the Test Class 407
44.7 Running the Test Locally 407
44.8 Firebase Console Testing 408
44.9 Adding the Screenshotter Library to the Project 409
44.10 Adding the Screenshotter Code 411
44.11 Running the Test from Android Studio 412
44.12 Summary 414

45. Firebase Dynamic Links **415**

45.1 An Overview of Firebase Dynamic Links 415
45.2 The Anatomy of a Dynamic Link 415
45.3 Creating Dynamic Links in the Firebase Console 416
45.4 Reviewing a Link in the Console 418
45.5 Creating a Dynamic Link in Code 420
45.6 Sharing a Dynamic Link 421
45.7 Receiving a Dynamic Link 422
45.8 Summary 425

46. Creating, Receiving and Testing a Firebase Dynamic Link **427**

46.1 About the Dynamic Links Example App 427
46.2 Creating the Dynamic Links Project 427
46.3 Designing the User Interface 427
46.4 Connecting the Project to Firebase 428
46.5 Performing Basic Initialization 428
46.6 Adding the Link Generation Code 429
46.7 Sharing the Dynamic Link 430
46.8 Adding the Main Activity Intent Filter 431
46.9 Detecting a Dynamic Link Launch 432
46.10 Parsing the Deep Link URL 434
46.11 Generating the Dynamic Link 434
46.12 Testing a Dynamic Link 435
46.13 Adding a Second Activity 436
46.14 Configuring Automatic Activity Launching 437
46.15 Testing Automatic Launching 438
46.16 Dynamic Link Analytics 438
46.17 Summary 439

47. Firebase Invites **441**

47.1 Creating a Firebase Invite Intent 441
47.2 Sending the Invitation 442
47.3 Handling the Activity Result 443
47.4 Testing Invitations 444
47.5 Summary... 444

48. Firebase App Indexing 445

48.1 An Overview of Firebase App Indexing... 445
48.2 Public Content Indexing... 445
48.3 Personal Content Indexing.. 446
48.4 User Action Logging... 446
48.5 Summary... 447

49. Implementing Firebase App Indexing... 449

49.1 Public Content Indexing... 449
49.2 Personal Content Indexing.. 450
49.3 App Indexing Service 451
49.4 Logging User Actions 452
49.5 Removing Index Entries 453
49.6 Summary... 453

50. A Firebase App Indexing Tutorial 455

50.1 About the Example App.. 455
50.2 The Database Schema 455
50.3 Loading and Running the Project... 456
50.4 Adding Firebase App Indexing Support 457
50.5 Logging User Actions 458
50.6 Adding Content Indexing.. 459
50.7 Testing Content Indexing.. 460
50.8 Indexing User Added Content 463
50.9 Testing Index Updates.. 466
50.10 Deleting Index Entries... 466
50.11 Summary.. 467

51. Firebase Performance Monitoring 469

51.1 An Overview of Firebase Performance Monitoring............................... 469
51.2 Adding Performance Monitoring to a Project 469
51.3 Defining Custom Traces 471
51.4 Enabling Logcat Output 472
51.5 Reviewing Performance Data in the Firebase Console 473
51.6 Turning Off Performance Monitoring.. 476
51.7 Summary... 476

52. Firebase Cloud Functions 479

52.1 A Cloud Functions Overview... 479
52.2 Firebase Authentication Functions... 479
52.3 Realtime Database Functions 480

52.4 Google Analytics Functions...481

52.5 HTTP Functions..482

52.6 Cloud Storage Functions..482

52.7 Performing External Operations...484

52.8 Modifying Cloud Function Settings..485

52.9 Summary...485

53. Installing the Firebase CLI..487

53.1 Installing Node.js..487

53.2 Installing the Firebase Tools Package..487

53.3 Logging into Firebase...487

53.4 Creating a Cloud Functions Project...488

53.5 Reviewing the Project..489

53.6 Deploying a Simple HTTP Cloud Function...489

53.7 Reviewing the Logs..490

53.8 Removing a Deployed Function...491

53.9 Summary...491

54. A Firebase Cloud Functions Tutorial...493

54.1 About the Example Project..493

54.2 Loading and Configuring the App..493

54.3 Trying out the App..494

54.4 Writing the Authentication Cloud Function..495

54.5 Writing the Realtime Database Function...496

54.6 Deploying the Cloud Functions...498

54.7 Testing the Cloud Functions...498

54.8 Summary...499

55. A Cloud Functions and Firebase Cloud Storage Example.............................501

55.1 The CloudStorage App...501

55.2 Setting Cloud Storage Rules...502

55.3 Installing Dependencies..503

55.4 Writing the Cloud Function..503

55.5 Testing the Cloud Function...506

55.6 Increasing Cloud Function Memory..506

55.7 Summary...509

Index...511

Chapter 1

1. Introduction

In 2014, Google completed the acquisition of a San Francisco-based company named Firebase, Inc. Firebase, Inc. provided a range of developer solutions designed to accelerate the integration of cloud-based features into mobile and web apps. After purchasing the company, Google combined the services provided by Firebase with a number of complementary features previously included as part of the Google Cloud Platform. The combined features from the two platforms are what is now known simply as *Firebase*.

In early 2017, Google acquired Fabric.io from Twitter, Inc. and is now in the process of integrating key Fabric features into Firebase.

This book covers the key features of Android app development using Firebase. Topics covered in this book include user authentication, realtime databases, cloud-based file storage, instant messaging, dynamic links, app indexing, cloud functions, analytics, performance monitoring and more.

The book is organized into chapter groups that focus on specific Firebase features, with each topic area consisting of a detailed overview followed by tutorial style examples that put theory into practice.

1.1 Downloading the Code Samples

The source code and Android Studio project files for the examples contained in this book are available for download at:

http://www.ebookfrenzy.com/print/firebase_android

The steps to load a project from the code samples into Android Studio are as follows:

1. From the Welcome to Android Studio dialog, select the Open an existing Android Studio project option.

2. In the project selection dialog, navigate to and select the folder containing the project to be imported and click on OK.

3. Before running the app, follow the steps in the corresponding chapter to connect the project to your Firebase account.

1.2 Download the eBook

Thank you for purchasing the print edition of this book. If you would like to download the eBook version of this book, please email proof of purchase to feedback@ebookfrenzy.com and we will provide you with a download link for the book in PDF format.

1.3 **Feedback**

We want you to be satisfied with your purchase of this book. If you find any errors in the book, or have any comments, questions or concerns please contact us at feedback@ebookfrenzy.com.

1.4 **Errata**

While we make every effort to ensure the accuracy of the content of this book, it is inevitable that a book covering a subject area of this size and complexity may include some errors and oversights. Any known issues with the book will be outlined, together with solutions, at the following URL:

http://www.ebookfrenzy.com/errata/firebase-android.html

In the event that you find an error not listed in the errata, please let us know by emailing our technical support team at feedback@ebookfrenzy.com. They are there to help you and will work to resolve any problems you may encounter.

2. Getting Started with Firebase

Working with Firebase requires a Google account and at least one Firebase project. This chapter will cover the steps that need to be taken in preparation for working with Firebase in the subsequent chapters of the book.

2.1 Signing into the Firebase Console

The first step in working with Firebase involves signing in to the Firebase console. Begin by opening a browser window and navigating to *https://firebase.google.com*, at which point a screen similar to the following will appear:

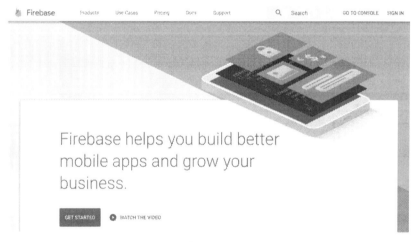

Figure 2-1

Click on either the *Sign In* link in the top right-hand corner, or the *Get Started* button and enter the credentials for your Google account. After signing in, the following screen will appear indicating that no Firebase projects yet exist for the account:

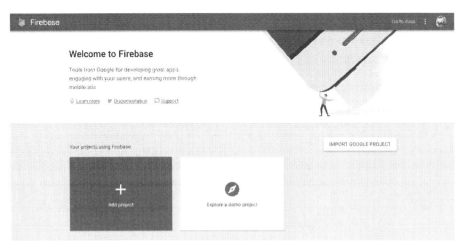

Figure 2-2

2.2 Creating a New Project

To create a new project, simply click on the *Add project* square in the console, enter *Firebase Examples* into the Project name field and select your country from the drop down list:

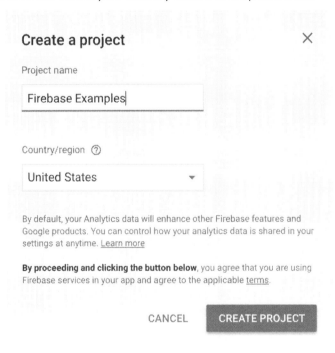

Figure 2-3

After completing the form, click on the *Create Project* button. There will be a short delay as the project is created after which the main Firebase console screen will appear as illustrated in Figure 2-4:

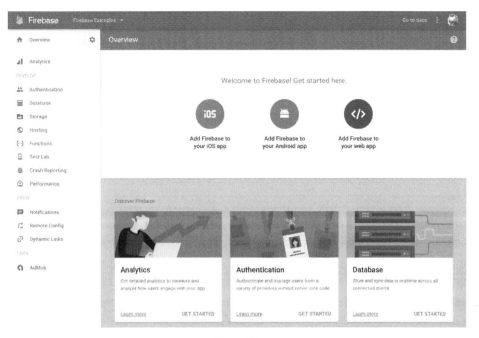

Figure 2-4

2.3 Firebase Projects

Before moving on to the next chapter, it is important to understand that a Firebase Project is different from an Android Studio project. While an Android Studio project contains a single app, a Firebase project typically contains multiple app projects. Google restricts the number of Firebase projects available to each account, so it is best to group multiple Android Studio app projects within a single Firebase project.

2.4 Firebase Pricing Plans

Google offers three pricing tiers for Firebase named Spark, Flame and Blaze, each of which provides increasing levels of database storage and usage quotas. All of the examples contained within this book have been designed to work with the free Spark plan level. Pricing details for the Flame and Blaze plans, which differ by region, can be found online at:

https://firebase.google.com/pricing/

All newly created Firebase accounts default to the Spark plan level.

2.5 Summary

As will become evident in future chapters, working with Firebase involves a considerable amount of time spent within the Firebase console. This chapter has outlined the process of logging into the console and creating an initial Firebase project.

Before any Firebase functionality can be built into an Android Studio app project, that app project must be associated with a Firebase project. A single Firebase project can contain multiple Android

Studio app projects. Since Google limits the number of Firebase projects available per account, a single Firebase project will typically be used to hold multiple app projects.

Firebase is available at three different pricing levels named Spark, Flame and Blaze. The free of charge Spark plan is used exclusively throughout this book.

3. Firebase User Authentication

Many apps and web services need to provide some form of authentication system in order to identify users, control access to premium content and to protect user data. Without some way to identify one user from another it would also be impossible for the app to know which data and settings belong to which user.

Authentication options can range from requiring an email address and a password to allowing users to sign in using credentials from third-party platforms such as Facebook, Google and Twitter.

Regardless of the motivations for adding user authentication to an app, developers often find that implementation is much more complex than it seems on the surface. Not only must authentication be performed securely and reliably, it must also allow for users to change their account settings, provide support for forgotten passwords and integrate with a range of vastly different third-party authentication APIs. Databases have to be implemented and stored securely and an administration interface developed for manually adding, editing and deleting users.

Fortunately there is an easier option than building all of this infrastructure. All of these requirements can be met with minimal effort by using Firebase Authentication.

3.1 An Overview of Firebase Authentication

Firebase authentication provides a way to add user account creation and sign in capabilities to an app with a minimal amount of coding. Once a user has been authenticated with Firebase, the user is assigned a unique Firebase user ID which can be used when integrating other Firebase services such as data storage and cloud messaging.

Firebase uses the concept of *authentication providers* to facilitate the identification and registration of users. The list of supported Firebase authentication providers currently consists of Google, Facebook, Twitter, GitHub, phone number and email/password authentication. Firebase also provides support for users to sign in anonymously with a temporary account and then subsequently link that account to an authentication provider-based account.

In addition to integrating with the supported authentication providers, Firebase also supports integration with custom authentication systems.

Firebase supports all of the standard authentication features such as handling forgotten passwords and managing user accounts and profiles both programmatically and through the Firebase console.

Two forms of Firebase authentication are available, one involving the use of FirebaseUI Auth and the other a lower level approach using the Firebase SDK. In practice, these involve the use of the following collection of Firebase authentication classes.

3.1.1 FirebaseAuth Instance

Much of the Firebase SDK authentication process involves the use of the FirebaseAuth shared instance. Once a reference to this object has been obtained, it can be used to perform a range of tasks such as creating accounts, signing users in and out and accessing or updating information relating to the current user.

A key function of the FirebaseAuth instance is the authentication state listener (AuthStateListener). When added to the FirebaseAuth instance, it is via this listener that the app receives notification of any changes to the user's authentication status.

Though useful for obtaining user information when using FirebaseUI Auth, the FirebaseAuth instance is primarily used in conjunction with the Firebase SDK approach to authentication.

3.1.2 AuthUI Instance

The AuthUI instance is used extensively in the FirebaseUI Auth authentication process. The class contains a range of methods including a sign-in intent builder and a sign out method. The intent builder method is called to create and configure an Intent object that is then used to launch the FirebaseUI authentication activity. This activity is responsible for all aspects of the user account creation and sign-in process. Configuration options available when using the builder method include changes to the color theme of the sign-in user interface, a logo for branding purposes and a list of the authentication providers that are to be offered as sign-in options to the user.

3.1.3 FirebaseUser Class

The FirebaseUser class is used to encapsulate the profile information for the currently authenticated user. An object of this type is returned, for example, when a call is made to the *getCurrentUser()* method of the FirebaseAuth instance. The data stored in the object will vary depending on which authentication provider is currently being used, but typically includes information such as the user's display name, email address, a URL to a profile photo and the ID of the authentication provider used to sign into the app. Methods are also included for performing tasks such as updating the user's profile information, verifying the user's email address, accessing the user's Firebase user ID and deleting the user's account.

3.1.4 AuthCredential Classes

The AuthCredential class is used to encapsulate user account credentials in a way that is compatible with Firebase. This class is used when exchanging a token from a third-party authentication provider for the credentials of a Firebase account. When a user signs in using the authentication provider for a third-party platform such as Facebook or Twitter, for example, the app is provided with a user token for that platform. Once obtained, this token needs to be passed to Firebase where it is used to create a Firebase account for the user. Before this can take place, however, the third-party provider token must be converted to an AuthCredential object by making a call to the *getCredential()* method of the corresponding authentication provider class. For each authentication provider there is a corresponding AuthCredential subclass:

- EmailAuthCredential

- PhoneAuthCredential
- FacebookAuthCredential
- GithubAuthCredential
- GoogleAuthCredential
- TwitterAuthCredential

3.1.5 Authentication Provider Classes

Each of the authentication providers has its own class that is used during the authentication process (specifically to create an AuthCredential object as outlined above). Firebase currently includes the following authentication provider classes:

- EmailAuthProvider
- PhoneAuthProvider
- FacebookAuthProvider
- GithubAuthProvider
- GoogleAuthProvider
- TwitterAuthProvider

3.2 FirebaseUI Auth Authentication

Of the two Firebase authentication options (namely FirebaseUI Auth and Firebase SDK), FirebaseUI Auth requires by far the least time and programming effort to integrate. In fact, configuring an Android Studio project to support Firebase authentication typically takes longer than writing the actual code to implement FirebaseUI authentication.

FirebaseUI Auth provides everything necessary to implement user authentication including all of the user interface screens that take the user through the account creation and sign-in process.

User authentication can be integrated into an app using FirebaseUI Auth by following a few simple steps:

1. Enable the required authentication providers in the Firebase console.

2. Register the app with the third-party authentication providers for which support is required (Google, Facebook, Twitter and GitHub).

3. Add the FirebaseUI Auth libraries to the Android Studio project.

4. Obtain a reference to the shared FirebaseAuth instance.

5. Use the AuthUI class to configure and build the FirebaseUI authentication intent.

6. Use the intent to launch the FirebaseUI Auth activity.

7. Handle the results returned by the activity.

Each of these steps will be covered in later chapters, beginning with the next chapter entitled *Email/Password Authentication using FirebaseUI Auth*.

3.3 **Firebase SDK Authentication**

Although integrating authentication using the Firebase SDK is more time consuming, it does have the advantage of flexibility. Unlike FirebaseUI Auth, the Firebase SDK provides full control over the look, feel and behavior of the authentication process (with the exception of any authentication screens presented by third-party authentication providers). In basic terms, Firebase SDK authentication is implemented using the following steps:

1. Enable the required authentication providers in the Firebase console.

2. Register the app with the third-party authentication providers for which support is required (Google, Facebook, Twitter and GitHub).

3. Add the Firebase SDK libraries to the Android Studio project.

4. Obtain a reference to the shared FirebaseAuth instance.

5. Implement and add an AuthStateListener instance to the FirebaseAuth instance and write callback methods.

6. Design the user interface layout for the sign-in screen including options for forgotten passwords.

7. Implement code to handle the account creation, sign-in, sign-out and password reset operations, including adaptations for each of the authentication providers to be supported.

8. Exchange tokens from third-party authentication providers for equivalent Firebase credentials.

9. Handle authentication results within the callback of the AuthStateListener instance.

Beginning with the chapter entitled *Email/Password Authentication using the Firebase SDK*, details on how to perform the above tasks will be covered for the more widely used authentication providers.

3.4 **Summary**

User authentication is vital both for controlling access to app content and features and protecting user data. Firebase Authentication allows user authentication to be added to an Android app with a minimum amount of time and effort with support for account management and built-in support for a range of popular third-party authentication providers including Google, Twitter and Facebook.

Authentication can be implemented using either FirebaseUI Auth, or the Firebase SDK. FirebaseUI Auth provides a quick and easy way to integrate authentication with minimal effort, while the Firebase SDK approach requires more work but provides greater flexibility.

Chapter 4

4. Email/Password Authentication using FirebaseUI Auth

With the basics of Firebase authentication covered in the previous chapter, this chapter will demonstrate the implementation of email/password based authentication within an Android app using the FirebaseUI Auth API. Subsequent chapters will extend this example to include Firebase user authentication using phone number verification, Google, Facebook and Twitter.

4.1 Creating the Example Project

The first step in this exercise is to create the new project. Begin by launching Android Studio and, if necessary, closing any currently open projects using the *File -> Close Project* menu option so that the Welcome screen appears.

Select the *Start a new Android Studio project* quick start option from the welcome screen and, within the new project dialog, enter *FirebaseAuth* into the Application name field and your domain as the Company Domain setting (or make up a fictitious domain for testing purposes) before clicking on the *Next* button.

On the form factors screen, enable the *Phone and Tablet* option and set the minimum SDK to API 16: Android 4.1 (Jellybean). Continue through the project setup screens, requesting the creation of an Empty Activity named *FirebaseAuthActivity* and a corresponding layout named *activity_firebase_auth*.

4.2 Connecting the Project to Firebase

Before an Android Studio project can make use of the Firebase features, it must first be connected to a Firebase project using the Firebase assistant panel. Open the Firebase assistant by selecting the *Tools -> Firebase* menu option. When the Firebase assistant panel appears, locate and select the *Authentication* section as illustrated in Figure 4-1:

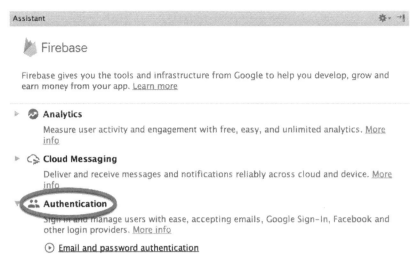

Figure 4-1

Click on the *Email and password authentication* link and, in the resulting panel, click on the *Connect to Firebase* button to display the Firebase connection dialog as shown in Figure 4-2 below.

Choose the option to store the app in an existing Firebase project and select the *Firebase Examples* project created in the *Getting Started with Firebase* chapter before clicking on the *Connect to Firebase* button:

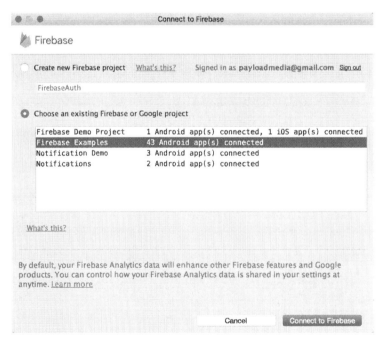

Figure 4-2

With the project's Firebase connection established, refer to the Firebase assistant panel once again, this time clicking on the *Add Firebase Authentication to your app* button. A dialog will appear (Figure

4-3) outlining the changes that will be made to the project build configuration to enable Firebase authentication:

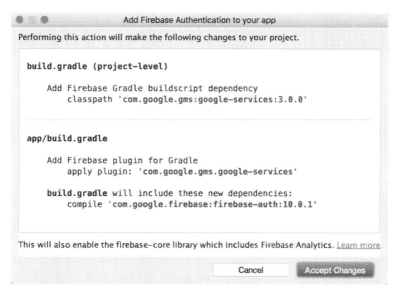

Figure 4-3

Click on the *Accept Changes* button to implement the changes to the project configuration.

After these steps are complete, the FirebaseAuth project will have been added to the *Firebase Examples* project. The core Firebase libraries necessary for adding authentication have also been added to the build configuration. An additional configuration file has also been downloaded and added to the project. This file is named *google-services.json* and is located under *FirebaseAuth -> app* within the project tree structure. To access this file, switch the Project tool window into *Project* mode and navigate to the file as shown in Figure 4-4 below:

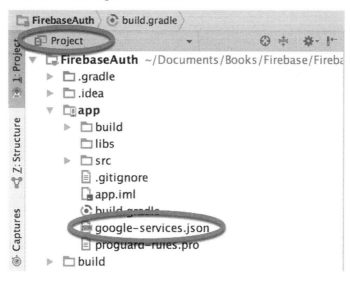

Figure 4-4

A review of the file content will reveal a wide range of Firebase client information that connects the app to the Firebase services including the project, app and client IDs, API keys and certificates. In general there is no need to manually edit this file. In the event that the file is deleted or corrupted, simply reconnect the app to Firebase using the Firebase assistant. Copies may also be downloaded from within the Firebase console.

Return the Project tool window to Android mode before proceeding.

4.3 Adding the FirebaseUI Project Dependencies

Since this project is going to make use of the FirebaseUI Auth API, two more dependencies need to be added to the module level *build.gradle* file for the project. Within the Project tool window, locate and double-click on the *build.gradle (Module: app)* file as shown in Figure 4-5 so that the file loads into the editor:

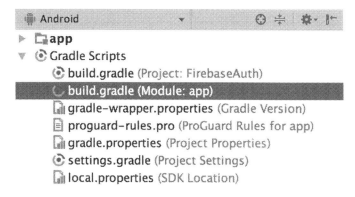

Figure 4-5

Once the Gradle file is open, modify the dependencies section to include the *firebase-ui* and *firebase-ui-auth* libraries (note that more recent versions of these libraries may have been released since this book was published):

```
dependencies {
    compile fileTree(dir: 'libs', include: ['*.jar'])
    androidTestCompile('com.android.support.test.espresso:espresso-
core:2.2.2', {
        exclude group: 'com.android.support', module: 'support-annotations'
    })
    compile 'com.android.support:appcompat-v7:25.3.1'
    compile 'com.android.support.constraint:constraint-layout:1.0.2'
    compile 'com.google.firebase:firebase-auth:10.0.1'
    compile 'com.firebaseui:firebase-ui:2.0.1'
    compile 'com.firebaseui:firebase-ui-auth:2.0.1'
    testCompile 'junit:junit:4.12'
}
```

In addition to the FirebaseUI dependencies, the build system will also need to download some additional libraries in order to be able to support Twitter-based authentication. These libraries are available via Google's Fabric.io platform and can be integrated into the Gradle build process for the project by adding a repository entry to the module level *build.gradle* file as follows:

```
.
.
.
    compile 'com.firebaseui:firebase-ui:2.0.1'
    compile 'com.firebaseui:firebase-ui-auth:2.0.1'
    testCompile 'junit:junit:4.12'
}

repositories {
    maven { url 'https://maven.fabric.io/public' }
}
.
.
.
```

4.4 Enabling Firebase Email/Password Authentication

Now that the Android Studio project has been configured to support Firebase authentication, some authentication settings need to be setup within the Firebase console. Open a browser window and navigate to your Firebase console at:

https://console.firebase.google.com/

Once signed into the Firebase console, select the *Firebase Examples* project from the list of available projects and note that the FirebaseAuth app has been added to the project.

In the left-hand navigation panel, select the *Authentication* option and, in the resulting panel, select the *Sign-In Methods* tab as highlighted in Figure 4-6:

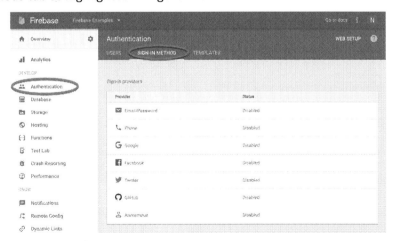

Figure 4-6

Note that by default none of the sign-in providers are enabled for apps residing within the *Firebase Examples* project. For the purposes of this example, only the Email/Password provider needs to be enabled. Click on the *Email/Password* entry in the providers list and turn on the *Enabled* switch when the settings dialog appears (Figure 4-7). Once the provider is enabled, click on the *Save* button to commit the change.

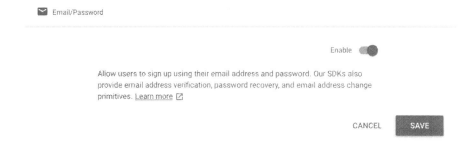

Figure 4-7

4.5 Adding the Signed-In Activity

The purpose of adding authentication to an app is to withhold access to functionality or content until a user's identity has been established and verified. This means that areas of the app need to be inaccessible to the user until the authentication process has successfully completed. In this example project, the restricted area of the app will be represented by a second activity which is only presented after the user has signed in to the app.

Add this second activity to the project now by locating the *app -> java -> <yourdomain>.firebaseauth* entry in the Project tool window and right-clicking on it. When the menu appears, select the *New -> Activity -> Empty Activity* menu option. In the *New Android Activity* dialog (Figure 4-8), name the activity *SignedInActivity*:

Figure 4-8

Before clicking on the *Finished* button, make sure that the *Generate Layout File* option is enabled and the *Launcher Activity* option disabled.

4.6 **Designing the SignedInActivity Layout**

The user interface layout for the SignedInActivity is going to need to be able to display the user's profile photo, email address and display name and also provide buttons for signing out of and deleting the account. Begin the design process by loading the *activity_signed_in.xml* file into the layout editor, turning off Autoconnect mode and adding and configuring widgets so that the layout matches Figure 4-9. When Android Studio requests an image to display on the ImageView, select the *common_google_signin_btn_icon_dark* icon from the list.

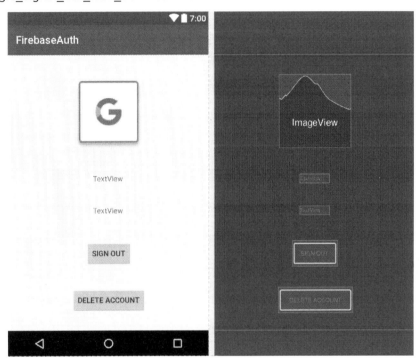

Figure 4-9

Select all five widgets, right-click on the ImageView and select *Center Horizontally* from the popup menu. Right-click on the ImageView again, this time selecting the *Center Vertically* menu option. The widgets should now be centered horizontally and constrained using a vertical chain configuration.

Using the Property tool window, change the IDs for the ImageView and two TextView widgets to *imageView*, *email* and *displayname* respectively. Also configure the two buttons to call onClick methods named *signOut* and *deleteAccount*.

4.7 **Firebase Initialization Steps**

Each time the app is launched, it will need to obtain an instance of the FirebaseAuth object and then check to verify whether the current user is already signed in to the app. If the user is already signed in, the app simply needs to launch SignedInActivity so that the user can interact with the app. In the event that the user has yet to sign in, the app will need to initiate the sign-in process.

Locate the FirebaseAuthActivty class within the Project tool window (*app -> java -> <yourdomain>.firebaseauth -> FirebaseAuthActivity*) and double click on it to load the Java file into the editor. Once loaded, modify the code so that it reads as follows:

```
package com.ebookfrenzy.firebaseauth;

import android.content.Intent;
import android.os.Bundle;
import android.support.v7.app.AppCompatActivity;

import com.google.firebase.auth.FirebaseAuth;

public class FirebaseAuthActivity extends AppCompatActivity {

    private FirebaseAuth auth;

    @Override
    protected void onCreate(Bundle savedInstanceState) {
        super.onCreate(savedInstanceState);
        setContentView(R.layout.activity_firebase_auth);

        auth = FirebaseAuth.getInstance();

        if (auth.getCurrentUser() != null) {
            startActivity(new Intent(this, SignedInActivity.class));
            finish();
        } else {
            authenticateUser();
        }
    }
}
```

The code has been implemented such that a method named *authenticateUser()* is called if the user is not currently signed in. Clearly the next step is to implement this method.

4.8 Initiating the Sign-in Process

It is the responsibility of the *authenticateUser()* method to present the user with options to sign into the app using existing email and password credentials, or to facilitate the creation of a new account if the user does not already have one. The authentication process also needs to take steps to verify that valid information has been entered and to allow the user to retrieve and reset a lost or forgotten password. In this example, all of these tasks will be performed for us by FirebaseUI Auth.

The code within the *authenticateUser()* method is going to use the *createSignInIntentBuilder()* method of the Firebase AuthUI instance to create a new intent object configured to meet the authentication requirements of our app. This intent will then be started using the *startActivityForResult()* method together with a request code that will be referenced when handling the activity result.

Remaining within the *FirebaseAuthActivity.java* file, implement the *authenticateUser()* method as follows:

```java
package com.ebookfrenzy.firebaseauth;

import android.content.Intent;
import android.os.Bundle;
import android.support.v7.app.AppCompatActivity;

import com.firebase.ui.auth.AuthUI;

import com.firebase.ui.auth.ErrorCodes;
import com.firebase.ui.auth.IdpResponse;
import com.firebase.ui.auth.ResultCodes;
import com.google.firebase.auth.FirebaseAuth;

import java.util.ArrayList;
import java.util.List;

public class FirebaseAuthActivity extends AppCompatActivity {

    private FirebaseAuth auth;
    private static final int REQUEST_CODE = 101;

    private void authenticateUser() {
        startActivityForResult(
                AuthUI.getInstance().createSignInIntentBuilder()
                        .setAvailableProviders(getProviderList())
                        .setIsSmartLockEnabled(false)
                        .build(),
                REQUEST_CODE);
    }
    .
    .
}
```

In the above code, the list of sign-in providers to be supported by the app is obtained via a call to a method named *getProviderList()*. This method now needs to be implemented within the FirebaseAuthActivity class:

```
private List<AuthUI.IdpConfig> getProviderList() {

    List<AuthUI.IdpConfig> providers = new ArrayList<>();

    providers.add(
        new AuthUI.IdpConfig.Builder(AuthUI.EMAIL_PROVIDER).build());

    return providers;
}
```

For this chapter, only the email/password provider is needed, though additional providers such as Google, Facebook and Twitter will be added to the list in subsequent chapters.

4.9 **Handling the Sign In Activity Result**

The next task is to add some code to handle the result of the sign-in process after control is returned to the app from the AuthUI activity. When an activity is launched using the *startActivityForResult()* method, the result is passed to the originating activity via a call to the *onActivityResult()* method if it has been implemented. This method is passed the request code originally included in the start request (represented by the value assigned to the REQUEST_CODE constant in this example) together with a result code indicating whether the activity was successful.

With the *FirebaseAuthActivity.java* file still in the editor, add the *onActivityResult()* method to the class so that it reads as follows:

```
@Override
protected void onActivityResult(int requestCode, int resultCode, Intent data)
{
    super.onActivityResult(requestCode, resultCode, data);

    IdpResponse response = IdpResponse.fromResultIntent(data);

    if (requestCode == REQUEST_CODE) {

        if (resultCode == ResultCodes.OK) {
            startActivity(new Intent(this, SignedInActivity.class));
            return;
        }
    } else {
        if (response == null) {
            // User cancelled Sign-in
            return;
        }

        if (response.getErrorCode() == ErrorCodes.NO_NETWORK) {
            // Device has no network connection
```

```
            return;
        }

        if (response.getErrorCode() == ErrorCodes.UNKNOWN_ERROR) {
            // Unknown error occurred
            return;
        }
    }
}
```

The method begins by calling the superclass, then checks that the request code matches that referenced when the activity was started. This step is recommended to ensure that the handler is not being called in response to any other activities that may have been launched by the app. The response code is then extracted from the data, evaluated and, in the event that the sign-in process was successful, the SignedInActivity is launched giving the user access to the previously restricted area of the app. Tests have also been added to detect when the user cancelled the sign-in process or when the device does not have an active network connection

4.10 Handling the Sign-in

When the user has successfully signed in, the SignedInActivity activity is launched. For the purposes of this tutorial, this activity will simply display a subset of the information known about the user and the sign-in provider. The SignedInActivity layout is also designed to display the profile picture associated with the user's account if one is available, though this will only be used in later chapters when Google, Facebook and Twitter sign-in support is added to the project. The layout also contains a button that allows the user to sign out of the app.

When the SignedInActivity activity starts, the FirebaseAuth object can be used to obtain a reference to the FirebaseUser object for the currently signed in user. It is from this object that details about the current user and sign-in provider can be obtained.

Locate the *SignedInActivity.java* class file within the project tool window and double click on it to load it into the code editor. Within the editor, modify the existing *onCreate()* method as follows:

```
package com.ebookfrenzy.firebaseauth;

import android.content.Intent;
import android.support.annotation.NonNull;
import android.support.v7.app.AppCompatActivity;
import android.os.Bundle;
import android.view.View;
import android.widget.TextView;

import com.firebase.ui.auth.AuthUI;
import com.google.android.gms.tasks.OnCompleteListener;
import com.google.android.gms.tasks.Task;
```

```
import com.google.firebase.auth.FirebaseAuth;
import com.google.firebase.auth.FirebaseUser;

public class SignedInActivity extends AppCompatActivity {

    @Override
    protected void onCreate(Bundle savedInstanceState) {
        super.onCreate(savedInstanceState);
        setContentView(R.layout.activity_signed_in);

        FirebaseUser currentUser =
                FirebaseAuth.getInstance().getCurrentUser();

        if (currentUser == null) {
            startActivity(new Intent(this, FirebaseAuthActivity.class));
            finish();
            return;
        }

        TextView email = (TextView) findViewById(R.id.email);
        TextView displayname = (TextView) findViewById(R.id.displayname);

        email.setText(currentUser.getEmail());
        displayname.setText(currentUser.getDisplayName());
    }
    .
    .
    .
}
```

The code added to the *onCreate()* method performs a check to verify that the user is actually signed in and, if not, returns control to the original activity where the sign-in process will repeat. If, on the other hand, the user is signed in, a reference to the FirebaseUser instance for that user is obtained and used to access the email and display name. These values are then displayed on the TextView widgets in the user interface layout.

4.11 **Signing Out**

When the user interface layout for the SignedInActivity activity was designed earlier in this chapter, it included a button intended to allow the user to sign out of the app. This button was configured to call a method named *signOut()* when tapped by the user. Remaining in the *SignedInActivity.java* file, implement this method now so that it reads as follows:

```
public void signOut(View view) {
    AuthUI.getInstance()
            .signOut(this)
```

```
        .addOnCompleteListener(new OnCompleteListener<Void>() {
            @Override
            public void onComplete(@NonNull Task<Void> task) {
                if (task.isSuccessful()) {
                    startActivity(new Intent(
                            SignedInActivity.this,
                            FirebaseAuthActivity.class));
                    finish();
                } else {
                    // Report error to user
                }
            }
        });
}
```

The method begins by calling the *signOut()* method of the AuthUI instance. The sign out process is handled asynchronously, so a completion handler is provided which will be called once the sign out is completed. In the case of a successful sign out, the user is returned to the main sign-in activity.

4.12 **User Account Removal**

The final task to be performed before testing the app is to implement the code for the Delete User button in the SignedInActivity layout. When added, this button was configured to call a method named *deleteAccount()* when tapped. The code for this method reads as follows and should now be added to the *SignedInActivity.java* file:

```
public void deleteAccount(View view) {
    AuthUI.getInstance()
            .delete(this)
            .addOnCompleteListener(new OnCompleteListener<Void>() {
                @Override
                public void onComplete(@NonNull Task<Void> task) {
                    if (task.isSuccessful()) {
                        startActivity(new Intent(SignedInActivity.this,
                                FirebaseAuthActivity.class));
                        finish();
                    } else {
                        // Notify user of error
                    }
                }
            });
}
```

As with the signing out process, the method begins by obtaining a reference to the AuthUI instance, this time making a call to the *delete()* method. The deletion process is, once again, an asynchronous task, requiring the provision of a completion handler to be called when the task completes. On a successful account deletion, the user is returned to the main activity.

With this task complete the example app is ready to be tested, an area that is covered in the next chapter entitled *Testing and Customizing FirebaseUI Auth Authentication*.

4.13 **Summary**

This chapter has provided a detailed tutorial to implementing email/password based authentication within an Android app using FirebaseUI Auth. FirebaseUI Auth provides a comprehensive, pre-built user authentication system including user interface and backend functionality that reduces the amount of code that needs to be written by the developer.

This authentication solution requires that a basic sequence of steps be performed consisting of connecting the Android Studio project to Firebase, adding Firebase build dependencies and enabling authentication for the project within the Firebase console. Once the configuration tasks are completed, the authentication process is initiated within the code of the Android app and listeners implemented to respond to results of the authentication process.

The next chapter, entitled *Testing and Customizing FirebaseUI Auth Authentication*, will focus on testing the app developed in this chapter and introduce some of the options available for customizing the user sign-in experience when using FirebaseUI Auth.

5. Testing and Customizing FirebaseUI Auth Authentication

The previous chapter worked through the development of an Android app that uses the FirebaseUI Auth API to implement email/password based user authentication. At the end of that chapter, the app was largely complete and ready to be tested. This chapter will work through the testing of the app and, in doing so, demonstrate both the account creation and sign-in features of FirebaseUI Auth and the user account management options within the Firebase console.

Once testing of the app is complete, this chapter will also introduce some of the options that are available to customize the appearance and behavior of the FirebaseUI Auth interface.

5.1 Authentication Testing Environment

The Firebase authentication features can be tested on either a physical device or a suitably configured emulator. In particular, the emulator must be running a version of Android that includes the Google APIs.

5.2 Firebase Console User Management

Before testing the FirebaseAuth app it is worth gaining some familiarity with the user management features located in the Authentication section of the Firebase console.

Log into the Firebase console and select the *Firebase Examples* project followed by the *Authentication* option located in the left-hand navigation panel. Within the Authentication screen, select the Users tab as illustrated in Figure 5-1:

Figure 5-1

Note that there are currently no users associated with this project. As users are added from within the app, they will be listed within this panel. A button is also provided for the manual addition of users. The list may be refreshed at any time by clicking on the reload button located to the right of the *Add User* button.

5.3 **Testing the FirebaseAuth App**

Compile and run the FirebaseAuth app, either on a physical device or a simulator session. Once the app has loaded, it will immediately prompt for the user to enter an email address as shown in Figure 5-2:

Figure 5-2

Start by entering an invalid email address (for example one containing spaces) and selecting the *Next* button. Note that the Firebase authentication system reports that the email address is not correctly formatted.

Enter your email address into the Email field and tap the *Next* button. When a valid email address is entered, the authentication process contacts Firebase to find out if the email address is already stored in the list of users for the *Firebase Examples* project. Since the email address is not yet associated with any existing users, the account creation screen (Figure 5-3) is displayed:

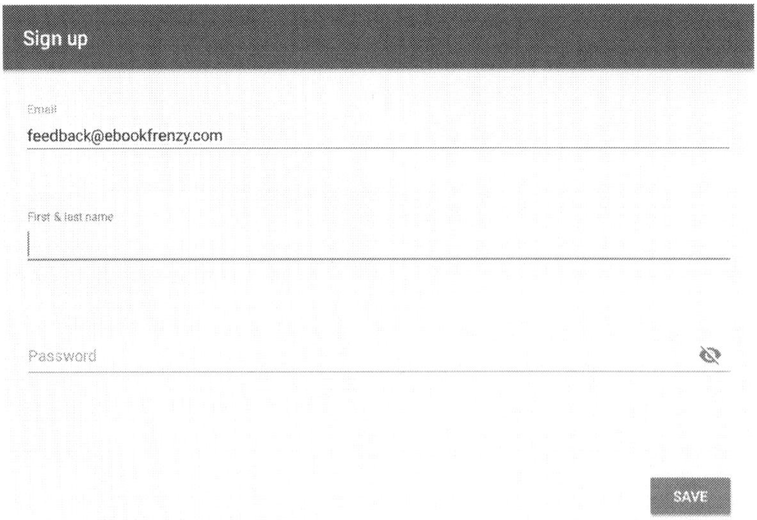

Figure 5-3

Enter your name and specify a password to be associated with the account before tapping the *Save* button. The account creation screen will insist on a password of at least 6 characters in length and provides the option to display the password by tapping the eye icon in the far right of the password field.

Once the name and password information have been saved, the account will be created and the user signed in, causing the SignedInActivity screen to appear displaying the email address and name associated with the newly created account.

Return to the browser window displaying the list of authenticated users and click on the refresh button. Once the list has updated the newly added account should be listed. This entry in the list will include the email address, an envelope icon indicating that this is an email address/password based account, the creation and last sign-in date and the user's unique identifier (UID). Moving the mouse pointer over the list entry will cause additional options to appear. The button containing three vertically arranged dots will, when clicked, present a menu of account management options as illustrated in Figure 5-4:

Figure 5-4

A deleted account cannot be subsequently restored, though a disabled account can be re-enabled at any time using the same menu. Requesting a password reset will result in a password reset email containing a link allowing the user to reset the password being sent to the email address associated with the account.

Within the running FirebaseAuth app, tap the *Sign Out* button to return to the original sign-in screen and enter the same email address before tapping the *Next* button. This time, Firebase will discover that an account associated with the email address exists and request the corresponding password:

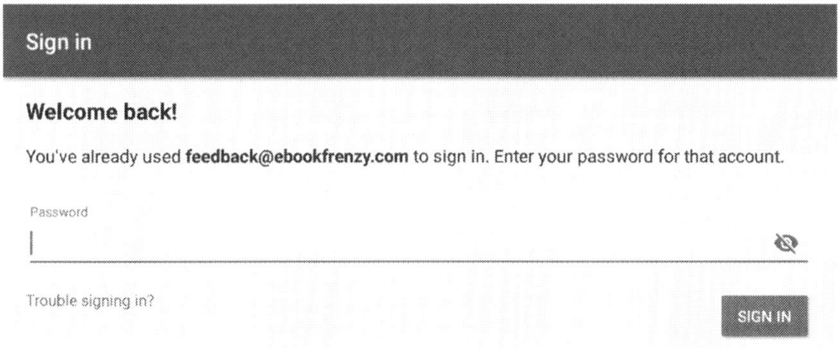

Figure 5-5

As can be seen in Figure 5-5 above, the password screen includes a *Trouble signing in?* link which, when selected will provide the user with the option to receive the same password reset email as that sent from within the Firebase console.

Enter the password for your account and wait to be logged into the SignedInActivity screen.

5.4 **Customizing the Password Reset Email Message**

Firebase provides three email templates for messages that will be sent to users for email address verification, password reset and email address change. These templates are customizable and accessible from the *Templates* tab within the Authentication screen of the Firebase console. Figure 5-6, for example, shows the standard message template that is sent when a user requests a password reset email:

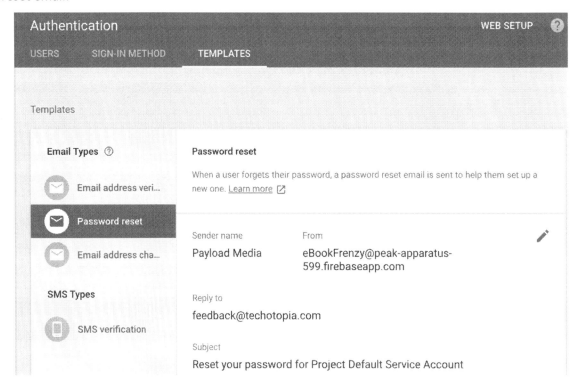

Figure 5-6

Click on the pencil icon to edit the settings for the message. By default, the email message will use the specified subject and title text. There will be no reply-to email address, no sender name and the message will appear to have been sent by *noreply@<app-identifier>.firebaseapp.com*. The email address settings can be changed within the top section of the template editing screen shown in Figure 5-7:

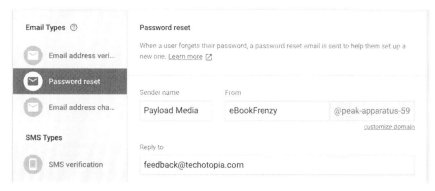

Figure 5-7

To change the domain containing the from email address it will be necessary to prove ownership of the domain. Click on the *customize domain* link, enter the URL of your web site domain, click on the *Continue* and edit the settings for the domain's DNS records as instructed. After the changes have been made click on the *Verify* button. It may take up to 48 hours before the DNS settings take effect and the domain is successfully verified.

The middle section of the screen allows the subject and message content to be customized:

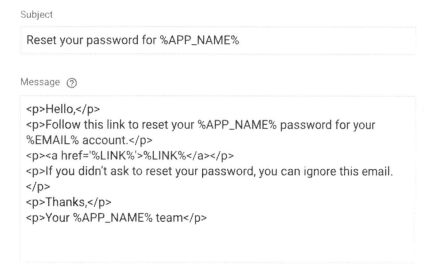

Figure 5-8

Both the subject and message content allow the use of the following placeholder variables which are automatically replaced by the corresponding values when the message is sent to the user:

- **%DISPLAY_NAME%** - The user's first name.
- **%APP_NAME%** - The name of the app for which the user is requesting a password reset.
- **%LINK%** - The link on which the user clicks to initiate the password change.
- **%EMAIL%** - The user's email address.

- **%NEW_EMAIL%** - Used only when the user is performing an email address change, this is replaced by the new email address.

The name used to replace the %APP_NAME% placeholder is set by default to "Project Default Service Account". To change this, click on the cog icon to the right of the *Firebase Examples* project name in the upper left-hand corner of the Firebase console and select the *Project Settings* option (highlighted in Figure 5-9):

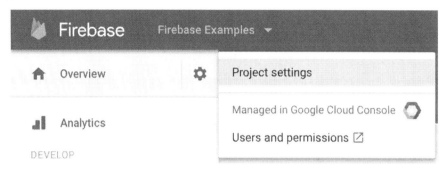

Figure 5-9

On the General screen of the Settings panel, click on the pencil icon to the right of the *Public-facing name* value, enter the new name into the resulting dialog and click *Save* to commit the change:

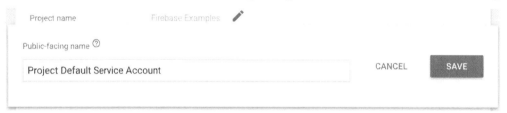

Figure 5-10

The final customization option (Figure 5-11) allows the password URL to be changed (also referred to as the action URL) to reference your own server instead of letting Firebase handle the password change. When a custom URL has been specified, this URL will be substituted for the %LINK% placeholder within the email message, with two additional parameters (mode and oobCode) appended to the end:

Figure 5-11

5.5 **Testing the Password Reset**

Take some time to customize the password reset email template, then return to the running FirebaseAuth app. Tap the *Sign Out* button to return to the sign-in screen, re-enter your email address and click *Next*. On the password screen, select the *Trouble signing in?* link and follow the steps to send a password reset email. When the email arrives in your inbox, review it to make sure it matches the changes before clicking on the provided link to change the password. The reset link may only be clicked once and expires shortly after the email has been sent to the user.

5.6 **Enabling Smart Lock for Passwords**

So far, the example app has not made use of Smart Lock for Passwords. Smart Lock is the technology behind the Google Chrome browser feature that remembers login and password information for the web sites visited by a user. This feature, when enabled, is also available to Android apps using Firebase authentication.

Smart Lock for Passwords allows the authentication system to present a list of credentials previously stored on the device by the user using Smart Lock. The user simply selects a previously stored identity to sign into or sign up for access to the app.

Smart Lock is enabled when calling the *createSignInIntentBuilder()* method on the AuthUI instance. To enable Smart Lock for the FirebaseAuth project, edit the *FirebaseAuthActivity.java* file, locate the *authenticateUser()* method and modify the *setIsSmartLockEnabled()* method to pass through a true value:

```
private void authenticateUser() {
    startActivityForResult(
            AuthUI.getInstance().createSignInIntentBuilder()
                    .setAvailableProviders(getProviderList())
                    .setIsSmartLockEnabled(true)
                    .build(),
            REQUEST_CODE);
}
```

When the app is run on a device, the user will be presented with a list of identities that have been previously saved to the user's Google account:

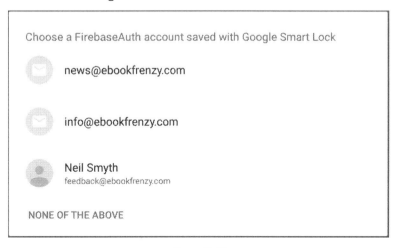

Figure 5-12

If an identity is selected from the list for which an account has already been created for the Firebase project, and for which Smart Lock has been used to save the password, the user will be directly logged into the device. If no account yet exists, the user will be required to create an account before proceeding.

The identities associated with the user's Google account may be reviewed and edited at any time by visiting the following URL:

https://passwords.google.com

Figure 5-13, for example, shows the Google Smart Lock entries for the FirebaseAuth app as stored by Google Smart Lock for passwords:

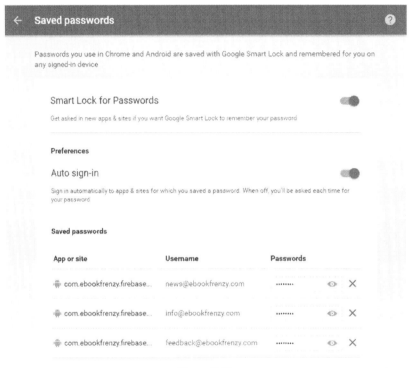

Figure 5-13

5.7 **Color Customization**

A different color theme may be specified for the FirebaseUI Auth account creation and sign-in screens. This is particularly useful when the screens are required to match the overall branding or color theme of the app. Where possible, it is recommended that the color selections chosen conform to the Material design guidelines.

Material design was created by the Android team at Google and dictates that the elements that make up the user interface of Android and the apps that run on it appear and behave in a certain way in terms of behavior, shadowing, animation and style. Details on Material color styles, color palettes and schemes can be found online at the following URL:

https://material.google.com/style/color.html

The referenced web page also includes a palette of colors that have been chosen to work together within the theme of an Android app.

Declaring a custom theme for the Firebase authentication UI is a two-step process which begins with adding a new style to the project's *styles.xml* file located under *app -> res -> values* within the project tool window:

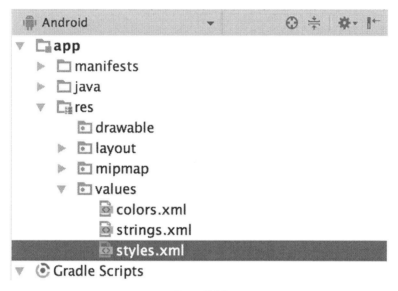

Figure 5-14

Within the FirebaseAuth project, edit this *styles.xml* file and add the following custom theme entry:

```xml
<style name="CustomTheme" parent="FirebaseUI">
    <item name="colorPrimary">@color/material_green_600</item>
    <item name="colorPrimaryDark">@color/material_green_700</item>
    <item name="colorAccent">@color/material_purple_a700</item>
    <item name="colorControlNormal">@color/material_green_500</item>
    <item name="colorControlActivated">@color/material_lime_a800</item>
    <item name="colorControlHighlight">@color/material_green_a200</item>
    <item name="android:windowBackground">@color/material_lime_50</item>
    <item name="colorButtonNormal">@color/material_purple_500</item>
</style>
```

The color values referenced above were all taken from the Material color palette. The next step is to declare the colors referenced in the above style. These need to be declared in *colors.xml* file located under *app -> res -> values*. Edit this file and add the following color entries:

```xml
<color name="material_green_600">#43A047</color>
<color name="material_green_500">#4CAF50</color>
<color name="material_green_700">#388E3C</color>
```

```
<color name="material_green_a200">#69F0AE</color>
<color name="material_lime_a800">#AFB42B</color>
<color name="material_lime_50">#F9FBE7</color>
<color name="material_purple_a700">#AA00FF</color>
<color name="material_purple_500">#9C27B0</color>
```

Once the style and colors have been declared, the new theme needs to be referenced during the building of the sign-in intend via a call to the *setTheme()* method. Edit the *FirebaseAuthActivity.java* file, locate the *authenticateUser()* method and modify it to change the theme:

```
private void authenticateUser() {
    startActivityForResult(
            AuthUI.getInstance().createSignInIntentBuilder()
                    .setTheme(R.style.CustomTheme)
                    .setAvailableProviders(getProviderList())
                    .setIsSmartLockEnabled(true)
                    .build(),
            REQUEST_CODE);
}
```

Compile and run the app and verify that the sign-in and account creation screens have adopted the specified theme. To gain a familiarity with the different color settings, experiment with different colors within the theme using the Material color palette as a guideline.

5.8 Specifying a Logo

In addition to changing the color theme, FirebaseUI Auth also allows a logo to be specified for presentation during the sign-in process. For this example, the *firelogo.png* image file contained within the *project_images* folder of the sample code download will be used. If you have not already downloaded the code samples, the archive can be downloaded using the following link:

http://www.ebookfrenzy.com/print/firebase_android

Locate the *firelogo.png* image in the file system navigator for your operating system and copy the image file. Right-click on the *app -> res -> drawable* entry in the Project tool window and select Paste from the menu to add the file to the folder. When the copy dialog appears, click on OK to accept the default settings:

Figure 5-15

With the logo added to the project, all that remains is to include it when the sign-in intent is constructed. In this case, the logo is added via a call to the *setLogo()* method as outlined in the following listing:

```
private void authenticateUser() {
    startActivityForResult(
            AuthUI.getInstance().createSignInIntentBuilder()
                    .setTheme(R.style.CustomTheme)
                    .setLogo(R.drawable.firelogo)
                    .setAvailableProviders(getProviderList())
                    .setIsSmartLockEnabled(true)
                    .build(),
            REQUEST_CODE);
}
```

Although the logo has been included in the activity, it would not be visible were the app to be run now. This is because the logo only appears when the authentication provider selection screen is displayed. Since the app is currently configured to use only one provider in the form of email and password authentication, this screen is not yet used. The logo will, however, become visible during the next chapter (entitled *Google Sign-In Authentication using FirebaseUI Auth*) when another authentication provider is added to the project.

5.9 Deleting the Test Account

The final area to test is the deletion of the user's account. The SignedInActivity screen contains a button configured to delete the current user from the list of registered users. Verify that the account deletion code works by launching the FirebaseAuth app and signing in using the previously registered account credentials. Once the SignedInActivity screen appears, tap the Delete Account button. The user will be signed out of the app and the account deleted. Open the Firebase console in a browser window, navigate to the Authentication page for the *Firebase Examples* project and verify that the account is no longer listed on the Users screen.

5.10 Summary

In the previous chapter, an example project was created that used the FirebaseUI Auth system to implement email and password based authentication. This chapter has performed a sequence of tests intended not only to verify that the code works but also to outline many of the features that are provided by default when using Firebase Authentication. This chapter has also explored the various ways in which the Firebase authentication process can be configured and customized, including the use of Smart Lock, customizing the password reset email message, changing color themes and adding a logo.

6. Google Sign-In Authentication using FirebaseUI Auth

The next area of Firebase authentication to cover involves the use of the Google Sign-in provider. As with the email and password provider, Google Sign-in uses an email address and a password to authenticate a user. In this case, however, the user's existing Google account credentials are used to create the user's account.

In this chapter, the FirebaseAuth project will be extended to include Google Sign-in authentication.

6.1 Preparing the Project

Most of the steps required to configure the project to work with Google Sign-in as an authentication provider have already been performed in the chapter entitled *Email/Password Authentication using FirebaseUI Auth*. These steps include connecting the project to Firebase from within Android Studio and adding the build dependencies to the Gradle build files.

Two additional steps are, however, required in preparation for adding Google Sign-in support to the project. These consist of adding the SHA-1 fingerprint for the app to the Firebase project and enabling Google Sign-in as a supported sign-in method.

6.2 Obtaining the SHA-1 Fingerprint

As an Android developer you have two unique certificates used to sign the apps you develop using Android Studio. The *debug certificate* is used to sign apps that are being developed and tested. The *release certificate* on the other hand, is used to sign the apps when they are ready to be uploaded to the Google Play store.

These certificates take the form of SHA-1 fingerprints. By default the debug key is stored in a file named *debug.keystore* and located in the *.android* folder of your home directory. The release keystore file is created when you first generate the release APK file for your app and will be placed in a location of your choosing.

Ultimately, both the release and debug fingerprints will need to be added to the Firebase project with which the Android app is associated in order to use the Google Sign-in provider. At this stage, however, only the debug fingerprint needs to be added.

There are a number of options for obtaining the SHA-1 fingerprint, the most common of which is to use the keytool command-line tool included with the Android SDK. On Windows, open a command prompt window and execute the following command to obtain the debug key:

```
keytool -exportcert -list -v -alias androiddebugkey -keystore
            %USERPROFILE%\.android\debug.keystore
```

The command will prompt for the password which, by default, set to *android*.

Similarly, the following command can be executed within a terminal window on macOS or Linux to obtain the debug key:

```
keytool -exportcert -list -v -alias androiddebugkey -keystore
            ~/.android/debug.keystore
```

The keytool utility may also be used to extract the release key as follows where *<key name>* and *<path to keystore>* are replaced by the name given to the key location of the release keystore file specified when the key was created:

```
keytool -exportcert -list -v
            -alias <key name> -keystore <path to keystore>
```

Before the key information is displayed, the utility will prompt for the password assigned to the keystore file. When prompted, enter the password specified when the keystore was generated.

The keytool command will output a number of values including the certificate fingerprints in a variety of encodings, one of which will be labeled SHA1, for example:

```
SHA1: 17:22:55:79:67:65:D6:3F:56:66:BF:A9:41:68:62:7A:CC:77:EE:A4
```

Copy the key so that it is ready to be pasted into the Firebase console.

6.3 Adding the SHA-1 Key to the Firebase Project

Having obtained at least the debug SHA-1 fingerprint, it must now be added to the project within the Firebase console. Open the console within a browser window and select the *Firebase Examples* project. Click on the settings gear icon to the right of the Overview title in the left-hand panel and select *Project settings* from the resulting menu:

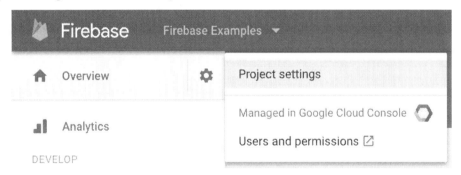

Figure 6-1

Within the settings screen, select the FirebaseAuth app from the list of apps, then locate and click on the Add Fingerprint button:

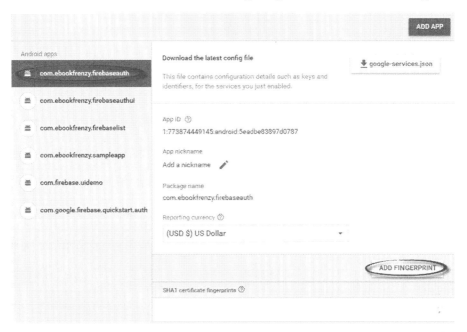

Figure 6-2

When the Add Fingerprint button is clicked, a dialog (Figure 6-3) will appear into which the SHA-1 fingerprint provided by the keytool utility must now be pasted. Once the key has been entered, click on the *Save* button and verify that the certificate is now listed in the settings screen.

Figure 6-3

6.4 Enabling the Google Sign-In Method

The next step to be performed within the Firebase console is to enable the Google Sign-In method within the project authentication settings. With the *Firebase Examples* project still selected within the console, select the Authentication option from the left-hand navigation panel followed by the Sign-In Method tab in the authentication panel.

Within the list of providers select the Google entry and, in the resulting panel, turn on the *Enable* switch as illustrated in Figure 6-4 before clicking on the *Save* button:

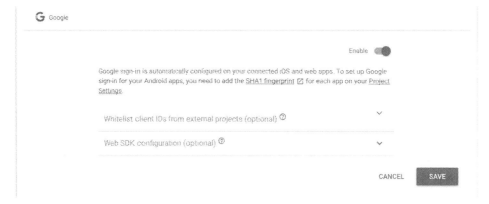

Figure 6-4

If you have other Google based projects (such as other Android apps or even web or Chrome-based apps) that you would like to use the same authentication settings, add the client IDs here. To find the ID for a Google Cloud Platform project, open the Google Cloud console (https://console.cloud.google.com), select the project name and navigate to *API Manager -> Credentials.* A list of projects and respective client IDs will appear listed under *OAuth 2.0 client IDs* as illustrated in Figure 6-5:

Figure 6-5

6.5 Adding the Google Sign-In Provider within the App

The final step before testing the Google Sign-in provider is to add some code within the app. Load the *FirebaseAuthActivity.java* file into the Android Studio code editor, locate the *getProvider()* list method and modify it to add the Google provider:

```
private List<AuthUI.IdpConfig> getProviderList() {

    List<AuthUI.IdpConfig> providers = new ArrayList<>();

    providers.add(new
        AuthUI.IdpConfig.Builder(AuthUI.EMAIL_PROVIDER).build());
    providers.add(new
        AuthUI.IdpConfig.Builder(AuthUI.GOOGLE_PROVIDER).build());

    return providers;
```

```
}
```

For initial testing purposes, edit the *authenticateUser()* method to disable Smart Lock:

```
private void authenticateUser() {
    startActivityForResult(
            AuthUI.getInstance().createSignInIntentBuilder()
                    .setTheme(R.style.CustomTheme)
                    .setLogo(R.drawable.firelogo)
                    .setAvailableProviders(getProviderList())
                    .setIsSmartLockEnabled(false)
                    .build(),
            REQUEST_CODE);
}
```

6.6 Testing Google Sign-In

With the code changes completed, compile and run the Firebase app on a device or emulator. This time when the app launches the app will behave differently. Now that there are two possible sign-in providers, the app no longer immediately displays the initial email and password sign-in screen. Instead, the user is presented with two buttons allowing the sign-in to be performed using either email or Google. Note also, that the logo added in the previous chapter is displayed above the buttons:

Figure 6-6

Begin the sign-in process by clicking on the *Sign in with Google* button. At this point the Firebase authentication process will check on the device to identify if any Google accounts have been configured. If no Google accounts have been set up on the device or emulator, the process of entering the credentials for an existing Google account, or creating a new one will begin, starting with the screen shown in Figure 6-7:

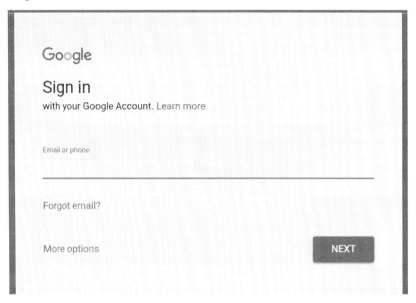

Figure 6-7

Once a valid Google account has been entered, or a new Google account created, those account details will be stored in the Firebase user database and the user signed into the app. The account will also be stored locally on the device or emulator and will be presented as a sign-in option next time the user needs to log into the app. On selecting a previously stored Google account, the user will be signed into the app without the need to enter the corresponding password.

If, on the other hand, one or more Google accounts have already been stored on the device, the authentication activity will present a list of those accounts.

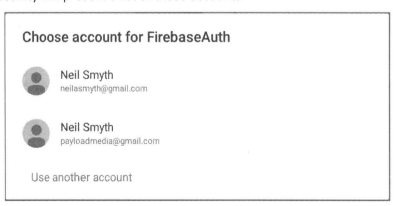

Figure 6-8

When the user selects an account from the list, it is added to the Firebase user database and the user signed into the app. If the required account is not listed, the user can select the *Add account* option and proceed through the steps of either entering the credentials for a different Google account or creating a new Google account as illustrated in Figure 6-7 above.

If you are testing the app on a device or emulator on which no pre-existing Google accounts have been configured, one or more may also be added by launching the Settings app, selecting the *Accounts* category and clicking on the *Add account* button.

Having created a new account for the FirebaseAuth app using a Google Sign-in, select the *Firebase Examples* project in the Firebase console and review the list of users on the Authentication page. Any Google accounts added to the project will appear in the list with a Google "G" in the Provider column indicating that these users used the Google Sign-in provider to create the account:

Figure 6-9

6.7 Displaying the User's Profile Photo

Unlike the email and password sign-in method, Google accounts are likely to have a profile photo, even if it is only the default photo comprised of a colored square containing the first letter of the user's name. The FirebaseAuth app can now be enhanced to extract the profile photo from the account and display it within the SignedInActivity screen.

When a profile picture is available, a URL will be included within the current user's FirebaseUser object along with the other information such as email address and display name. The photo URL can be extracted via a call to the *getPhotoUrl()* method of the FirebaseUser object.

Edit the *SignedInActivity.java* file, locate the *onCreate()* method and add code to check for the presence of a photo URL:

```
@Override
protected void onCreate(Bundle savedInstanceState) {
    super.onCreate(savedInstanceState);
    setContentView(R.layout.activity_signed_in);

    FirebaseUser currentUser = FirebaseAuth.getInstance().getCurrentUser();

    if (currentUser == null) {
        startActivity(new Intent(this, FirebaseAuthActivity.class));
        finish();
```

```
        return;
    }

    TextView email = (TextView) findViewById(R.id.email);
    TextView displayname = (TextView) findViewById(R.id.displayname);

    email.setText(currentUser.getEmail());
    displayname.setText(currentUser.getDisplayName());

    if (currentUser.getPhotoUrl() != null) {
        displayImage(currentUser.getPhotoUrl());
    }
}
```

If the method identifies the presence of a photo URL, that URL is passed to a method named *displayImage()*. It will be the responsibility of this method to download the image using the provided URL and display it on the ImageView object within the SignedInActivity layout. Remaining within the *SignedInActivity.java* file, add the code to download and display the photo image so that it reads as follows:

```
package com.ebookfrenzy.firebaseauth;

import android.content.Intent;
import android.support.annotation.NonNull;
import android.support.v7.app.AppCompatActivity;
import android.os.Bundle;
import android.view.View;
import android.widget.TextView;
import android.graphics.Bitmap;
import android.graphics.BitmapFactory;
import android.net.Uri;
import android.os.AsyncTask;
import android.widget.ImageView;

import java.io.InputStream;

import com.firebase.ui.auth.AuthUI;
import com.google.android.gms.tasks.OnCompleteListener;
import com.google.android.gms.tasks.Task;
import com.google.firebase.auth.FirebaseAuth;
import com.google.firebase.auth.FirebaseUser;

public class SignedInActivity extends AppCompatActivity {

.
```

```
    void displayImage(Uri imageUrl) {

        // show The Image in a ImageView
        new DownloadImageTask((ImageView) findViewById(R.id.imageView))
                .execute(imageUrl.toString());
    }

    private class DownloadImageTask extends AsyncTask<String, Void, Bitmap> {
        ImageView bmImage;

        public DownloadImageTask(ImageView bmImage) {
            this.bmImage = bmImage;
        }

        protected Bitmap doInBackground(String... urls) {
            String urldisplay = urls[0];
            Bitmap bitmap = null;
            try {
                InputStream in = new java.net.URL(urldisplay).openStream();
                bitmap = BitmapFactory.decodeStream(in);
            } catch (Exception e) {
                e.printStackTrace();
            }
            return bitmap;
        }

        protected void onPostExecute(Bitmap result) {
            bmImage.setImageBitmap(result);
        }
    }
    .
    .
    .
}
```

The added code runs an asynchronous task in the background to download the image data from the photo URL. Once the download completes, the downloaded image data is converted to a bitmap and displayed on the ImageView object.

Compile and run the app and once again sign in using a Google account. When the SignedInActivity screen appears the profile picture associated with the account should be displayed on the ImageView object:

Figure 6-10

Finally, edit the *onCreate()* method within the *FirebaseAuthActivity.java* file to re-enable Smart Lock:

```
private void authenticateUser() {
    startActivityForResult(
            AuthUI.getInstance().createSignInIntentBuilder()
                    .setTheme(R.style.CustomTheme)
                    .setLogo(R.drawable.firelogo)
                    .setProviders(getProviderList())
                    .setIsSmartLockEnabled(true)
                    .build(),
            REQUEST_CODE);
}
```

The next time the app is run, the Smart Lock dialog will appear providing the option to sign in using account credentials saved for both Google Sign-in and email/password based accounts.

6.8 **Summary**

Firebase authentication provides a number of different ways in which a user's identity can be established. While the previous chapter explored the use of email and password authentication, this chapter has covered the use of Google account credentials to authenticate users.

The first step in implementing Google Sign-in as an authentication option is to add your developer debug certificate SHA-1 key to the Firebase project containing the app and enable the Google Sign-in method via the Firebase console. Once these steps are completed, all that remains is to add Google as a supported provider while performing the initialization of FirebaseUI Auth within the app code.

When Google Sign-in is fully implemented and enabled, users will be able to create new accounts for the app based on existing Google accounts. Users without a Google account are also given the option to create a new one as part of the signup process for the app.

7. Facebook Login Authentication using FirebaseUI Auth

So far in this book we have covered two different types of Firebase user authentication for Android apps. The first involved the creation of user accounts based solely on the user's email address and a password. These accounts apply only to the Firebase project with which the Android app is associated and are unconnected to any accounts the user might have on other platforms.

The second approach, which was covered in the previous chapter, allows users to create an account and sign into Android apps based on existing Google account credentials. This has the advantage that the user does not have yet another login and password to keep track of along with those of other apps and web sites for which the user has signed up over the years.

This chapter will continue the theme of using third-party credentials to create an account and sign into the example FirebaseAuth app by making use of the Facebook Login provider.

7.1 Preparing the Project

As with the Google Sign-in example covered in the previous chapter, most of the steps required to configure the project to work with Facebook Login have already been performed in the chapter entitled *Email/Password Authentication using FirebaseUI Auth*. These steps include connecting the project to Firebase from within Android Studio and adding the build dependencies to the Gradle build files.

A number of additional steps are, however, required in preparation for adding Facebook Login support to the project. These steps will be outlined in detail throughout the remainder of this chapter.

7.2 Obtaining the Facebook App ID and App Secret

The Facebook App ID and App Secret serve as the connection between the Android app and the Facebook Login service. Each app that makes use of Facebook developer services in any way must have a unique ID and secret, both of which are assigned by Facebook via the Facebook for Developers site.

To generate the ID and secret, begin by logging into the Facebook for Developers portal at the following URL:

https://developers.facebook.com/

Log into the developer portal using your Facebook account information (or create a Facebook account if you do not already have one) and, after signing in, navigate to the Facebook Login Apps page:

Facebook Login Authentication using FirebaseUI Auth

https://developers.facebook.com/apps/

On the apps page, click on the *Add a New App* button as highlighted in Figure 7-1:

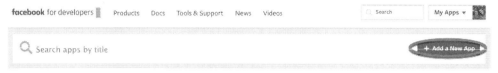

Figure 7-1

In the resulting dialog fill in values for the Display Name, Contact Email and Category settings before clicking on the *Create App ID* button:

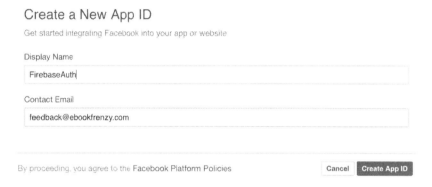

Figure 7-2

If prompted, perform the security check task in the next dialog before clicking on the Submit button.

Once the app has been created, return to the Facebook apps screen and select the newly added app. From the left-hand navigation panel, select the *Settings* option. The app settings screen (Figure 7-3) will display a range of values, including the App ID and App Secret. If the App Secret is concealed, click on the *Show* button to reveal the value:

Figure 7-3

Select the Advanced option in the navigation panel and enable the *Native or desktop app?* switch before clicking on the Save Changes button:

Figure 7-4

7.3 Adding the App ID and Secret to the Firebase Project

Open a second browser window and navigate to the Firebase console. Select the *Firebase Examples* project followed by the Authentication option. On the authentication screen, choose the *Sign-In Method* tab and click on the Facebook provider option. When the Facebook provider dialog appears (Figure 7-5) turn on the *Enable* switch and cut and paste the App ID and App Secret values from the Facebook for Developers app settings screen into the corresponding fields of the Firebase dialog:

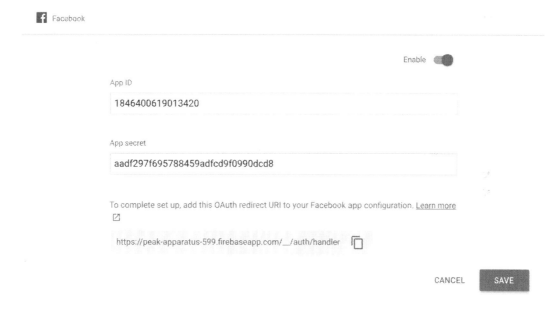

Figure 7-5

Copy the OAuth redirect URI shown at the bottom of the dialog in preparation for a later step, then click on the *Save* button to commit the settings and enable the Facebook provider.

7.4 Adding the Facebook Login Product to the App

Once a new app has been created, the Facebook products that are to be supported by the app need to be added. Within the Settings page, locate the Products section in the navigation panel and click on the *+ Add Product* entry as illustrated in Figure 7-6:

Figure 7-6

When the Add Product link is clicked the Product Setup screen will appear containing a list of products that are available to be added to the app. Locate and click on the *Get Started* button next to the Facebook Login product and choose Android from the platform selection screen.

On the Android startup screen, click on the link that reads *I already installed the SDK*.

7.5 Setting the OAuth Redirect URI

The OAuth Redirect URI copied from the Firebase console in a previous section now needs to be setup for the app within the Facebook for Developers portal. Select the *Settings* option listed under Facebook Login in the Products section of the navigation panel:

Figure 7-7

On the settings screen, paste the Uri into the *Valid OAuth redirect URIs* field as shown in Figure 7-8 and turn on the *Login from Devices* option. Click on the *Save Changes* button before proceeding.

Figure 7-8

7.6 **Adding the Debug and Release Key Hash**

The final task before modifying the code for the app is to add the debug release key for your Android development environment to the Facebook app configuration. This once again requires the use of the *keytool* utility together with the *openssl* tool. On macOS and Linux, open a terminal window and execute the following command to obtain the debug key hash:

```
keytool -exportcert -alias androiddebugkey -keystore
     ~/.android/debug.keystore | openssl sha1 -binary | openssl base64
```

The default password for the debug keystore is *android*.

On Windows it will be necessary to install OpenSSL before the key hash can be generated. A copy of OpenSSL for Windows can be downloaded using the following link:

https://sourceforge.net/projects/openssl

Once OpenSSL has been installed, run the following command within a Command Prompt window to generate the debug key hash:

```
keytool -exportcert -alias androiddebugkey -keystore
  %HOMEPATH%\.android\debug.keystore | openssl sha1 -binary | openssl base64
```

To generate the release key hash before uploading an app to the app store, the following command will need to be executed (where *<key name>* and *<path to keystore>* are replaced by the name given to the key and the location of the release keystore file specified when the key was created):

```
keytool -exportcert -alias <key name>  -keystore <path to keystore> |
            openssl sha1 -binary | openssl base64
```

Once the key hash has been generated, it needs to be added to the app configuration within the Facebook for Developers portal. With the app selected in the Facebook portal, select the basic settings option in the navigation panel. Within the settings screen, click on the *Add Platform* option as shown in Figure 7-9:

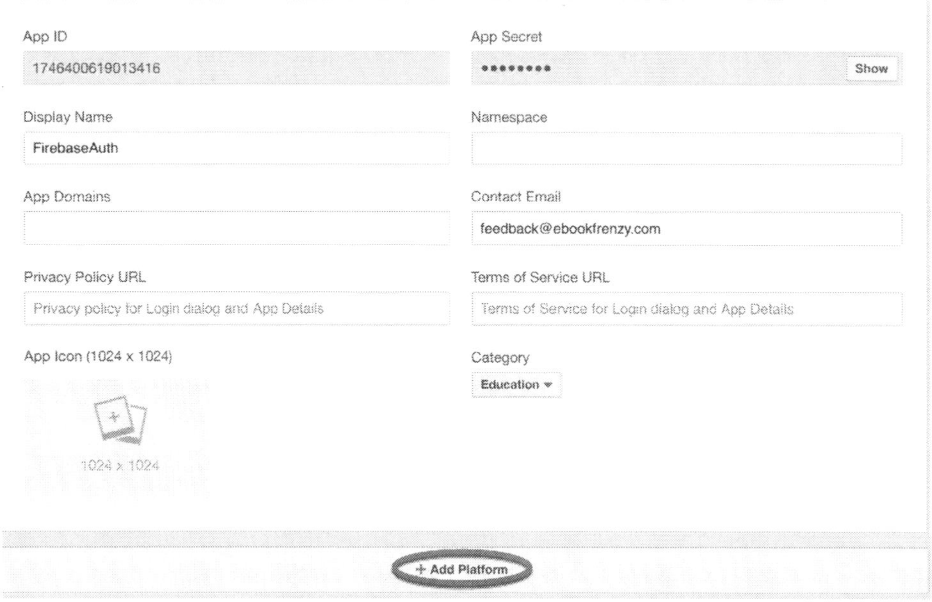

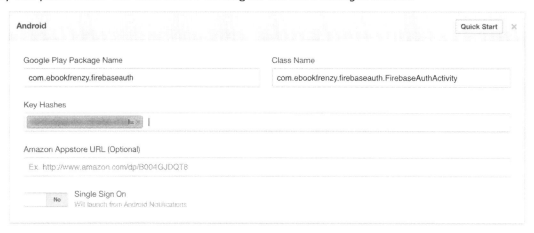

Figure 7-9

From the list of platforms, select the Android option. An additional section will then appear within the settings screen including a field titled *Key Hashes*. Copy the debug key hash generated by the keytool utility and paste it into this field before clicking on the *Save Changes* button:

Figure 7-10

When you have an app ready to be published, return to these settings and paste in the release hash key into the same field.

7.7 **Modifying the App**

With the work complete in the Firebase console and Facebook for Developers portal, there are now three more tasks that need to be accomplished before Facebook Login can be used within the example app. The first task is to add a string declaration within the *strings.xml* file containing the Facebook App

ID. With the FirebaseAuth project loaded into Android Studio, use the project tool window to open the *app -> res -> values -> strings.xml* file. With the file loaded into the editor, add a new string entity with the name *facebook_application_id* as follows where *<your_fb_app_id>* is replaced by the actual App ID assigned within the Facebook portal:

```
<resources>
    <string name="app_name">FirebaseAuth</string>
    <string name="facebook_application_id"
                translatable="false"><your_fb_app_id></string>
</resources>
```

Next, two new elements need to be added to the project manifest file, one to grant internet access permission to the app, and the other to assign the *facebook_application_id* string created above to the ApplicationId property of the Facebook SDK. Within the project tool window, select the *manifests -> AndroidManifest.xml* file and edit it to add these additional elements:

```
<?xml version="1.0" encoding="utf-8"?>
<manifest xmlns:android="http://schemas.android.com/apk/res/android"
    package="com.ebookfrenzy.firebaseauth">

    <uses-permission android:name="android.permission.INTERNET"/>

    <application
        android:allowBackup="true"
        android:icon="@mipmap/ic_launcher"
        android:label="@string/app_name"
        android:supportsRtl="true"
        android:theme="@style/AppTheme">
        <activity
            android:name=".FirebaseAuthActivity"
            android:label="@string/app_name"
            android:theme="@style/AppTheme.NoActionBar">
            <intent-filter>
                <action android:name="android.intent.action.MAIN" />

                <category android:name="android.intent.category.LAUNCHER" />
            </intent-filter>
        </activity>
        <activity android:name=".SignedInActivity"></activity>

        <meta-data android:name="com.facebook.sdk.ApplicationId"
            android:value="@string/facebook_application_id"/>

    </application>
```

```
</manifest>
```

Next, edit the module level *build.gradle* file and add a dependency for the facebook-android-sdk library:

```
compile 'com.android.support:appcompat-v7:25.3.1'
compile 'com.android.support.constraint:constraint-layout:1.0.2'
compile 'com.google.firebase:firebase-auth:10.0.1'
compile 'com.firebaseui:firebase-ui:2.0.1'
compile 'com.firebaseui:firebase-ui-auth:2.0.1'
compile('com.facebook.android:facebook-android-sdk:4.23.0')
testCompile 'junit:junit:4.12'
```

The final task before testing the Facebook Login provider is to add a single line of code to include Facebook Login in the list of supported providers. Remaining within Android Studio, edit the *FirebaseAuthActivity.java* file, locate the *getProviderList()* method and modify it to add the Facebook Login provider:

```
private List<AuthUI.IdpConfig> getProviderList() {

    List<AuthUI.IdpConfig> providers = new ArrayList<>();

    providers.add(new
        AuthUI.IdpConfig.Builder(AuthUI.EMAIL_PROVIDER).build());
    providers.add(new
        AuthUI.IdpConfig.Builder(AuthUI.GOOGLE_PROVIDER).build());
    providers.add(new
        AuthUI.IdpConfig.Builder(AuthUI.FACEBOOK_PROVIDER).build());

    return providers;
}
```

7.8 Testing Facebook Login Authentication

Compile and run the FirebaseAuth app on a physical Android device or emulator. If the Smart Lock dialog appears, tap on the *None of the Above* option to display the provider selection screen where a Facebook button will now be shown along with the Google and email provider options:

Figure 7-11

After selecting the *Sign in with Facebook* button, the exact Facebook sign in screen that appears will depend on whether the Facebook app is also installed on the device. If the Facebook app is not currently installed on the device, the screen shown in Figure 7-12 will appear. This is known as the fallback login screen and is actually a login screen loaded into a WebView instance:

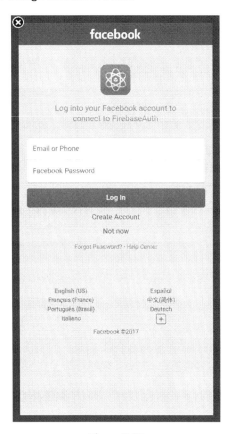

Figure 7-12

If, on the other hand, the Facebook app is installed on the device, the provider will redirect the login to the app and the sign-in screen will resemble Figure 7-13:

Figure 7-13

Sign in using a valid Facebook account and note that the account name, email address and profile photo all appear within the SignedInActivity layout.

Open a browser window and navigate to the list of users on the Authentication page for the *Firebase Examples* project where the Facebook account used to gain access to the app will now listed. Since this account was created using the Facebook Login provider, a Facebook logo is included in the Provider column:

Figure 7-14

7.9 Summary

Integrating Facebook Login as a provider within a Firebase authentication configuration is a multistep process which involves creating and configuring an app within the Facebook developer portal, implementing the correct settings within the Firebase console and making project and code changes to the app project within Android studio. Once these steps have been performed as outlined in this chapter, users are able to create accounts and sign into the app using their Facebook credentials.

8. Twitter Sign-In Authentication using FirebaseUI Auth

Now that Firebase sign-in authentication using Google and Facebook have been covered in the preceding chapters, this chapter will focus on integrating Twitter based user authentication into the example FirebaseAuth app.

As with the Facebook authentication provider, this is a multistep process consisting primarily of configuring settings within the Firebase and Twitter developer consoles.

8.1 Preparing the Project

As with the previous authentication chapters, many of the steps required to configure the project to work with Twitter as an authentication provider have already been performed in the chapter entitled *Email/Password Authentication using FirebaseUI Auth*. Assuming that these steps have been performed, the next step is to enable Twitter authentication within the Firebase console.

8.2 Enabling Twitter Authentication

Navigate to the Firebase console in a browser window and select the *Authentication* option in the navigation panel followed by the Sign-In Method tab. Click on the Twitter entry in the list of sign-in providers and turn on the *Enable* switch. The field at the bottom of the dialog will contain the callback URL for the authentication process which will need to be added within the Twitter Application Management console in the next step. Click on the button to the right of the callback URL to copy this to the clipboard:

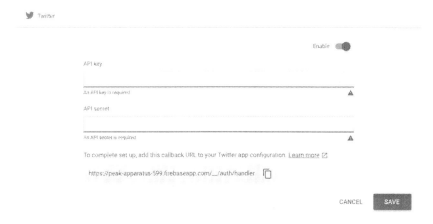

Figure 8-1

Leave the Twitter dialog open so that it is ready to paste in the API key and API secret in a later section.

8.3 **Creating a Twitter App**

Twitter authentication using Firebase requires that a consumer API key and API secret be obtained for the app from within the Twitter developer environment. This will require that you have a Twitter account with which to sign into the Twitter Application Management console. Open another browser window and navigate to the following URL to access the Application Management console:

https://apps.twitter.com/

When the page has loaded, sign into the console using your Twitter account credentials. Once signed in, click on the *Create New App* button which will display the screen shown in Figure 8-2:

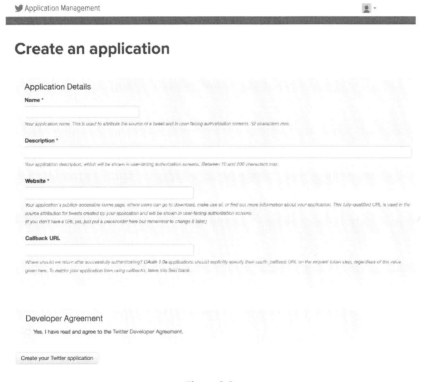

Figure 8-2

Enter a name, description and website URL into the corresponding fields of the form, then paste the callback URL copied from the Firebase console into the Callback URL field. Enable the box indicating acceptance of the developer agreement, then click on the *Create your Twitter application* button.

8.4 **Obtaining the Twitter API Keys**

After the app has been created within the management console, a screen will load displaying the details of the app. From within this screen, click on the *Keys and Access Tokens* tab:

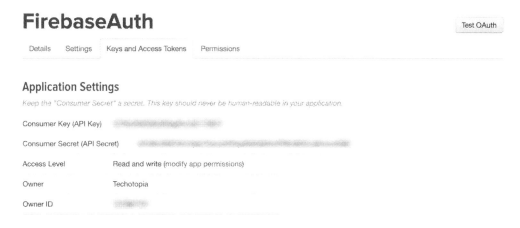

Figure 8-3

Highlight and copy the Consumer API key, return to the browser window containing the Firebase console and paste the key into the API Key field of the Twitter settings dialog. Repeat this step, this time copying the Consumer API Secret from the Twitter page and pasting it into the API Secret field within the Firebase console.

Once the keys have been added to the Firebase console, click on the Save button in the Twitter dialog of the Firebase console to commit the changes before returning to the Twitter Application Management browser window.

8.5 Generating the Access Token

Before Twitter authentication can be used, one more step is required within the Twitter Application Management console. Located beneath the Application Settings on the *Keys and Access Tokens* screen is a section entitled *Your Access Token* as shown in Figure 8-4:

Figure 8-4

To generate the access token for the app, simply click on the *Create my access token* button. After a short delay, the screen will refresh and display the generated access token information. This token information is used internally by the authentication process so no further action is needed on this screen. The consumer API key data will be needed one more time so leave this browser window open.

8.6 **Adding the API Keys to the Project**

The consumer API key and secret now need to be embedded into the Android Studio project in the form of string resources. Launch Android Studio, open the FirebaseAuth project and use the project tool window to locate and edit the *app -> res -> values -> string.xml* resource file and add entries for the consumer API key and secret as generated within the Twitter Application Management portal. These entries should read as follows where *<consumer api key>* and *<consumer api secret>* are replaced by the keys for your app:

```
<resources>
    <string name="app_name">FirebaseAuth</string>
    .
    .
    .
    <string name="twitter_consumer_key" translatable="false">
                                <consumer api key></string>

    <string name="twitter_consumer_secret" translatable="false">
                                <consumer api secret></string>
</resources>
```

8.7 **Adding Twitter to the Provider List**

The final step in implementing Twitter sign-in is to add a single line of code to the app to include Twitter in the list of sign-in providers. Edit the *FirebaseAuthActivity.java* file, locate the *getProviderList()* method and modify it so that it reads as follows:

```
private List<AuthUI.IdpConfig> getProviderList() {

    List<AuthUI.IdpConfig> providers = new ArrayList<>();

    providers.add(new
        AuthUI.IdpConfig.Builder(AuthUI.EMAIL_PROVIDER).build());
    providers.add(new
        AuthUI.IdpConfig.Builder(AuthUI.GOOGLE_PROVIDER).build());
    providers.add(new
        AuthUI.IdpConfig.Builder(AuthUI.FACEBOOK_PROVIDER).build());
    providers.add(new
        AuthUI.IdpConfig.Builder(AuthUI.TWITTER_PROVIDER).build());

    return providers;
}
```

8.8 Adding the Twitter Library Dependency

Edit the module level *build.gradle* file and add an entry to the dependencies section to reference the Twitter API SDK library as follows:

```
compile("com.twitter.sdk.android:twitter-core:3.0.0@aar") { transitive = true
}
```

8.9 Testing Twitter Authentication

Compile and run the app on a device or emulator and dismiss the Smart Lock dialog if it appears. When the login screen displays, Twitter should now be included in the list of available providers as outlined in Figure 8-5:

Figure 8-5

Choosing the Twitter sign-in option will cause a second screen to appear in which authorization must be given to access the user's Twitter account:

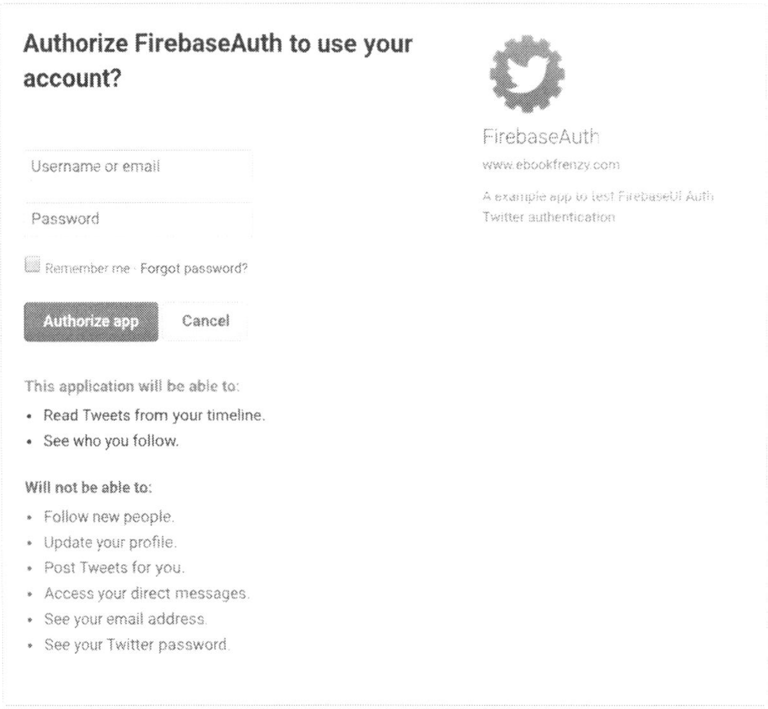

Authorize FirebaseAuth to use your account?

FirebaseAuth
www.ebookfrenzy.com

A example app to test FirebaseUI Auth Twitter authentication

Username or email

Password

Remember me · Forgot password?

Authorize app   Cancel

This application will be able to:

- Read Tweets from your timeline.
- See who you follow.

Will not be able to:

- Follow new people.
- Update your profile.
- Post Tweets for you.
- Access your direct messages.
- See your email address.
- See your Twitter password.

Figure 8-6

Enter your Twitter account credentials into the appropriate sign-in fields before clicking on the *Authorize app* button to initiate the sign-in process. Firebase will authenticate the account credentials with Twitter and, assuming a successful result, load the *SignedInActivity* screen populated with the user's profile photo and Twitter user name.

After the account has been created, return to the list of authenticated users within the Firebase console and note that the new account has been added with a Twitter logo positioned in the Providers column.

8.10 Summary

In this chapter we have explored the mechanism for implementing user authentication using the user's Twitter credentials. Similar in many ways to Facebook authentication, this involved registering the app within the Twitter Application Management console and the generation of API key data, embedding those keys into the Android project and adding Twitter as a supported authentication provider.

9. Phone Number Sign-in Authentication using FirebaseUI Auth

Firebase Phone Number Authentication allows users to sign into an app by providing a phone number. After the phone number has been entered, Firebase sends an SMS message to that number containing a one-time code that must be entered within the app to sign in. This chapter will extend the now familiar FirebaseAuth example app to include phone number authentication using FirebaseUI Auth.

9.1 Preparing the Project

As with the previous authentication chapters, most of the steps required to configure the project to work with phone verification as an authentication provider have already been performed in the chapter entitled *Email/Password Authentication using FirebaseUI Auth*. Assuming that these steps have been performed, the next step is to enable phone number authentication within the Firebase console.

9.2 Enabling Phone Number Authentication

Before phone authentication can be used, it must be enabled as an authentication provider in the Firebase console. In a browser window, navigate to the *Firebase Examples* project within the Firebase console, select the *Authentication* option in the navigation panel followed by the Sign-In Method tab. Click on the Phone entry in the list of sign-in providers and turn on the *Enable* switch in the resulting dialog before saving the new setting:

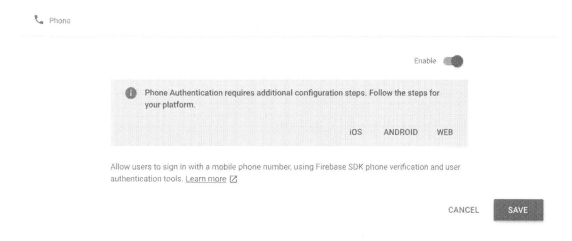

Figure 9-1

9.3 **Adding Phone Verification to the Provider List**

The final step in implementing phone authentication is to add a single line of code to the app to add phone verification to the list of sign-in providers. Edit the *FirebaseAuthActivity.java* file, locate the *getProviderList()* method and modify it so that it reads as follows:

```
private List<AuthUI.IdpConfig> getProviderList() {

    List<AuthUI.IdpConfig> providers = new ArrayList<>();

    providers.add(new
        AuthUI.IdpConfig.Builder(AuthUI.EMAIL_PROVIDER).build());
    providers.add(new
        AuthUI.IdpConfig.Builder(AuthUI.GOOGLE_PROVIDER).build());
    providers.add(new
        AuthUI.IdpConfig.Builder(AuthUI.FACEBOOK_PROVIDER).build());
    providers.add(new
        AuthUI.IdpConfig.Builder(AuthUI.TWITTER_PROVIDER).build());
    providers.add(new
        AuthUI.IdpConfig.Builder(AuthUI.PHONE_VERIFICATION_PROVIDER).build());
    return providers;
}
```

9.4 **Testing Phone Number Authentication**

Compile and run the app on a device or emulator and dismiss the Smart Lock dialog if it appears. When the login screen displays, phone verification should now be included in the list of available providers as outlined in Figure 9-2:

Figure 9-2

Choosing the Phone sign-in option will cause a second screen to appear in which a phone number must be entered:

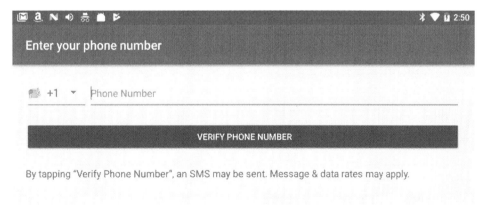

Figure 9-3

Enter a phone number capable of receiving SMS messages and click on the *Verify Phone Number* button. After a short delay, the 6-digit verification code will arrive on the phone ready to be entered into the screen shown in Figure 9-4:

Figure 9-4

Once the code has been entered, the *SignedInActivity* screen will appear. After the account has been created, return to the list of authenticated users within the Firebase console and note that the new account has been added with a Phone icon positioned in the Providers column.

9.5 **Summary**

In this, the final chapter looking at authentication using FirebaseUI Auth, we have explored the mechanism for implementing user authentication using phone number verification. Now that the use of FirebaseUI Auth has been covered, the following chapters will introduce user authentication using the Firebase SDK.

10. Email/Password Authentication using the Firebase SDK

There are many advantages to using the FirebaseUI Auth mechanism of user authentication, not the least of which being that all of the work involved in presenting the authentication user interface, verifying the validity of user input such as email addresses and handling email reset and account recovery is performed automatically.

That being said, situations may arise where an app needs complete control over the appearance and behavior of the authentication process. For such situations, authentication may also be implemented by making direct calls to the Firebase SDK.

As with FirebaseUI Auth, the exact steps to implementing authentication using this approach vary between authentication providers. This chapter, therefore, will begin by focusing on email/password based authentication before moving on to other providers in later chapters.

10.1 Creating the PasswordAuth Project

The first step in this exercise is to create the new project. Begin by launching Android Studio and, if necessary, closing any currently open projects using the *File -> Close Project* menu option so that the Welcome screen appears.

Select the *Start a new Android Studio project* quick start option from the welcome screen and, within the new project dialog, enter *PasswordAuth* into the Application name field and your domain as the Company Domain setting before clicking on the *Next* button.

On the form factors screen, enable the *Phone and Tablet* option and set the minimum SDK to API 16: Android 4.1 (Jellybean). Continue to proceed through the screens, requesting the creation of an Empty Activity named *PasswordAuthActivity* with a corresponding layout named *activity_password_auth.*

10.2 Enabling Authentication Providers

The steps in this chapter and the subsequent authentication chapters assume that the necessary sign-in methods have been enabled in the Firebase console for the *Firebase Examples* project.

Verify the current configuration by opening the Firebase console in a browser window, selecting the *Firebase Examples* project and navigating to the Sign-in Methods page of the Authentication screen. Review the current settings and enable the Email/Password, Phone, Google, Facebook and Twitter sign-in methods as outlined in Figure 10-1:

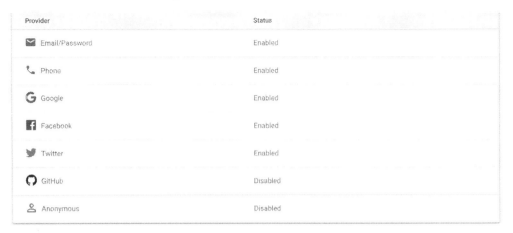

Provider	Status
✉ Email/Password	Enabled
📞 Phone	Enabled
G Google	Enabled
f Facebook	Enabled
🐦 Twitter	Enabled
⚫ GitHub	Disabled
👤 Anonymous	Disabled

Figure 10-1

10.3 **Connecting the Project to Firebase**

Once the project has been created, use the *Tools -> Firebase* menu to display the Firebase assistant panel, locate and click on the Authentication category, select the *Email and password authentication* link and then click on the *Connect to Firebase* button to display the Firebase connection dialog.

Choose the option to store the app in an existing Firebase project and select the *Firebase Examples* project created in the beginning of the book.

With the project's Firebase connection established, refer to the Firebase assistant panel once again, this time clicking on the *Add Firebase Authentication to your app* button. A dialog will appear outlining the changes that will be made to the project build configuration to enable Firebase authentication. Click on the *Accept Changes* button to commit the changes to the project configuration.

10.4 **Designing the User Interface Layout**

Locate the *app -> res -> layout -> password_auth_sdk.xml* file and load it into the layout editor.

Select and delete the "Hello World!" TextView object and, in the layout editor toolbar, make sure that the Autoconnect feature (Figure 10-2) is switched off.

Figure 10-2

With a blank layout, locate the E-mail EditText widget from Text category of the palette and drag and drop it so that it is positioned near the top of the layout canvas and centered horizontally. Using the Properties tool window, set the ID of the widget to *emailText*.

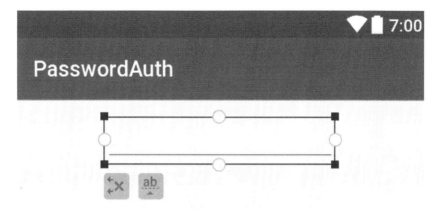

Figure 10-3

Drag and drop a Password EditText widget so that it is positioned beneath the email field and set the ID property to *passwordText*.

Next, drag and drop two TextView objects from the widget palette Text category positioned in a vertical arrangement beneath the bottom EditText object:

Figure 10-4

Starting with the top TextView widget, set the ID property on the views to *userText* and *statusText* respectively.

Repeat these steps to add two Button widgets positioned vertically beneath the TextView widgets. Using the Properties tool window, change the text on the buttons to read *Sign In*, and *Sign Out*.

Click in the upper left corner of the layout canvas and drag the resulting selection rectangle so that it encompasses all of the widgets added to the layout. Release the mouse button and verify that all of the widgets are currently selected. Right-click on the uppermost of the EditText fields and select the *Center Horizontally* menu option. Right click on the widget once again, this time selecting the *Center Vertically* menu option. On completion of these steps, the layout should resemble that illustrated in Figure 10-5:

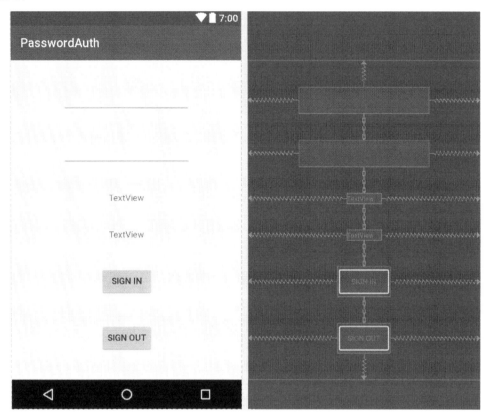

Figure 10-5

Two more Button objects are required to complete the user interface layout for the project.

Begin by re-enabling Autoconnect mode, then drag a Button object from the palette and position it in the bottom left-hand corner of the layout canvas. Before dropping the button into place, make sure that it is positioned so that the dashed lines indicating the left and bottom margins appear indicated by the black arrows in Figure 10-6:

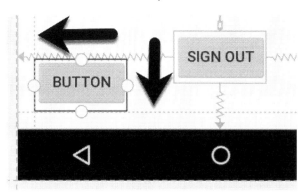

Figure 10-6

On releasing the Button widget, Autoconnect will establish constraints on the left and bottom edges of the button view.

Repeat these steps to position a Button widget in the lower right-hand corner of the layout aligned with reference to the right-hand and bottom margin guidelines. Using the properties tool window, change the text on these buttons to read *Create\nAccount* and *Reset\nPassword*. On completion of these steps, the layout should resemble that of Figure 10-7:

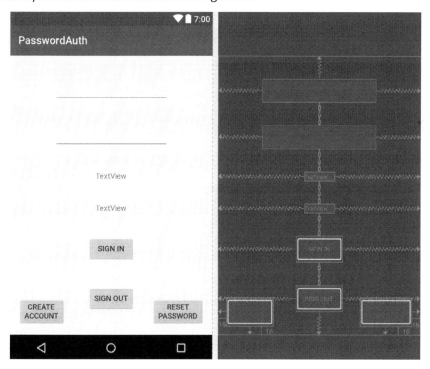

Figure 10-7

Select the *Sign In* button and, using the properties panel, configure the *onClick* property to call a method named *signIn*. Configure the appropriate *onClick* properties for the remaining buttons to call methods named *signOut, createAccount* and *resetPassword*.

10.5 **Getting View Object References**

Later in this chapter, the code will need access to some of the view objects declared within the user interface layout. In preparation for this, some variables and code need to be added to the *PasswordAuthActivity.java* class file. Locate this class within the project tool window, load it into the code editing tool and modify it so that it reads as follows:

```
package com.ebookfrenzy.passwordauth;

import android.support.v7.app.AppCompatActivity;
import android.os.Bundle;
import android.view.View;
import android.widget.EditText;
import android.widget.TextView;

public class PasswordAuthActivity extends AppCompatActivity {

    private TextView userText;
    private TextView statusText;
    private EditText emailText;
    private EditText passwordText;

    @Override
    protected void onCreate(Bundle savedInstanceState) {
        super.onCreate(savedInstanceState);
        setContentView(R.layout.activity_password_auth);

        userText = (TextView) findViewById(R.id.userText);
        statusText = (TextView) findViewById(R.id.statusText);
        emailText = (EditText) findViewById(R.id.emailText);
        passwordText = (EditText) findViewById(R.id.passwordText);
        userText.setText("");
        statusText.setText("Signed Out");
    }
    .
    .
    .
}
```

10.6 **Adding a User Notification Method**

At various points within this project it will be necessary to convey information to the user in the form of short Toast messages. In order to avoid code repetition a convenience method needs to be added to the main activity class. This method will be named *notifyUser()* and will construct and display a Toast message based on the string passed through as an argument when the method is called. Implement this method as follows in the *PasswordAuthActivity.java* file:

```
import android.widget.Toast;
.
.
.
private void notifyUser(String message) {
    Toast.makeText(PasswordAuthActivity.this, message,
            Toast.LENGTH_SHORT).show();
}
```

10.7 Accessing the FirebaseAuth Instance

The two key components of Firebase SDK based authentication are the FirebaseAuth instance and the authentication state listener. The first step in implementing Firebase authentication is to obtain a reference to the FirebaseAuth instance. Within Android Studio, edit the *PasswordAuthActivity.java* file to obtain a reference to the FirebaseAuth instance:

```
package com.ebookfrenzy.passwordauth;
.
.
.
import android.support.annotation.NonNull;

import com.google.android.gms.tasks.OnCompleteListener;
import com.google.android.gms.tasks.Task;
import com.google.firebase.auth.AuthResult;
import com.google.firebase.auth.FirebaseAuth;
import com.google.firebase.auth.FirebaseUser;

public class PasswordAuthActivity extends AppCompatActivity {

    private TextView userText;
    private TextView statusText;
    private EditText emailText;
    private EditText passwordText;

    private FirebaseAuth fbAuth;
    private FirebaseAuth.AuthStateListener authListener;

    @Override
    protected void onCreate(Bundle savedInstanceState) {
        super.onCreate(savedInstanceState);
        setContentView(R.layout.activity_password_auth);

        userText = (TextView) findViewById(R.id.userText);
        statusText = (TextView) findViewById(R.id.statusText);
```

```
        emailText = (EditText) findViewById(R.id.emailText);
        passwordText = (EditText) findViewById(R.id.passwordText);
        userText.setText("");
        statusText.setText("Signed Out");


    fbAuth = FirebaseAuth.getInstance();
    .
    .
    .
}
```

10.8 Adding the Authentication State Listener

The authentication state listener is the mechanism by which the app receives notification of the changes to the status of the sign-in process. The listener takes the form of a method that is attached to the FirebaseAuth object and is called each time one of the following events occurs:

- The authentication listener has just been registered
- A user has signed in
- The current user has signed out
- The current user changes
- A change is detected to the current user's token

With the *PasswordAuthActivity.java* file still open in the Android Studio code editor, further modify the *onCreate()* method to declare the authentication state listener method:

```
@Override
protected void onCreate(Bundle savedInstanceState) {
    super.onCreate(savedInstanceState);
    setContentView(R.layout.activity_password_auth);

    userText = (TextView) findViewById(R.id.userText);
    statusText = (TextView) findViewById(R.id.statusText);
    emailText = (EditText) findViewById(R.id.emailText);
    passwordText = (EditText) findViewById(R.id.passwordText);
    userText.setText("");
    statusText.setText("Signed Out");

    fbAuth = FirebaseAuth.getInstance();

    authListener = new FirebaseAuth.AuthStateListener() {
        @Override
        public void onAuthStateChanged(@NonNull FirebaseAuth firebaseAuth) {

            FirebaseUser user = firebaseAuth.getCurrentUser();

            if (user != null) {
```

```
            userText.setText(user.getEmail());
            statusText.setText("Signed In");

        } else {
            userText.setText("");
            statusText.setText("Signed Out");
        }
    }
};


}
```

The listener method begins by getting a reference to the FirebaseUser object for the current user. If the user object is not null then the code assumes that a user has just successfully signed into the app. The user's email address is accessed and displayed on the userText TextView object. The text displayed on the statusText object is then changed to indicate that the user is currently signed in.

A null value assigned to the user object, on the other hand, indicates the authentication change involved the user signing out of the app. The email address is removed from the email text view and the status text is updated to reflect that the user has signed out.

10.9 Adding and Removing the Listener

At this point, the authentication state listener has been declared but has not yet been added to the FirebaseAuth instance. Without this vital step, the method will never be called in response to changes in the authentication state. For the purposes of this example, the standard *onStart()* Android lifecycle method will be overridden and used to add the listener. The *onStart()* method is called immediately after the call to the *onCreate()* method and before the activity is to become visible to the user. Within the *FirebaseAuthActivity.java* file, add this method so that it reads as follows:

```
@Override
public void onStart() {
    super.onStart();
    fbAuth.addAuthStateListener(authListener);
}
```

In addition to adding the listener, it is equally important to remove the listener when it is no longer needed. To achieve this, the *onStop()* method will be used:

```
@Override
public void onStop() {
    super.onStop();
    if (authListener != null) {
        fbAuth.removeAuthStateListener(authListener);
    }
}
```

10.10 **Creating the User Account**

The user will create an account for the app by entering an email address and a password into the two EditText fields and tapping on the Create Account button. Within the user interface layout, this button was configured to call a method named *createAccount()* when clicked. Add this method to the main activity class file now so that it reads as follows:

```
public void createAccount(View view) {
    String email = emailText.getText().toString();
    String password = passwordText.getText().toString();

    if (email.length() == 0) {
        emailText.setError("Enter an email address");
        return;
    }

    if (password.length() < 6) {
        passwordText.setError("Password must be at least 6 characters");
        return;
    }

    fbAuth.createUserWithEmailAndPassword(email, password)
            .addOnCompleteListener(this,
                        new OnCompleteListener<AuthResult>() {
                @Override
                public void onComplete(@NonNull Task<AuthResult> task) {

                    if (!task.isSuccessful()) {
                        notifyUser("Account creation failed");
                    }
                }
            });

}
```

The method begins by obtaining the email address and password entered by the user. When using the Firebase SDK to authenticate users, and unlike the FirebaseUI Auth approach to authentication, it is the responsibility of the app to verify that a valid email address has been entered and that the password meets general security guidelines. For the purposes of this example, however, it will suffice to ensure something has been entered into the email address field and that the password selected by the user exceeds 5 characters. If either of these requirements are not met, the *setError()* method of the EditText class is called to prompt the user to correct the issue before the method returns.

The user account creation process is then initiated via a call to the *createUserWithEmailAndPassword()* method of the FirebaseAuth instance, passing through the email address and password string as arguments. The account creation process is performed asynchronously, requiring that a completion handler be provided to be called when the process completes. In this case, the completion handler checks that the task was complete and displays a Toast message in the case of a failure. The attempt to create the account (successfully or otherwise) will result in a call to the authentication listener implemented earlier in the chapter where a check for a valid current user will be performed and the user interface updated accordingly to indicate that the account has been created and that the new user is signed in.

10.11 Implementing the Sign-In Method

When the user interface layout was designed, the onClick property of the Sign-in button was configured to call a method named *signIn()*. This method now needs to be added to the *PasswordAuthActivity.java* class file as follows:

```
public void signIn(View view) {

    String email = emailText.getText().toString();
    String password = passwordText.getText().toString();

    if (email.length() == 0) {
        emailText.setError("Enter an email address");
        return;
    }

    if (password.length() < 6) {
        passwordText.setError("Password must be at least 6 characters");
        return;
    }

    fbAuth.signInWithEmailAndPassword(email, password)
            .addOnCompleteListener(this,
                    new OnCompleteListener<AuthResult>() {
                        @Override
                        public void onComplete(@NonNull
                                        Task<AuthResult> task) {

                            if (!task.isSuccessful()) {
                                notifyUser("Authentication failed");
                            }
                        }
                    });

}
```

After performing some rudimentary validation on the email and password entered by the user, email and password based authentication is then initiated by a call to the *signInWithEmailAndPassword()* method of the FirebaseAuth instance, passing through the email address and password strings as arguments. The sign-in process is performed asynchronously, requiring the addition of a completion handler to be called when the process is completed. In the event that the sign-in failed, the user is notified via a Toast message.

The attempt to sign-in, whether successful or not, will also trigger a call to the authentication state listener method. As designed, the listener will check if the user is signed in and update the user interface accordingly.

10.12 **Signing Out**

Now that the user account creation and sign-in functionality of the app is complete, the user now needs a way to sign out of the app. This requires the implementation of the *signOut()* method which has been configured to be called when the user clicks on the Sign Out button:

```
public void signOut(View view) {
    fbAuth.signOut();
}
```

All that this method needs to do is call the *signOut()* method of the FirebaseAuth object. The signing out process will subsequently trigger a call to the authentication listener which will, in turn, identify that there is no current user and update the TextViews in the user interface layout accordingly.

10.13 **Implementing the Password Reset Option**

When using FirebaseUI Auth, a password reset option was provided automatically as part of the authentication user interface flow. When using Firebase SDK authentication this feature has to be added manually. The user interface layout already contains a button titled Reset Password with the onClick property set to call a method named *resetPassword()*. The last task in this phase of the project is to implement this method. The method will need to extract the email address entered by the user before passing that address as an argument to the *sendPasswordResetEmail()* method of the FirebaseAuth instance. A completion handler may also be specified to check that the email has been sent. Remaining in the *PasswordAuthActivity.java* file, add the following method:

```
public void resetPassword(View view) {

    String email = emailText.getText().toString();

    if (email.length() == 0) {
        emailText.setError("Enter an email address");
        return;
    }

    fbAuth.sendPasswordResetEmail(email)
            .addOnCompleteListener(new OnCompleteListener<Void>() {
```

```
            @Override
            public void onComplete(@NonNull Task<Void> task) {
                if (task.isSuccessful()) {
                    notifyUser("Reset email sent");
                }
            }
        });
}
```

10.14 Testing the Project

Before testing the project, log into the Firebase console, select the *Firebase Examples* project and display the Users panel on the Authentication page. If user accounts already exist from earlier chapters of this book, take the time to delete these accounts to avoid account creation conflicts while testing this latest project.

Compile and run the app, either on a physical Android device, or an emulator session. Enter an email address to which you have inbox access (a password reset email will be sent to this address later) and password into the two text fields and click on the Create Account button. After a short delay the TextView objects should update to reflect that the account has been created and the user signed in.

Click on the Sign Out button and verify that the app responds appropriately by clearing the TextView displaying the user's email address and displaying a "Signed Out" message on the status TextView.

Next, try signing in with an unregistered email address and password and verify that the failed authentication message appears.

Sign in with the correct credentials, then click the password reset button. Check the email inbox for the email address and use the provided link to reset the password to a different string:

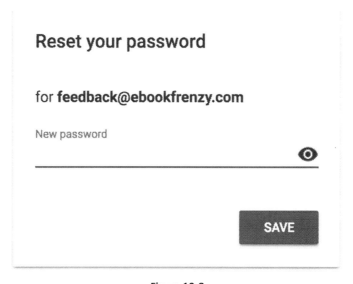

Figure 10-8

10.15 **Summary**

The FirebaseUI Auth approach to user authentication automates much of the work involved in allowing users to create accounts and sign-in to gain access to restricted areas of functionality and content within an Android app. An alternative to this approach is to make use of the classes and methods contained within the Firebase SDK to implement user authentication. This chapter has focused on the use of the Firebase SDK to implement email and password authentication. This involves designing the user interface for handling the authentication, implementing an authentication state listener and writing code to verify user input, create and sign into user accounts.

Although later chapters will address the use of the Firebase SDK to perform user authentication using other providers, the next chapters will outline some of the other user account management features available with the Firebase SDK and introduce Firebase authentication error handling techniques.

11. Managing User Accounts using the Firebase SDK

The previous chapter demonstrated the use of the authentication features of the Firebase SDK to provide email and password-based account creation and sign-in features for Android apps. In addition to providing the ability to create and sign into accounts, it is also important to gain an understanding of the account management features provided by the Firebase SDK, including the ability to change a user's email address or password, delete accounts and add user profile information such as a display name and photo. The goal of this chapter is to outline these account management features including sample code designed to work with the example created in the previous chapter.

11.1 Enhancing the User's Profile Information

When a new email and password based account is created using Firebase SDK authentication no display name or profile photo is initially assigned to the user's account. Once the account has been created, however, these properties may be assigned to the account by creating a UserProfileChangeRequest object containing a display name and photo Uri and then passing this object through to the *updateProfile()* method of the current user object.

Assuming a profile photo image named *photo.jpg* located in the *app -> res -> drawable* location within the project, the following code would assign this image as the profile photo along with a display name of "Ann D. Roid" within the profile of the current user where *<your pkg name here>* is replaced by the package name for your project (for example *com.example.firebaseauth*):

```
FirebaseUser user = fbAuth.getCurrentUser();

UserProfileChangeRequest profileUpdates =
        new UserProfileChangeRequest.Builder()
          .setDisplayName("Ann D. Roid")
          .setPhotoUri(Uri.parse(
                "android.resource://<your pkg name>/drawable/photo"))
        .build();

user.updateProfile(profileUpdates)
        .addOnCompleteListener(new OnCompleteListener<Void>() {
            @Override
            public void onComplete(@NonNull Task<Void> task) {
                Toast.makeText(FirebaseAuthActivity.this,
```

```
                                         "Profile updated.",
                        Toast.LENGTH_SHORT).show();
                }
        });
```

11.2 Changing a User's Email Address

It is not uncommon for a user to want to change the email address associated with an account. This feature can be added to an app by making a call to the *updateEmail()* method of the current user object, passing through as an argument the new email address. It is important to note that this method call will only work if the user is already signed in. The code to implement this reads as follows:

```
String email = emailText.getText().toString();

FirebaseUser user = fbAuth.getCurrentUser();

user.updateEmail(email)
        .addOnCompleteListener(new OnCompleteListener<Void>() {
            @Override
            public void onComplete(@NonNull Task<Void> task) {
                if (task.isSuccessful()) {
                    Toast.makeText(FirebaseAuthActivity.this,
                            "Email address updated",
                        Toast.LENGTH_SHORT).show();
                }
            }
        });
```

When a user successfully changes the email address associated with an account, the Firebase authentication system will send the user an email to the old email address containing notification of the change and providing a link to reverse the update. The default template for this email may be modified within Email Templates screen of the Authentication section of the Firebase console by selecting the Password Reset category followed by the edit button as indicated in Figure 11-1:

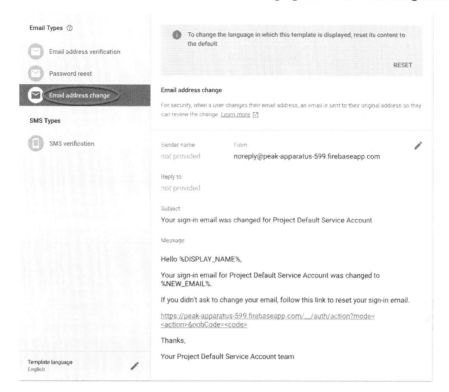

Figure 11-1

For details on customizing this message, refer to the earlier chapter entitled *Testing and Customizing FirebaseUI Auth Authentication*.

11.3 **Changing a User's Password**

Not to be confused with the password reset option, this feature of the Firebase SDK allows the password of a currently signed in user to be changed from within a running app. This involves a call to the *updatePassword()* method of the current user object passing through the new password as an argument. In common with other Firebase SDK methods a completion handler may be assigned to receive notification of the result of the request.

```
String password = passwordText.getText().toString();

FirebaseUser user = fbAuth.getCurrentUser();

user.updatePassword(password)
        .addOnCompleteListener(new OnCompleteListener<Void>() {
            @Override
            public void onComplete(@NonNull Task<Void> task) {
                if (task.isSuccessful()) {
                    Toast.makeText(FirebaseAuthActivity.this,
                            "Password updated",
```

```
                              Toast.LENGTH_SHORT).show();
               }
          }
     });
```

11.4 **Deleting a User Account**

The currently signed-in user's account may be deleted from the Firebase Authentication system via a call to the *delete()* method of the current user object as follows:

```
FirebaseUser user = FirebaseAuth.getInstance().getCurrentUser();

user.delete()
        .addOnCompleteListener(new OnCompleteListener<Void>() {
            @Override
            public void onComplete(@NonNull Task<Void> task) {
                if (task.isSuccessful()) {
                    Toast.makeText(FirebaseAuthActivity.this,
                            "Account deleted",
                        Toast.LENGTH_SHORT).show();
                }
            }
        });
```

11.5 **Verifying the User's Email Address**

When using email and password authentication it usually makes sense to take some steps to verify that the email address provided actually belongs to the user. The best way to do this is to send an email to the provided address containing a verification link. Until the user has clicked the link, access to the app can be denied even though an account has been created.

To instruct Firebase Authentication to send a verification email, simply call the *sendEmailVerification()* method of a FirebaseUser instance as follows:

```
FirebaseUser user = fbAuth.getCurrentUser();

user.sendEmailVerification()
        .addOnCompleteListener(this, new OnCompleteListener() {
            @Override
            public void onComplete(@NonNull Task task) {

                if (task.isSuccessful()) {
                    // Verification sent successfully
                } else {
                    // Failed to send verification email.
                }
            }
```

```
    });
```

When the user subsequently attempts to sign into the app, code can be added to check that the user's email address has been verified by calling the *isEmailVerified()* method of the FirebaseUser instance:

```
if (user.isEmailVerified() == true) {
    // User has verified email address
} else {
    // User has not verfied email address
}
```

The template for the email address verification email may be modified within the Firebase console by selecting the Templates tab in the Authentication screen and selecting the *Email address verification* category.

11.6 **Understanding Security Sensitive Actions**

With the exception of making updates to the user's profile information, each of the account management tasks outlined in this chapter are categorized as security-sensitive actions. Although all of the actions outlined above require that the user be signed into the account for which changes are being made, security-sensitive actions impose the additional requirement that a limited amount of time must have elapsed since the user signed into the account. If this time restriction has been exceeded, the method calls to delete or update the accounts will fail with an exception.

One option would be to force the user to sign out of the app and then sign back in before performing a security sensitive action. Fortunately, the FirebaseUser class includes a method named *reauthenticate()* which can be used to refresh the user's credentials when making a security-sensitive account change. In order to know when re-authentication is required, however, it is important to be able to detect and identify authentication failure exceptions, a topic which will be covered in the next chapter.

11.7 **Summary**

There is more to user authentication than simply creating user accounts and providing a sign-in interface. Users also need to be given the ability to make changes to, or even delete, their accounts. Fortunately, the FirebaseUser class provides a range of methods that allow such features to be integrated into Android apps with relative ease.

With the exception of profile updates, all of the management tasks outlined in this chapter are considered to be security-sensitive, requiring user re-authentication if too much time has elapsed since the user signed in. Detecting and responding to this situation, along with other authentication failures will be covered in the next chapter.

12. Handling Firebase Authentication Errors and Failures

A key part of providing a good user experience involves not just letting users know when something has failed, but also providing a useful explanation as to why the failure occurred. The more information that is provided about a failure, the greater the likelihood that the user will be able to resolve the problem.

In the Firebase authentication examples created in this book so far, very little effort has been made beyond simply notifying the user that a failure occurred. The apps will, for example, let the user know that a login attempt has failed without giving an explanation as to why.

This chapter will introduce the use of Firebase authentication failure listeners in terms of identifying not just that a failure has occurred, but also the nature of the failure.

12.1 Completion Listeners and Basic Failure Detection

User authentication using Firebase primarily consists of obtaining a reference to the FirebaseAuth instance or a FirebaseUser object on which method calls are made to create accounts, sign-in users and perform account management tasks. All of these methods perform the requested task asynchronously. This essentially means that immediately after the method is called, control is returned to the app while the task is performed in the background. As is common with asynchronous tasks of this type, it is possible for the app to be notified that the authentication task has finished by providing a completion listener method to be called when the task completes.

Consider, for example, the following code fragment from the FirebaseAuth project:

```
fbAuth.signInWithEmailAndPassword(email, password)
      .addOnCompleteListener(this,
            new OnCompleteListener<AuthResult>() {
        @Override
        public void onComplete(@NonNull Task<AuthResult> task) {

            if (!task.isSuccessful()) {
                // Notify user of failure
            }
        }
    });
```

This code performs an email and password based user sign-in operation involving the use of a completion listener to be called when the task completes. As currently implemented, the only status information available is a success or failure value on the task object of the completion handler method. This allows the app to tell the user the sign-in failed, but does not provide any context as to why. To be able to obtain more information about the reason for the failure, a failure listener needs to be added to the call.

12.2 The Failure Listener

In much the same way that a completion handler is called when an asynchronous task completes, a failure handler is called when the task fails to complete due to a problem or error. Failure listeners are added to Firebase authentication method calls via the *addOnFailureListener()* method. The above code, for example, can be extended to add a failure listener as follows:

```
fbAuth.signInWithEmailAndPassword(email, password)
        .addOnCompleteListener(this, new OnCompleteListener<AuthResult>() {
            @Override
            public void onComplete(@NonNull Task<AuthResult> task) {

                if (!task.isSuccessful()) {
                    // Notify user of failure
                }
            }
        }).addOnFailureListener(new OnFailureListener() {
            @Override
            public void onFailure(@NonNull Exception e) {

            }
        });
```

Open the FirebaseAuth project in Android Studio, load the *FirebaseAuthActivity.java* file into the editing panel and make the above changes to the *signInWithEmail()* method.

When using the *addOnFailureListener()* method within an activity, it will also be necessary to import the Android OnFailureListener package:

```
import com.google.android.gms.tasks.OnFailureListener;
```

When a failure occurs during the sign-in process, the *onFailure()* method will be called and passed an Exception object containing information about the reason for the failure. The exact type of the exception thrown will depend on the nature of the error. An invalid password, for example, will throw a different type of exception than that generated when trying to create an account using an email address that conflicts with an existing account.

The simplest form of the user notification is to simply display the localized description to the user as outlined in the following code fragment:

```
fbAuth.signInWithEmailAndPassword(email, password)
```

```
        .addOnCompleteListener(this, new OnCompleteListener<AuthResult>() {
            @Override
            public void onComplete(@NonNull Task<AuthResult> task) {

                if (!task.isSuccessful()) {
                            // Notify user of failure
                }
            }
        }).addOnFailureListener(new OnFailureListener() {
            @Override
            public void onFailure(@NonNull Exception e) {
                notifyUser(e.getLocalizedMessage());
            }
        });
```

Note that when using a failure listener it is no longer necessary to check for failure within the completion listener method. Doing so will likely result in duplicated app behavior. Make this change to the *signInWithEmailAndPassword()* method and build, run and test the new behavior in the app.

If an attempt is now made to sign in using an email address for which no account yet exists, the above code displays a message which reads as follows:

```
There is no user record corresponding to this identifier. The user may have
been deleted.
```

If, on the other hand, a correct email address is used with an incorrect password, the localized description string will read as follows:

```
The password is invalid or the user does not have a password.
```

While useful as a quick way to notify the user of the nature of the problem, it is quite likely that greater control over how the failure is reported and what actions are taken next will often be required. This involves identifying the type of the Exception object and accessing the error code.

12.3 FirebaseAuth Exception Types

The type of exception thrown by the Firebase SDK in the event of an authentication failure can be used to identify more information about the cause of the failure. In the previous section, the built-in failure description was presented to the user, but the app itself made no attempt to identify the cause of the failure. While this may be acceptable for many situations, it is just as likely that the app will need more information about what went wrong.

In the event of an authentication failure, the Firebase SDK will throw one the following types of exception:

- **FirebaseAuthInvalidUserException** – This exception indicates a problem with the email address entered by the user. For example, the account does not exist or has been disabled in the Firebase console. The precise reason for the exception can be identified by accessing the error code as outlined later in this chapter.

- **FirebaseAuthInvalidCredentialsException** – This exception is thrown when the password entered by the user does not match the email address.
- **FirebaseAuthUserCollisionException** – Thrown during account creation, this exception indicates a problem with the email address entered by the user. The exact reason for the failure can be identified by accessing the error code.
- **FirebaseAuthWeakPasswordException** – Indicates that the password specified during an account creation or password update operation is insufficiently strong. A string describing the reason that the password is considered too weak can be obtain via a call to the *getReason()* method of the exception object.
- **FirebaseAuthRecentLoginRequiredException** – The user has attempted to perform a security sensitive operation but too much time has elapsed since signing in to the app. When this exception is detected the user will need to be re-authenticated as outlined later in this chapter.

With knowledge of the different exception types, the previous sample code can be modified to identify if the sign-in failure was due to an issue with the email or password entry. This can be achieved by finding out the type of the Exception object. To see this in action, modify the *onFailure()* method located in the *signInWithEmail()* method so that it reads as follows:

```
.
.
@override
public void onFailure(@NonNull Exception e) {
    if (e instanceof FirebaseAuthInvalidCredentialsException) {
        notifyUser("Invalid password");
    } else if (e instanceof FirebaseAuthInvalidUserException) {
        notifyUser("Incorrect email address");
    } else {
        notifyUser(e.getLocalizedDescription());
    }
}
.
.
```

Compile and run the app once again and try signing in with invalid email and password combinations. The error notifications displayed by the app will now differentiate between an email address problem and an invalid password. The code also makes use of the localized description string contained within the exception to catch instances that do not match the credential and user exceptions.

Although this is an improvement on the original code, it would be helpful to provide yet more detail. The code, for example, does not provide any information about why email address was found to be incorrect. Adding this level of information involves the use of the exception error codes.

12.4 **FirebaseAuth Error Codes**

In addition to identifying the cause of a failure by finding the type of the exception, additional information can be obtained by inspecting the error code contained within the exception object. Error codes are currently available for the invalid user and user collision exceptions.

The error codes supported by FirebaseAuthInvalidUserException are as follows:

- **ERROR_USER_DISABLED** – The account with which the email is associated exists but has been disabled.
- **ERROR_USER_NOT_FOUND** – No account could be found that matches the specified email address. The user has either entered the wrong email address, has yet to create an account or the account has been deleted.
- **ERROR_USER_TOKEN_EXPIRED** – The user's token has been invalidated by the Firebase system. This usually occurs when the user changes the password associated with the account from another device or platform (such as a web site associated with the app).
- **ERROR_INVALID_USER_TOKEN** – The system does not recognize the user's token as being correctly formed.

FirebaseAuthUserCollisionException, on the other hand, supports the following error codes:

- **ERROR_EMAIL_ALREADY_IN_USE** – Indicates that the user is attempting to create a new account, or change the email address for an existing account that is already in use by another account.
- **ERROR_ACCOUNT_EXISTS_WITH_DIFFERENT_CREDENTIAL** – When attempting to sign in to an account using the *signInWithCredential()* method passing through an AuthCredential object, this error indicates that the email associated with the AuthCredential instance is already in use by another account that does not match the provided credentials.
- **ERROR_CREDENTIAL_ALREADY_IN_USE** – It is quite possible for one user to establish multiple accounts by using different authentication providers. As will be outlined in *Linking and Unlinking Firebase Authentication Providers*, Firebase provides the ability for these separate accounts to be consolidated together through a process of account linking. This error indicates that an attempt has been made to link a credential to an account that is already linked to another account.

These error codes are provided in the form of string objects containing the error code name. Testing for an error, therefore, simply involves performing string comparisons against the error code.

By using error codes, the previous code to identify an invalid user exception within the *onFailure()* method can be improved to identify the exact cause of the failure simply by accessing the error code in the exception object. For example:

```
@Override
public void onFailure(@NonNull Exception e) {
    if (e instanceof FirebaseAuthInvalidCredentialsException) {
        notifyUser("Invalid password");
    } else if (e instanceof FirebaseAuthInvalidUserException) {

        String errorCode =
```

```
                ((FirebaseAuthInvalidUserException) e).getErrorCode();

        if (errorCode.equals("ERROR_USER_NOT_FOUND")) {
            notifyUser("No matching account found");
        } else if (errorCode.equals("ERROR_USER_DISABLED")) {
            notifyUser("User account has been disabled");
        } else {
            notifyUser(e.getLocalizedMessage());
        }
    }
}
```

With these changes implemented, compile and run the app and try to sign in with an unregistered email address. The app should respond with the message indicating that no matching account could be found.

Next, open the Firebase console in a browser window and navigate to the Users screen of the Authentication section for the *Firebase Examples* project. Using the menu to the right of one of the existing user account entries, select the *Disable Account* menu option as outlined in Figure 12-1:

Figure 12-1

With the account disabled, return to the app and attempt to sign in using the email address assigned to the disabled account. This time the app will display the account disabled error message.

12.5 Handling Secure Action Exceptions

Now that the basics of authentication exception handling have been covered, it is time to return to the subject of secure actions. The topic of secure actions was introduced in the chapter entitled *Managing User Accounts using the Firebase SDK*. In summary, secure actions are a category of account management operation that may only be performed if the current user recently signed in. Such operations include changing the user's password or email address via calls to the Firebase SDK. If the user recently signed into the app, these operations will complete without any problems. If it has been a few hours since the current user signed in, however, the operation will fail with a FirebaseAuthRecentLoginRequiredException exception.

Consider, for example, the code that allows a user to update the account password:

```
FirebaseUser user = fbAuth.getCurrentUser();

user.updatePassword(newPassword)
```

```
            .addOnCompleteListener(new OnCompleteListener<Void>() {
                @Override
                public void onComplete(@NonNull Task<Void> task) {
                    if (task.isSuccessful()) {
                        notifyUser("Password updated");
                    }
                }
            });
```

Clearly, given the fact that this is categorized as a secure action, some code needs to be added to identify when the recent login required exception is thrown. This, once again, involves the use of a failure listener to check for the type of exception:

```
user.updatePassword(newPassword)
            .addOnCompleteListener(new OnCompleteListener<Void>() {
                @Override
                public void onComplete(@NonNull Task<Void> task) {
                    if (task.isSuccessful()) {
                        notifyUser("Password updated");
                    }
                }
            }).addOnFailureListener(new OnFailureListener() {
                @Override
                public void onFailure(@NonNull Exception e) {
                    if (e instanceof FirebaseAuthRecentLoginRequiredException) {
                        notifyUser("Re-authentication needed");
                    }
                }
            });
```

As implemented above, when the user attempts to perform a password update after having been signed in for too long, the exception will be caught and the user notified of the problem. One less than optimal solution to this problem would be to instruct the user to sign out, sign back in again and perform the password update a second time. A far more user friendly approach, however, is to re-authenticate the user.

The first step in the re-authentication process involves obtaining the current user's credentials in the form of an AuthCredential object. This is achieved by passing the user's email and password through to the *getCredential()* method of the appropriate authentication provider which, depending on the form of authentication, will be one of the following:

- EmailAuthProvider
- GoogleAuthProvider
- FacebookAuthProvider
- TwitterAuthProvider

- GitHubAuthProvider

When obtaining the user's credentials during the re-authentication for a password update action, it is important to be aware that it is the user's current password that must be used, not the new password to which the user is attempting to change. If the app has not stored the existing password internally, the user will need to be prompted to enter it before the credentials can be obtained and the account re-authenticated. The following code obtains the AuthCredential object using the email authentication provider:

```
AuthCredential credential = EmailAuthProvider
        .getCredential(email, currentPassword);
```

Once the updated credentials have been obtained, the re-authentication is ready to be performed by making a call to the *reauthenticate()* method of the current user's FirebaseUser instance, passing through the AuthCredential object as an argument:

```
final FirebaseUser user = fbAuth.getCurrentUser();

user.updatePassword(newPassword)
        .addOnCompleteListener(new OnCompleteListener<Void>() {
            @Override
            public void onComplete(@NonNull Task<Void> task) {

            }
        }).addOnFailureListener(new OnFailureListener() {

    @Override
    public void onFailure(@NonNull Exception e) {
        if (e instanceof FirebaseAuthRecentLoginRequiredException) {
            AuthCredential credential = EmailAuthProvider
                    .getCredential(email, currentPassword);

            user.reauthenticate(credential)
                .addOnCompleteListener(new OnCompleteListener<Void>() {
                    @Override
                    public void onComplete(@NonNull Task<Void> task) {
                        // Re-authentication was successful
                        // Re-attempt secure password update action
                    }
                }).addOnFailureListener(new OnFailureListener() {
                    @Override
                    public void onFailure(@NonNull Exception e) {
                        notifyUser(e.getLocalizedMessage());
                    }
                });
        }
}
```

```
    }
});
```

As implemented, the code obtains the user's credentials and initiates the re-authentication. A completion listener is added to the operation where appropriate code can be added to re-attempt the secure action (in this case a password update). A failure listener is also added to the re-authentication method call and used to display the localized error description from any exception that is thrown during the re-authentication procedure.

12.6 **Summary**

There are few issues more annoying to a user than problems encountered when creating an account for, or signing in to an app. While it is impossible to eliminate all potential errors during the user authentication process, providing useful and informative feedback on the nature of any problems goes a long way toward alleviating the user's frustration. In order to provide information about the problem it is first necessary to be able to identify the cause. As outlined in this chapter, this can be achieved by adding failure listeners when making calls to Firebase SDK methods. When called, these failure listeners will be passed an exception object. By identifying the type of the exception and accessing error codes and description strings, an app can provide detailed information to the user on the cause of an authentication failure.

As also demonstrated in this chapter, the ability to identify recent login required exceptions when performing secure actions is a key requirement when a user needs to be re-authenticated.

13. Google Authentication using the Firebase SDK

Having covered Firebase SDK email and password authentication and error handling in the previous chapters, this chapter will focus on the use of the Google Play Services Sign In API to validate a user's identity via a Google account in order to create a matching Firebase user account.

The chapter will begin with an overview of the Google sign-in process and the way it integrates into the Firebase authentication process. An example project will then be created that demonstrates the practical steps involved in implementing this within an Android app.

13.1 Firebase Authentication with the Google Sign-In API

The Google Play Services library includes a set of APIs that provide access to a range of Google services. One such API is the Google Sign-In API which, as the name suggests, allows app developers to provide users the ability to sign into Google accounts from with an Android app. Once a user has successfully signed into a Google account, the ID token for that Google account can then be used to register the user via the Firebase authentication system. In effect this connects the user's Google account with a corresponding Firebase authentication account, allowing the user to continue signing into the app as a Firebase registered user using the Google account details.

The core elements of Google sign-in are the GoogleSignInOptions and GoogleApiClient classes. GoogleSignInOptions is used to configured the way in which the Google sign-in operation is handled, and specifies the Google account information that is required by the Android app.

GoogleApiClient provides a convenient interface for working with Google Play Services APIs without having to write extensive code and error handling logic. A GoogleApiClient instance is initialized with a suitably configured GoogleSignInOptions instance and then used to launch the Google sign-in activity. This activity takes the user through the Google sign-in process and returns the result to the app.

If the user successfully signed into a Google account using the Google user sign-in activity, the resulting data returned to the app will include the user's Google account ID token. The Firebase SDK is then used to exchange this ID for a Firebase credential object which is, in turn, used to register the user within the Firebase authentication system and subsequently sign into the app.

13.2 Creating the GoogleAuth Project

The first step in this exercise is to create the new project. Launching Android Studio, select the *Start a new Android Studio project* quick start option from the welcome screen and, within the new project dialog, enter *GoogleAuth* into the Application name field and your domain as the Company Domain setting before clicking on the *Next* button.

On the form factors screen, enable the *Phone and Tablet* option and set the minimum SDK to API 16: Android 4.1 (Jellybean). Proceed through the setup screens, requesting the creation of an Empty Activity named *GoogleAuthActivity* and a corresponding layout named *activity_google_auth*.

13.3 **Connecting the Project to Firebase**

As usual, the project will need to be connected to Firebase. Within Android Studio, use the *Tools -> Firebase* menu to display the Firebase Assistant panel, locate and click on the Authentication category, select the *Email and password authentication* link and then click on the *Connect to Firebase* button to display the Firebase connection dialog.

Choose the option to store the app in an existing Firebase project and select the *Firebase Examples* project created at the beginning of the book.

With the project's Firebase connection established, refer to the Firebase assistant panel once again, this time clicking on the *Add Firebase Authentication to your app* button. A dialog will appear outlining the changes that will be made to the project build configuration to enable Firebase authentication. Click on the *Accept Changes* button to commit the changes to the project configuration.

13.4 **Configuring the SHA-1 Fingerprint Key**

It is likely that the SHA-1 fingerprint will already be configured for all apps within the *Firebase Examples* project. Verify this is the case for the current project by navigating to the Firebase console within a browser window, clicking on the gear icon next to the *Overview* item and selecting *Project Settings* from the menu:

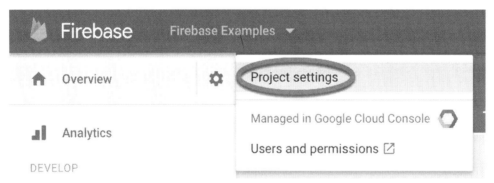

Figure 13-1

Within the resulting panel, select the General tab, locate the GoogleAuth app from the list and scroll to the SHA1 certificate fingerprints section. If the SHA-1 fingerprint is not already configured for the app, use the steps outlined in the chapter entitled *Google Sign-In Authentication using FirebaseUI Auth* to extract the SHA-1 Fingerprint key for your development environment and add it within the console.

Before returning to Android Studio, display the Authentication page within the Firebase console, select the *Sign-in Method* tab and verify that the Google provider is enabled.

13.5 Adding the Google Play Authentication Library

The Google authentication provider makes use of the Google Play Services authentication library. To avoid undefined symbols later in this tutorial, this library must be added to the Gradle configuration. Within the Android Studio project tool window, locate and open the *build.gradle (app: module)* build file (located under *Gradle Scripts*) and add the library to the *dependencies* section of the file:

```
apply plugin: 'com.android.application'
.
.
dependencies {
    compile fileTree(dir: 'libs', include: ['*.jar'])
    androidTestCompile('com.android.support.test.espresso:espresso-
core:2.2.2', {
        exclude group: 'com.android.support', module: 'support-annotations'
    })
    compile 'com.android.support:appcompat-v7:25.3.1'
    compile 'com.android.support.constraint:constraint-layout:1.0.2'
    compile 'com.google.firebase:firebase-auth:11.0.1'
    compile 'com.google.android.gms:play-services-auth:11.0.1'
    testCompile 'junit:junit:4.12'
}
.
.
```

13.6 Designing the User Interface Layout

The user interface layout is going to consist of an ImageView, two TextViews and two Buttons. Begin by loading the *activity_google_auth.xml* file into the layout editor tool and turning off Autoconnect mode.

Select and delete the "Hello World" TextView object and drag and drop an ImageView component from the Palette onto the layout canvas. When the ImageView is released onto the layout, a resources dialog will appear providing a list of images available to be displayed on the ImageView object. Addition of the Google libraries to the project build configuration has provided access to a range of Google related images for use within the project. Within the resources dialog locate the *common_google_signin_btn_icon_dark* image (Figure 13-2):

Google Authentication using the Firebase SDK

Figure 13-2

With the image selected, click on the *OK* button to apply the image to the ImageView and dismiss the resources dialog.

Remaining within the layout editor, add the TextView and Button widgets to the layout so that it resembles the layout shown in Figure 13-3. Shift-click on the TextView buttons so that both are selected and increase the *textSize* attribute in the properties window to 18sp:

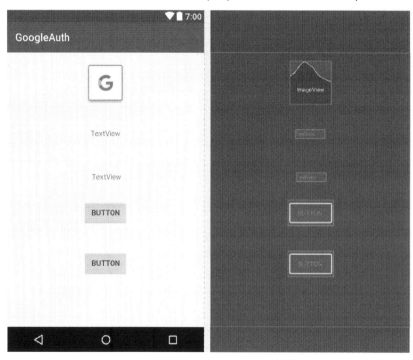

Figure 13-3

Select the ImageView and, using the properties tool panel, change the ID to *profileImage*. Also change the IDs of the two TextView objects to *emailText* and *statusText*. Change the text on the two buttons to *Google Sign-in* and *Sign Out* and configure onClick properties so that the buttons are configured to call methods named *signIn* and *signOut* respectively.

With the view components added to the layout it is now time to add some constraints. Click in the upper right-hand corner of the layout canvas and drag the resulting rectangle until it encompasses all of the widgets. On releasing the mouse button, all four widgets should now be selected. Right-click on the ImageView object and, from the resulting menu, select the *Center Horizontally* menu option. Repeat this step once again, this time selecting the *Center Vertically* menu option.

At this stage, appropriate constraints should have been added such that the layout will be responsive to different screen sizes and device orientations:

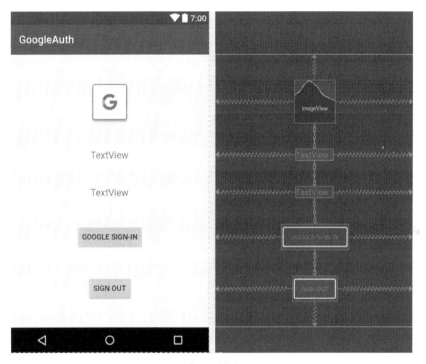

Figure 13-4

13.7 Adding a User Notification Method

A method named *notifyUser()* will once again be used to display Toast messages from within the app. Implement this method as follows in the *GoogleAuthActivity.java* file:

```
import android.widget.Toast;
.
.
.
private void notifyUser(String message) {
    Toast.makeText(GoogleAuthActivity.this, message,
```

```
                Toast.LENGTH_SHORT).show();
}
```

13.8 Accessing the FirebaseAuth Instance

As with all forms of Firebase SDK authentication, the two key components are the FirebaseAuth instance and the authentication state listener. The next step in implementing Firebase authentication for the Google provider is to obtain a reference to the FirebaseAuth instance. Within Android Studio, edit the *GoogleAuthActivity.java* file to obtain a reference to the FirebaseAuth instance and to perform some basic initialization tasks:

```
package com.ebookfrenzy.googleauth;

import android.support.v7.app.AppCompatActivity;
import android.os.Bundle;
import android.widget.Toast;
import android.widget.ImageView;
import android.widget.TextView;

import com.google.android.gms.tasks.OnCompleteListener;
import com.google.android.gms.tasks.Task;
import com.google.firebase.auth.AuthResult;
import com.google.firebase.auth.FirebaseAuth;
import com.google.firebase.auth.FirebaseUser;
import android.support.annotation.NonNull;

public class GoogleAuthActivity extends AppCompatActivity {

    private ImageView profileImage;
    private TextView emailText;
    private TextView statusText;
    private FirebaseAuth fbAuth;
    private FirebaseAuth.AuthStateListener authListener;

    @Override
    protected void onCreate(Bundle savedInstanceState) {
        super.onCreate(savedInstanceState);
        setContentView(R.layout.activity_google_auth);

        profileImage = (ImageView) findViewById(R.id.profileImage);
        emailText = (TextView) findViewById(R.id.emailText);
        statusText = (TextView) findViewById(R.id.statusText);

        emailText.setText("");
        statusText.setText("Signed Out");
```

```
        fbAuth = FirebaseAuth.getInstance();
    }
    .
    .
    .
}
```

13.9 Adding the Authentication State Listener

With the *GoogleAuthActivity.java* file still open in the Android Studio code editor, further modify the *onCreate()* method to declare the authentication state listener method:

```
@Override
protected void onCreate(Bundle savedInstanceState) {
    super.onCreate(savedInstanceState);
    setContentView(R.layout.activity_google_auth);

    emailText = (TextView) findViewById(R.id.emailText);
    statusText = (TextView) findViewById(R.id.statusText);

    emailText.setText("");
    statusText.setText("Signed Out");

    fbAuth = FirebaseAuth.getInstance();

    authListener = new FirebaseAuth.AuthStateListener() {
        @Override
        public void onAuthStateChanged(@NonNull FirebaseAuth firebaseAuth) {

            FirebaseUser user = firebaseAuth.getCurrentUser();

            if (user != null) {
                emailText.setText(user.getEmail());
                statusText.setText("Signed In");
                if (user.getPhotoUrl() != null) {
                    displayImage(user.getPhotoUrl());
                }
            } else {
                emailText.setText("");
                statusText.setText("Signed Out");
                profileImage.setImageResource(
                        R.drawable.common_google_signin_btn_icon_dark);
            }

        }
    }
```

```
    };
}
```

The listener method begins by getting a reference to the FirebaseUser object for the current user. If the user object is not null then the code assumes that a user has just successfully signed into the app. The user's email address is accessed and displayed on the emailText TextView object. The text displayed on the statusText object is then changed to indicate that the user is currently signed in and the user's profile photo is passed to a method named *displayImage()* which needs to be added to the Java class file as follows:

```
.
.
import android.net.Uri;
import android.graphics.Bitmap;
import android.os.AsyncTask;
import android.graphics.BitmapFactory;

import java.io.InputStream;
.
.
void displayImage(Uri imageUrl) {
    new DownloadImageTask((ImageView) findViewById(R.id.profileImage))
            .execute(imageUrl.toString());
}

private class DownloadImageTask extends AsyncTask<String, Void, Bitmap> {
    ImageView bmImage;

    public DownloadImageTask(ImageView bmImage) {
        this.bmImage = bmImage;
    }

    protected Bitmap doInBackground(String... urls) {
        String urldisplay = urls[0];
        Bitmap bitmap = null;
        try {
            InputStream in = new java.net.URL(urldisplay).openStream();
            bitmap = BitmapFactory.decodeStream(in);
        } catch (Exception e) {
            e.printStackTrace();
        }
        return bitmap;
    }
```

```
protected void onPostExecute(Bitmap result) {
    bmImage.setImageBitmap(result);
}
}
```

A null value assigned to the user object, on the other hand, indicates the authentication change involved the user signing out of the app. The email address is removed from the email text view, the status text is updated to reflect that the user has signed out and the ImageView updated to once again display the Google icon.

13.10 **Adding and Removing the Listener**

At this point, the authentication state listener has been declared but has not yet been added to the FirebaseAuth instance. Without this vital step, the method will never be called in response to changes in the authentication state. Once again, the standard *onStart()* Android lifecycle method will be overridden and used to add the listener. The *onStart()* method is called immediately after the call to the *onCreate()* method and before the activity is to become visible to the user. Within the *GoogleAuthActivity.java* file, add this method so that it reads as follows:

```
@Override
public void onStart() {
    super.onStart();
    fbAuth.addAuthStateListener(authListener);
}
```

In addition to adding the listener, it is equally important to remove the listener when it is no longer needed. To achieve this, the *onStop()* method will be used:

```
@Override
public void onStop() {
    super.onStop();
    if (authListener != null) {
        fbAuth.removeAuthStateListener(authListener);
    }
}
```

13.11 **Initializing the Google API Client**

Before a Google authentication can be performed, a GoogleSignInOptions instance needs to be created and used to initialize a GoogleApiClient object. This object is configured with options that define how the authentication will be handled and the types of user information required by the app. The GoogleSignInOptions class includes a builder method which is used to create an instance of the class. For example:

```
GoogleSignInOptions signInOptions = new
    GoogleSignInOptions.Builder(GoogleSignInOptions.DEFAULT_SIGN_IN)
        .requestIdToken(getString(R.string.default_web_client_id))
```

```
        .requestEmail()
        .requestProfile()
        .build();
```

The above example builds a GoogleSignInOptions instance using the default configuration for performing a Google sign in operation. The instance is also configured to request the user's Google account ID token, email address and profile information. The ID token will be used later in exchange for a Firebase authentication credential.

In order to request the ID token the value assigned to the *default_web_client_id* resource was passed through to the builder. This resource is generated automatically based on the content of the *google-services.json* file added to the project during the Firebase setup.

Once the GoogleSignInOptions instance has been created, it can be used in the creation of a GoogleApiClient object, once again using the builder provided with the class:

```
GoogleApiClient googleApiClient = new GoogleApiClient.Builder(this)
        .enableAutoManage(this, this)
        .addApi(Auth.GOOGLE_SIGN_IN_API, signInOptions)
        .build();
```

GoogleApiClient is a class designed specifically to make it easier for app developers to use the many APIs provided by the Google Play Services library. In this case, a GoogleApiClient instance is being created in order to access the Google Sign-In API using the configuration parameters previously assigned to the *signInOptions* object.

The *enableAutoManage* setting indicates that the Google API client should automatically handle all aspects of the connection to the Google sign-in services, including automatically resolving any non-fatal errors. While this greatly simplifies the implementation of Google services features, it does require that a handler be designated to act as the listener for unresolvable failures. This handler must, in turn, implement the GoogleApiClient OnConnectionFailedListener interface. For this example, this role will be performed by the GoogleAuthActivity class.

With the *GoogleAuthActivity.java* file loaded into the Android Studio code editor, modify the class to perform these initialization tasks as follows:

```
.
.
import com.google.android.gms.auth.api.Auth;
import com.google.android.gms.auth.api.signin.GoogleSignInOptions;
import com.google.android.gms.common.api.GoogleApiClient;
.
.
import com.google.android.gms.common.ConnectionResult;
.
.
public class GoogleAuthActivity extends AppCompatActivity implements
```

```
        GoogleApiClient.OnConnectionFailedListener {
.
.

    private GoogleApiClient googleApiClient;
    private static final int RC_SIGN_IN = 1001;
.
.

    @Override
    protected void onCreate(Bundle savedInstanceState) {
        super.onCreate(savedInstanceState);
        setContentView(R.layout.activity_google_auth_sdk);

        emailText = (TextView) findViewById(R.id.emailText);
        statusText = (TextView) findViewById(R.id.statusText);
        emailText.setText("");
        statusText.setText("Signed Out");

        GoogleSignInOptions signInOptions =
                new GoogleSignInOptions.Builder(
                        GoogleSignInOptions.DEFAULT_SIGN_IN)
                .requestIdToken(getString(R.string.default_web_client_id))
                .requestEmail()
                .requestProfile()
                .build();

        googleApiClient = new GoogleApiClient.Builder(this)
                .enableAutoManage(this, this)
                .addApi(Auth.GOOGLE_SIGN_IN_API, signInOptions)
                .build();
.
.
```

Having declared that the GoogleAuthActivity class implements the OnConnectionFailedListener interface, the *onConnectionFailed()* method now needs to be overridden within the class to notify the user that an unresolvable error occurred:

```
@Override
public void onConnectionFailed(@NonNull ConnectionResult connectionResult) {
    notifyUser("Google Play Services failure.");
}
```

13.12 Implementing the Sign In Method

With both the Firebase and Google initialization tasks completed, the next step is to begin adding the code to perform the user sign-in. During the design of the user interface layout, the sign-in button was configured to call a method named *signIn()* when clicked. Remaining within the GoogleAuthActivity class file, add this method now so that it matches the following:

```
.
.
import android.content.Intent;
import android.view.View;
.
.
import com.google.android.gms.auth.api.signin.GoogleSignInAccount;
import com.google.android.gms.auth.api.signin.GoogleSignInOptions;
import com.google.android.gms.auth.api.signin.GoogleSignInResult;
.
.
public void signIn(View view) {
    Intent signInIntent =
                Auth.GoogleSignInApi.getSignInIntent(googleApiClient);
    startActivityForResult(signInIntent, RC_SIGN_IN);
}
```

The above method creates a new Google sign-in Intent object based on the Google Client API object built during the initialization phase. This intent is then used to launch the Google sign-in activity. Since the activity is launched using the *startActivityForResult()* method, the *onActivityResult()* method will also now need to be added in order to receive the results of the activity:

```
@Override
public void onActivityResult(int requestCode, int resultCode, Intent data) {
    super.onActivityResult(requestCode, resultCode, data);

    if (requestCode == RC_SIGN_IN) {
        GoogleSignInResult result =
                Auth.GoogleSignInApi.getSignInResultFromIntent(data);

        if (result.isSuccess()) {
            GoogleSignInAccount account = result.getSignInAccount();
            authWithFirebase(account);
        } else {
            this.notifyUser("Google sign-in failed.");
        }
    }
}
```

The code begins by comparing the result code to the one provided when the sign-in activity was started. If the code matches, the result of the sign-in operation is obtained from the result data in the form of a GoogleSignInResult object. The *isSuccess()* method of the result object is called to identify whether the user's attempt to sign in using a Google account succeeded. If the sign-in was successful, the GoogleSignInAccount object for the user is extracted from the result object and passed to a yet to be implemented method named *authWithFirebase()*. It is within this method that the user's Google account ID needs to be exchanged for a Firebase authentication credential.

13.13 Registering the User with Firebase

With the user successfully signed into a Google account, it is now time to obtain the ID token for the user's Google account and pass it to Firebase in return for a corresponding Firebase AuthCredential object. This credential will then be used to sign the user into the app using Firebase authentication. These steps will be performed within the *authWithFirebase()* method as follows:

```
.
.
import com.google.firebase.auth.AuthCredential;
import com.google.firebase.auth.GoogleAuthProvider;
.
.
private void authWithFirebase(GoogleSignInAccount acct) {

    AuthCredential credential = GoogleAuthProvider.getCredential(
                        acct.getIdToken(), null);

    fbAuth.signInWithCredential(credential)
            .addOnCompleteListener(this,
                    new OnCompleteListener<AuthResult>() {
                @Override
                public void onComplete(@NonNull Task<AuthResult> task) {
                    if (!task.isSuccessful()) {
                        notifyUser("Firebase authentication failed.");
                    }
                }
            });
}
```

The code extracts the user's Google ID token from the GoogleSignInAccount object and uses it to request a Firebase AuthCredential object from the Google authentication provider. The credential object is then used to sign into Firebase, including the creation of a new account if one does not already exist. A completion listener is attached to the request and used to notify the user of a failure should one occur.

13.14 Signing Out

All that remains before testing the app is to implement the *signOut()* method to be called when the user clicks the Sign Out button in the user interface:

```
.
```

```
.
import com.google.android.gms.common.api.ResultCallback;
import com.google.android.gms.common.api.Status;
.

.
public void signOut(View view) {
    fbAuth.signOut();

    Auth.GoogleSignInApi.signOut(googleApiClient).setResultCallback(
            new ResultCallback<Status>() {
                @Override
                public void onResult(@NonNull Status status) {

                }
            });
}
```

After successfully completing the sign-in process, the user is actually signed in using both Google and Firebase authentication. When it comes to signing out, therefore, the user must be signed out of both accounts. In the method outlined above, the *signOut()* method of the FirebaseAuth instance is called to sign out of the app via Firebase. The *signOut()* method of the Google SignIn API is then called and passed a reference to the *GoogleApiClient* object in order to sign out of the Google account. The call is assigned a callback where code may be added to verify that the sign out operation completed successfully.

13.15 **Testing the Project**

Log into the Firebase console within a browser window, select the *Authentication* option in the left-hand navigation panel followed by the *Users* tab on the Authentication screen. If a user already exists for the Google account you intend to use for testing purposes, delete it from Firebase before proceeding.

Compile and run the app on a physical Android device or emulator session and tap the Sign In button to launch the Google sign-in activity. If the device or emulator already has Google accounts configured, a dialog will appear providing a list of known accounts from which to choose. In the absence of previously configured Google accounts, the Google sign-in activity will instead provide the option either to add an existing account to the device or create a new one:

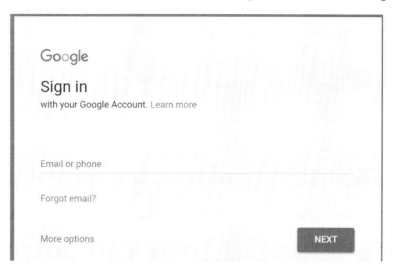

Figure 13-5

After successfully signing in to the app using a Google account the user interface should update to reflect the user's email address and profile image. Return to the Firebase console browser window and verify both that the corresponding account has been created, and that it is listed as using the Google provider:

Figure 13-6

13.16 **Summary**

This chapter has outlined the use of the Google Sign API, part of the Google Play Services library, to allow users to create and sign into Firebase authentication accounts using Google accounts. This involves the use of the GoogleSignInOptions and GoogleApiClient classes to initiate the sign-in process. Once the user has successfully signed into a Google account, the ID token for that account is then exchanged for a Firebase authentication credential which is then used to register the user with Firebase and sign into the app using Firebase authentication.

14. Facebook Authentication using the Firebase SDK

The previous chapter covered Firebase SDK based authentication using the Google provider. While some concepts are the same, there are also a number of different requirements that must be fulfilled when implementing Firebase SDK authentication using Facebook to identify and authenticate app users.

This chapter will begin by outlining the general steps to achieve Facebook-based authentication by combining both the Firebase and Facebook SDKs. Once these basics have been covered, the chapter will work through the creation of an example project.

14.1 Authentication with the Firebase and Facebook SDKs

Implementing Firebase authentication using both the Firebase and Facebook SDKs is a multistep process which can be broken down into a sequence of steps involving a number of different classes.

As with the Google authentication process outlined in the previous chapter, this form of authentication requires that the user first sign into a valid Facebook account in order to receive an access token from the Facebook SDK. This access token is then used to create a Firebase authentication credential. The Firebase credential is then used to sign into a Firebase authentication user account (including the creation of a new account if one does not already exit).

The cornerstone to performing the Facebook phase of the authentication is the LoginButton class. This class provides a button for inclusion within a user interface which, when appropriately configured, serves the dual role of being both the login and logout button. Callbacks are then registered on the LoginButton instance which are called by the Facebook SDK to notify the app of the status of Facebook sign-in requests. On a successful Facebook sign-in, the appropriate callback method is called and passed a LoginResult object containing the user's access token which is then used to register the user in Firebase.

14.2 Creating the FacebookAuth Project

The first step in this exercise is to create the new project. Begin by launching Android Studio and, if necessary, closing any currently open projects using the *File -> Close Project* menu option so that the Welcome screen appears.

Select the *Start a new Android Studio project* quick start option from the welcome screen and, within the new project dialog, enter *FacebookAuth* into the Application name field and your domain as the Company Domain setting before clicking on the *Next* button.

On the form factors screen, enable the *Phone and Tablet* option and set the minimum SDK to API 16: Android 4.1 (Jellybean). Continue to proceed through the screens, requesting the creation of an Empty Activity named *FacebookAuthActivity* with a corresponding layout named *activity_facebook_auth.*

14.3 **Connecting the Project to Firebase**

As with previous examples, the project will need to be connected to Firebase. Within Android Studio, use the *Tools -> Firebase* menu to display the Firebase Assistant panel, locate and click on the Authentication category, select the *Email and password authentication* link and then click on the *Connect to Firebase* button to display the Firebase connection dialog.

Choose the option to store the app in an existing Firebase project and select the *Firebase Examples* project created in the beginning of the book.

With the project's Firebase connection established, refer to the Firebase assistant panel once again, this time clicking on the *Add Firebase Authentication to your app* button. A dialog will appear outlining the changes that will be made to the project build configuration to enable Firebase authentication. Click on the *Accept Changes* button to commit the changes to the project configuration.

14.4 **Firebase and Facebook Console Configuration**

Many of the steps for configuring the project to support Facebook authentication are the same as those outlined in the chapter entitled *Facebook Login Authentication using FirebaseUI Auth*. In fact, if you have already completed the steps outlined in that chapter, then the following steps will already have been performed and do not need to be repeated for this example:

1. Obtain the Facebook App ID and App Secret from the Facebook for Developers portal.

2. Enable the Facebook provider in the Firebase console.

3. Add the App ID and App Secret to the project in the Firebase console.

4. Add the Facebook login product to the app within the Facebook portal.

5. Obtain the OAuth Redirect URI from the Firebase console and adding it to the app settings in the Facebook portal.

6. Generate the debug key hash for the project and adding to app configuration in Facebook portal.

If these steps have yet to be performed within your development environment, refer to the initial sections in the *Facebook Login Authentication using FirebaseUI Auth* chapter and follow the instructions to complete this phase of the project configuration before proceeding.

14.5 **Configuring the Android Studio Project**

With the work complete in the Firebase console and Facebook for Developers portal, there are now some tasks that need to be accomplished before Facebook Login can be used within the example app. Note that, unlike the console settings above, these steps are specific to each Android Studio project and must be performed for this project regardless of whether they were performed for a previous project.

The first task is to add a string declaration within the *strings.xml* file containing the Facebook App ID. With the FacebookAuth project loaded into Android Studio, use the project tool window to open the *app -> res -> values -> strings.xml* file. With the file loaded into the editor, add a new string entity with the name *facebook_application_id* as follows where *<your_fb_app_id>* is replaced by the actual App ID assigned within the Facebook portal:

```
<resources>
    <string name="app_name">FacebookAuth</string>
    <string name="facebook_application_id"
             translatable="false"><your_fb_app_id></string>
    <string name="action_settings">Settings</string>
</resources>
```

Next, two new elements need to be added to the project manifest file, one to grant internet access permission to the app, and the other to assign the *facebook_application_id* string created above to the *ApplicationId* property of the Facebook SDK. Within the project tool window, select the *manifests -> AndroidManifest.xml* file and edit it to add these additional elements:

```
<?xml version="1.0" encoding="utf-8"?>
<manifest xmlns:android="http://schemas.android.com/apk/res/android"
    package="com.ebookfrenzy.facebookauth">

    <uses-permission android:name="android.permission.INTERNET"/>

    <application
        android:allowBackup="true"
        android:icon="@mipmap/ic_launcher"
        android:label="@string/app_name"
        android:supportsRtl="true"
        android:theme="@style/AppTheme">
        <activity
            android:name=".FacebookAuthActivity"
            android:label="@string/app_name"
            android:theme="@style/AppTheme.NoActionBar">
            <intent-filter>
                <action android:name="android.intent.action.MAIN" />

                <category android:name="android.intent.category.LAUNCHER" />
            </intent-filter>
        </activity>
        <meta-data android:name="com.facebook.sdk.ApplicationId"
            android:value="@string/facebook_application_id"/>
```

```
        </application>
</manifest>
```

14.6 Adding the Facebook SDK Library

Facebook authentication when using the Firebase SDK makes extensive use of support provided by the Facebook SDK. The module level *build.gradle* file must, therefore, be modified to ensure that this library is included as part of the project build process.

Locate the module level *build.gradle* file in the project tool window (*Gradle Scripts -> build.gradle (Module: app)*) and load it into the code editor. Within the file, scroll down to the *dependencies* section and add the directive to include the Facebook SDK:

```
.
.
dependencies {
    compile fileTree(dir: 'libs', include: ['*.jar'])
    androidTestCompile('com.android.support.test.espresso:espresso-
core:2.2.2', {
        exclude group: 'com.android.support', module: 'support-annotations'
    })
    compile 'com.android.support:appcompat-v7:25.3.1'
    compile 'com.android.support.constraint:constraint-layout:1.0.2'
    compile 'com.google.firebase:firebase-auth:11.0.1'
    compile 'com.facebook.android:facebook-android-sdk:[4,5)'
    testCompile 'junit:junit:4.12'
}
.
.
```

When the yellow warning bar appears indicating that a project sync may be necessary, click on the *Sync Now* link and allow the project to be rebuilt to reflect the new Gradle build settings.

14.7 Designing the User Interface Layout

Initially, the user interface is going to consist of an ImageView, two TextViews and a Button. Begin by loading the *activity_facebook_auth.xml* file into the layout editor tool and turning off Autoconnect mode.

Select and delete the default "Hello World" TextView object and drag and drop an ImageView component from the Palette onto the layout canvas. When the ImageView is released onto the layout, a resources dialog will appear providing a list of images available to be displayed on the ImageView object. Inclusion of the Facebook SDK into the project has provided a range of Facebook related images from which to choose. Scroll down the rows of images in the resources dialog until the Facebook blank square profile picture image comes into view (highlighted in Figure 14-1):

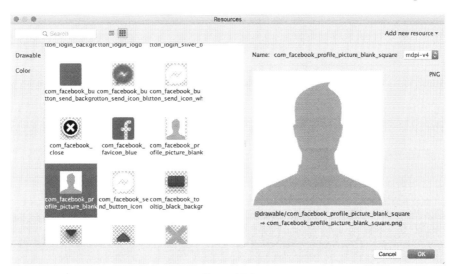

Figure 14-1

With the image selected, click on the *OK* button to apply the image to the ImageView and dismiss the resources dialog.

Remaining within the layout editor, add the TextView and Button widgets to the layout so that it resembles the layout shown in Figure 14-2. Shift-click on the TextView buttons so that both are selected and increase the *textSize* attribute in the Properties tool window to 18sp:

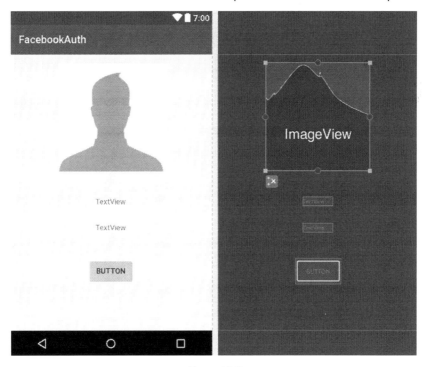

Figure 14-2

Select the ImageView and, using the Properties tool window, change the ID to *profileImage*. Also change the IDs of the two TextView objects and the Button to *emailText*, *statusText* and *loginButton* respectively.

With the view components added to the layout it is now time to add some constraints. Click in the upper right-hand corner of the layout canvas and drag the resulting rectangle until it encompasses all of the widgets. On releasing the mouse button, all four widgets should now be selected. Right-click on the ImageView object and, from the resulting menu, select the *Center Horizontally* menu option. Repeat this step once again, this time selecting the *Center Vertically* menu option.

At this stage, appropriate constraints should have been added such that the layout will be responsive to different screen sizes and device orientations:

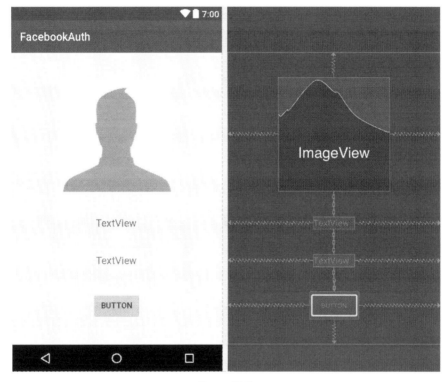

Figure 14-3

14.8 **Adding the Facebook LoginButton**

The Button object added to the layout in the previous section was used as a placeholder and now needs to be replaced by an instance of the Facebook LoginButton. With the *activity_facebook_auth_sdk.xml* layout resource file still open in the layout editor, switch the editor to text mode, locate the Button widget in the XML and change the class type from Button to *com.facebook.login.widget.LoginButton* as follows:

```
<com.facebook.login.widget.LoginButton
    android:text="Button"
```

```
android:layout_width="wrap_content"
android:layout_height="wrap_content"
android:id="@+id/loginButton"
app:layout_constraintRight_toRightOf="parent"
app:layout_constraintLeft_toLeftOf="parent"
app:layout_constraintBottom_toBottomOf="parent"
app:layout_constraintTop_toBottomOf="@+id/statusText" />
```

Return the layout editor to design mode and note the button appearance has changed to a Facebook LoginButton button:

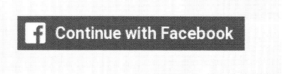

Figure 14-4

14.9 Facebook SDK Initialization Steps

Facebook authentication setup involves initialization of the Facebook SDK, the creation of a CallbackManager and the registration of callback methods with the LoginButton instance. The callback manager and callback methods act as the bridge between the app and the Facebook SDK, allowing the SDK to notify the app of events relating to the authentication process.

Begin by loading the *FacebookAuthActivity.java* file into the Android Studio code editor and adding some variables and import directives that will be used later in the code:

```
package com.ebookfrenzy.facebookauth;

import android.support.v7.app.AppCompatActivity;
import android.os.Bundle;
import android.content.Intent;
import android.util.Log;
import android.widget.ImageView;
import android.widget.TextView;

import com.facebook.CallbackManager;
import com.facebook.FacebookCallback;
import com.facebook.FacebookException;
import com.facebook.FacebookSdk;
import com.facebook.login.LoginResult;
import com.facebook.login.widget.LoginButton;

public class FacebookAuthActivity extends AppCompatActivity {
```

```
    private CallbackManager callbackManager;

    private LoginButton loginButton;
    private TextView emailText;
    private TextView statusText;
    private ImageView imageView;

    private static final String TAG = "FacebookAuth";
    .
    .
    .
}
```

Next, modify the *onCreate()* method to perform some initialization tasks. When making the changes, be sure to place the Facebook SDK initialization call before the call to the *setContentView()* method. Failure to do so will cause the app to crash when the activity is launched:

```
@Override
protected void onCreate(Bundle savedInstanceState) {
    super.onCreate(savedInstanceState);

    callbackManager = CallbackManager.Factory.create();

    setContentView(R.layout.activity_facebook_auth);

    emailText = (TextView) findViewById(R.id.emailText);
    statusText = (TextView) findViewById(R.id.statusText);
    imageView = (ImageView) findViewById(R.id.profileImage);
    loginButton = (LoginButton) findViewById(R.id.loginButton);

    loginButton.setReadPermissions("email", "public_profile");
}
```

The purpose of the last line of code added to the method above is to configure the LoginButton instance with the permissions that will be required by our app during authentication. For the purposes of this example access will be required to the email address and public profile information associated with the user's Facebook account.

14.10 **Handling Authentication Results and Callbacks**

Regardless of the fact that the Facebook authentication process is handled entirely in the background by the Facebook SDK, the app still needs a way to be notified of whether or not the authentication was successful.

When the user clicks the LoginButton, the Facebook SDK essentially uses the Android Intents mechanism to launch an activity which presents the user with the Facebook login interface and carries out the authentication process. Intents (*android.content.Intent*) are the messaging system by which one activity is able to launch another activity.

When another activity is launched by an intent, it can be configured such that a call to the *onActivityResult* of the originating activity is made when the launched activity finishes. It is via this mechanism that the Facebook SDK returns data to the app containing the results of the authentication.

Implement the *onActivityResult()* method within the FacebookAuthActivity class as follows:

```
@Override
protected void onActivityResult(int requestCode, int resultCode, Intent data)
{
    super.onActivityResult(requestCode, resultCode, data);
    callbackManager.onActivityResult(requestCode, resultCode, data);
}
```

The key line of code within the above method is the call to the *onActivityResult()* method of the callbackManager instance created during the Facebook SDK initialization process earlier in this chapter. Before this will do anything useful, a callback handler needs to be registered on the LoginButton and assigned to the CallbackManager instance.

This handler needs to contain methods to be called in the event of successful, failed and cancelled Facebook authentication requests.

Code to register and implement this handler this should now be added to the *onCreate()* method so that it reads as follows:

```
@Override
protected void onCreate(Bundle savedInstanceState) {
    .
    .
    .
    imageView = (ImageView) findViewById(R.id.profileImage);
    loginButton = (LoginButton) findViewById(R.id.loginButton);

    loginButton.setReadPermissions("email", "public_profile");

    loginButton.registerCallback(callbackManager,
            new FacebookCallback<LoginResult>() {

        @Override
        public void onSuccess(LoginResult loginResult) {
            Log.d(TAG, "onSuccess: " + loginResult);
        }

        @Override
```

```
        public void onCancel() {
            Log.d(TAG, "onCancel: User cancelled sign-in");
        }

        @Override
        public void onError(FacebookException error) {
            Log.d(TAG, "onError: " + error);
        }
    });
}
```

In the event of a successful authentication, the *onSuccess()* callback method will be called and passed an object of type LoginResult. This object will be used later in this chapter to extract the access token and use it to authenticate the user with Firebase. For now, however, the methods are implemented to simply output information to the Android Studio logcat console.

14.11 Testing Facebook Authentication

At this point the Facebook phase of the authentication process is fully implemented and may be tested by running the app. Once launched, the user interface should appear, including the Facebook LoginButton. The result of clicking the button will depend on whether or not the Facebook app is installed on the device.

If the app is launched on a device on which the Facebook app is installed and set up with the user's Facebook credentials, a dialog similar to that shown in Figure 14-5 may appear allowing the user to immediately sign in without entering a username and password:

Figure 14-5

If the Facebook app is installed, but does not have any existing Facebook account credentials configured, the standard Facebook app sign-in screen will be displayed prompting for the user's account information.

Alternatively, if the app is running on an emulator or a device on which the Facebook app is absent, a WebView instance (Figure 14-6) will be launched requesting the user's account information:

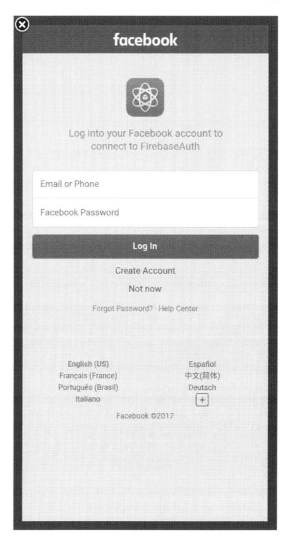

Figure 14-6

With the app running, tap the Facebook LoginButton and sign in to a valid Facebook account. Once the sign-in is complete, check the logcat output in the Android Studio Android Monitor panel for either a success or failure message. If the login was successful, the LoginButton will switch to "Log out" mode shown in Figure 14-7:

Figure 14-7

14.12 **Initializing Firebase**

Performing the Facebook login is, of course, only part of the Firebase authentication process. So far the app has been able to obtain a valid Facebook access token for the user, but no attempt has been made to exchange that token for a Firebase credential and register the user within the Firebase ecosystem. Before doing this, however, the now familiar steps of initializing the Firebase SDK and adding the authentication state listener must be completed.

Edit the *FacebookAuthActivity.java* file and add some more import statements and variables as follows:

```
package com.ebookfrenzy.facebookauth;

import android.content.Intent;
import android.support.v7.app.AppCompatActivity;
import android.os.Bundle;
import android.util.Log;
import android.widget.ImageView;
import android.widget.TextView;

import com.facebook.CallbackManager;
import com.facebook.FacebookCallback;
import com.facebook.FacebookException;
import com.facebook.FacebookSdk;
import com.facebook.login.LoginResult;
import com.facebook.login.widget.LoginButton;

import com.google.firebase.auth.FirebaseAuth;
import android.support.annotation.NonNull;
import com.google.firebase.auth.FirebaseUser;

public class FacebookAuthActivity extends AppCompatActivity {

    private CallbackManager callbackManager;
    private FirebaseAuth fbAuth;
    private FirebaseAuth.AuthStateListener authListener;
.
.
.
```

Remaining in the FacebookAuthActivity class file, add the following code to the bottom of the *onCreate()* method to obtain a reference to the FirebaseAuth instance and install the authentication state listener:

```
@Override
protected void onCreate(Bundle savedInstanceState) {
```

```
    super.onCreate(savedInstanceState);
.
.
.

    fbAuth = FirebaseAuth.getInstance();

    authListener = new FirebaseAuth.AuthStateListener() {
        @Override
        public void onAuthStateChanged(@NonNull FirebaseAuth firebaseAuth) {
            FirebaseUser user = firebaseAuth.getCurrentUser();
            if (user != null) {
                emailText.setText(user.getEmail());
                statusText.setText("Signed In");

                if (user.getPhotoUrl() != null) {
                    displayImage(user.getPhotoUrl());
                }
            } else {
                emailText.setText("");
                statusText.setText("Signed Out");
                imageView.setImageResource(
                    R.drawable.com_facebook_profile_picture_blank_square);
            }
        }
    };
}

@Override
public void onStart() {
    super.onStart();
    fbAuth.addAuthStateListener(authListener);
}

@Override
public void onStop() {
    super.onStop();
    if (authListener != null) {
        fbAuth.removeAuthStateListener(authListener);
    }
}
```

On detection of a change to the authentication state, the above listener code checks for the presence of a valid user account. Depending on whether a valid user is detected, the user interface is updated accordingly, including displaying the user's Facebook profile photo using a method named *displayImage()* which also now needs to be added to the class. Begin by adding import statements for the packages that will be needed by the image handling code:

```
package com.ebookfrenzy.facebookauth;

import android.content.Intent;
import android.support.annotation.NonNull;
import android.support.v7.app.AppCompatActivity;
import android.os.Bundle;
import android.util.Log;
import android.widget.ImageView;
import android.widget.TextView;
import android.graphics.Bitmap;
import android.graphics.BitmapFactory;
import android.net.Uri;
import android.os.AsyncTask;

import com.google.firebase.auth.FirebaseAuth;

import com.facebook.CallbackManager;
import com.facebook.FacebookCallback;
import com.facebook.FacebookException;
import com.facebook.FacebookSdk;
import com.facebook.login.LoginResult;
import com.facebook.login.widget.LoginButton;
import com.google.firebase.auth.FirebaseUser;

import java.io.InputStream;
.
.
```

Next, add the code to download the user's profile photo and display it on the ImageView object in the user interface layout:

```
void displayImage(Uri imageUrl) {
    new DownloadImageTask((ImageView) findViewById(R.id.profileImage))
            .execute(imageUrl.toString());
}

private class DownloadImageTask extends AsyncTask<String, Void, Bitmap> {
    ImageView bmImage;

    public DownloadImageTask(ImageView bmImage) {
        this.bmImage = bmImage;
    }
```

```
protected Bitmap doInBackground(String... urls) {
    String urldisplay = urls[0];
    Bitmap bitmap = null;
    try {
        InputStream in = new java.net.URL(urldisplay).openStream();
        bitmap = BitmapFactory.decodeStream(in);
    } catch (Exception e) {
        e.printStackTrace();
    }
    return bitmap;
}


protected void onPostExecute(Bitmap result) {
    bmImage.setImageBitmap(result);
}
}
```

With the appropriate steps implemented to detect authentication state changes, the next step is to use the Facebook access token to obtain a matching Firebase authentication credential, and then use that credential to sign the user in to the app.

14.13 Registering the User in Firebase

When the user's Facebook identity has been successfully verified, the *onSuccess()* callback method previously registered on the LoginButton instance is called and passed a LoginResult object. Contained within this object is the user's Facebook access token which needs to be exchanged for a corresponding Firebase AuthCredential object. This credential object will then be used to sign the user in to the app using the Firebase authentication system. If this is the first time that the user has signed into the app using a Facebook account, this process will automatically create a new Firebase authentication account for that user.

Begin by modifying the *onSuccess()* callback method to call a new method named *exchangeAccessToken()* which takes as an argument a Facebook AccessToken object:

```
.
.
loginButton.registerCallback(callbackManager, new
FacebookCallback<LoginResult>() {

    @Override
    public void onSuccess(LoginResult loginResult) {
        Log.d(TAG, "onSuccess: " + loginResult);
        exchangeAccessToken(loginResult.getAccessToken());
    }
.
```

.

With the call to the method added to the callback, the method must now also be added to the class, beginning with the task of importing some additional packages:

.

.

```
import android.widget.Toast;

import com.facebook.AccessToken;
import com.google.android.gms.tasks.OnCompleteListener;
import com.google.android.gms.tasks.Task;
import com.google.firebase.auth.AuthCredential;
import com.google.firebase.auth.AuthResult;
import com.google.firebase.auth.FacebookAuthProvider;
```

.

.

Next, add the *exchangeAccessToken()* method so that it reads as follows:

```
private void exchangeAccessToken(AccessToken token) {

    AuthCredential credential =
            FacebookAuthProvider.getCredential(token.getToken());

    fbAuth.signInWithCredential(credential)
        .addOnCompleteListener(this, new OnCompleteListener<AuthResult>() {
            @Override
            public void onComplete(@NonNull Task<AuthResult> task) {

                if (!task.isSuccessful()) {
                    Toast.makeText(FacebookAuthActivity.this,
                            "Authentication failed.",
                        Toast.LENGTH_SHORT).show();
                }
            }
        });
}
```

The code begins by generating Firebase credentials for the user by calling the *getCredential()* method of the FacebookAuthProvider class, passing through the Facebook access token as the sole argument. These credentials are passed through to the *signInWithCredential()* method of the FirebaseAuth instance. A completion handler is then used to check whether the sign-in was successful and to report any failure that may have occurred.

A successful Firebase authentication sign-in will trigger a call to the authentication state listener and the user interface will be updated to reflect the change in status and to display the user's email address and profile photo.

14.14 Testing the Project

Open the Firebase console in a browser window, select the *Authentication* option in the left-hand navigation panel following by the *Users* tab on the Authentication screen. If a user already exists for the Facebook account you intend to use for testing purposes, delete it from Firebase before proceeding.

Compile and run the app on a physical Android device or emulator and tap the *Log in with Facebook* button. Depending on the configuration of the device, take the appropriate steps to authenticate using a valid Facebook account. On signing in, the user interface should update and the LoginButton should change to read "Log out".

Return to the Firebase console, refresh the Users list and verify that the account has been created using the Facebook provider.

Click on the Log out button within the app, at which point the Facebook SDK will display a dialog seeking confirmation that you wish to log out:

Figure 14-8

Tap the log out option and note that the Log out button has now reverted to a Sign in with Facebook button. There is, however, a problem in that the user interface has not been updated to reflect that the user has signed out. The photo ImageView and the two TextView objects still suggest that the same user is still signed in. This is because the app has not noticed that the user selected the sign out option. Clearly some more work is required before this project is complete.

14.15 Detecting the Facebook Log Out

It is important to keep in mind when performing authentication of this nature that there are actually two authentications taking place, one with Facebook and another with Firebase. Although the Facebook LoginButton has callbacks registered within the app to receive notification of the status of a login attempt, no such callback is available for detecting when the user logs out of Facebook using the LoginButton. After signing out of Facebook, therefore, the user is still signed in using Firebase.

To resolve this problem, a way is needed to detect when the user has signed out of Facebook and, having detected this change, also sign out of Firebase. This can easily be achieved by creating an *access token tracker* instance within the app. An access token tracker is an instance of the AccessTokenTracker class of the Facebook SDK and provides a way for an app to receive notification when the status of an access token changes, such as a user signing out of an account.

Facebook Authentication using the Firebase SDK

Add an access token tracker to the app by editing the *FacebookAuthActivity.java* file and modifying the code as follows:

```java
package com.ebookfrenzy.facebookauth;
.
.
import com.facebook.AccessTokenTracker;
.
.
public class FacebookAuthActivity extends AppCompatActivity {
.
.
    private AccessTokenTracker accessTokenTracker;
.
.
    @Override
    protected void onCreate(Bundle savedInstanceState) {
        super.onCreate(savedInstanceState);

        FacebookSdk.sdkInitialize(getApplicationContext());
        callbackManager = CallbackManager.Factory.create();

        accessTokenTracker = new AccessTokenTracker() {
            @Override
            protected void onCurrentAccessTokenChanged(
                        AccessToken oldAccessToken,
                        AccessToken currentAccessToken) {

                if (currentAccessToken == null) {
                    fbAuth.signOut();
                }
            }
        };
.
.
}
```

The new code creates an access token tracker instance which simply checks to find out if a valid token still exists. In the event that the current token is null, the code assumes that the user has logged out of Facebook and takes the necessary action to also sign out of the corresponding Firebase account. This, in turn, will trigger the authentication state listener which will update the user interface to reflect that the user has now signed out.

Test the app once more and confirm that logging out now works as expected.

14.16 **Summary**

The chapter has outlined the use of the Facebook SDK to allow users to create and sign into Firebase authentication accounts using Facebook accounts. This involves obtaining an access token from Facebook for the user, then exchanging that token for corresponding Firebase credentials. These credentials are then used to register the user within Firebase. Interaction between the app, the Facebook SDK and Firebase is handled through a series of callbacks and listeners together with an access token tracker.

15. Twitter Log In Authentication using the Firebase SDK

In addition to Google and Facebook, Firebase user authentication may also be performed using the Twitter SDK. As with Google and Facebook integration, the user is instructed to sign in to a Twitter account, the details of which are then used to create a new account within the project's Firebase authentication user database. Once a Firebase authentication account has been associated with the user's Twitter identity, the user will be able to sign into the app using those Twitter credentials.

15.1 Authentication using Firebase and the Twitter SDK

Twitter-based authentication requires that the user first sign into a Twitter account in order to receive an access token from the Twitter SDK. This access token is then used to create a Firebase authentication credential. The Firebase credential is then used to create a Firebase authentication user account. Once the account has been created, the user may continue to use the Twitter Log In process to sign into the app. Each time, the Twitter access token will be exchanged for the user's Firebase credentials which, in turn, will be used to sign into the app.

Similar to the Facebook LoginButton class, the Twitter SDK provides the TwitterLoginButton. This class provides a Twitter-branded button for inclusion within a user interface layouts. Unlike the Facebook LoginButton, however, the Twitter button does not also serve as a "Sign Out" button.

Once integrated with the user interface of an app, callbacks are registered on the TwitterLoginButton instance which are called by the Twitter SDK to notify the app of the status of sign-in requests. On a successful Twitter account sign-in, the appropriate callback method is called and passed a TwitterSession object containing the users access token which is then used to register the user in Firebase via the TwitterAuthProvider class.

15.2 Creating the TwitterAuth Project

Begin by launching Android Studio and selecting the *Start a new Android Studio project* quick start option from the welcome screen.

Within the new project dialog, enter *TwitterAuth* into the Application name field and your domain as the Company Domain setting before clicking on the *Next* button.

On the form factors screen, enable the *Phone and Tablet* option and set the minimum SDK to API 16: Android 4.1 (Jellybean). Continue to proceed through the screens, requesting the creation of an Empty Activity named *TwitterAuthActivity* with a corresponding layout named *activity_twitter_auth*.

15.3 **Connecting the Project to Firebase**

Within Android Studio, use the *Tools -> Firebase* menu to display the Firebase assistant panel, locate and click on the Authentication category, select the *Email and password authentication* link and then click on the *Connect to Firebase* button to display the Firebase connection dialog.

Choose the option to store the app in an existing Firebase project and select the *Firebase Examples* project created in the beginning of the book.

With the project's Firebase connection established, refer to the Firebase assistant panel once again, this time clicking on the *Add Firebase Authentication to your app* button. A dialog will appear outlining the changes that will be made to the project build configuration to enable Firebase authentication. Click on the *Accept Changes* button to commit the changes to the project configuration.

15.4 **Enabling Twitter Authentication**

This tutorial will make use of the app created in the Twitter Application Management console in the chapter entitled *Twitter Sign-in Authentication using FirebaseUI Auth*, including the previously generated Twitter Consumer Key and Consumer Secret values. If you have not yet completed these steps, return to the earlier chapter and complete these initial setup steps.

15.5 **Adding the Twitter Library Dependency**

With the app configured in both the Firebase and Twitter Application Management consoles, return to Android Studio, edit the module level *build.gradle* file and add an entry to the dependencies section to reference the Twitter API SDK library as follows:

```
compile 'com.twitter.sdk.android:twitter:3.0.0'
```

15.6 **Designing the User Interface Layout**

The user interface for the main activity is going to consist of an ImageView, two TextViews and two Buttons. Begin by loading the *activity_twitter_auth.xml* file into the layout editor tool and turning off Autoconnect mode.

Select and delete the default "Hello World" TextView object and drag and drop an ImageView component from the Palette onto the layout canvas. When the ImageView is released onto the layout, a resources dialog will appear providing a list of images available to be displayed on the ImageView object. Scroll down the rows of images in the resources dialog and select *tw_composer_logo_blue* icon as the placeholder.

With the image selected, click on the *OK* button to apply the image to the ImageView and dismiss the resources dialog.

Remaining within the layout editor increase the size of the ImageView object and add the TextView and Button widgets to the layout so that it resembles the layout shown in Figure 15-1. Shift-click on the TextView buttons so that both are selected and increase the *textSize* attribute in the properties window to 18sp:

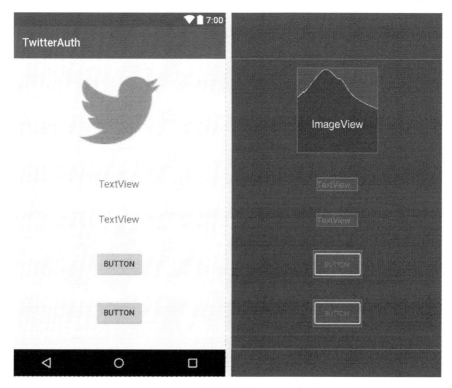

Figure 15-1

Using the Properties tool window, change the text attribute on the lower of the two Button objects so that it reads "Sign Out" and is assigned an onClick method named *signOut*.

Select the ImageView and, using the properties tool panel, change the ID to *profileImage*. Also change the IDs of the two TextView objects and the Button to *userText*, *statusText* and *loginButton* respectively.

With the view components added to the layout it is now time to add some constraints. Click in the upper right-hand corner of the layout canvas and drag the resulting rectangle until it encompasses all of the widgets. On releasing the mouse button, all four widgets should now be selected. Right-click on the ImageView object and, from the resulting menu, select the *Center Horizontally* menu option. Repeat this step once again, this time selecting the *Center Vertically* menu option.

At this stage, appropriate constraints should have been added such that the layout will be responsive to different screen sizes and device orientations:

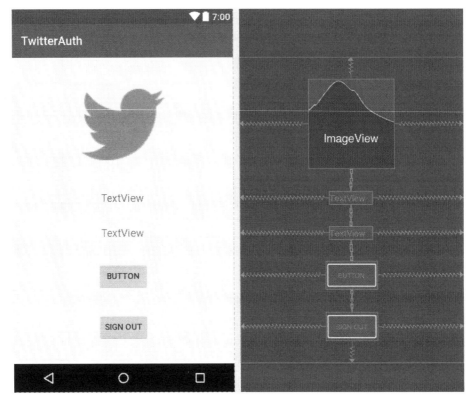

Figure 15-2

15.7 **Adding the Twitter Login Button**

The first of the two Button objects added to the layout in the previous section was used as a placeholder and now needs to be replaced by an instance of the TwitterLoginButton. With the *activity_twitter_auth.xml* layout resource file still open in the layout editor, switch the editor to text mode, locate the first Button widget in the XML description and change the class type from *Button* to *com.twitter.sdk.android.core.identity.TwitterLoginButton* as follows:

```
<com.twitter.sdk.android.core.identity.TwitterLoginButton
    android:id="@+id/loginButton"
    android:layout_width="wrap_content"
    android:layout_height="wrap_content"
    android:text="Button"
    app:layout_constraintRight_toRightOf="parent"
    app:layout_constraintLeft_toLeftOf="parent"
    app:layout_constraintBottom_toTopOf="@+id/button3"
    app:layout_constraintTop_toBottomOf="@+id/statusText" />
```

Return the layout editor to design mode and note the button appearance has changed to a Twitter LoginButton button:

Figure 15-3

15.8 Performing Initialization Tasks

A few more initialization tasks now need to be performed within the main activity class. Begin by loading the *TwitterAuthActivity.java* file into the Android Studio code editor and adding some variables and import directives that will be used later in the code:

```
package com.ebookfrenzy.twitterauth;

import android.content.Intent;
import android.support.v7.app.AppCompatActivity;
import android.os.Bundle;

import android.view.View;
import android.widget.ImageView;
import android.widget.TextView;
import android.util.Log;

import com.google.firebase.auth.FirebaseAuth;
import android.support.annotation.NonNull;
import com.google.firebase.auth.FirebaseUser;

import com.twitter.sdk.android.core.DefaultLogger;
import com.twitter.sdk.android.core.Twitter;
import com.twitter.sdk.android.core.TwitterAuthConfig;
import com.twitter.sdk.android.core.Callback;
import com.twitter.sdk.android.core.Result;
import com.twitter.sdk.android.core.TwitterAuthConfig;
import com.twitter.sdk.android.core.TwitterConfig;
import com.twitter.sdk.android.core.TwitterException;
import com.twitter.sdk.android.core.TwitterSession;
import com.twitter.sdk.android.core.identity.TwitterLoginButton;

public class TwitterAuthActivity extends AppCompatActivity {

    private static final String TWITTER_KEY = "<Your Twitter Key Here>";
    private static final String TWITTER_SECRET =
                                "<Your Twitter Secret Here>";
```

```
    private static final String TAG = "TwitterAuth";

    private FirebaseAuth fbAuth;
    private FirebaseAuth.AuthStateListener authListener;

    private TwitterLoginButton loginButton;
    private TextView userText;
    private TextView statusText;
    private ImageView imageView;

    @Override
    protected void onCreate(Bundle savedInstanceState) {
        super.onCreate(savedInstanceState);
        TwitterConfig config = new TwitterConfig.Builder(this)
            .logger(new DefaultLogger(Log.DEBUG))
            .twitterAuthConfig(new TwitterAuthConfig(TWITTER_KEY,
                                            TWITTER_SECRET))
            .debug(true)
            .build();
        Twitter.initialize(config);

        setContentView(R.layout.activity_twitter_auth);

        userText = (TextView) findViewById(R.id.userText);
        statusText = (TextView) findViewById(R.id.statusText);
        imageView = (ImageView) findViewById(R.id.profileImage);

        loginButton = (TwitterLoginButton) findViewById(R.id.loginButton);
    }
    .
    .
    .
}
```

15.9 Handling Callbacks and Activity Results

As with the Facebook integration, a set of callback methods act as the bridge between the app and the Twitter SDK, allowing the SDK to notify the app of events relating to the authentication process.

With the activity TwitterAuthActivity class file still loaded into the Android Studio code editor add code to register a callback handler on the TwitterLoginButton instance within the *onCreate()* method. This will need to contain both *success()* and *failure()* callback methods:

```
@Override
protected void onCreate(Bundle savedInstanceState) {
    super.onCreate(savedInstanceState);
```

```
TwitterConfig config = new TwitterConfig.Builder(this)
        .logger(new DefaultLogger(Log.DEBUG))
        .twitterAuthConfig(new TwitterAuthConfig(TWITTER_KEY,
                            TWITTER_SECRET))
        .debug(true)
        .build();
Twitter.initialize(config);


setContentView(R.layout.activity_twitter_auth);

userText = (TextView) findViewById(R.id.userText);
statusText = (TextView) findViewById(R.id.statusText);
imageView = (ImageView) findViewById(R.id.profileImage);

loginButton = (TwitterLoginButton) findViewById(R.id.loginButton);

loginButton.setCallback(new Callback<TwitterSession>() {

    @Override
    public void success(Result<TwitterSession> result) {
        Log.d(TAG, "loginButton Callback: Success");
    }

    @Override
    public void failure(TwitterException exception) {
        Log.d(TAG, "loginButton Callback: Failure " +
                exception.getLocalizedMessage());
    }
});
}
```

When the TwitterLoginButton is tapped by the user the Twitter activity will launch another activity to handle the authentication of the user's Twitter identity. The *onActivityResult()* method must now be overridden within the TwitterAuthActivity class so that it will be called when the Twitter authentication activity returns. This method must, in turn, call the *onActivityResult()* method of the TwitterLoginButton instance, passing through the activity results to notify the button of the status of the Twitter login operation. Without this method the callback methods on the login button will not be called and the app will unaware of the results of the Twitter authentication:

```
@Override
protected void onActivityResult(int requestCode, int resultCode, Intent data)
{
```

```
    super.onActivityResult(requestCode, resultCode, data);
    loginButton.onActivityResult(requestCode, resultCode, data);
}
```

15.10 **Testing the Twitter Authentication**

The Twitter phase of the authentication process is now ready to be tested. Compile and run the app on a device or emulator. When the app is launched and running, tap the *Log in with Twitter* button to launch the Twitter authorization activity. If the device does not have the Twitter app installed, the screen shown in Figure 15-4 will appear seeking Twitter account access authorization:

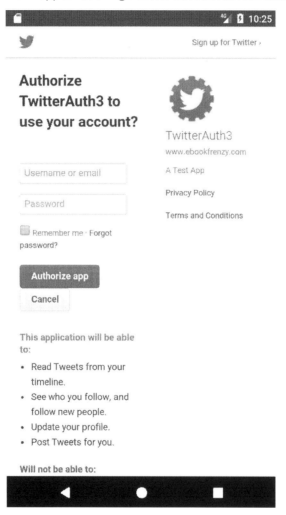

Figure 15-4

Enter the username and password for a valid Twitter account before selecting the *Authorize app* button. After a short pause control will return to the main activity. Within Android Studio, check the logcat output in the Android Monitor tool window for evidence that the *success()* method was called:

```
D/TwitterAuth: loginButton Callback: Success
```

If the Twitter app is installed and the user has already signed in with a Twitter account, the screen shown in Figure 15-5 will appear requesting permission to connect the Twitter account to the TwitterAuth app:

Figure 15-5

Clicking on the *Connect* button will authorize the connection and log the user in.

Assuming that the code added so far is functioning correctly, it is time to implement the code to exchange the Twitter token for a Firebase authentication credential.

15.11 **Initializing Firebase**

Before undertaking the steps to exchange the user's Twitter identity for a Firebase user account, the standard tasks of initializing the Firebase SDK and adding the authentication state listener to the activity must be completed.

Remaining in the TwitterAuthActivity class file, add the following code to the bottom of the *onCreate()* method to obtain a reference to the FirebaseAuth instance and install the authentication state listener:

```
@Override
protected void onCreate(Bundle savedInstanceState) {
    super.onCreate(savedInstanceState);
.
```

```
        fbAuth = FirebaseAuth.getInstance();

        authListener = new FirebaseAuth.AuthStateListener() {
            @Override
            public void onAuthStateChanged(
                                @NonNull FirebaseAuth firebaseAuth) {
                FirebaseUser user = firebaseAuth.getCurrentUser();
                if (user != null) {
                    userText.setText(user.getDisplayName());
                    statusText.setText("Signed In");

                    if (user.getPhotoUrl() != null) {
                        displayImage(user.getPhotoUrl());
                    }
                } else {
                    userText.setText("");
                    statusText.setText("Signed Out");
                    imageView.setImageResource(
                        R.drawable.tw__composer_logo_blue);

                }
            }
        };
    }

    @Override
    public void onStart() {
        super.onStart();
        fbAuth.addAuthStateListener(authListener);
    }

    @Override
    public void onStop() {
        super.onStop();
        if (authListener != null) {
            fbAuth.removeAuthStateListener(authListener);
        }
    }



}
```

On detection of a change to the authentication state, the above listener code checks for the presence of a valid user account. Depending on whether a valid user is detected, the user interface is updated accordingly, including displaying the user's Twitter profile image using the *displayImage()* method which now needs to be added to the class. Begin by adding import statements for the packages that will be needed by the image handling code:

```
package com.ebookfrenzy.twitterauth;
.
.
import android.graphics.Bitmap;
import android.graphics.BitmapFactory;
import android.net.Uri;
import android.os.AsyncTask;
.
.
import java.io.InputStream;
.
.
```

Next, add the usual code to download the user's profile photo and display it on the ImageView object in the user interface layout:

```
void displayImage(Uri imageUrl) {
    new DownloadImageTask((ImageView) findViewById(R.id.profileImage))
            .execute(imageUrl.toString());
}


private class DownloadImageTask extends AsyncTask<String, Void, Bitmap> {
    ImageView bmImage;

    public DownloadImageTask(ImageView bmImage) {
        this.bmImage = bmImage;
    }

    protected Bitmap doInBackground(String... urls) {
        String urldisplay = urls[0];
        Bitmap bitmap = null;
        try {
            InputStream in = new java.net.URL(urldisplay).openStream();
            bitmap = BitmapFactory.decodeStream(in);
        } catch (Exception e) {
            e.printStackTrace();
        }
        return bitmap;
    }
```

```
protected void onPostExecute(Bitmap result) {
    bmImage.setImageBitmap(result);
}
}
```

With steps taken to detect authentication state changes, the next step is to use the credentials stored in the TwitterSession object to obtain a matching Firebase authentication credential, and then use that credential to sign the user in to the app.

15.12 **Registering the User in Firebase**

When the user completes a successful Twitter sign-in, the *success()* callback method assigned to the TwitterLoginButton instance is called and passed a TwitterSession object. This object contains the user's Twitter authentication token and secret. Both of these items will need to be passed to the Firebase TwitterAuthProvider class in exchange for a corresponding Firebase AuthCredential instance. The AuthCredential object will then be used to create a Firebase authentication account if one does not already exist and sign the user in.

Begin by modifying the *success()* callback method to call a new method named *exchangeTwitterToken()* which takes as an argument a TwitterSession object:

.
.

```
        loginButton.setCallback(new Callback<TwitterSession>() {


        @Override
        public void success(Result<TwitterSession> result) {
            Log.d(TAG, "loginButton Callback: Success");
            exchangeTwitterToken(result.data);
        }


        @Override
        public void failure(TwitterException exception) {
            Log.d(TAG, "loginButton Callback: Failure " +
                            exception.getLocalizedMessage());
        }
    });
```

.
.

With the call to the method added to the callback, the method must now also be added to the class, beginning with the task of importing some additional packages:

.
.

```
import android.widget.Toast;

import com.google.android.gms.tasks.OnCompleteListener;
import com.google.android.gms.tasks.Task;
import com.google.firebase.auth.AuthCredential;
import com.google.firebase.auth.AuthResult;
import com.google.firebase.auth.TwitterAuthProvider;
.
.
```

Next, add the *exchangeTwitterToken()* method so that it reads as follows:

```
private void exchangeTwitterToken(TwitterSession session) {

    AuthCredential credential = TwitterAuthProvider.getCredential(
            session.getAuthToken().token,
            session.getAuthToken().secret);

    fbAuth.signInWithCredential(credential)
        .addOnCompleteListener(this, new OnCompleteListener<AuthResult>() {
                @Override
                public void onComplete(@NonNull Task<AuthResult> task) {

                    if (!task.isSuccessful()) {
                        Log.w(TAG, "signInWithCredential",
                                    task.getException());
                        Toast.makeText(TwitterAuthActivity.this,
                            "Authentication failed.",
                                Toast.LENGTH_SHORT).show();
                    }
                }
            });
}
```

The code begins by generating a Firebase AuthCredential instance for the user by calling the *getCredential()* method of the TwitterAuthProvider class, passing through the user's Twitter access token and secret as arguments. These credentials are then passed through to the *signInWithCredential()* method of the FirebaseAuth instance. A completion handler is then used to check whether the sign-in was successful and to report any failure that may have occurred.

A successful Firebase authentication sign-in will trigger a call to the authentication state listener and the user interface will be updated to reflect the change of status and to display the user's display name and profile image.

15.13 **Signing Out**

When the user interface layout was designed earlier in this chapter, a Sign Out button was added and configured to call a method named *signOut()*. The next coding task in this project is to add this method to the *TwitterAuthActivity.java* file:

```
.
.
.
public void signOut(View view) {
    fbAuth.signOut();
}
```

15.14 **Testing the Project**

Open the Firebase console in a browser window, select the *Authentication* option in the left-hand navigation panel followed by the *Users* tab on the Authentication screen. If a user already exists for the Twitter account you intend to use for testing purposes, delete it from Firebase before proceeding.

Compile and run the app on a physical Android device or emulator and tap the *Log in with Twitter* button and take the appropriate steps to authenticate using a valid Twitter account. On signing in, the user interface should update to display the user's profile image and Twitter name.

Return to the Firebase console, refresh the Users list and verify that the account has been created using the Twitter provider:

Figure 15-6

Click on the Log Out button within the app and verify the user interface updates accordingly.

As indicated by the blank entry in the email column for the Firebase user account in Figure 15-6 above, Twitter has not yet provided access to the email address associated with the user's Twitter account. Additional steps are required to gain access to the email address of users when using Twitter log in.

15.15 **Configuring Privacy and Terms of Service URLs**

Before Twitter will allow email address information to be provided to the app, two additional steps are necessary within the Twitter Application Management console. First, both privacy and terms of service URLs must be provided for the app. With the app still selected in the management console, select the *Settings* tab and enter URLs into the *Privacy Policy URL* and *Terms of Service URL* fields as illustrated in Figure 15-7:

Privacy Policy URL

http://www.ebookfrenzy.com

The URL for your application or service's privacy policy. The URL will be shared with users authorizing this application.

Terms of Service URL

http://www.ebookfrenzy.com

The URL for your application or service's terms of service. The URL will be shared with users authorizing this application.

Figure 15-7

For the purposes of testing, it is acceptable to enter temporary placeholder URLs for these fields. Once the URLs have been entered, click on the *Update Settings* button to commit the changes.

15.16 Enabling Email Address Permission

With privacy and terms of service URLs configured, select the *Permissions* tab within the Twitter Application Management console, locate the *Additional Permissions* section, enable the *Request email addresses from users* option (Figure 15-8) and click on the *Update Settings* button.

Figure 15-8

With the app settings configured to enable email address requests, the final step before testing the project involves the addition of code to perform the request.

15.17 Requesting the User's Email Address

The final task before testing the project is to add the code that performs the email address request during the authentication. This involves a call to the *requestEmail()* method of an instance of the TwitterAuthClient class. Add the code to perform this task within the *exchangeTwitterToken()* method located in the *TwitterAuthActivity.java* file as follows:

```
.

.

import com.twitter.sdk.android.core.identity.TwitterAuthClient;

.

.

private void exchangeTwitterToken(TwitterSession session) {

    TwitterAuthClient authClient = new TwitterAuthClient();
    authClient.requestEmail(session, new Callback<String>() {
```

```
        @Override
        public void success(Result<String> result) {
            Log.d(TAG, "EMAIL = " + result.data);
        }

        @Override
        public void failure(TwitterException exception) {
            // Do something on failure
        }
    });
  .
  .
  .
}
```

The code creates an instance of the TwitterAuthClient class and calls the *requestEmail()* method on that instance, passing through the current user's TwitterSession object as an argument. A callback handler is also assigned containing both success and failure callback methods. If the email request is successful, code has been added to output the email address to the logcat panel within the Android Studio Android Monitor tool window.

15.18 **Testing Email Permission**

Return to the Firebase console in a browser window, select the *Authentication* option in the left-hand navigation panel followed by the *Users* tab on the Authentication screen. If the user already exists for the Twitter account used previously for testing, delete it from Firebase before proceeding.

Compile and run the app and sign in using a Twitter account. After authenticating the app within the Twitter login activity, an additional screen (Figure 15-9) may appear seeking email access permission from the user:

Share your email address

Allow TwitterAuthSDK to access the email address associated with your Twitter account @Techotopia so that TwitterAuthSDK can use it according to its privacy policy. For example, TwitterAuthSDK could send you updates and other information at that address.

| NOT NOW | ALLOW |

Figure 15-9

Tap on the Allow button and verify that the email address associated with the Twitter account appears in the diagnostic output in the Android Monitor logcat panel. Assuming the account has an email address (some Twitter accounts may have only a telephone number) return to the Firebase console and refresh the list of users within the Authentication panel. The account information should now include the user's Twitter email address:

15.19 **Summary**

The chapter has outlined the use of the Twitter SDK to allow users to create and sign into Firebase authentication accounts using Twitter accounts.

The TwitterLoginButton class provides a Twitter-branded button which launches the Twitter Log In activity. The results of this activity are then passed back to the app including the Twitter authentication token for the user's Twitter account. This token is then exchanged for corresponding Firebase credentials. These credentials are used to register the user within Firebase and to allow the user to continue signing into the app using the Twitter Log In activity.

By default, the Twitter SDK does not provide the app with access to the user's email address.

To access the user's email address, the privacy and terms of services URLs need to be configured for the app within the Twitter Application Management console and the email permission request option enabled. Finally code needs to be added to the project to perform the request.

16. Phone Number Authentication using the Firebase SDK

As previously outlined in the *Phone Number Sign-in Authentication using FirebaseUI Auth* chapter of this book, Firebase Phone Number Authentication allows users to sign into an app by providing a phone number. Before the user can sign in, a one-time code is sent via SMS to the provided number which must be entered into the app to gain access.

Having covered Phone number authentication using FirebaseUI Auth in the earlier chapter, this chapter will explain how to achieve similar results using the Firebase SDK.

16.1 Phone Number Authentication

Phone authentication using the Firebase SDK involves asking the user for a phone number, sending a 6-digit verification code via SMS message, and then verifying that the code is valid. If the code entered is valid, the app can take the usual steps to sign the user in. In the event that the code is not received by the user, the app should typically provide the user the option to resend the code.

All of the work involved in generating the code and sending the SMS message is handled by a call to the *verifyPhoneNumber()* method of the PhoneAuthProvider instance. This will trigger a call to one of the following callback methods:

- **onVerificationCompleted()** – Called only on certain device configurations (typically devices containing a SIM card) where the verification code can be verified automatically on the device without the user having to manually enter it.
- **onVerificationFailed()** – Indicates that an error occurred when sending the activation code. This is usually the result of the user entering an invalid or incorrectly formatted phone number.
- **onCodeSent()** – Called after the code has been sent. This method is passed a verification ID and a resend token that should be referenced when making a code resend request.
- **onCodeAutoRetrievalTimeOut()** – When the *verifyPhoneNumber()* method is called it is passed a timeout value. This method is called if the verification process is not completed within the given timescale.

Once the verification code has been entered by the user, the code and the verification ID provided to the *onCodeSent()* callback are passed through to the *getCredential()* method of the *PhoneAuthProvider* class. This returns a PhoneAuthCredential object which can be used to sign the user into the app in the usual way via a call to the *signInWithCredential()* method of the FirebaseAuth class.

16.2 **Creating the Example Project**

Launch Android Studio and select the *Start a new Android Studio project* quick start option from the welcome screen.

Within the new project dialog, enter *PhoneAuth* into the Application name field and your domain as the Company Domain setting before clicking on the *Next* button.

On the form factors screen, enable the *Phone and Tablet* option and set the minimum SDK to API 16: Android 4.1 (Jellybean). Continue to proceed through the screens, requesting the creation of an Empty Activity named *PhoneAuthActivity* with a corresponding layout named *activity_phone_auth.*

16.3 **Connecting the Project to Firebase**

Within Android Studio, use the *Tools -> Firebase* menu to display the Firebase assistant panel, locate and click on the Authentication category, select the *Email and password authentication* link and then click on the *Connect to Firebase* button to display the Firebase connection dialog.

Choose the option to store the app in an existing Firebase project and select the *Firebase Examples* project.

With the project's Firebase connection established, refer to the Firebase assistant panel once again, this time clicking on the *Add Firebase Authentication to your app* button. A dialog will appear outlining the changes that will be made to the project build configuration to enable Firebase authentication. Click on the *Accept Changes* button to commit the changes to the project configuration.

16.4 **Updating the firebase-auth Package**

Phone verification makes use of the latest version of the firebase-auth library. At the time of writing, Android Studio is defaulting to an older version of the library in the module level *build.gradle* file. To resolve this issue, edit the *build.gradle (Module: app)* file and update the version on the firebase-auth library to version 11.0.1 or newer:

```
compile 'com.google.firebase:firebase-auth:11.0.1'
```

After making the change, click on the *Sync Now* link that appears at the top of the editor window.

16.5 **Designing the User Interface**

The user interface for the main activity is going to consist of four Buttons, two EditText views and a TextView object. Open the *activity_phone_auth.xml* file in the layout editor, delete the default Hello World TextView and turn off Autoconnect mode.

Drag and drop components from the palette on the layout canvas and set the text and hint properties on the views so that the layout resembles Figure 16-1. Starting from the top, the widgets selected are a TextView, Phone EditText, two Buttons, Number EditText and, finally, two more Buttons:

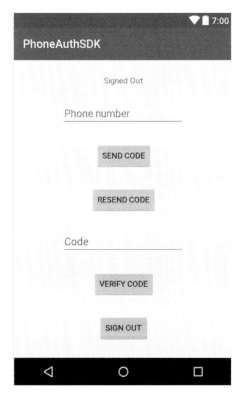

Figure 16-1

Select all seven widgets in the layout, right-click on the TextView widget and choose the *Center Horizontally* menu option. Repeat this step, this time selecting the *Center Vertically* menu option.

Using the properties tool window, configure the buttons to call onClick methods named *sendCode()*, *resendCode()*, *verifyCode()* and *signOut()* respectively.

Starting at the top widget and working down, configure the ID property for each view to *statusText*, *phoneText*, *sendButton*, *resendButton*, *codeText*, *verifyButton* and *signoutButton*.

16.6 Performing Initialization Tasks

Before starting work on the onClick and callback handlers, some preparatory initialization work needs to be performed within the PhoneAuthActivity class. Locate the *PhoneAuthActivty.java* file in the Project tool window and load it into the code editor. Begin by adding some import directives, variable declarations and initialization code:

```
import android.support.v7.app.AppCompatActivity;
import android.os.Bundle;
import android.util.Log;
import android.view.View;
import android.widget.Button;
import android.widget.EditText;
import android.widget.TextView;
```

```java
import com.google.firebase.auth.FirebaseAuth;
import com.google.firebase.auth.PhoneAuthProvider;

public class PhoneAuthActivity extends AppCompatActivity {

    private static final String TAG = "PhoneAuth";

    private EditText phoneText;
    private EditText codeText;
    private Button verifyButton;
    private Button sendButton;
    private Button resendButton;
    private Button signoutButton;
    private TextView statusText;

    private String phoneVerificationId;
    private PhoneAuthProvider.OnVerificationStateChangedCallbacks
                                        verificationCallbacks;
    private PhoneAuthProvider.ForceResendingToken resendToken;

    private FirebaseAuth fbAuth;

    @Override
    protected void onCreate(Bundle savedInstanceState) {
        super.onCreate(savedInstanceState);
        setContentView(R.layout.activity_phone_auth);

        phoneText = (EditText) findViewById(R.id.phoneText);
        codeText = (EditText) findViewById(R.id.codeText);
        verifyButton = (Button) findViewById(R.id.verifyButton);
        sendButton = (Button) findViewById(R.id.sendButton);
        resendButton = (Button) findViewById(R.id.resendButton);
        signoutButton = (Button) findViewById(R.id.signoutButton);
        statusText = (TextView) findViewById(R.id.statusText);

        verifyButton.setEnabled(false);
        resendButton.setEnabled(false);
        signoutButton.setEnabled(false);
        statusText.setText("Signed Out");

        fbAuth = FirebaseAuth.getInstance();
    }
}
```

```
.
}
```

16.7 **Sending the Verification Code**

Code now needs to be added to the project to send the verification code to the user's phone when the user clicks the Send Code button. Remaining within the *PhoneAuthActivity.java* file, implement the *sendCode()* method as follows:

```
.
.
import com.google.firebase.auth.PhoneAuthCredential;

import java.util.concurrent.TimeUnit;
.
.
public void sendCode(View view) {

    String phoneNumber = phoneText.getText().toString();

    setUpVerificatonCallbacks();

    PhoneAuthProvider.getInstance().verifyPhoneNumber(
            phoneNumber,            // Phone number to verify
            60,                     // Timeout duration
            TimeUnit.SECONDS,       // Unit of timeout
            this,                   // Activity (for callback binding)
            verificationCallbacks);
}
```

The *sendCode()* method calls the *verifyPhoneNumber()* method of the PhoneAuthProvider instance to send the code to the phone number entered into the phoneText EditText view. Before doing this, however, a call is made to set up the verification callbacks which are referenced in the final argument passed to the *verifyPhoneNumber()* method call. The next step, therefore, is to implement this method.

16.8 **Adding the Verification Callbacks**

Staying within the PhoneAuthActivity class file, add the *setUpVerificationCallbacks()* method so that it reads as follows:

```
import com.google.firebase.FirebaseException;
import com.google.firebase.FirebaseTooManyRequestsException;
import com.google.firebase.auth.FirebaseAuthInvalidCredentialsException;

public class PhoneAuthActivity extends AppCompatActivity {
```

```java
    private void setUpVerificatonCallbacks() {

        verificationCallbacks =
            new PhoneAuthProvider.OnVerificationStateChangedCallbacks() {

            @Override
            public void onVerificationCompleted(
                        PhoneAuthCredential credential) {

                signoutButton.setEnabled(true);
                statusText.setText("Signed In");
                resendButton.setEnabled(false);
                verifyButton.setEnabled(false);
                codeText.setText("");
                signInWithPhoneAuthCredential(credential);
            }

            @Override
            public void onVerificationFailed(FirebaseException e) {

                if (e instanceof FirebaseAuthInvalidCredentialsException) {
                    // Invalid request
                    Log.d(TAG, "Invalid credential: "
                                    + e.getLocalizedMessage());
                } else if (e instanceof FirebaseTooManyRequestsException) {
                    // SMS quota exceeded
                    Log.d(TAG, "SMS Quota exceeded.");
                }
            }

            @Override
            public void onCodeSent(String verificationId,
                        PhoneAuthProvider.ForceResendingToken token) {

                phoneVerificationId = verificationId;
                resendToken = token;

                verifyButton.setEnabled(true);
                sendButton.setEnabled(false);
                resendButton.setEnabled(true);
            }
        };
    }
```

```
.
.
}
```

In the event that the verification code sent successfully, the *onCodeSent()* method stores the verification ID and token for later use before enabling and disabling some of the buttons in the user interface.

If the code was verified automatically, the *onVerificationCompleted()* method makes some changes to the user interface and calls a method to initiate the sign-in process using the provided credential.

Finally, a failed verification attempt will result in a call to the *onVerificationFailed()* method where code has been added to differentiate between an invalid credential and the SMS quota being exceeded.

16.9 **Verifying the Code**

After the code arrives via SMS message and has been entered it into the code text field, the user is expected to click on the Verify Code button. When the user interface was designed, this button as configured to call a method named *verifyCode()* which now needs to be added:

```
public void verifyCode(View view) {

    String code = codeText.getText().toString();

    PhoneAuthCredential credential =
        PhoneAuthProvider.getCredential(phoneVerificationId, code);
    signInWithPhoneAuthCredential(credential);
}
```

The method obtains the code from the EditText view and passes it, along with the verification ID saved within the *onCodeSent()* method to the *getCredential()* method of the PhoneAuthProvider instance. The credential returned by this method call is then passed to the *signInWithPhoneCredential()* method which now also needs to be implemented.

16.10 **Signing In with the Credential**

Regardless of whether the user manually verified the code, or if verification was automatic, the app has been provided with a PhoneAuthCredential object which can be used to sign into the app. The code for this is similar to that required for other authentication providers and should be added as follows:

```
import android.support.annotation.NonNull;
import com.google.android.gms.tasks.OnCompleteListener;
import com.google.android.gms.tasks.Task;
import com.google.firebase.auth.AuthResult;
import com.google.firebase.auth.FirebaseUser;
.
```

```
private void signInWithPhoneAuthCredential(PhoneAuthCredential credential) {
    fbAuth.signInWithCredential(credential)
            .addOnCompleteListener(this, new OnCompleteListener<AuthResult>()
{
            @Override
            public void onComplete(@NonNull Task<AuthResult> task) {
                if (task.isSuccessful()) {
                    signoutButton.setEnabled(true);
                    codeText.setText("");
                    statusText.setText("Signed In");
                    resendButton.setEnabled(false);
                    verifyButton.setEnabled(false);
                    FirebaseUser user = task.getResult().getUser();

                } else {
                    if (task.getException() instanceof
                            FirebaseAuthInvalidCredentialsException) {
                        // The verification code entered was invalid
                    }
                }
            }
        });
}
```

16.11 Resending the Verification Code

The next step in this tutorial is to add the *resendCode()* method. This method is called when the Resend Code button is clicked and simply makes another call to the *verifyPhoneNumber()* method of the PhoneAuthProvider instance. This time, however, the method is also passed the resend token which was saved within the *onCodeSent()* callback method:

```
public void resendCode(View view) {

    String phoneNumber = phoneText.getText().toString();

    setUpVerificatonCallbacks();

    PhoneAuthProvider.getInstance().verifyPhoneNumber(
            phoneNumber,
            60,
            TimeUnit.SECONDS,
            this,
            verificationCallbacks,
            resendToken);
```

}

16.12 **Signing Out**

The final step before testing the project is to implement the *signOut()* onClick method as follows:

```
public void signOut(View view) {
    fbAuth.signOut();
    statusText.setText("Signed Out");
    signoutButton.setEnabled(false);
    sendButton.setEnabled(true);
}
```

16.13 **Testing the App**

Compile and run the app, enter a phone number and click on the Send Code button. After the SMS message arrives, enter it into the code text field and click the Verify Code button. If the code is valid, the status TextView will change to indicate that the user is signed in. Click on the Sign Out button and send another verification code. Make a note of the code, tap the Resend Code button and verify that the provider has resent the previous code instead of generating a new one.

16.14 **Summary**

Firebase Phone Number Authentication allows users to be authenticated via a phone number and a verification code. This chapter has demonstrated the use of the Firebase SDK to implement phone authentication within an Android app, including sending the verification code, performing the verification and handling requests to resend the code.

Chapter 17

17. Anonymous Authentication using the Firebase SDK

All of the Firebase authentication examples covered in the book so far require that the user provide an identity in the form of an email address, phone number or third party account such as Facebook before gaining access to restricted content or features. Situations might arise, however, where having the user authenticate with an identity is not the first priority. A retail app, for example, might allow a user to browse products and place potential items in a shopping cart prior to purchase. In this scenario, the app will need some temporary way to identify the user in order to keep track of the items in the shopping cart. Only at the point of checkout would the user be required to create a permanent account using an established identity or email address.

To address this requirement, Firebase provides the ability to perform anonymous authentications, a topic which will be covered in the rest of this chapter.

17.1 Anonymous Firebase Authentication

As the name suggests, anonymous authentication provides a way for the user to authenticate using a temporary anonymous identity. This allows users to gain access to an app without the need to go through the process of authenticating with an identity. Anonymous authentication can be performed with a single button click, or even in the background when the user launches the app.

Once signed in anonymously, the user is assigned a temporary account which can be used by the app when performing tasks such as storing data for the user during the current session. Once the user signs out of the anonymous account, the anonymous account continues to exist within the Firebase account database, but is unreachable by that, or any other user. If the same user signs in anonymously again, an entirely new anonymous account will be created and assigned to the user for the current app session.

If the user wishes to create a non-temporary account and continue using the same Firebase stored data, the anonymous account must be associated with a permanent email or third-party authentication account. This will typically involve prompting the user to authenticate using an identity using one or more of the options outlined in preceding chapters and then linking that account to the user's anonymous account. Going forward, the user will be able to sign in using the permanent account while continuing to have access to any data associated with the anonymous account.

As will be revealed in the remainder of this chapter, anonymous authentication is a straightforward process that makes use of many of the Firebase authentication concepts outlined in earlier chapters.

In fact, implementation is almost identical to email based authentication except the user is not required to enter an email and password and the *signInAnonymously()* method is called in place of *signInWithEmailAndPassword()*.

The rest of this chapter is dedicated to the task of creating an example project that implements Firebase anonymous authentication. Once these basics have been covered, the next chapter (entitled *Linking and Unlinking Firebase Authentication Providers*) will cover the topic of linking Firebase accounts.

17.2 Creating the AnonAuth Project

Begin by launching Android Studio and selecting the *Start a new Android Studio project* quick start option from the welcome screen.

Within the new project dialog, enter *AnonAuth* into the Application name field and your domain as the Company Domain setting before clicking on the *Next* button.

On the form factors screen, enable the *Phone and Tablet* option and set the minimum SDK to API 16: Android 4.1 (Jellybean). Continue to proceed through the screens, requesting the creation of an Empty Activity named *AnonAuthActivity* with a corresponding layout named *activity_anon_auth.*

17.3 Connecting the Project to Firebase

As with previous examples, the project will need to be connected to Firebase. Within Android Studio, use the *Tools -> Firebase* menu to display the Firebase assistant panel, locate and click on the Authentication category, select the *Email and password authentication* link and then click on the *Connect to Firebase* button to display the Firebase connection dialog.

Choose the option to store the app in an existing Firebase project and select the *Firebase Examples* project created in the beginning of the book.

With the project's Firebase connection established, refer to the Firebase assistant panel once again, this time clicking on the *Add Firebase Authentication to your app* button. A dialog will appear outlining the changes that will be made to the project build configuration to enable Firebase authentication. Click on the *Accept Changes* button to commit the changes to the project configuration.

17.4 Enabling Anonymous Authentication

Before anonymous authentication can be used it must first be enabled for the project within the Firebase console. Open the Firebase console in a browser window, select the *Firebase Examples* project and display the Authentication screen. Select the *Sign-in Method* tab and edit the setting for Anonymous authentication. In the settings panel, change the *Enable* switch to the on position:

Figure 17-1

17.5 Designing the User Interface Layout

The user interface layout is going to consist of two EditText fields, two TextViews and three Buttons. Begin by loading the *activity_anon_auth.xml* file into the layout editor tool and turning off Autoconnect mode.

Add Email and Password EditText objects to the layout together with the TextView and Button widgets to the layout so that it resembles the layout shown in Figure 17-2. Shift-click on the TextView buttons so that both are selected and increase the *textSize* attribute in the properties window to 18sp:

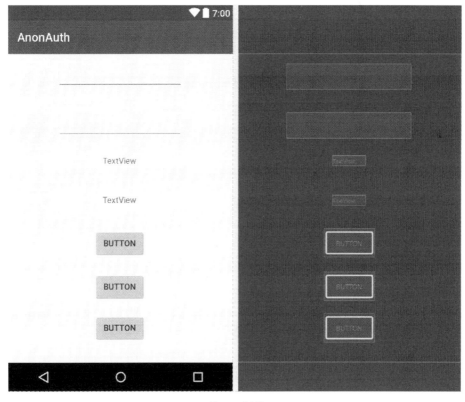

Figure 17-2

Assign IDs of *emailText* and *passwordText* to the two EditText objects and *userText* and *statusText* to the TextView widgets. Select the uppermost of the three buttons and change the ID to *softButton*.

Change the text on the three buttons to *Anonymous Sign-in*, *Sign In* and *Sign Out*. Configure onClick properties so that the buttons are configured to call methods named *softButtonClick*, *signIn* and *signOut* respectively.

With the view components added to the layout it is now time to add some constraints. Click in the upper right-hand corner of the layout canvas and drag the resulting rectangle until it encompasses all of the widgets. On releasing the mouse button, all four widgets should now be selected. Right-click on the ImageView object and, from the resulting menu, select the *Center Horizontally* menu option. Repeat this step once again, this time selecting the *Center Vertically* menu option.

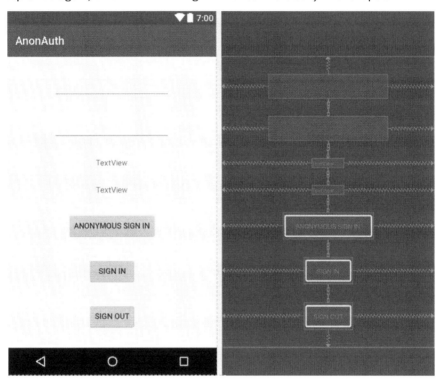

Figure 17-3

The uppermost of the three buttons is going to be implemented as a dual mode button. In the default mode, clicking the button will sign the user into the app anonymously. After the user has been assigned an anonymous account, the button will change to display text which reads *Create an Account* which, when clicked, will create an email/password based account for the user and link it to the anonymous account. The two remaining buttons will perform standard email and password authentication sign-in and sign-out operations.

17.6 Accessing the FirebaseAuth Instance

As with all forms of Firebase SDK authentication, the two key components are the FirebaseAuth instance and the authentication state listener. The next step in implementing Firebase anonymous authentication is to obtain a reference to the FirebaseAuth instance. Within Android Studio, edit the

AnonAuthActivity.java file to obtain a reference to the FirebaseAuth instance and to perform some
basic initialization tasks:

```
package com.ebookfrenzy.anonauth;

import android.support.annotation.NonNull;
import android.support.v7.app.AppCompatActivity;
import android.os.Bundle;
import android.view.View;
import android.widget.Button;
import android.widget.EditText;
import android.widget.TextView;
import android.widget.Toast;

import com.google.android.gms.tasks.OnCompleteListener;
import com.google.android.gms.tasks.OnFailureListener;
import com.google.android.gms.tasks.Task;
import com.google.firebase.auth.AuthCredential;
import com.google.firebase.auth.AuthResult;
import com.google.firebase.auth.EmailAuthProvider;
import com.google.firebase.auth.FirebaseAuth;
import com.google.firebase.auth.FirebaseAuthInvalidCredentialsException;
import com.google.firebase.auth.FirebaseAuthInvalidUserException;
import com.google.firebase.auth.FirebaseUser;

public class AnonAuthActivity extends AppCompatActivity {

    private static final int ANON_MODE = 100;
    private static final int CREATE_MODE = 101;
    private int buttonMode = ANON_MODE;

    private static final String TAG = "AnonAuth";
    private TextView userText;
    private TextView statusText;
    private EditText emailText;
    private EditText passwordText;
    private Button softButton;

    private FirebaseAuth fbAuth;
    private FirebaseAuth.AuthStateListener authListener;

    @Override
    protected void onCreate(Bundle savedInstanceState) {
        super.onCreate(savedInstanceState);
```

```
        setContentView(R.layout.activity_anon_auth);

        userText = (TextView) findViewById(R.id.userText);
        statusText = (TextView) findViewById(R.id.statusText);
        emailText = (EditText) findViewById(R.id.emailText);
        passwordText = (EditText) findViewById(R.id.passwordText);
        softButton = (Button) findViewById(R.id.softButton);


        fbAuth = FirebaseAuth.getInstance();
    }
.
.
.
}
```

17.7 Adding the Authentication State Listener

With the *AnonAuthActivity.java* file still open in the Android Studio code editor, further modify the *onCreate()* method to declare the authentication state listener method:

```
@Override
protected void onCreate(Bundle savedInstanceState) {
    super.onCreate(savedInstanceState);
    setContentView(R.layout.activity_anon_auth_sdk);

    userText = (TextView) findViewById(R.id.userText);
    statusText = (TextView) findViewById(R.id.statusText);
    emailText = (EditText) findViewById(R.id.emailText);
    passwordText = (EditText) findViewById(R.id.passwordText);
    softButton = (Button) findViewById(R.id.softButton);

    fbAuth = FirebaseAuth.getInstance();

    authListener = new FirebaseAuth.AuthStateListener() {
        @Override
        public void onAuthStateChanged(@NonNull FirebaseAuth firebaseAuth) {

            FirebaseUser user = firebaseAuth.getCurrentUser();

            if (user != null) {
                userText.setText(user.getEmail());
                statusText.setText("Signed In");

            } else {
                userText.setText("");
                statusText.setText("Signed Out");
```

```
            softButton.setText("Anonymous Sign-in");
            buttonMode = ANON_MODE;
        }
    }
};
}
```

The authentication state listener tests for a valid user account and updates the user interface accordingly. If no valid user is found, the code assumes that the user has signed out and reverts the *softButton* instance to anonymous sign-in mode.

Within the *AnonAuthActivity.java* file, override the *onStart()* and *onStop()* methods to add and remove the listener:

```
@Override
public void onStart() {
    super.onStart();
    fbAuth.addAuthStateListener(authListener);
}

@Override
public void onStop() {
    super.onStop();
    if (authListener != null) {
        fbAuth.removeAuthStateListener(authListener);
    }
}
```

17.8 Performing the Anonymous Authentication

The softButton is configured to call a method named *softButtonClicked()* when tapped by the user. It is the responsibility of this method to identify whether the button is currently in anonymous sign-in or account creation mode and then call the appropriate method to complete the authentication task. Implement this method now within the *AnonAuthActivity.java* file so that it reads as follows:

```
public void softButtonClick(View view) {
    if (buttonMode == ANON_MODE) {
        anonSignIn();
    } else {
        createAccount();
    }
}
```

When the button is in anonymous sign-in mode, the *anonSignIn()* method is called, the code for which must now be added to the AnonAuthActivity class:

```
public void anonSignIn() {
```

```
    fbAuth.signInAnonymously()
            .addOnCompleteListener(this,
                    new OnCompleteListener<AuthResult>() {
                @Override
                public void onComplete(@NonNull Task<AuthResult> task) {

                    if (!task.isSuccessful()) {
                        Toast.makeText(AnonAuthActivity.this,
                                "Authentication failed. "
                                        + task.getException(),
                                Toast.LENGTH_SHORT).show();
                    } else {
                        softButton.setText("Create an Account");
                        buttonMode = CREATE_MODE;
                    }
                }
            });
}
```

The *anonSignIn()* method calls the *signInAnonymously()* method of the FirebaseAuth instance and uses a completion listener to receive the result of the authentication. If the authentication fails, a message is displayed to the user. In the event of a successful anonymous authentication, the softButton instance is switch to account creation mode. The successful authentication will have also triggered a call to the authentication state listener causing the user interface to be updated accordingly.

The code for the *createAccount()* method will be implemented in the next chapter as part of the account linking process. For now, add a template for this method to the class file to avoid errors during the project compilation.

```
public void createAccount() {

}
```

17.9 Signing Out

The final task before testing the project is to add the *signOut()* method as follows:

```
public void signOut(View view) {
    fbAuth.signOut();
}
```

17.10 Testing the Project

Build and run the app and tap the anonymous sign-in button. After a short delay the status TextView widget should update to indicate that the user is signed in and the soft button should switch to account creation mode.

Within a browser window, navigate to the Authentication page of the Firebase console and select the option to list user accounts. In addition to any previously added accounts, a new anonymous account should now also be listed as illustrated in Figure 17-4:

Figure 17-4

This account will be assigned to the user until the user signs out. To demonstrate the transient nature of the user's association with this anonymous account, click the *Sign Out* button then perform a second anonymous sign-in. Return to the Firebase console, refresh the user account list and note that the user now has an entirely new anonymous account.

To preserve the user's association with an anonymous account, together with any data stored within Firebase, the user must first authenticate using either an email address or a third-party authentication provider. Once that account has been established it must be linked to the anonymous account, a topic that will be covered in the next chapter.

17.11 **Summary**

In addition to providing authentication using an email address and password or an account from a third-party platform such as Twitter and Facebook, Firebase also allows users to be authenticated anonymously.

Anonymous authentication allows the user to be temporarily registered as an app user without the need to enter account credentials. The user's association to an anonymous account is temporary and is lost when the user either signs out or the app exits. The only way to preserve the association between the anonymous account and the user is to register a permanent account and then link that account to the anonymous account.

18. Linking and Unlinking Firebase Authentication Providers

Firebase account linking allows users to sign into the same account using different authentication providers. By linking the user's Facebook and Twitter credentials, for example, the user can sign into the same account using either sign-in provider. As discussed in the previous chapter, linking is also key to preserving a user's anonymous account.

This chapter will introduce the concepts of Firebase authentication account linking before extending the project created in the previous chapter to add the ability to link an email and password account to an anonymous account.

18.1 Firebase Authentication Account Linking

The average user today probably has an email address and a multitude of online accounts including Google, Facebook and Twitter. All of the examples so far in this book have restricted the user to using one of these identities to sign into an account. Account linking allows the user to link an account from one provider to an account from another provider. Having linked these accounts, the user is then able to sign into the app using either of those accounts.

Consider, for the purposes of an example, a user registered to access an app using an account created via the Firebase Facebook authentication provider. If the user creates a new account using the Google authentication provider and links that new account to the original Facebook-based account, either account can then be used to sign into the app.

As outlined in the previous chapter, establishing a link involving an anonymous account is a special case. In order for a user to gain permanent access to any data stored while signed in with an anonymous account, the user must link that account with an account associated with an authentication provider (in other words an email, Google, Facebook, Twitter or GitHub account).

18.2 Limitations of Firebase Account Linking

When using account linking it is important to be aware that some limitations exist. First, only two accounts can participate in a link. If an attempt is made to link to an account which is already linked, the new link will replace the original link.

It is also not possible to link two accounts associated with the same authentication provider. While a Facebook account may be linked with a Google account, for example, it is not possible to link two Google provider based accounts. An attempt to link accounts from the same provider will result in an exception containing a message which reads as follows:

```
User has already been linked to the given provider
```

Account linking can only be performed at the point at which a new account is created. It is not possible, in other words, to link two pre-existing accounts. A workaround to this limitation is to delete one of the two accounts and then establish the link while re-creating the account.

18.3 Implementing Email/Password Authentication

At the end of the preceding chapter, the AnonAuth project allowed the user to sign in to an app as an anonymous user and then sign out. The user interface was designed such that the user is provided with the option of creating an account using the email authentication provider and linking that account to the anonymous account and includes fields into which the user may enter an email address and password.

The project already contains a placeholder for a method named *createAccount()* which is called when the user requests the creation of an account. Open the project, edit the *AnonAuthActivity.java* file and modify the *createAccount()* method as follows:

```java
public void createAccount() {
    String email = emailText.getText().toString();
    String password = passwordText.getText().toString();

    if (email.length() == 0) {
        emailText.setError("Enter an email address");
        return;
    }

    if (password.length() < 6) {
        passwordText.setError("Password must be at least 6 characters");
        return;
    }

    AuthCredential credential =
                    EmailAuthProvider.getCredential(email, password);

    fbAuth.getCurrentUser().linkWithCredential(credential)
            .addOnCompleteListener(this,
                            new OnCompleteListener<AuthResult>() {
                @Override
                public void onComplete(@NonNull Task<AuthResult> task) {
                    if (!task.isSuccessful()) {
                        Toast.makeText(AnonAuthActivity.this,
                                "Authentication failed.",
                                Toast.LENGTH_SHORT).show();
                    }
                }
```

```
    });
}
```

The code begins with the familiar step of extracting the user's email and password entries from the EditText objects and performing some rudimentary validation to ensure the fields contain content. The email and password are then used to obtain authentication credentials for the new account from Firebase.

Once the credentials have been obtained, the FirebaseUser object for the current user (in this case the anonymous account) is obtained and the *linkWithCredential()* method of that object called, passing through the credentials for the new email and password account. If an error is encountered, the user is notified via a Toast message. A successful linking operation, on the other hand, will trigger a call to the authentication state listener which will update the user interface with the user's email address and switch the soft button back to anonymous sign-in mode.

18.4 **Testing the Project**

Open the Firebase console within a browser window, navigate to the Authentication page and select the user account list. To avoid confusion during testing, delete any existing anonymous accounts from the list.

Build and run the app and click the sign out button if the app is currently signed into an account.

Create an anonymous account and refer to the Firebase console to verify that the anonymous account has been created:

Figure 18-1

Make a note of the User UID assigned to the anonymous account, then return to the app and enter an email address and password into the appropriate EditText fields before clicking on the *Create an Account* button.

After a brief delay, the user interface should update to display the user's email address.

Reload the list of users within the Authentication panel of the Firebase console at which point the anonymous account should have been replaced by the new email and password based account using the same User UID as originally assigned to the anonymous account. There can sometimes be a delay before the change appears in the Firebase console. If the link is not reflected immediately, try switching to another area of the Firebase console then returning to the Authentication panel:

Figure 18-2

18.5 **Linking Other Account Types**

Obviously, account linking is not restricted to anonymous accounts. Links can be established between accounts regardless of the authentication provider used to create the account (assuming the two accounts are from different authentication providers). All that is required is the AuthCredential object for the new account and the FirebaseUser instance for the account with which the link is to be established. The following code, for example, links a Google account to the current user account:

```
AuthCredential credential =
        GoogleAuthProvider.getCredential(acct.getIdToken(), null);

fbAuth.getCurrentUser().linkWithCredential(credential)
        .addOnCompleteListener(this, new OnCompleteListener<AuthResult>() {
            @Override
            public void onComplete(@NonNull Task<AuthResult> task) {

                if (!task.isSuccessful()) {
                    // Report failure to user
                }
            }
        });
```

18.6 **Unlinking an Authentication Provider**

An existing link can be removed from an account by calling the *unlink()* method of the FirebaseUser object for the current user, passing through the provider ID of the account to be unlinked.

A list of provider IDs associated with an account can be obtained by calling the *getProviderData()* method of the current user's FirebaseUser object as follows:

```
FirebaseUser user = fbAuth.getCurrentUser();

List<? extends UserInfo> providerData = user.getProviderData();
```

The above method call returns a list of UserInfo objects, each containing the provider for the corresponding account. The following code iterates through the UserInfo objects in the above providerData list and outputs the provider ID for each to the console:

```
for (UserInfo userInfo : providerData ) {
```

```
    String providerId = userInfo.getProviderId();
    Log.d(TAG, "providerId = " + providerId);
}
```

The provider ID takes the form of a string which represents the authentication provider used to create the account ("firebase", "twitter.com", "facebook.com", "google.com", "password" etc). When identifying the authentication providers assigned to a user, there will always be a "firebase" entry regardless of which other providers have also been configured. A user that only has an email/password based account will, for example, return two UserInfo objects within the provider data containing provider ids of "firebase" and "password" respectively. It is not possible to unlink the "firebase" provider.

Unlinking code should be implemented such that it identifies a specific provider and then unlinks it from the current user account. The following code, for example, unlinks the user's Google provider-based account:

```
for (UserInfo userInfo : providerData ) {

    String providerId = userInfo.getProviderId();
    Log.d(TAG, "providerId = " + userInfo.getProviderId());

    if (providerId.equals("google.com")) {
        user.unlink(providerId)
                .addOnCompleteListener(this,
                        new OnCompleteListener<AuthResult>() {
                    @Override
                    public void onComplete(@NonNull Task<AuthResult> task) {
                        if (!task.isSuccessful()) {
                            // Handle error
                        }
                    }
                });
    }
}
```

Once the Google authentication provider account has been unlinked, the user will no longer be able to sign into the app using those credentials leaving only the original account available for signing in.

Unlinking the only authentication provider registered for a user account will turn the account into an anonymous account. As such, the user will only have access to the account and associated Firebase stored data for the remainder of the current log in session and once the user logs out, that access will be lost. The user should either be prompted to link a different provider based account to the anonymous account before logging out or, more preferably, prevented from unlinking the last remaining authentication provider.

18.7 **Summary**

Firebase account linking serves two purposes. The first is to allow a temporary anonymous account to be converted into a permanent account. Account linking also allows a user to sign in using the credentials of more than one authentication provider. By linking Google and Facebook accounts together, for example, the user is able to use either to log into the app in future.

Only two accounts can be linked together and those accounts cannot be from the same authentication provider. It is also not possible to link two existing accounts. A link may only be established during the creation of a new account. Linking between two pre-existing accounts is not possible unless one of the accounts is deleted and recreated.

In addition to linking accounts, accounts may also be unlinked by identifying the ID of the authentication provider to be removed and passing it through to the *unlink()* method of the current user's Firebase User object.

19. Firebase Realtime Database

The Firebase Realtime Database allows data to be stored securely on Google cloud servers and synchronized in realtime across all clients sharing the same database.

This chapter will introduce the key concepts and capabilities of the Firebase Realtime Database within the context of Android app development. Subsequent chapters will work through the practical application of these concepts.

19.1 An Overview of the Firebase Realtime Database

The purpose of the Realtime Database feature of Firebase is to allow data to be shared between multiple clients, where a "client" can take the form of apps running on Android and iOS mobile devices, or JavaScript running on web server.

The main goal of the system is to provide a secure, reliable and fast way to synchronize data with a minimal amount of coding effort on the part of the developer. The database system is also designed to scale to support millions of users.

The database is referred to as being "realtime" because the speed with which the data is synchronized across clients is probably as close to realtime as is currently achievable (taking into consideration the physical limitation of transmitting data over the internet and wireless connections). As will be demonstrated in later chapters, the elapsed time while a data change on one client propagates to another is visually imperceptible.

The Realtime Database also provides data persistence by storing data locally, thereby enabling the data to remain accessible even when a device is offline. When connectivity is re-established, the local data is automatically synchronized and merged with the remote data.

19.2 How is the Data Stored?

Firebase uses what is known as a *NoSQL* database for storing data in a Realtime Database. As the name suggest this means that data is not stored in the tables and rows found in relational database management systems (RDBMS) such as Oracle Database or Microsoft SQL Server. Nor is the data accessed using Structured Query Language (SQL) statements. Instead, the data is stored in the form of a *JSON object*.

JSON is an acronym for JavaScript Object Notation and it defines a syntax used to transmit data in a format that is both lightweight and easy for both humans and software to read, write and understand.

JSON objects typically consist of a key/value pair, where the key uniquely identifies the object within the database and the value represents the data that is being stored. Multiple JSON objects are structured in the form of a JSON tree.

The following JSON syntax, for example, declares a very simple JSON object:

```
{ "name" : "Peter" }
```

19.3 Nesting Data

In the above example, "name" is the key and "Peter" is the value. JSON objects may also be nested. The following JSON declaration provides the structure for storing the profile information for a user:

```
{
  "profile" : {
    "name" : "Peter",
    "email" : {
              "address" : "pete@demo.com",
              "verified" : true
        }
    }
}
```

In this case, a JSON object has been declared with "profile" as the key. This object consists of two child nodes identified by keys which read "name" and "email". The "email" object, in turn, contains two child objects containing the user's email address and a value indicating whether or not the email address has been verified. Figure 19-1 illustrates this nested structure in the form of a tree diagram:

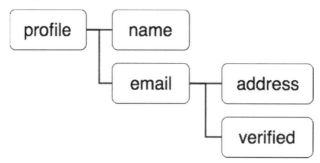

Figure 19-1

Rather like the directory structure of a computer filesystem, each node within a JSON tree is referenced by a path. Within the path each path component is represented by the key element of the corresponding node. The paths to the email address and verified nodes in the above structure, for example, would read as follows:

```
/profile/email/address
/profile/email/verified
```

19.4 **Separating User Data**

The user profile JSON tree outlined in the previous section would only be suitable if an app had one user since storing profile information for a second user would simply overwrite the data for the first. In order to scale the database to support multiple users, some changes need to be made to the structure. The easiest way to store data for multiple users within the same database is to make use of Firebase Authentication. All registered users are assigned a Firebase user identifier that uniquely identifies each user within the Firebase ecosystem. By using this identifier as the key for a tree node each user will, as illustrated in Figure 19-2, have a unique branch within the tree.

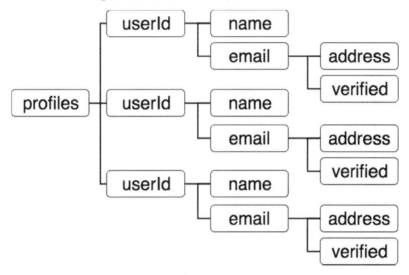

Figure 19-2

When a user has signed into the app using Firebase Authentication, the user ID can be obtained from the FirebaseUser object and used to construct a path to the user's profile data. The following path, for example, represents the "verified" node for a specific user's email address:

```
/profiles/<users firebase id>/email/verified
```

An important point to note here is that while the child nodes are implemented as key/value pairs, the user ID node contains only a key with no value. This is because the key itself is sufficient to uniquely identify the node since all user IDs are themselves unique. In this scenario, the key essentially serves as both the key and the value. The JSON structure for an entry in this database might read as follows where *<user's unique id>* is replaced by the user's actual user ID:

```
{
  "profile" : {
    "<user's unique id>" : {
        "name" : "Peter",
         "email" : {
              "address" : "pete@demo.com",
              "verified" : true
```

```
                    }
            }
        }
}
```

19.5 Avoiding Deep Nesting

Although nesting is a useful way both to structure a database and separate user data, care should be taken to avoid nesting too deeply wherever possible. When accessing data from a location within the tree, all of the child nodes for that location are also retrieved by the database whether that data is currently required by the app or not. Keeping the tree structure as flat as possible will ensure that the database operates at peak performance. To avoid deep nesting, consider separating nested data into separate trees and establishing relationships between the two trees using key references.

Consider, for example, an app that allows users to report bugs encountered while testing the beta version of a software application. The app will need a way to store the contact details of each user together with a list of bugs reported by that user. Each bug report will, in turn, consist of an ID that uniquely identifies the report, a brief title and a detailed explanation of how to reproduce the problem. At first glance, it might be tempting to structure the database as outlined in the partial JSON tree diagram illustrated in Figure 19-3 below:

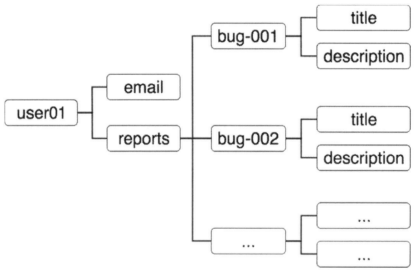

Figure 19-3

Although this looks like a logical way to structure the data, there is a potential flaw that is unique to the way in which the Firebase Realtime Database system works. Imagine, for example, that the app includes a feature allowing all of the user's bug reports to be listed, and that this list is only required to display the IDs and titles for those reports. The description for a particular bug report is not required unless the user taps the report in the list.

As currently structured, however, accessing the list of bugs for a particular user will also download all of the description data. If a user has filed many thousands of bug reports this will clearly download much more data than is actually needed, resulting in unnecessary bandwidth use and degraded database response times.

A better approach is to store only the bug report IDs within the user data tree, while storing the title and description information in a separate tree indexed by the same bug report ID:

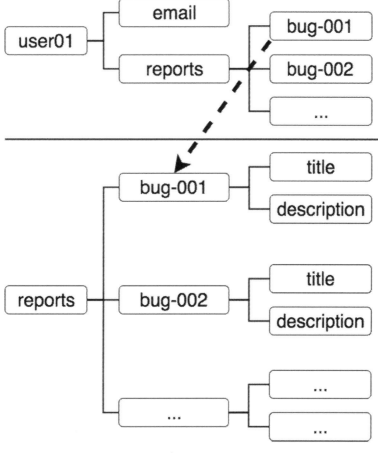

Figure 19-4

As indicated by the arrow in the above tree hierarchies, the bug report ID from the user tree can be used to cross-reference the corresponding title and description data from the reports tree. Using this *flat tree* approach, only the necessary tree nodes are downloaded.

19.6 **Supported Data Types**

Having outlined the way in which data is stored in a Firebase Realtime Database, the next step is to explore the types of data that can be stored. Currently, the following data types can be stored within a realtime database:

- String
- Long
- Double

- Boolean
- Map<String, Object>
- List<Object>
- Null (empty)
- Java object

In order to be eligible for realtime database storage, the Java object must be based on a class containing a default constructor that takes no arguments and with public properties for any encapsulated data items for which storage is required. The following Java class, for example, would be eligible for storage:

```
import com.google.firebase.database.IgnoreExtraProperties;

@IgnoreExtraProperties
public class Profile {

    public String name;
    public String address;
    public String phone;

    public Profile() {
    }

    public Profile(String name, String address, String phone) {
        this.name = name;
        this.address = address;
        this.phone = phone;
    }
}
```

When a Java object is stored in a realtime database, it is converted to the equivalent JSON structure. If a Java object based on the above class were to be stored within a database, therefore, it would be structured as follows:

```
{
  "address" : "1 Infinite Loop",
  "name" : "Peter Wilson",
  "phone" : "555-123-1234"
}
```

19.7 Adding Realtime Database Support to Projects

To add Firebase realtime database support to an Android Studio project, select the *Tools -> Firebase* menu option and click on the Realtime Database entry in the list. Once selected, click on the *Save and retrieve data* link (Figure 19-5):

▽ ▤ **Realtime Database**

     Store and sync data in realtime across all connected clients. More info

    ⊙ Save and retrieve data

Figure 19-5

Within the resulting panel, click on the Connect to Firebase button and select the *Firebase Examples* project to contain the app. Return to the Firebase panel and click on the *Add the Realtime Database to your app* button:

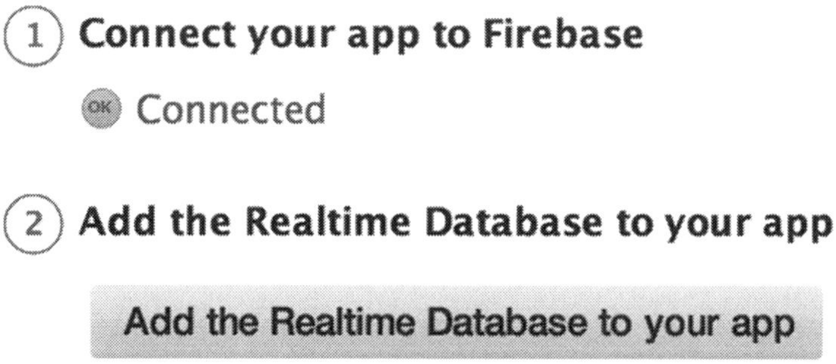

(1) **Connect your app to Firebase**

    🆗 Connected

(2) **Add the Realtime Database to your app**

        Add the Realtime Database to your app

Figure 19-6

A dialog will appear listing the changes that will be made to the project build files to add realtime database support to the project. Review these changes before clicking on the *Accept Changes* button:

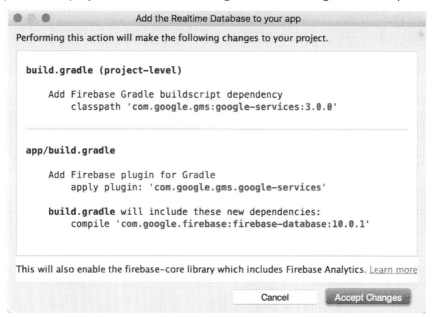

Figure 19-7

Once these steps have been taken, the app is ready to begin writing data to the database.

19.8 **Offline Data Handling**

The Firebase realtime database maintains a local copy of any data currently being used by the app for use in the event that connectivity is lost by the device. For the duration of time that the device is without connectivity, all transactions performed by the app are made to the local copy of the data. When the connection is re-established, the local data will be synchronized with the remote Firebase database servers. The app will also receive any events that occurred during the offline period so that the local data can be updated to match the state of the remote database.

19.9 **Summary**

The Firebase Realtime Database provides a platform for storing and retrieving data on Firebase cloud servers. This provides a secure, reliable and fast way to share and synchronize data between apps that is scalable to support millions of users. The data is stored in a tree structure based on JSON, typically comprising data in key/value pairs. The database supports the storage of a range of native data types in addition to Java objects.

Chapter 20

20. Writing Firebase Realtime Database Data

Now that the basics of the Firebase Realtime Database have been covered, the next step is to explore the ways in which data can be written to a database tree from within an Android app. This chapter will provide details on how to write and delete database tree nodes and also outline some techniques for handling database write errors.

20.1 Obtaining the Database Reference

Before any tasks can be performed on a database, a reference to that database must first be obtained. Each Firebase project has its own dedicated realtime database, details of which can be reviewed by opening the project within the Firebase console and selecting the *Database* option. Within the console, panels can be selected to view the current data trees stored in the database, the rules configured for access, database usage statistics and database backups:

Figure 20-1

In the above example, a basic data tree is shown containing nodes for address, name and phone values. At the top of the tree is an entry which reads *peak-apparatus-599*. This is the unique identifier assigned to the Firebase project and serves as the *root* element (/) for the database tree.

From the point of view of an Android app, a Firebase database is represented by an instance of the FirebaseDatabase class, a reference to which is obtained via a call to the *getInstance()* method of the class, for example:

```
FirebaseDatabase database = FirebaseDatabase.getInstance();
```

The FirebaseDatabase instance can then be used to get a *database reference*. This is a reference to a specific point within the database tree at which read and write operations may be performed. A database reference is represented by an instance of the DatabaseReference class and is obtained via a call to the *getReference()* method of the FirebaseDatabase instance:

```
DatabaseReference dbRef = database.getReference();
```

When the *getReference()* method is called without arguments, the path for the reference within the database is set to the root of the tree. Any write operations performed using this reference would, therefore, be performed relative to the tree root. In Figure 20-1 above, the address, name and phone tree nodes were all added as direct children of the root element.

If, on the other hand, a path is passed as an argument, all write operations will be performed relative to that path into the tree. In the following line of code, for example, the database reference is set to a specific path within the current database:

```
dbRef = database.getReference("/test/data/message1");
```

If the specified path does not already exist, it is created automatically within the tree as soon as data is written at that location.

20.2 Performing a Basic Write Operation

The most basic of write operations involves the use of the *setValue()* method of the database reference object, passing through the data to be stored. The data must be of a supported type (as outlined in the previous chapter). Assuming the above configured database reference, a string value may be written to the database using the following line of code:

```
dbRef.setValue("Hello");
```

After execution, the data tree as represented within the Firebase console will appear as shown in Figure 20-2:

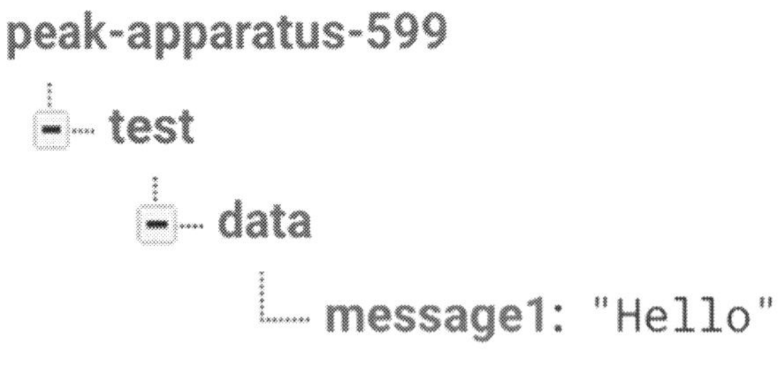

peak-apparatus-599

    ⊟··· **test**

        ⊟··· **data**

            └··· **message1:** "Hello"

Figure 20-2

If data already exists at the specified path, it will be overwritten by the write operation.

20.3 Accessing Child Nodes

In addition to writing data using the path defined within the database reference, the *child()* method may be called on each node to navigate and write to a specific node within a tree. Assuming a database reference set to the root of the tree shown in Figure 20-2 above, the following code would change the string value assigned to the message1 key:

```
dbRef = database.getReference();
    dbRef.child("test").child("data").child("message1").setValue("Goodbye");
```

This approach is ideal for situations where only a single value needs to be changed without rewriting large amounts of data to a tree. When writing to the database in this way it is important to understand how this interacts with the database reference.

As with all write operations, if the path specified by the *child()* method calls does not yet exist, it will be created at the point that the *setValue()* method is called. In the above code, the database reference was first configured to point to the root (/) of the database tree. The second line of code then assembles a path *relative* to the database reference, in other words /test/data/message1. When executed, the above code will result in the following tree where only the value assigned to the message1 key has changed:

Figure 20-3

Had the database reference not been reset to the root of the tree (in other words the reference was still pointing to /test/data/message1), the setValue operation would have entirely different results. Consider, for example, the following variation to the previous code fragment:

```
dbRef = database.getReference("/test/data/message1");
dbRef.child("test").child("data").child("message1").setValue("Goodbye");
```

This time, the database reference is being set to /test/data/message1 before the setValue operation is performed. When executed, the code will result in the creation of the following tree structure:

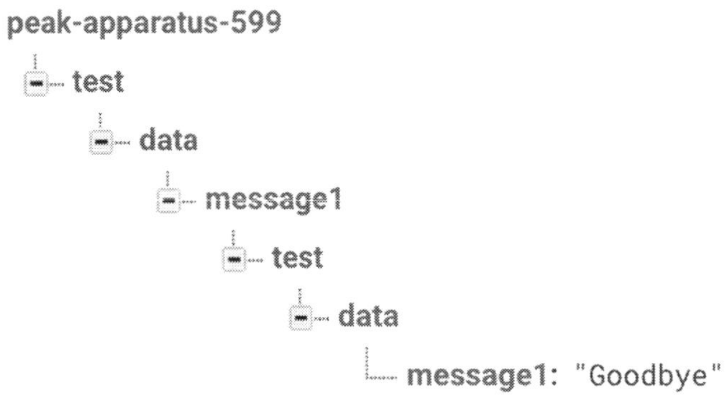

peak-apparatus-599
|
└── **test**
    |
    └── **data**
        |
        └── **message1**
            |
            └── **test**
                |
                └── **data**
                    └── **message1**: "Goodbye"

Figure 20-4

In this case, the write operation has been performed relative to the /test/data/message1 path, resulting in an entirely new path being appended to the existing path. Since the combined path did not previously exist, Firebase has created it for us before setting the "Goodbye" value.

When working with paths, therefore, it is important to be aware of where the database reference is pointing at all times.

20.4 **Writing to Multiple Nodes**

The *setValue()* method is useful for writing values to the database one at a time. Another common scenario is likely to involve writing values to multiple nodes simultaneously. This type of update operation can be performed using the *updateChildren()* method of the database reference. In the following code fragment, this method is used to update title and content nodes for both message1 and message2:

```
dbRef = database.getReference("/test/data");

Map<String, Object> childUpdates = new HashMap<>();

childUpdates.put("message1/title", "Title 1");
childUpdates.put("message1/content", "Content string 1");
childUpdates.put("message2/title", "Title 2");
childUpdates.put("message2/content", "Content string 2");

dbRef.updateChildren(childUpdates);
```

20.5 **Storing a Java Object**

The previous chapter (*An Introduction to the Firebase Realtime Database*) outlined the requirements that must be met in order to be able to store the content of a Java object in a Firebase database. Assuming these requirements have been met, the data within a Java object can be stored using the *setValue()* method. The previous chapter identified the following example Java class as being suitable for storage in a realtime database:

```
import com.google.firebase.database.IgnoreExtraProperties;

@IgnoreExtraProperties
public class Profile {
    public String name;
    public String address;
    public String phone;

    public Profile() {
    }

    public Profile(String name, String address, String phone) {
        this.name = name;
        this.address = address;
        this.phone = phone;
    }
}
```

Code to store an instance of this class would read as follows:

```
Profile profile = new Profile("Tim Cook", "Infinite Loop", "555-123-1234");
dbRef = database.getReference();
dbRef.setValue(profile);
```

As will be outlined in the next chapter, this data can subsequently be read back from the database in the form of a Java object.

20.6 **Deleting Data**

In addition to reading, writing and updating the data in a realtime database, data may also be deleted using a variety of options. Data can be deleted, for example, by passing a null value through to a *setValue()* method call:

```
dbRef.child("message1").child("content").setValue(null);
```

Similarly, data may be deleted using the *removeValue()* method:

```
dbRef.child("message1").child("content").removeValue();
```

Alternatively, data can be deleted from multiple nodes in a single operation using null values in conjunction with the *updateChildren()* method:

```
Map<String, Object> childUpdates = new HashMap<>();

childUpdates.put("message1/title", null);
childUpdates.put("message1/content", null);
childUpdates.put("message2/title", null);
childUpdates.put("message2/content", null);
```

```
dbRef.updateChildren(childUpdates);
```

20.7 Handling Write Errors

As with any operation, it is important for an app to notify the user in the event that a realtime database write operation failed. The success or failure of a write operation can be tracked by the app through the use of a completion handler. Completion handlers are created using the CompletionListener interface of the DatabaseReference class as follows:

```
DatabaseReference.CompletionListener completionListener = new
            DatabaseReference.CompletionListener() {

    @Override
    public void onComplete(DatabaseError databaseError,
                    DatabaseReference databaseReference) {

        if (databaseError != null) {
            // Notify user of failure
        }
    }
};
```

In the event of a failure, the *getMessage()* method of the DatabaseError object may be used to obtain the description of the error that occurred to display the user.

Once the completion listener has been added, it needs to be referenced when data is being written to the database using the *setValue()* or *updateChildren()* methods, for example:

```
dbRef.child("message1").child("content").setValue("hello",
                                        completionListener);

dbRef.updateChildren(childUpdates, completionListener);
```

20.8 Summary

The first step in writing to a database involves obtaining a reference to the FirebaseDatabase instance. This instance is then used to generate a DatabaseReference object which points to a specific location within the tree. Write operations may then be performed by making calls to the *setValue()* method of the DatabaseReference object. The database tree hierarchy can be traversed during a write operation by making calls to the *child()* method. To write to multiple nodes simultaneously, simply specify the data to be updated within a Map object and pass it through to the *updateChildren()* method of the database reference.

Database write failures can be detected by implementing a completion listener and referencing it during write operations.

21. Reading Firebase Realtime Database Data

Clearly a database system is of little use if the data it stores cannot be read. Now that the basics of writing data to a Firebase Realtime database have been outlined, this chapter will explore the reading of data from a database tree. As will become clear early in this chapter, reading data from a Firebase Realtime Database differs from most database systems in that it involves the passive approach of listening for data value changes as opposed to actively making database retrieval requests.

21.1 Detecting Value Changes

When working with Firebase realtime databases, there is no way to specifically read the value assigned to a particular database node. Instead, an app must register listeners in order to be informed when a value within a database changes. When changes are made to the database, a listener method is called and passed a snapshot containing relevant tree data.

Value change listeners are represented by the ValueEventListener class and are added by calling either the *addValueEventListener()* or *addListenerForSingleValueEvent()* method of an existing database reference object. Once added, the listener methods will be called when changes are detected either at the path specified by the database reference object, or on any descendent nodes of that path.

If the *addValueEventListener()* method is used to add the listener, the app will be notified every time the data changes in the specified subtree. The *addListenerForSingleValueEvent()*, on the other hand, only reports the first time that a value change occurs and then removes itself from the database reference. In both cases, the listener will be called once when first added to the database reference in addition to any calls made as the result of value changes.

For the purpose of an example, we will assume that an app needs to be notified of any changes made to the value assigned to the message1 node from the example described in the previous chapter. To achieve this, a value event listener would need to be added to the database reference as follows:

```
dbRef = database.getReference("/test/data/message1");
dbRef.addValueEventListener(changeListener);
```

The above code references a listener named changeListener which now needs to be implemented to contain callback methods to handle both value changes and errors encountered during a database operation:

```
ValueEventListener changeListener = new ValueEventListener() {
    @Override
```

```
    public void onDataChange(DataSnapshot dataSnapshot) {


    }

    @Override
    public void onCancelled(DatabaseError databaseError) {


    }
};
```

Having detected that a value has changed, code now needs to be added to obtain the new value. This involves the extraction of data from the DataSnapshot object passed by Firebase to the *onDataChange()* listener method.

When a listener is no longer needed it should be detached from the database reference object as follows:

```
dbRef.removeEventListener(changeListener);
```

21.2 Working with a DataSnapshot Object

Value change events are configured to notify an app of changes to the data taking place at a particular path within the database tree. It is important to note that this includes changes to any descendent nodes (in other words the subtree beginning at the designated path). A listener added to a database reference path of */data/test* would, therefore, also detect a change that occurred in a node with a path of */test/data/messages/content1*.

When a data snapshot is delivered to the listener, it will contain the nodes for the entire subtree in which the value change occurred. It is also important to keep in mind that the data snapshot may contain value changes that have occurred at multiple node locations within the subtree. Given these potential value change scenarios, it is necessary to be able to obtain information from the DataSnapshot instance.

The simplest form of snapshot is one where only one value could have changed. In fact, this is the case for the example used so far in this chapter. With the listener added to the */test/data/message1* path, the only possible value change is for the message1 node (unless, of course, additional descendent nodes are being added). This new value can simply be extracted from the snapshot as follows:

```
String change = dataSnapshot.getValue(String.class);
```

Database operations are rarely, if ever, this simple. Figure 21-1, for example, shows another database tree as rendered within the Firebase console.

peak-apparatus-599

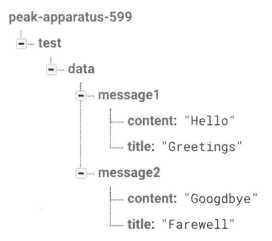

Figure 21-1

Suppose that a value change event listener has been added to the database reference path of */test/data* as follows:

```
dbRef = database.getReference("/test/data");
dbRef.addValueEventListener(changeListener);
```

As configured, any changes that take place in the tree beneath the */test/data* level will trigger a call to the *onDataChange()* method of the change event listener. The data snapshot passed to this method will contain the entire subtree located beneath the */test/data* node.

This presents the challenge of obtaining information about the snapshot and extracting data. Fortunately the DataSnapshot class provides a number of methods that can be used to interrogate and navigate the snapshot tree.

Before looking at these methods, the concept of the root node within a data snapshot needs to be explained. Continuing with the same example, the path of */test/data* is considered to represent the root of the tree and, as such, all operations performed on the snapshot will be relative to this location in the tree. It is possible to identify the path to the root of the snapshot by calling the *getRef()* method of the snapshot object. This will return a DatabaseReference object from which the path string can be obtained. For example:

```
String path = dataSnapshot.getRef().toString();
```

When executed, the path returned will resemble the following:

```
https://<firebase project id>.firebaseio.com/test/data
```

Whether or not the root node of the snapshot contains child nodes can be found by making a call to the *hasChildren()* method as follows:

```
if (dataSnapshot.hasChildren()) {
    // The root node of the snapshot has children
```

```
}
```

Based on the example tree in Figure 21-1 above, the *hasChildren()* method will return a true value since the */test/data* node has two direct descendants (message1 and message2).

A count of the number of direct children of the root can be identified by making a call to the *getChildrenCount()* method of the snapshot object:

```
long count = dataSnapshot.getChildrenCount();
```

In the example scenario this call will, of course, return a count of two children.

The presence or otherwise of a child node at a particular path within a snapshot can be identified via a call to the *hasChild()* method. The following code, for example, checks that the snapshot contains a node for the message1 title:

```
if (dataSnapshot.hasChild("message1/title")) {
    // The snapshot contains a node at the specified path
}
```

This is one of a number of areas where it is important to remember that the snapshot tree paths are relative to the root path at which the listener is attached. The above code will return a true result given the structure of the example tree. The following, however, will report that the path does not exist since neither the test nor data nodes are stored within the snapshot tree:

```
if (dataSnapshot.hasChild("/test/data/message1/title")) {
    // The snapshot contains a node at the specified path
}
```

21.3 Extracting Data from a DataSnapshot Object

A range of different options are available for extracting data from a DataSnapshot object. As outlined in the previous section, the *getValue()* method may be used to extract a specific value from the tree:

```
String change = dataSnapshot.getValue(String.class);
```

Much as when using the *setValue()* method to write data, the *child()* method may also be used to navigate to a specific path within the snapshot tree before accessing the value at that location. The following code, for example, extracts the String value stored for the message1 title key:

```
String title =
    dataSnapshot.child("message1").child("title").getValue(String.class);
```

All of the direct children of the snapshot root can be requested using the *getChildren()* method. This returns the immediate child nodes in the form of an Iterable list of DataSnapshot objects which can be looped through using a *for* construct as follows:

```
for (DataSnapshot child : dataSnapshot.getChildren()) {
    Log.i(TAG, child.getKey());
    Log.i(TAG, child.getValue(String.class));
```

}

In addition to the values, the above code makes use of the *getKey()* method to display the keys for the two immediate children in the example tree (i.e. message1 and message2). Because each element returned by the *getChildren()* method is itself a DataSnapshot instance, code can be written to recursively call the *getChildren()* method on each child to eventually extract keys and values from the entire snapshot tree.

21.4 Reading Data into a Java Object

In addition to retrieving data values as native types (for example String, int, long, Boolean etc.), the data may also be extracted from a data snapshot in the form of a Java object. In the previous chapter, data was written to a database in the form of a Java object based on an example Profile Java class. The following code extracts the data associated with this class from a snapshot in the form of a Profile object before displaying the name, address and phone data:

```
Profile profile = dataSnapshot.getValue(Profile.class);

Log.i(TAG, profile.name);
Log.i(TAG, profile.address);
Log.i(TAG, profile.phone);
```

Data does not have to have been written to the database in the form of a Java object in order to have the data retrieved in object form. The message nodes used as an example throughout this chapter can be extracted into a Java object even though a Java object was not used when writing the data. All that is required is a Java class that matches the structure of the data snapshot. The following class, for example, would be suitable for containing the example message data from a snapshot:

```
import com.google.firebase.database.IgnoreExtraProperties;

@IgnoreExtraProperties
public class Message {
    public String title;
    public String content;

    public Message() {
    }

    public Message(String title, String content) {
        this.title = title;
        this.content = content;
    }
}
```

This class could then be used in a *for* loop to output the title and content values of all the messages in a snapshot:

```
for (DataSnapshot child : dataSnapshot.getChildren()) {

    Message message = child.getValue(Message.class);

    Log.i(TAG, "Title = " + message.title);
    Log.i(TAG, "Content = " + message.content);
}
```

21.5 Summary

Unlike traditional database systems, data is read from a Firebase Realtime Database by implementing a listener to be called each time a change takes place within a designated database subtree. The *onDataChanged()* listener callback method is passed a DataSnapshot containing the data for the specified subtree. This object can then be traversed and the modified data values extracted using the *child()* and *getValue()* methods of the snapshot object.

22. Firebase Realtime Database Rules

Firebase database rules control the way in which the data stored in a Firebase Realtime Database data is secured, validated and indexed. These rules are defined using a rules expression language similar to JSON which may be configured on a per-project basis using either the Firebase console or Firebase command-line interface.

In this chapter we will review the basics of implementing database rules using the Firebase console.

22.1 Accessing and Changing the Database Rules

The current database rules for a Firebase project may be viewed within the Firebase console by selecting the project and clicking on the Database option in the left-hand navigation panel followed by the *Rules* tab in the main panel as illustrated in Figure 22-1 below:

Figure 22-1

The rules may be changed within this screen simply by editing the declarations. Once modifications have been made, the console will display buttons providing the option to either discard the changes or publish them so that they become active. A simulator is also provided that allows the rules to be tested before they are published. If the rules contain syntax errors, these will be reported when the Publish button is clicked.

By default, all new Firebase projects are configured with the following database rules:

```
{
  "rules": {
    ".read": "auth != null",
    ".write": "auth != null"
  }
}
```

When a user is authenticated, the *auth* variable referenced in the above rules will contain the user's authentication identity. A null value, on the other hand, indicates that the current user is not signed in using any of the Firebase authentication providers. As declared, these rules dictate that only authenticated app users are allowed read and write access to the project's realtime database data.

To test these rules, click on the Simulator button, verify that the Read option is selected and the Authenticated switch turned off before clicking on the Run button:

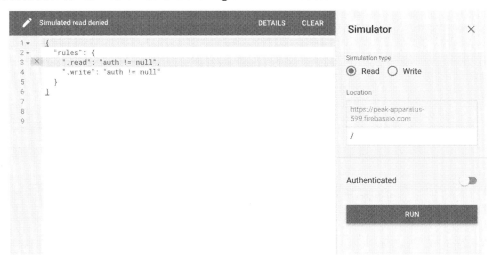

Figure 22-2

The console will display a status bar across the top of the rules panel indicating that the read request has been denied. Clicking on the Details button will display a panel containing more information on the simulation results.

Remaining within the Rules screen, edit the *.read* rule to allow full read access to the database as follows:

```
{
  "rules": {
    ".read": true,
    ".write": "auth != null"
  }
}
```

With the rule changed (there is no need to publish rules in order to test them) click on the Run button in the simulator panel and note that the status bar changes to indicate the read operation was permitted.

Since only the read rule was changed, writing to the database will still require that the user be authenticated. To verify this is the case, select the Write simulation type in the simulator panel, move the Authenticated switch to the on position and choose an authentication provider from the drop down menu. Finally, click on the Run button and note that the write request was allowed.

22.2 Understanding Database Rule Types

Database rules are grouped into the following four categories:

22.2.1 Read and Writing Rules

As previously outlined, the *.read* and *.write* rule types are used to declare the circumstances under which the data in a realtime database may be read and written by users.

22.2.2 Data Validation Rules

The *.validate* rule type allows rules to be declared that validate data values before they are written to the database. This provides a flexible way to ensure that any data being written to the database conforms to specific formats and structures. Validation may, for example, be used to ensure that the value written to a particular database node is of type String and does not exceed a specific length, or whether a set of child node requirements have been met.

22.2.3 Indexing Rules

The Firebase database allows child nodes to be specified as indexes. This can be useful for speeding up ordering and querying operations in databases containing large amounts of data. The *.indexOn* rule type provides a mechanism by which you, as the app developer, notify Firebase of the database nodes to be indexed.

22.3 Structuring Database Rules

So far in this chapter the only rules that have been explored have applied to the entire database tree. Very rarely will this "all or nothing" approach to implementing database rules be sufficient. In practice, rules will typically need to be applied in different ways to different parts of a database hierarchy. A user's profile information might, for example, be restricted such that it is only accessible to that user, while other data belonging to the user may be required to be accessible to other users of the app.

Database rules are applied in much the same way that Firebase databases are structured, using paths to define how and where rules are to be enforced. Consider the database structure illustrated in the following figure:

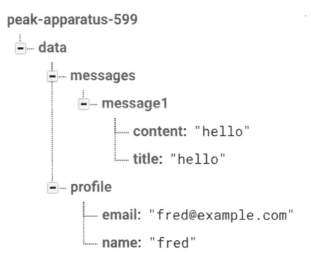

peak-apparatus-599

data

messages

message1

content: `"hello"`

title: `"hello"`

profile

email: `"fred@example.com"`

name: `"fred"`

Figure 22-3

Now assume that the following database rules have been declared for the project within the Firebase console:

```
{
  "rules": {
    ".read": true,
    ".write": false
  }
}
```

Since no path is specified, the above rules apply to the root of the tree. A key point to be aware of when working with rules is that read and write rules *cascade* (unlike validation rules which do not cascade). This essentially means that rules defined at a specific point in the database tree are also applied to all descendent child nodes. As currently configured, all users have read (but not write) permission to all nodes in the tree.

Instead of allowing read access to all data for all users, the rules could instead be changed to allow all users to read the message data while permitting only authenticated users to access the profile data. This involves mirroring the data structure when declaring the database rules.

The JSON tree for the database shown in Figure 22-3 above reads as follows:

```
{
  "data" : {
    "messages" : {
      "message1" : {
        "content" : "hello",
        "title" : "Hi"
      }
    },
```

```
    "profile" : {
      "email" : "fred@example.com",
      "name" : "Fred"
    }
  }
}
```

If we want to create rules that prohibit writing, but allow reading of messages data, the rules would need to be declared as follows:

```
{
  "rules": {
    ".write" : false,
    "data" : {
      "messages" : {
        ".read" : true
      }
    }
  }
}
```

To test out these rules, enter them into the Rules panel of the Firebase console and display the simulator panel. Within the simulator, select the Read simulation type and enter /data/messages/message1 into the Location field as shown in Figure 22-4:

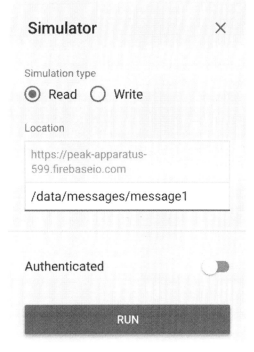

Figure 22-4

Click on the Run button and verify that the read request was allowed. Next, change the location to /data/profile/email and run the simulation again. This time the request will be denied because read permission has been configured only for the messages branch of the tree.

Modify the rules once again to add read permission to the profile node, this time restricting access to authenticated users only:

```
{
  "rules": {
    ".write" : false,
    "data" : {
      "messages" : {
      ".read" : true
      },
      "profile" : {
       ".read" : "auth != null"
      }
    }
  }
}
```

Within the simulator panel, enable authentication and attempt a read operation on the /data/profile/email tree location. The request should now be allowed.

As a final test, turn off authentication in the simulator, re-run the test and verify that read access is now denied.

22.4 Securing User Data

An important part of implementing database rules involves ensuring that data that is private to a user is not accessible to any other users. The key to this involves the use of Firebase Authentication together with the *auth* variable. The auth variable is one of a number of predefined variables available for use within database rules. It contains information about the authentication provider used, the Firebase Auth ID token and, most importantly, the user's unique ID (uid). This allows rules to be defined which, when applied to an appropriately structured database tree, restrict access to data based on the user identity.

As outlined in the chapter entitled *An Introduction to the Firebase Realtime Database*, uid information can be used to separate user data. Figure 22-5, for example, shows a basic example of this approach to data separation:

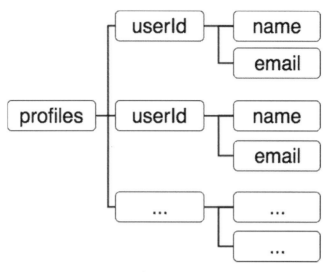

Figure 22-5

Since the uids are contained within the database, the database rules can be configured to compare the uid stored in the database against the uid of the current user, thereby ensuring that only the owner of the data is given access:

```
{
  "rules": {
    "profiles": {
      "$uid": {
        ".read": "auth != null && auth.uid == $uid"
      }
    }
  }
}
```

The above example establishes a rule that checks the uid in the profiles section of the database. If the auth variable is null (in other words the user has not been authenticated), or the uid read from the database node for which access is being requested does not match the uid of the current user access is denied. In order to fully explain the way in which the rule works, it is first necessary to understand the concept of $ variables.

22.5 $ Variables

In establishing the rule outlined in the previous section, use is made of a variable named $uid. Variables of this type, referred to as *$ variables* or *capture variables*, are used to represent the value assigned to a node location within a requested database path. The path being requested in this case might, for example, read as follows:

```
/profiles/userid/name
```

The value assigned to the userid key will, of course, depend on which node is being read (since each user ID node will have a unique value assigned to it). The $ variable provides a way to store the value assigned to the key and reference it within rule expressions.

A $ variable can be given any name as long as it is prefixed with a $ character, though a name that clearly describes the value is recommended.

In the case of the $uid example, the sequence of events when an app tries to read a profile entry from the database will unfold as follows:

1. The app will request access to one of the userid nodes in the profiles branch of the tree.
2. Firebase will receive the request and refer to the database rules for the Firebase project associated with the app.
3. The $uid variable will be assigned the uid value stored in the requested database node.
4. The rule compares the uid from the requested database node with the uid of the current user and either allows or denies access to that section of the tree.
5. Firebase either returns the requested data or reports an access denial depending on whether the user's ID matches the uid stored in the userid node of the requested database path.

22.6 Predefined Variables

In addition to allowing $ variables to be created, Firebase also provides a number of pre-defined variables available for use when declaring database rules, including the auth variable covered earlier in the chapter. The full list of pre-defined variables is as follows:

- **auth** – Contains data if the current user has signed in using a Firebase Authentication provider. The variable contains fields for the authentication provider used, the uid and the Firebase Auth ID token. A null value assigned to this variable indicates that the user has not been authenticated.
- **now** – The current time in milliseconds elapsed since 1 January 1970.
- **data** – A snapshot of the current data in the database associated with the current read or write request. The data is supplied in the form of a RuleDataSnapshot instance on which a range of methods can be called to extract and identify the data content.
- **newData** - A RuleDataSnapshot instance containing the new data to be written to the database in the event that the write request is approved.
- **root** – RuleDataSnapshot of the root of the current database tree.

22.7 RuleDataSnapShot Methods

Both the *data* and *newData* predefined variables provide the rule with database data in the form of a RuleDataSnapshot instance. RuleDataSnapshot provides a range of methods (Table 22-1) that may called within the rule.

Method	Description
child()	Returns a RuleDataSnapshot of the data at the specified path.

parent()	Returns a RuleDataSnapshot of the parent node of the current path location.
hasChild(childPath)	Returns a Boolean value indicating whether or not the specified child exists.
hasChildren([children])	Returns a Boolean value indicating whether or not the children specified in the array exist.
exists()	Returns a Boolean value indicating whether the RuleDataSnapshot contains any data.
getPriority()	Returns the priority of the data contained in the snapshot.
isNumber()	Returns a true value if the RuleDataSnapshot is a numeric value.
isString()	Returns a true value if the RuleDataSnapshot contains a String value.
isBoolean()	Returns a true value if the RuleDataSnapshot contains a Boolean value.
val()	Used in conjunction with the *child()* method to extract a value from a RuleDataSnapshot.

Table 22-1

Combining the predefined variable with these RuleDataSnapshot methods provides significant flexibility when writing database rules. The following rule, for example, only allows write access if the node at path /profiles/userid/email exists:

```
".write" : "data.child('profiles').child('userid').child('email').exists()"
```

Similarly, the following rule allows write access if the value of the node at /profiles/userid/name is of type string:

```
".write" : "data.child('profiles').child('userid').child('name').isString()"
```

The *val()* method is used in the rule below to restrict read access unless the value assigned to the node at /profiles/userid/name is a set to "John Wilson":

```
".read" : "data.child('profiles').child('userid').child('name').val()
          === 'John Wilson'"
```

The above examples test whether data already contained within the database meets specified criteria. The newData variable can be used in a similar manner to verify that the data about to be written to the database complies with the database rule declaration. In the following example, the rule requires that the data being written to the database contain a string value at the path /data/username and that the existing database has a true Boolean value at the /data/settings/updates key path:

```
".write" : "newData.child('data').child('username').isString() &&
    data.child('data').child('settings').child('updates').val() === true"
```

When testing complex .write rules it is useful to know that these can also be tested with real data within the Firebase console rules simulator. When the Write simulation type is selected, an additional field is displayed titled Data (JSON) into which JSON data structures may be entered to be used during the write simulations:

Figure 22-6

22.8 Data Validation Rules

The purpose of data validation rules is to ensure that data is formatted and structured correctly before it is written to the database. Validation rules are enforced only after requirements have been met for .write rules. The .validate rule type differs from .write and .read rules in that validation rules do not cascade to child nodes allowing validation to be enforced with greater precision. Otherwise, validation rules have access to the same predefined variables and methods as the read and write rule types covered earlier in the chapter.

The following validation rule, for example, verifies that the value being written to the database at path location /data/username is a string containing less than 30 characters:

```
{
  "rules": {
```

```
        ".write": true,
        ".validate" : "newData.child('data').child('username').isString() &&
                newData.child('data').child('username').val().length < 30"
    }
}
```

As a general guideline, validation rules should not be used as a substitute for validating user input within the app. It is much more efficient to catch formatting errors within the app than to rely entirely on the Firebase database rules system to catch errors and pass them back to the app.

22.9 Indexing Rules

The Firebase realtime database allows data to be queried and ordered based on key and value data. To make sure that the performance of these operations do not degrade as the database grows in size, Google recommends the use of indexing rules to declare any nodes that are likely to be used frequently to query and order data.

Indexing rules are declared using the *.indexOn* rule type and can be implemented for ordering either by *child* or *value*.

Consider the following sample data structure for a database designed to store the driving range and pricing of electric and hybrid cars:

```
{
"cars" : {
        "Model S" : {
                "range" : 210,
                "price" : 68000
        },
        "Leaf" : {
                "range" : 107,
                "price" : 30000
        },
        "Volt" : {
                "range" : 420,
                "price" : 33000
        }
    }
}
```

The model names are categorized as key only nodes (in other words the key essentially serves as both the key and the value, much like user IDs in earlier examples). Nodes of this type are indexed automatically by Firebase and do not need to be indexed specifically in indexing rule declarations. If queries are likely to be performed on the price and range child nodes, however, an indexing rule could be declared as follows:

```
{
```

```
"rules": {
  "cars": {
      ".indexOn": ["range", "price"]
  }
 }
}
```

By default, Firebase assumes that indexes are to be created for ordering by child which is appropriate for the above rule. In other situations it may make more sense to index by value. The following JSON represents a different data structure where key-value pairs are used to store the model name and price of each car:

```
{
    "cars" : {
        "Model S" : 68000,
        "Model X" : 90000,
        "Leaf" : 30000,
        "Volt" : 33000
    }
}
```

If an app needed to list cars ordered by price from lowest to highest, it makes more sense to index the value (i.e. the price) than the key (the car model name). To achieve this, the *.value* keyword is used when declaring the rule:

```
{
  "rules": {
    "cars": {
        ".indexOn" : ".value"
    }
  }
}
```

22.10 **Summary**

Firebase provides three types of database rules to control read and write access, data validation and to designate nodes to be indexed for improved querying and data ordering performance. These rules may be configured using either the Firebase console or command-line tool and are declared using JSON, much like database tree structures. A wide range of variables and methods are available for use within declarations, allowing for considerable flexibility in controlling data access and maintaining database integrity and performance.

23. Working with Firebase Realtime Database Lists

So far we have only looked at the reading and writing of individual data items within the Firebase Realtime Database. Firebase also provides support for working with lists of data within the database tree. This system allows items to be appended to and removed from a list, and also for query operations to be performed to extract one or more items from a list based on filtering and matching criteria.

The key elements of Firebase database list handling are the *push()* method, the Query class, child and value event listeners and a range of filtering options.

This chapter will provide an overview of working with lists with the Firebase Realtime Database in preparation for the tutorial outlined in a later chapter entitled *A Firebase Realtime Database List Data Tutorial*.

23.1 The push() Method

As with all realtime database implementations, an app must first obtain a database reference instance before working with lists:

```
FirebaseDatabase database = FirebaseDatabase.getInstance();
DatabaseReference dbRef = database.getReference("/data");
```

The *push()* method of the database reference allows child nodes to be appended to a list of items in the database. Each time the *push()* method is called, it creates a new node at the path location of the database reference instance and assigns it an auto-generated key. This key is unique and includes timestamp information so that all keys in the list are automatically ordered based on the time of creation.

Once the push method has created a new child, it returns a DatabaseReference object initialized with the path to that child. Calling the *getKey()* method on this reference will return the auto-generated key which may then be used to store a corresponding value.

The following code, for example, uses the *push()* method to add a new child at the path stored within the database reference instance:

```
DatabaseReference newChildRef = dbRef.push();
```

With access to the database reference for the new child, the corresponding key may be obtained and used to store a value as follows:

```
String key = newChildRef.getKey();
dbRef.child(key).setValue("An Item");
```

When executed, the database tree created by this code will resemble that shown below:

peak-apparatus-599

⊟··· **data**

└··· **-Knyaj2DEncnXhwaXqh4:** `"An Item"`

Figure 23-1

The code to perform the push operation may be simplified in a number of ways. One option is to extract the key directly from the database reference:

```
String key = dbRef.push().getKey();
dbRef.child(key).setValue("An Item");
```

Alternatively, the *setValue()* method may be called on the database reference instance for the new child:

```
DatabaseReference newChildRef = dbRef.push();
newChildRef.setValue("An Item");
```

Each time the *push()* method is called, it will create a new node with a unique key which may be used to store a data value. Figure 23-2, for example, shows multiple children appended to the list using this technique:

peak-apparatus-599

⊟··· **data**

├··· **-KnybYx5-5j-9xkNVOUq:** `"An Item"`

├··· **-KnyblJo938C11rBA3Z7:** `"Item 2"`

├··· **-Knybxyt7B-YgrEEOUuq:** `"Item 3"`

├··· **-KnybzY6qpN2h8XGNVtY:** `"Item 4"`

└··· **-Knybzr4laPSQPTVij3a:** `"Item 5"`

Figure 23-2

Using Firebase to generate unique keys in this way is also of particular use when an app has multiple users creating child nodes at the same path in the tree. Since each key is guaranteed to be unique, there is no risk of multiple users attempting to save data using the same key.

23.2 **Listening for Events**

In addition to being able to append children to a database list, it is also important for an app to receive notifications when changes occur within the list. This can be achieved by setting up event listeners. Previous chapters have already outlined the use of the *value event listener*. As the name suggests, a value event listener is triggered when the value stored within a database tree node changes. In addition to value event listeners, working with Firebase Realtime Database lists will typically also require the use of *child event listeners*. These listeners notify the app when child nodes are added, deleted or moved within a list.

Child event listeners are created as instances of the ChildEventListener class and added via a call to the *addChildEventListener()* method of the database reference instance.

The following callback methods must be implemented within the child event listener:

- **onChildAdded()** – This method is called each time a new child is added to a list. When the method is called it is passed a DataSnapshot object containing the newly added data.
- **onChildChanged()** – Called when the data assigned to a node in the list changes, or new children are added to that node. When called, the method is passed a DataSnapshot instance containing the modified data.
- **onChildRemoved()** – When a child node is removed from a list, this method is called and passed a DataSnapshot object containing the data for the deleted node.
- **onChildMoved()** – This method is called when any changes result in alterations to the order of the items in a list.

The following code declares and then adds a child event listener to a database reference:

```
ChildEventListener childListener = new ChildEventListener() {

    @Override
    public void onChildAdded(DataSnapshot dataSnapshot, String s) {

    }

    @Override
    public void onChildChanged(DataSnapshot dataSnapshot, String s) {

    }

    @Override
    public void onChildMoved(DataSnapshot dataSnapshot, String s) {

    }

    @Override
    public void onChildRemoved(DataSnapshot dataSnapshot) {
```

```
    }

    @Override
    public void onCancelled(DatabaseError databaseError) {

    }
};
```

```
dbRef.addChildEventListener(childListener);
```

When no longer required, child event listeners should be removed from the database reference:

```
dbRef.removeEventListener(childListener);
```

23.3 Performing List Queries

The Firebase Query class allows apps to retrieve items from a database list based on specified criteria. A range of query options are available including retrieving items in a list in a particular order, or retrieving only certain items based on data matching. Options are also available to control the number and position of the list items to be retrieved (for example the first three or last four items in a list).

Once a query has been configured, an event listener is attached which will be called when the operation is complete. The listener will be passed a DataSnapshot object containing the data result of the query.

Consider, for example, a list structured as illustrated in Figure 23-3 which consists of keys generated by the *push()* method, each of which has a child node consisting of a key/value pair:

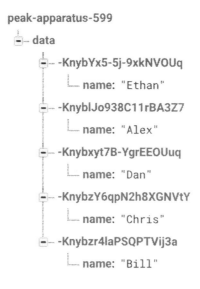

Figure 23-3

The items are listed in the order that they were appended to the list, starting with the oldest entry at the top. To retrieve these items from the list in chronological order, the query would need to be configured using *order by key* (since the *push()* method included timestamp information in the keys as items were appended to the list). The code to initialize the query would, therefore, read as follows:

```
Query query = dbRef.orderByKey();
query.addListenerForSingleValueEvent(queryValueListener);
```

Note the event listener has been added using the single value event listener method. Since queries are usually onetime events this is more convenient than having to remove the listener after the query completes.

The *queryValueListener* referenced in the above code could be implemented as follows:

```
ValueEventListener queryValueListener = new ValueEventListener() {

    @Override
    public void onDataChange(DataSnapshot dataSnapshot) {

        Iterable<DataSnapshot> snapshotIterator = dataSnapshot.getChildren();
        Iterator<DataSnapshot> iterator = snapshotIterator.iterator();

        while (iterator.hasNext()) {
            DataSnapshot next = (DataSnapshot) iterator.next();
            Log.i(TAG, "Value = " + next.child("name").getValue());
        }
    }

    @Override
    public void onCancelled(DatabaseError databaseError) {

    }
};
```

The *onDataChanged()* callback method is passed a DataSnapshot object containing all of the children that matched the query. As implemented above, the method iterates through the children, outputting the name value for each node to the logcat console. Assuming the data list shown in Figure 23-3 above, the resulting output would read as follows:

```
Ethan
Alex
Dan
Chris
Bill
```

To retrieve the data ordered based on the values, an *order by child* query needs to be performed referencing the "name" key in the child nodes:

```
Query query = dbRef.orderByChild("name");
```

When executed, the names will be retrieved and output in alphabetical order:

```
Alex
Bill
Chris
Dan
Ethan
```

The items matching specified criteria may be retrieved using the *equalTo()* filter. The following code will extract only those list items that match the name "Chris":

```
Query query = dbRef.orderByChild("name").equalTo("Chris");
```

Segments of the list may also be retrieved using the *startAt()* and *endAt()* filters. These filters may be used independently, or as in the following example, combined to specify both start and end points:

```
Query query = dbRef.orderByChild("name").startAt("Bill").endAt("Dan");
```

The above query, when performed on the example name list, will generate the following output (note that ordering by child is still being used so the results are presented in alphabetical order):

```
Bill
Chris
Dan
```

Specific numbers of list items may be retrieved using the *limitToFirst()* and *limitToLast()* filters. Unlike the start and end filters, these filters may not be combined into a single query operation. In the following example, only the first two list entries will be retrieved:

```
Query query = dbRef.orderByChild("name").limitToFirst(2);
```

23.4 **Querying and Indexes**

If an app is expected to make frequent database queries it will be important to declare appropriate indexing rules to maintain the performance of the database. This is achieved using the *.onIndex* rule type as outlined in the *Firebase Realtime Database Rules* chapter of this book.

23.5 **Summary**

In addition to the reading and writing of individual data items, Firebase also includes support for working with data in list form. When working with lists, new items are appended to a list using the *push()* method of the DatabaseReference class. This method creates a child node with an auto-generated key into which data may be written. The Query class, when combined with value and child event listeners allows for a wide range of querying and filtering operations to be performed on lists of data stored using the Firebase Realtime Database.

24. A Basic Firebase Realtime Database Tutorial

With the basics of the Firebase Realtime Database covered in the previous chapters, this chapter will step through the creation of an Android Studio project that makes use of the realtime database to store data. The app created in this chapter will demonstrate the key elements of the Firebase Realtime Database, including reading and writing data, implementing database rules, adding a data change listener and the separation of user data using Firebase user ids as node keys.

24.1 About the Realtime Database Project

The example app created in this chapter will require the user to sign in using Firebase email/password based authentication. Once authenticated, the user will be able to enter text into an EditText field and store that text in a realtime database tree. Database rules will also be declared to ensure that the data is readable by all users but writable only by the owner, and to validate certain aspects of the user's input.

24.2 Creating the Realtime Database Project

Launch Android Studio and select the *Start a new Android Studio project* quick start option from the welcome screen.

Within the new project dialog, enter *RealtimeDB* into the Application name field and your domain as the Company Domain setting before clicking on the *Next* button.

On the form factors screen, enable the *Phone and Tablet* option and set the minimum SDK to API 16: Android 4.1 (Jellybean). Continue to proceed through the screens, requesting the creation of an Empty Activity named *RealtimeDBActivity* with a corresponding layout named *activity_realtime_db*.

24.3 Adding User Authentication

As previously outlined, access to the data stored by this app will only be available to authenticated users. Though only email/password authentication will be used in this project, the mechanism for accessing the user's data are the same regardless of choice of authentication provider. Begin the authentication implementation process by opening the Firebase console in a browser window and selecting the *Firebase Examples* project created at the beginning of the book. Navigate to the Authentication screen, select the *Sign-In Method* tab and enable the Email/Password provider if it is currently disabled.

Return to the project in Android Studio and select the *Tools -> Firebase* menu option. When the Firebase assistant panel appears, locate and select the *Authentication* section and click on the *Email and password authentication* link.

In the resulting panel, click on the *Connect to Firebase* button to display the Firebase connection dialog.

Choose the option to store the app in an existing Firebase project and select the *Firebase Examples* project before clicking on the *Connect to Firebase* button.

With the project's Firebase connection established, refer to the Firebase assistant panel once again, this time clicking on the *Add Firebase Authentication to your app* button. A dialog will appear outlining the changes that will be made to the project build configuration to enable Firebase authentication. Click on the *Accept Changes* button to implement the changes to the project configuration.

Since this project is going to make use of the FirebaseUI Auth API, two more dependencies need to be added to the module level *build.gradle* file for the project. Within the Project tool window, locate and double-click on the *build.gradle (Module: app)* file so that it loads into the editor.

Once the Gradle file has loaded, modify the dependencies section to include the *firebase-ui* and *firebase-ui-auth* libraries (note that more recent versions of these libraries may have been released since this book was published):

```
dependencies {
    compile fileTree(dir: 'libs', include: ['*.jar'])
    androidTestCompile('com.android.support.test.espresso:espresso-
core:2.2.2', {
        exclude group: 'com.android.support', module: 'support-annotations'
    })
    compile 'com.android.support:appcompat-v7:25.3.1'
    compile 'com.android.support.constraint:constraint-layout:1.0.2'
    compile 'com.google.firebase:firebase-auth:11.0.1'
    compile 'com.firebaseui:firebase-ui:2.0.1'
    compile 'com.firebaseui:firebase-ui-auth:2.0.1'
    testCompile 'junit:junit:4.12'
}
```

24.4 Adding the Second Activity

The RealtimeDBActivity class will be used to authenticate the user. Once the user has signed in to the app, a second activity will be launched to present the user interface within which the user will enter text and save it to the database.

Add this second activity to the project now by locating the *app -> java -> <yourdomain>.realtimedb* entry into the project tool window and right-clicking on it. When the menu appears, select the *New -> Activity -> Empty Activity* menu option. In the *New Android Activity* dialog (Figure 24-1), name the activity *SignedInActivity*:

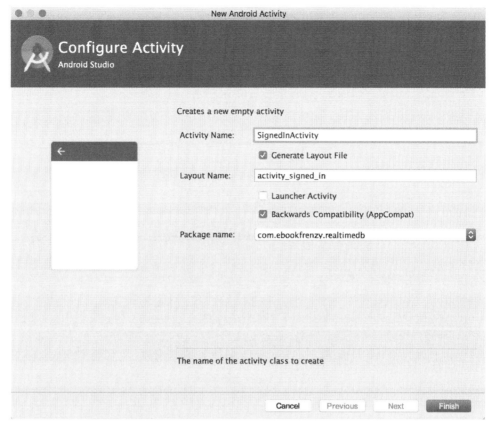

Figure 24-1

Before clicking on the *Finish* button, make sure that the *Generate Layout File* option is enabled and the *Launcher Activity* option disabled.

24.5 Designing the SignedInActivity User Interface

The user interface for the second activity is going to consist of the Plain Text EditText view into which the user will enter text together with two Button objects. Locate the *activity_signed_in.xml* file, load it into the layout editor and turn off Autoconnect mode.

With Autoconnect mode disabled, drag and drop the three components from the palette onto the layout canvas so that the layout resembles Figure 24-2. Note that the text properties on the two buttons have been changed to "Save" and "Sign Out" and that the text property on the EditText view has been modified to remove the default "Name" string.

Figure 24-2

With the views positioned and configured, click on the Infer Constraints button (indicated in Figure 24-3) to apply appropriate constraints to the layout.

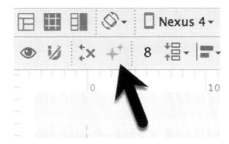

Figure 24-3

Edit the onClick properties for the two buttons to call methods named *saveData()* and *signOut()* when clicked by the user. Finally, select the EditText view and change the ID to *userText*.

24.6 **Configuring the Project for Realtime Database Access**

Before code can be written to make use of the realtime database some library dependencies need to be added to the build configuration.

To add Firebase realtime database support, select the *Tools -> Firebase* menu option and click on the Realtime Database entry in the resulting Firebase assistant panel. Once selected, click on the *Save and retrieve data* link. In the next panel, click on the *Add the Realtime Database to your app* button.

A dialog will appear listing the changes that will be made to the project build files to add realtime database support to the project. Review these changes before clicking on the *Accept Changes* button.

24.7 **Performing the Authentication**

With the project suitably configured to make use of Firebase Authentication and the realtime database, code can now be added to the project to perform the user authentication. Edit the *RealtimeDBActivity.java* file and modify it as follows to initiate the authentication process:

```
package com.ebookfrenzy.realtimedb;

import android.content.Intent;
import android.support.v7.app.AppCompatActivity;
import android.os.Bundle;

import com.firebase.ui.auth.ErrorCodes;
import com.firebase.ui.auth.IdpResponse;
import com.firebase.ui.auth.ResultCodes;
import com.firebase.ui.auth.AuthUI;
import com.google.firebase.auth.FirebaseAuth;

import java.util.ArrayList;
import java.util.List;

public class RealtimeDBActivity extends AppCompatActivity {

    FirebaseAuth auth;
    private static final int REQUEST_CODE = 101;

    @Override
    protected void onCreate(Bundle savedInstanceState) {
        super.onCreate(savedInstanceState);
        setContentView(R.layout.activity_realtime_db);

        auth = FirebaseAuth.getInstance();

        if (auth.getCurrentUser() != null) {
            startActivity(new Intent(this, SignedInActivity.class));
            finish();
        } else {
            authenticateUser();
        }


    }
```

```
.
}
```

As in the example covered in the chapter entitled *Email/Password Authentication using FirebaseUI Auth*, the code added above will call a method named *authenticateUser()* if the current user is not already signed in. The next step is to add this method:

```
private void authenticateUser() {

    List<AuthUI.IdpConfig> providers = new ArrayList<>();

    providers.add(
            new AuthUI.IdpConfig.Builder(AuthUI.EMAIL_PROVIDER).build());


    startActivityForResult(
            AuthUI.getInstance().createSignInIntentBuilder()
                    .setAvailableProviders(providers)
                    .setIsSmartLockEnabled(false)
                    .build(),
            REQUEST_CODE);
}
```

When the authentication activity is completed, the *onActivityResult()* method will be called. Implement this method now to launch the SignedInActivity on a successful authentication:

```
@Override
protected void onActivityResult(int requestCode, int resultCode, Intent data)
{
    super.onActivityResult(requestCode, resultCode, data);

    IdpResponse response = IdpResponse.fromResultIntent(data);

    if (requestCode == REQUEST_CODE) {
        if (resultCode == ResultCodes.OK) {
            startActivity(new Intent(this, SignedInActivity.class));
            return;
        }
    } else {
        if (response == null) {
            // User cancelled Sign-in
            return;
        }

        if (response.getErrorCode() == ErrorCodes.NO_NETWORK) {
```

```
            // Device has no network connection
            return;
        }

        if (response.getErrorCode() == ErrorCodes.UNKNOWN_ERROR) {
            // Unknown error occurred
            return;
        }
    }
}
```

24.8 Accessing the Database

Code now needs to be added to the SignedInActivity class to obtain both a database reference and the uid of the current user. Load the *SignedInActivity.java* file into the editor and modify it as follows:

```java
package com.ebookfrenzy.realtimedb;

import android.content.Intent;
import android.support.annotation.NonNull;

import android.support.v7.app.AppCompatActivity;
import android.os.Bundle;
import android.view.View;
import android.widget.EditText;
import android.widget.Toast;

import com.firebase.ui.auth.AuthUI;
import com.google.android.gms.tasks.OnCompleteListener;
import com.google.android.gms.tasks.Task;
import com.google.firebase.auth.FirebaseAuth;
import com.google.firebase.auth.FirebaseUser;
import com.google.firebase.database.DataSnapshot;
import com.google.firebase.database.DatabaseError;
import com.google.firebase.database.DatabaseReference;
import com.google.firebase.database.FirebaseDatabase;
import com.google.firebase.database.ValueEventListener;

public class SignedInActivity extends AppCompatActivity {

    private static FirebaseUser currentUser;
    private static final String TAG = "RealtimeDB";
    private FirebaseDatabase database;
    private DatabaseReference dbRef;
    private EditText userText;
```

```
.
.
.
}
```

Next, locate and edit the *onCreate()* method to identify the current user and to obtain the database reference:

```
@Override
protected void onCreate(Bundle savedInstanceState) {
    super.onCreate(savedInstanceState);
    setContentView(R.layout.activity_signed_in);

    userText = (EditText) findViewById(R.id.userText);

    currentUser =
            FirebaseAuth.getInstance().getCurrentUser();

    if (currentUser == null) {
        startActivity(new Intent(this, RealtimeDBActivity.class));
        finish();
        return;
    }

    database = FirebaseDatabase.getInstance();
    dbRef = database.getReference("/data");
    dbRef.addValueEventListener(changeListener);
}
```

The above code also adds the value event listener to the database reference so that the app will receive notification when changes occur to the data stored in the database. Remaining within the *RealtimeDBActivity.java* file, add this listener now:

```
ValueEventListener changeListener = new ValueEventListener() {

    @Override
    public void onDataChange(DataSnapshot dataSnapshot) {

        String change = dataSnapshot.child(
                currentUser.getUid()).child("message")
                            .getValue(String.class);

        userText.setText(change);
    }

    @Override
```

```
public void onCancelled(DatabaseError databaseError) {
    notifyUser("Database error: " + databaseError.toException());
}
};
```

The *onDataChange()* listener method will be called when the data stored at /data within the database tree changes and is passed a DataSnapshot instance containing the data. The code within this method extracts the String object from the DataSnapshot instance located at the <user id>/message node. This string is then assigned to the EditText field so that it is visible to the user.

The *onCancelled()* listener method notifies the user of any errors that have occurred using a method named *notifyUser()* which also needs to be added to the SignedInActivity class:

```
private void notifyUser(String message) {
    Toast.makeText(SignedInActivity.this, message,
            Toast.LENGTH_SHORT).show();
}
```

24.9 Writing to the Database

When the user interface layout for the SignedInActivity class was designed, the Save button was configured to call a method named *saveData()* when clicked. This method now needs to be implemented to save the text entered by the user to the database. Edit the *RealtimeDBActivity.java* file once again to implement this method:

```
public void saveData(View view) {
    dbRef.child(currentUser.getUid()).child("message")
            .setValue(userText.getText().toString(), completionListener);
}
```

In the *onCreate()* method, the database reference was initialized with the /data path. The above code adds to this path using the user's ID and a node with the key set to "message" and the value based on the current text in the EditText view. This will result in the text being saved at the following location in the database tree (where <user id> is replaced by the Firebase uid of the current user):

```
/data/<user id>/message
```

Note also that the *setValue()* method call is passed a reference to a completion listener which now needs to be implemented:

```
DatabaseReference.CompletionListener completionListener =
                    new DatabaseReference.CompletionListener() {
    @Override
    public void onComplete(DatabaseError databaseError,
                DatabaseReference databaseReference) {

        if (databaseError != null) {
            notifyUser(databaseError.getMessage());
```

```
            }
        }
};
```

24.10 Signing Out

The final method to be added to the SignedInActivity class is the *signOut()* method which is configured to be called when the user clicks the Sign Out button. This method needs to sign the user out of the app using the *signOut()* method of the AuthUI instance:

```
public void signOut(View view) {
    AuthUI.getInstance()
            .signOut(this)
            .addOnCompleteListener(new OnCompleteListener<Void>() {
                @Override
                public void onComplete(@NonNull Task<Void> task) {
                    if (task.isSuccessful()) {
                        startActivity(new Intent(
                                SignedInActivity.this,
                                RealtimeDBActivity.class));
                        finish();
                    } else {
                        // Report error to user
                    }
                }
            });
}
```

24.11 Configuring the Database Rules

With coding work complete, the next step is to configure the database rules. The requirements for this app are that any user can read another user's message text, but only the owner of the message can write to it.

Load the Firebase console into a browser window and select the *Firebase Examples* project. Choose the Database option in the navigation panel and select the Rules tab:

Figure 24-4

Edit the rules to read as follows before clicking on the Publish button to commit the changes:

```
{
  "rules": {
    "data" : {
        ".read" : true,
        "$uid" : {
            ".write" : "auth != null && auth.uid == $uid"
        }
      }
  }
}
```

As declared, the /data node of the tree (and all of its descendants) is readable by any user. A second rule is then declared for the user ID node allowing only the owner of the data to perform write operations on this or any child nodes.

Remaining in the console window, select the Data tab to display the database tree for the project.

24.12 Testing the App

Compile and run the app on a physical device, create a test account and sign in so that the SignedInActivity screen appears. With the Data page of the Firebase console visible in the browser window, enter some text into text field of the app and click the Save button. In realtime the Firebase console should update the database tree to reflect the newly added data nodes as shown in Figure 24-5:

Figure 24-5

Launch a second instance of the app on a simulator session and sign in using the same account credentials created above. Change the text in the text field, click the Save button and note that the instance of the app running on the device changes instantly to reflect the new text.

Sign out of one of the instances of the app and create a second test account. Once signed in with the new account, enter some text and save the data. Refer to the Firebase console and note that a new branch has been created within the database tree using the uid of the second account:

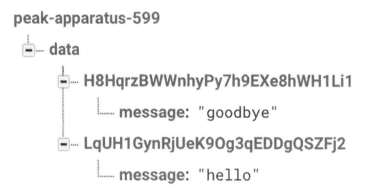

Figure 24-6

Try changing the text within the two instances of the app and verify that a text change in one app is not reflected in the other app indicating that the data is now separated based on user ids.

24.13 Adding a Validation Rule

The final step is to implement a validation rule to verify that the data being saved to /data/<userid>/message is a string containing no more than nine characters. Within the Rules screen of the Firebase console, modify the database rules to include a *.validate* declaration as follows:

```
{
  "rules": {
    "data" : {
        ".read" : true,
          "$uid" : {
```

```
            ".write" : "auth != null && auth.uid == $uid",
            "message" : {
              ".validate" : "newData.isString() &&
                                    newData.val().length < 10"
            }
         }
      }
   }
}
```

With the changes made, click on the Publish button within the Firebase console to activate the rule changes and then test the app once again. When attempting to save a string that exceeds nine characters in length, a message should now appear indicating that permission has been denied.

24.14 Summary

This chapter has demonstrated the combination of the Firebase authentication and realtime database features to store and access data assigned to a specific user. This includes the integration of database and authentication support into the Android Studio project and the implementation of code to store data and receive realtime notifications of data changes. The example project also made use of Firebase database rules to restrict data access and perform data validation.

25. A Firebase Realtime Database List Data Tutorial

The preceding chapters have introduced the Firebase realtime database and explored the concepts of reading and writing data before working through a tutorial outlining the steps in reading and writing individual data items.

In this, the final chapter covering the Firebase Realtime Database, we will build on the information covered in the *Working with Firebase Realtime Database Lists* chapter by creating an example app that makes use of many of the list data features of the realtime database.

25.1 About the Data List App Project

The project created in this chapter takes the form of a simple To Do list app in which items may be added to, or removed from a list stored in a Firebase realtime database. In addition to these features, the app will also allow the user to search for items contained in the list.

25.2 Creating the Data List Project

Launch Android Studio and select the *Start a new Android Studio project* quick start option from the welcome screen.

Within the new project dialog, enter *RealtimeDBList* into the Application name field and your domain as the Company Domain setting before clicking on the *Next* button.

On the form factors screen, enable the *Phone and Tablet* option and set the minimum SDK to API 16: Android 4.1 (Jellybean). Continue through the screens, requesting the creation of an Empty Activity named *RealtimeDBListActivity* with a corresponding layout named *activity_realtime_dblist*.

25.3 Configuring the Project for Realtime Database Access

Before code can be written to make use of the realtime database, some library dependencies need to be added to the build configuration.

To add Firebase Realtime Database support, select the *Tools -> Firebase* menu option and click on the *Realtime Database* entry in the resulting Firebase assistant panel. Once selected, click on the *Save and retrieve data* link followed by the *Connect to Firebase* button followed by the *Add the Realtime Database to your app* button once the connection has been established.

A dialog will appear listing the changes that will be made to the project build files to add realtime database support to the project. Review these changes before clicking on the *Accept Changes* button.

25.4 **Designing the User Interface**

Once Android Studio has finished creating the new project, locate the *activity_realtime_dblist.xml* layout file and load it into the layout editor. Begin by selecting and deleting the default "Hello World!" TextView widget so that the layout canvas is blank. Before adding any components to the view, turn off Autoconnect mode.

The completed layout for the user interface is going to consist of a ListView, a Plain Text EditText and three Button views. Begin by dragging, dropping, positioning and sizing the widgets on the layout canvas so that the layout resembles that shown in Figure 25-1:

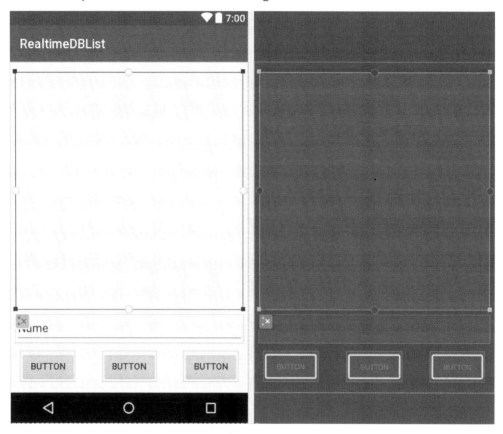

Figure 25-1

With the ListView component selected in the layout, use the Properties tool window to change the ID to *dataListView*.

Click and drag from the constraint anchor located in the center of the top edge of the ListView to the top edge of the parent container and release. This will establish a constraint from the top of the ListView to the top of the parent ConstraintLayout. Repeat these steps to attach the left and right-hand edges of the ListView to the corresponding sides of the parent, and to attach the bottom edge of the ListView to the top of the EditText widget.

With the ListView still selected, set the *layout_width* and *layout_height* properties to 0dp. This switches the component to *match constraint* mode causing the widget to resize based on the constraints applied to it:

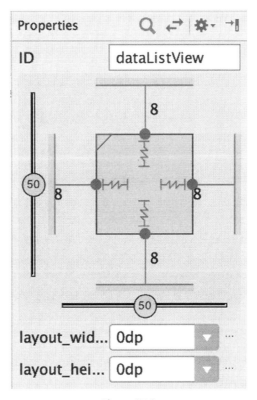

Figure 25-2

Next, establish constraints from the left and right-hand edges of the EditText widget to the matching sides of the parent and from the bottom of the EditText to the top of the center button.

Click on the left-most Button widget, then hold down the shift-key while clicking on the two remaining buttons so that all three are selected. Right-click on any of the Button widgets and select the *Center Horizontally* option from the popup menu.

Add constraints from the bottom of each button to the bottom of the parent layout.

Using the properties tool window, delete the "Name" text from the EditText view and set the text properties of the three buttons to Add, Find and Delete and configure the *onClick* properties to call methods named *addItem*, *findItems*, and *deleteItem* respectively.

On completion of these steps, the layout should resemble that illustrated in Figure 25-3:

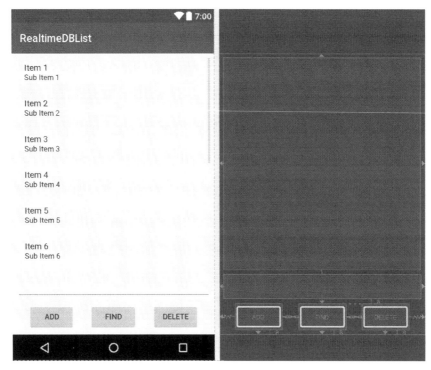

Figure 25-3

Before proceeding, change the ID for the EditText component to *itemText* and the IDs for the Find and Delete buttons to *findButton* and *deleteButton*.

25.5 Performing Initialization Tasks

As is now customary, a number of initialization tasks will need to be performed within the *onCreate()* method located in the *RealtimeDBListActivity.java* file. Locate this file, load it into the Android Studio code editor and modify it as follows to declare variables, import required packages and perform some basic initialization:

```
package com.ebookfrenzy.realtimedblist;

import android.support.v7.app.AppCompatActivity;
import android.os.Bundle;
import android.widget.Button;
import android.widget.EditText;
import android.widget.ListView;

import com.google.firebase.database.DatabaseReference;
import com.google.firebase.database.FirebaseDatabase;

public class RealtimeDBList extends AppCompatActivity {
```

```
    private ListView dataListView;
    private EditText itemText;
    private Button findButton;
    private Button deleteButton;
    private Boolean searchMode = false;
    private Boolean itemSelected = false;
    private int selectedPosition = 0;

    private FirebaseDatabase database = FirebaseDatabase.getInstance();
    private DatabaseReference dbRef = database.getReference("todo");

    @Override
    protected void onCreate(Bundle savedInstanceState) {
        super.onCreate(savedInstanceState);
        setContentView(R.layout.activity_realtime_dblist);

        dataListView = (ListView) findViewById(R.id.dataListView);
        itemText = (EditText) findViewById(R.id.itemText);
        findButton = (Button) findViewById(R.id.findButton);
        deleteButton = (Button) findViewById(R.id.deleteButton);
        deleteButton.setEnabled(false);

    }
}
```

The above code changes obtain references to the user interface components together with an instance of the database reference configured with a path of "/todo". The Delete button is then disabled to prevent the user from attempting to delete an item from the list without first selecting one. Other variables have also been declared that will be used in later code to track the status of the user interface in terms of the currently selected ListView item and whether or not the user is searching for items.

25.6 Implementing the ListView

The list of items will be displayed to the user via the ListView component. The ListView class requires an ArrayAdapter instance and an ArrayList object containing the items to be displayed. This example app will also use an array to store the keys assigned to each child node in the list. Remaining within the *RealtimeDBListActivity.java* file make the following additions:

```
package com.ebookfrenzy.firebaselist;
.
.
.
import android.widget.ArrayAdapter;
import android.widget.AdapterView;
import android.view.View;
```

```
.
.
import java.util.ArrayList;
import java.util.Iterator;

public class MainActivity extends AppCompatActivity {

    ArrayList<String> listItems = new ArrayList<String>();
    ArrayList<String> listKeys = new ArrayList<String>();
    ArrayAdapter<String> adapter;

    @Override
    protected void onCreate(Bundle savedInstanceState) {
        super.onCreate(savedInstanceState);
        setContentView(R.layout.activity_realtime_dblist);

        dataListView = (ListView) findViewById(R.id.dataListView);
        itemText = (EditText) findViewById(R.id.itemText);
        addButton = (Button) findViewById(R.id.addButton);
        findButton = (Button) findViewById(R.id.findButton);
        deleteButton = (Button) findViewById(R.id.deleteButton);
        deleteButton.setEnabled(false);

        adapter = new ArrayAdapter<String>(this,
                    android.R.layout.simple_list_item_single_choice,
                            listItems);
        dataListView.setAdapter(adapter);
        dataListView.setChoiceMode(ListView.CHOICE_MODE_SINGLE);

        dataListView.setOnItemClickListener(
                new AdapterView.OnItemClickListener() {
            public void onItemClick(AdapterView<?> parent,
                        View view, int position, long id) {
                selectedPosition = position;
                itemSelected = true;
                deleteButton.setEnabled(true);
            }
        });

        addChildEventListener();
    }
}
```

The code added to the *onCreate()* method initializes an ArrayAdapter instance with the content of the listItems array and configures the adapter for single item selection. The adapter is then assigned to the ListView component and the ListView component also configured for single item selection (it will only be possible for the user to select and delete items one at a time). An item click listener is then attached to the ListView which records the currently selected item number in the previously declared *selectedPosition* variable, indicates that an item has been selected and then enables the Delete button.

Code has also been added to call an additional method, the purpose of which is to add a child event listener to the database reference. This method now needs to be added to the project.

25.7 **Implementing Child Event Listener**

The app will need to receive notifications whenever new child nodes are added to the data list. A call to a method named *addChildEventListener()* has already been added to the *onCreate()* method and now needs to be added to the *RealtimeDBListActivity.java* file:

```
.

.
import com.google.firebase.database.ChildEventListener;
import com.google.firebase.database.DataSnapshot;
import com.google.firebase.database.DatabaseError;
import com.google.firebase.database.Query;
import com.google.firebase.database.ValueEventListener;

.

.
private void addChildEventListener() {
    ChildEventListener childListener = new ChildEventListener() {

        @Override
        public void onChildAdded(DataSnapshot dataSnapshot, String s) {
            adapter.add(
                (String) dataSnapshot.child("description").getValue());

            listKeys.add(dataSnapshot.getKey());
        }

        @Override
        public void onChildChanged(DataSnapshot dataSnapshot, String s) {

        }

        @Override
        public void onChildMoved(DataSnapshot dataSnapshot, String s) {
        }
```

```
        @Override
        public void onChildRemoved(DataSnapshot dataSnapshot) {
            String key = dataSnapshot.getKey();
            int index = listKeys.indexOf(key);

            if (index != -1) {
                listItems.remove(index);
                listKeys.remove(index);
                adapter.notifyDataSetChanged();
            }
        }


        @Override
        public void onCancelled(DatabaseError databaseError) {
        }
    };
    dbRef.addChildEventListener(childListener);
}
.
.
```

For the purposes of this project, only the *onChildAdded()* and *onChildRemoved()* callback methods need to do any work. The *onChildAdded()* method will be called when a new child is added to the data list and will be passed a DataSnapshot object containing the key and value of the new child. As implemented above, the value is added to the ListView adaptor so that it will appear in the list, and the key is stored in the listKeys array for use when deleting items from the data list.

The *onChildRemoved()* method will, as the name suggests, be called when a child is removed from the list. This method will be called under two different circumstances. The first, and most obvious scenario, is when the current instance of the app removes a child from the list. This will be the result of the user clicking on the Delete button which will, in turn, trigger a call to the *deleteItem()* method which will be added later in the chapter. This method will remove the item from the database, thereby triggering a call to the *onChildRemoved()* callback method where the deleted node will be provided in the form of a data snapshot. The code in the *onChildRemoved()* method extracts the key from the snapshot, identifies the position of the node in the listKeys array and, if it exists, removes the entry from both the listKeys and listItems array.

In the second scenario, the app will receive notification that the child has been removed by another instance of the app. In this situation the child will already have been removed from the database, so only the local data arrays need to be updated to remove the data. As currently written, the *onChildRemoved()* method is designed to handle both of these possibilities.

25.8 **Adding Items to the List**

When the user taps the Add button, any text entered into the EditText view needs to be added as a new child to the data list within the database tree. During the design of the user interface layout, the onClick property of the Add button was configured to call a method named *addItem()* which must now be added to the activity Java class:

```
public void addItem(View view) {

    String item = itemText.getText().toString();
    String key = dbRef.push().getKey();

    itemText.setText("");
    dbRef.child(key).child("description").setValue(item);

    adapter.notifyDataSetChanged();
}
```

The method extracts the string entered into the EditText view before calling the *push()* method of the database reference to create a new child. The key generated for the new child is stored in the listKeys array, the EditText view is cleared and the value saved to the following path:

```
/todo/<key>/description
```

The addition of the new child to the list will trigger a call to the *onChildAdded()* method of the child event listener which was added to the project earlier in the chapter. This method will extract the value from the data snapshot and add it to the ListView adapter array. The key will also be stored in the listKeys array.

The last task performed by the *addItem()* method is to notify the adapter that the data has changed, thereby triggering an update of the list displayed to the user.

25.9 **Deleting List Items**

The Delete button is configured to call the *deleteItem()* method. This method is responsible for deleting the currently selected item from the database.

The code for this method, which now needs to be added to the *RealtimeDBListActivity.java* file reads as follows:

```
public void deleteItem(View view) {
    dataListView.setItemChecked(selectedPosition, false);
    dbRef.child(listKeys.get(selectedPosition)).removeValue();
}
```

The above code deselects the currently selected item in the ListView and then uses the selectedPosition variable as an index into the listKeys array. Having identified the key associated with the item to be deleted, that key is used to remove the child node from the database. The remaining steps of the deletion process will be completed by the code in the *onChildRemoved()* callback method which will be called as a result of the child node being removed from the list.

25.10 **Querying the List**

The last task before testing the app is to implement the code for the Find button. This button is configured to call a method named *findItems()* when clicked and will need to make use of the Query class to find list items that match the current text in the EditText widget. The list items that match the search criteria will be displayed in the ListView in alphabetical order.

The Find button is intended to be dual purpose. Once the user has initiated a search, it will change into a Clear button which, when clicked, will clear the filtered results and display the full list of items in the original chronological order. This is achieved by performing a second query using "order by key" with no additional filtering:

```
public void findItems(View view) {

    Query query;

    if (!searchMode) {
        findButton.setText("Clear");
        query = dbRef.orderByChild("description").
                        equalTo(itemText.getText().toString());
        searchMode = true;
    } else {
        searchMode = false;
        findButton.setText("Find");
        query = dbRef.orderByKey();
    }

    if (itemSelected) {
        dataListView.setItemChecked(selectedPosition, false);
        itemSelected = false;
        deleteButton.setEnabled(false);
    }

    query.addListenerForSingleValueEvent(queryValueListener);
}
```

The line of code at the end of the method attaches a single value event listener named *queryValueListener* to the Query object. This listener will be called when the query operation returns with the results of the search. Implement this listener now so that it reads as follows:

```
ValueEventListener queryValueListener = new ValueEventListener() {

    @Override
```

```
public void onDataChange(DataSnapshot dataSnapshot) {

    Iterable<DataSnapshot> snapshotIterator = dataSnapshot.getChildren();
    Iterator<DataSnapshot> iterator = snapshotIterator.iterator();

    adapter.clear();
    listKeys.clear();

    while (iterator.hasNext()) {
        DataSnapshot next = (DataSnapshot) iterator.next();

        String match = (String) next.child("description").getValue();
        String key = next.getKey();
        listKeys.add(key);
        adapter.add(match);
    }

}

@Override
public void onCancelled(DatabaseError databaseError) {

}
};
```

The *onDataChanged()* method of the listener will be called when the query returns and will be passed a data snapshot containing the items that match the search criteria. The method clears both the adapter and listKeys arrays and then iterates through the children in the snapshot. For each child, the key is stored on the listKeys array and the value added to the adapter so that it will appear in the ListView.

25.11 Changing the Database Rules

As this example app does not use Firebase Authentication, some changes need to be made to the database rules. Within the Firebase console, temporarily modify the rules as follows and then click on the Publish button:

```
{
  "rules": {
    ".read": true,
    ".write": true
  }
}
```

25.12 **Testing the App**

Open a browser window, navigate to the Firebase console and open the Data page of the Database panel. Compile and run the app on a physical device or emulator and enter several items to the list by entering text into the EditText field and tapping the Add button:

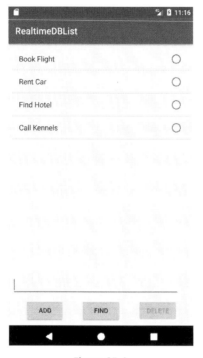

Figure 25-4

Note that in addition to appearing in the ListView within the app, the items also appear in the database tree within the Firebase console:

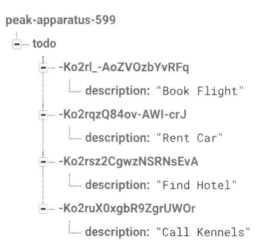

Figure 25-5

Select an item from the list and click the Delete button to remove it from the database. Verify that the item is removed from both the ListView and the tree in the Firebase console.

Next, perform a search for an item currently included in the list. Clear the search results, add duplicate items to the list and perform another search verifying that both instances of the item are listed.

Finally, run the app concurrently, using multiple devices or emulator sessions, and test that any data additions or deletions are reflected in realtime in both instances of the app.

25.13 **Summary**

This chapter contained a tutorial intended to demonstrate the use of the Firebase Realtime Database to store and manage data in list form including saving, deleting and searching for list items. This has involved the use of the *push()* method of the DatabaseReference class together with the Query class and both value and child event listeners.

26. Firebase Cloud Messaging

Firebase Cloud Messaging (FCM) provides a platform for sending messages to and from client apps and web sites. This platform is ideal for sending notifications to users and implementing realtime instant messaging solutions with minimal coding effort.

This chapter will walk through the addition of Firebase Cloud Messaging support to an Android Studio app project and then make use of the Firebase console to test the sending and receiving of notification messages targeted at specific Android devices and user segments. The app created in this chapter will be extended in later chapters as more aspects of the Firebase Messaging system are introduced including message topics, device groups and both upstream and server-side messaging.

26.1 An Overview of Firebase Cloud Messaging

FCM provides an environment for sending and receiving messages from within mobile apps and web sites. The simplest form of messaging involves the transmission of notifications to app users. This can be achieved either using the Firebase console, or programmatically from a trusted server environment via HTTP, XMPP or Node.js code. Notifications can take the form of informational messages, a data payload or a combination of both. Messages can be targeted to individual devices or specific groups of users.

Two way messaging is possible through the implementation of *upstream messaging* support. This allows messages to be sent from client devices, through a message server for delivery to other devices.

26.2 Creating the Firebase Messaging Project

Launch Android Studio and select the *Start a new Android Studio project* quick start option from the welcome screen.

Within the new project dialog, enter *Messaging* into the Application name field and your domain as the Company Domain setting before clicking on the *Next* button.

On the form factors screen, enable the *Phone and Tablet* option and set the minimum SDK to API 16: Android 4.1 (Jellybean). Continue to proceed through the screens, requesting the creation of an Empty Activity named *MessagingActivity* with a corresponding layout named *activity_messaging*.

26.3 Adding Firebase Messaging Support to the Project

To add Firebase Messaging support to the Android Studio project, select the *Tools -> Firebase* menu option and click on the Cloud Messaging entry in the Firebase assistant panel. Once selected, click on the *Set up Firebase Messaging* link. In the next panel, connect the project to Firebase using the provided connection button and select the *Firebase Examples* project from the list of existing projects. Once the project has been connected, click on the *Add FCM to your app* button.

A dialog will appear listing the changes that will be made to the project build files to add cloud messaging support to the project. Review these changes before clicking on the *Accept Changes* button.

26.4 **Designing the User Interface**

This example project will use the existing "Hello World" TextView in the activity layout to display the data associated with incoming messages. All that is required is to change the ID for the view.

Load the *activity_messaging.xml* file into the Android Studio layout editor, select the TextView object and change the ID in the Properties tool window to *myTextView*.

26.5 **Obtaining and Monitoring the Registration Token**

When an app first makes use of cloud messaging, it is assigned a registration token which uniquely identifies the app and the device on which it is running. This allows messages to be sent that target a specific app running on a specific device.

The registration token takes the form of a string and may be accessed by implementing a service within the project that extends the FirebaseInstanceIdService class. This service needs to implement a method named *onTokenRefresh()* which is called when the app is first assigned a registration token, and then subsequently any time the token changes. Events that typically cause the token to change include the user uninstalling and then re-installing the app, the app being restored during a device recovery operation (or a move to a new device), or the user clearing the app data from the device. Given these possibilities it is important to ensure that the app is always using the current registration token.

Add a new service to the project by right clicking on the *app -> java -> <package name>* entry in the project tool window and selecting the *New -> Java Class...* menu option. In the New Class dialog, enter *FirebaseIDService* into the Class Name field and select the FirebaseInstanceIdService class as the superclass before clicking on the OK button:

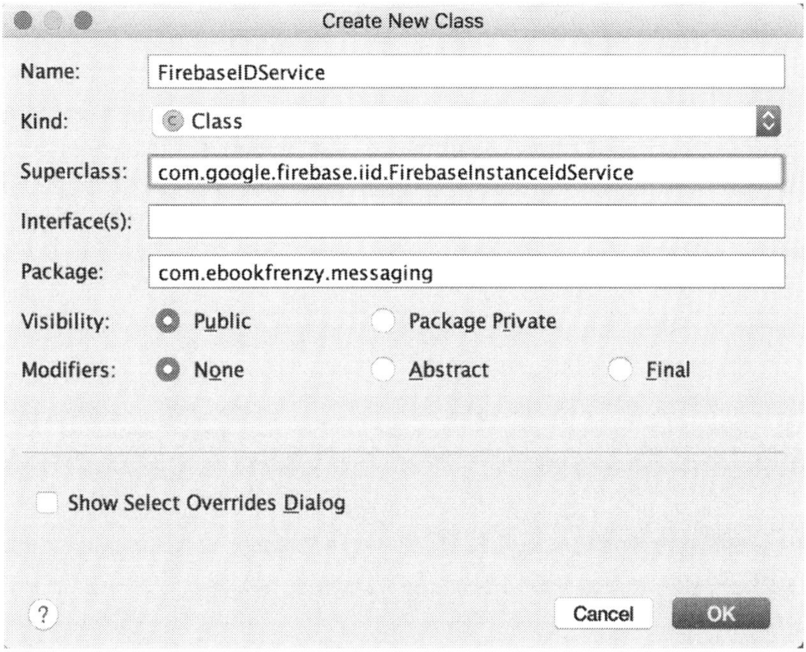

Figure 26-1

Edit the newly created *FirebaseIDService.java* file and modify it so that it reads as follows:

```
.

.
import android.util.Log;

import com.google.firebase.iid.FirebaseInstanceId;
import com.google.firebase.iid.FirebaseInstanceIdService;

public class FirebaseIDService extends FirebaseInstanceIdService {

    private static final String TAG = "FirebaseIDService";

    @Override
    public void onTokenRefresh() {

        String token = FirebaseInstanceId.getInstance().getToken();
        Log.d(TAG, "Registration Token: = " + token);

        sendRegistrationToServer(token);
    }

    private void sendRegistrationToServer(String token) {
```

```
    }
}
```

The service implements the *onTokenRefresh()* callback method and extracts the current token via a call to the *getToken()* method of the FirebaseInstanceId object. The token is then output to the Android Studio logcat panel. The *onTokenRefresh()* method also calls a method named *sendRegistrationToServer()*, passing through the token string as an argument. This method provides an opportunity for the token to be provided to an application server that may, for example, be maintaining a database of messaging clients and tokens. At the moment an empty version of this method is provided in the class, though code will be added to this method in later chapters when we look at the server side aspects of cloud messaging.

Now that the service has been added to the project, it needs to be declared within the project manifest file so that it will be triggered in the event of a change to the token. Within the Project tool window, locate the *AndroidManifest.xml* file, load it into the editor and add the service entry:

```xml
<?xml version="1.0" encoding="utf-8"?>
<manifest xmlns:android="http://schemas.android.com/apk/res/android"
    package="com.ebookfrenzy.messaging">

    <application
        android:allowBackup="true"
        android:icon="@mipmap/ic_launcher"
        android:label="@string/app_name"
        android:roundIcon="@mipmap/ic_launcher_round"
        android:supportsRtl="true"
        android:theme="@style/AppTheme">
        <activity android:name=".MessagingActivity">
            <intent-filter>
                <action android:name="android.intent.action.MAIN" />

                <category android:name="android.intent.category.LAUNCHER" />
            </intent-filter>
        </activity>

        <service
            android:name=".FirebaseIDService">
            <intent-filter>
                <action
                    android:name="com.google.firebase.INSTANCE_ID_EVENT"/>
            </intent-filter>
        </service>
    </application>
</manifest>
```

With the code and manifest changes completed, compile and run the app on a device or emulator and review the output in the logcat panel of the Android Monitor tool window to locate the registration token string. The output will resemble the following (though the token will, of course, be different):

```
Registration Token: =
cxpKdykhQeY:APA91bEl3LnBTnEzaWTUoW7aGARytp2KeOMuE_lZ496msWhQ5EjRRH75WYFO4Fwq91
Dp7_KGcK8B9mnwAJ2E2sF5QcoXTl5eQ7PCspfYkHSgWlEFQr91t2PxXMwgOyGdPQlFPa65dCIu
```

Take this opportunity to cut and paste the token string into a safe place so that it can be referenced in the next section.

26.6 Sending a Notification to the Device

The next step is to use the registration token to send a message directly to the device. The quickest way to test this is to use the Notifications feature of the Firebase console. By default, notifications only appear when the target app is in the background. If the app is still in the foreground on the device or emulator session, tap the home button to place it into the background before taking the next steps.

Open a browser window, navigate to the Firebase console and select the *Notifications* entry in the navigation bar.

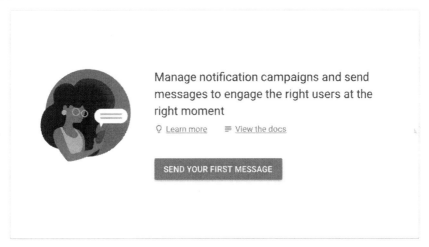

Figure 26-2

Click on the *Send your First Message* button to display the message composition screen. Enter some text into the Message text field and select the *Single device* option in the Target section (highlighted in Figure 26-3). Cut and paste the registration token obtained in the previous section into the FCM registration token box, leave the other settings unchanged and click the *Send Message* button.

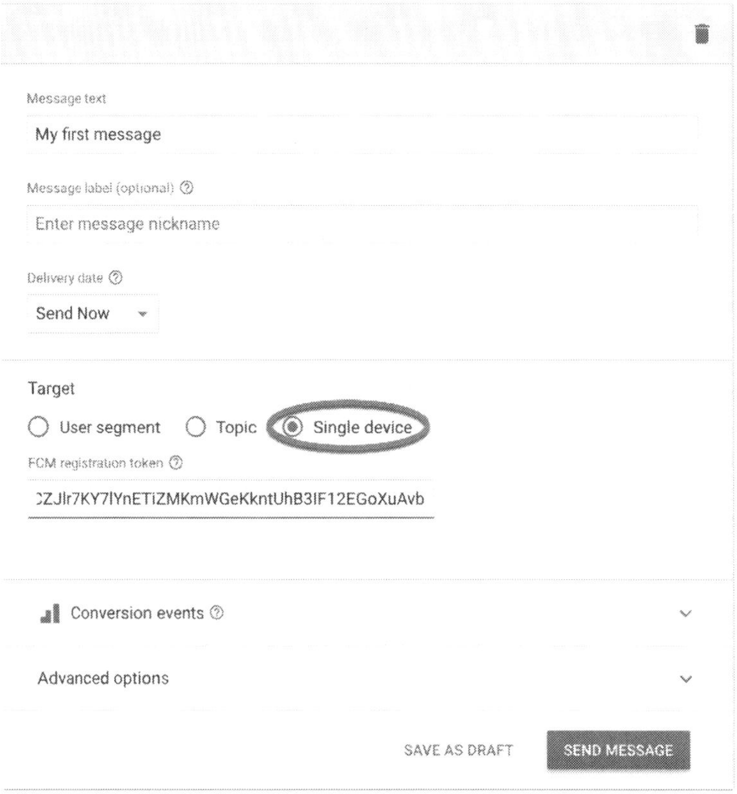

Message text

My first message

Message label (optional) ⑦

Enter message nickname

Delivery date ⑦

Send Now   ▾

Target

○ User segment   ○ Topic   ⊙ Single device

FCM registration token ⑦

ⅭZJlr7KY7lYnETiZMKmWGeKkntUhB3IF12EGoXuAvb

.ıl Conversion events ⑦   ⌄

Advanced options   ⌄

SAVE AS DRAFT   **SEND MESSAGE**

Figure 26-3

Review the message in the resulting dialog then click on the Send button.

26.7 Receiving the Notification

After the message has been sent, return to the device or emulator on which the app is running and look for a notification indicator in the top status bar (the indicator will take the form of an Android robot icon). Once the indicator appears, slide downward from the status bar to view the notification which will contain the message text entered when the notification was composed within the Firebase console:

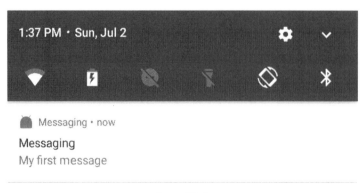

Figure 26-4

Tapping the notification will launch the Messaging app.

26.8 Including Custom Data within the Notification

Firebase cloud messaging also provides the option to pass key-value based data within the message payload. This data can then be retrieved by the activity that is launched when the notification is selected on the device. The key-value data pairs to be included with the message are specified from within the Advanced options section of the Firebase console message composition screen. Figure 26-5, for example, shows two custom data pairs configured for a message:

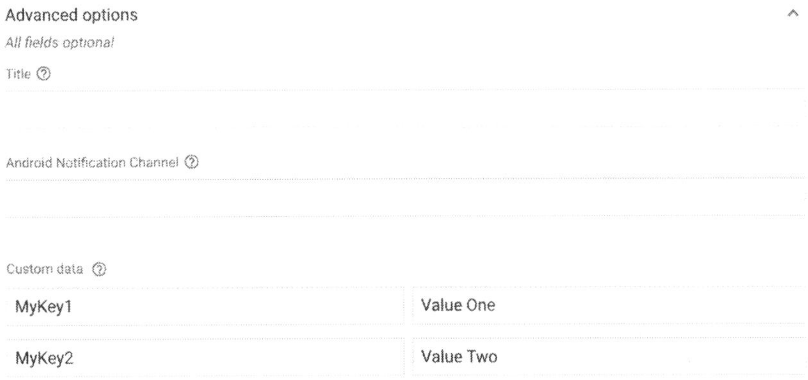

Advanced options
All fields optional
Title ⑦

Android Notification Channel ⑦

Custom data ⑦

| MyKey1 | Value One |
| MyKey2 | Value Two |

Figure 26-5

Within the activity launched when the user taps the notification on the device, the *getIntent()* method may be used to obtain a reference to the Intent object that triggered the launch. Calling the *getExtras()* method on that Intent will return a Bundle object containing the custom data.

The value associated with each key may be accessed by passing through the key value to the *getString()* method of the Bundle object.

Edit the *MessagingActivity.java* file and modify the *onCreate()* method to extract the value for a key of "MyKey1" and display that value on the myTextView widget in the activity user interface layout:

```
.
.
import android.widget.TextView;
.
.
.
@Override
protected void onCreate(Bundle savedInstanceState) {
    super.onCreate(savedInstanceState);
    setContentView(R.layout.activity_firebase_notify);

    Bundle customData = getIntent().getExtras();

    if (customData != null) {
```

```
        TextView textView = (TextView) findViewById(R.id.myTextView);
        textView.setText(customData.getString("MyKey1"));
    }
}
```

Build and run the app and place it into the background. Using the Firebase console, compose a new message targeted at a single device using the registration token. Before sending the notification, open the Advanced options panel and enter MyKey1 as the key and a string of your choice as the corresponding value. Send the message, refer to the device on which the app is running and pull down the notification shade when the notification icon appears in the status bar. Tap the notification to launch the activity and note that the string entered into the value field is now displayed on the TextView widget. Custom data has successfully been passed from the Firebase console via a cloud message to the main activity of the app.

26.9 Foreground App Notification Handling

As previously outlined an app will not, by default, receive a Firebase message notification if it is currently the foreground app. In order for a foreground app to receive the message, it must implement a service that extends the FirebaseMessagingService class and override the *onMessageReceived()* callback method within that class.

Add a new service to the project by right clicking on the *app -> java -> <package name>* entry in the project tool window and selecting the *New -> Java Class...* menu option. In the New Class dialog, enter *FirebaseMsgService* into the Class Name field and select the FirebaseMessagingService class as the superclass before clicking on the OK button.

Edit the newly created *FirebaseMsgService.java* file and modify it so that it reads as follows:

```
.

.

import android.util.Log;

import com.google.firebase.messaging.FirebaseMessagingService;
import com.google.firebase.messaging.RemoteMessage;

public class FirebaseMsgService extends FirebaseMessagingService {

    private static final String TAG = "FirebaseMsgService";

    public FirebaseMsgService() {
    }

    @Override
    public void onMessageReceived(RemoteMessage remoteMessage) {
```

```
    Log.d(TAG, "From: " + remoteMessage.getFrom());

    if (remoteMessage.getNotification() != null) {
          Log.d(TAG, "Notification Title: " +
                  remoteMessage.getNotification().getTitle());

          Log.d(TAG, "Notification Message: " +
                  remoteMessage.getNotification().getBody());
    }

    if (remoteMessage.getData().size() > 0) {
        Log.d(TAG, "Message data payload: " +
                  remoteMessage.getData().get("MyKey1"));
    }
  }
}
```

When the *onMessageReceived()* method is called, it is passed as an argument a RemoteMessage object containing the details of a Firebase cloud message.

In the above code, the *getFrom()* method of the RemoteMessage object is called to identify where the message originated. The *getNotification()* method of the RemoteMessage object is called to access the RemoteMessage.Notification object and used to obtain both the title and notification body.

Finally, the method checks whether a data payload was included in the message and, if so, extracts the value assigned to MyKey1 using the RemoteMessage *getData()* method. All of this information is sent to the Android Studio logcat panel.

The final task before testing the code is to add an entry within the *AndroidManifest.xml* file for the service:

```
<service android:name=".FirebaseMsgService">
    <intent-filter>
        <action android:name="com.google.firebase.MESSAGING_EVENT"/>
    </intent-filter>
</service>
```

Once the changes have been made, build and run the app and display the Android Monitor tool window so that the logcat output from the app is visible. Leaving the app in the foreground, and using the Firebase console, send a new message to the app using the steps outlined earlier in the chapter, making sure to include the text message, a title and a key/value data pair. Once the notification has arrived on the device, output should appear in the Android Monitor tool window containing the message data similar to the following:

```
D/FirebaseMsgService: Notification Title: This is an example title
D/FirebaseMsgService: Notification Message: This is some message text
D/FirebaseMsgService: Message data payload: Value One
```

26.10 **Sending to Apps and User Segments**

So far in this chapter, the Firebase console has been used to send messages to specific devices defined by registration token. It is also possible to send a message to all instances of a particular app by referencing the app's package name. To target all instances of a specific app, compose a new message within the Firebase console and select the User Segment option located in the Target section of the composition screen. Once selected, choose the destination app from the drop down menu as shown in Figure 26-6:

Figure 26-6

To target more than one app, click on the *Target Another App* button and select the next app from the menu. Repeat this step until all the required target apps have been selected before sending the message.

Once at least one target app has been selected, a range of other user segments are available for fine tuning the message recipients. To view the full list of segmentation options, click on the AND entry next to the app package name as highlighted in Figure 26-7:

Figure 26-7

Clicking on the AND button will add an additional row to the list of segments from which other criteria may be selected:

Firebase Cloud Messaging

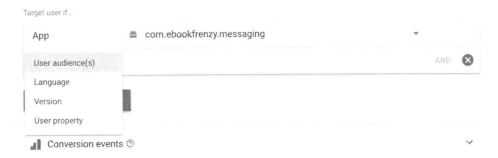

Figure 26-8

Firebase currently supports the following segmentation options:

- **Audience** – A group of users that has been defined within the Firebase Analytics system.
- **User Properties** – Used in conjunction with Firebase Analytics, user properties allow specific groups of users to be identified.
- **Version** – Targets a specific version of an app. Useful when notifying users of an older app version that it is time to upgrade.
- **Language** – The language supported by the user's device.

26.11 Conversion Events

Conversion events allow user engagement with notification messages to be evaluated. By default, Firebase will automatically track notifications sent and opened events. Additional events (for example tracking users who made an in app purchase in response to a notification) may be configured using Firebase Analytics, a topic which will be covered in the chapter entitled *An Introduction to Firebase Analytics*.

26.12 Summary

Firebase messaging allows notifications and messages to be sent to devices on which specific Firebase-enabled apps have been installed. Adding Firebase cloud messaging support to an app is a multistep process involving adding support to the Android Studio project, obtaining the registration token for the app on the device and implementing handlers to identify when a message has arrived for the app. Notification messages may be sent using the Firebase console which provides a range of targeting and user segmentation options. As will be demonstrated in the following chapters, greater messaging flexibility is available by implementing a server-based messaging system.

257

27. Sending Firebase Cloud Messages from a Node.js Server

The previous chapter created an example Firebase Cloud Messaging client app and outlined the steps involved in obtaining the registration token for an app and device combination. The tutorial then demonstrated the use of that token to send notification messages targeted to the specific device using the Notifications section of the Firebase console.

While the Firebase console is useful for manually sending downstream notification messages to client apps, more complex development projects will typically need to send messages programmatically from a server. The Firebase console is also limited to sending so called "notification" messages. While these messages can contain a data payload, they always result in a notification appearing within the Android status bar and notifications shade when the app is in the background. Server based message sending, on the other hand, allows *data only* messages to be sent to devices, allowing data to be delivered to client apps without triggering a notification.

As discussed in earlier chapters a number of options are available for sending messages from a server. One such option, and the topic of this chapter, involves the use of the Firebase Admin SDK and Node.js.

27.1 An Introduction to Node.js

JavaScript began as a scripting language intended to provide interactive behavior to web pages. Traditionally JavaScript code was embedded into the content of a web page, downloaded into a web browser and executed using a JavaScript engine built into the browser. In the case of the Google Chrome browser, this engine is known as the V8 JavaScript engine.

In very basic terms, Node.js takes the V8 JavaScript engine and repurposes it to provide a server-side runtime environment for executing JavaScript code. The result is an extremely fast, efficient and scalable environment in which to create and serve dynamic web content.

Node.js includes a range of modules that provide specific functionality such as networking and database access. One such module is the Firebase Admin Node.js SDK provided by Google to allow Firebase cloud messaging to be implemented within Node.js code.

In the following sections of this chapter steps will be outlined demonstrating how to install Node.js on macOS, Windows and Linux before outlining the use of Node.js to send messages using Firebase cloud messaging. Regardless of which platform you choose to use to run Node.js, think of it as fulfilling the role of the server and the Android app as the client.

Node.js can be downloaded pre-built for most platforms from the following URL:

https://nodejs.org/en/download/

27.2 **Installing Node.js on macOS**

From the Node.js download page, select and download the macOS Installer (.pkg) file. Once the package has downloaded, locate it in a Finder window and double-click on it to launch the installer. Work through the installation process, accepting the default selections unless you have specific requirements. On completion of the installation, both the *npm* and *node* executable binaries will be installed in the /usr/local/bin folder and will be accessible from the command-prompt within a Terminal window.

27.3 **Installing Node.js on Windows**

Download the appropriate Windows Installer (.msi) package (either 32-bit or 64-bit depending on your hardware platform) and launch the installer once the download is complete. Windows Installer will unpack the Node.js files and present a dialog within which the installation may be performed. Accept the license terms and choose a filesystem location into which the Node.js files should be installed. On the custom setup screen, accept the default package selection, then click *Next* followed by the *Install* button. Once the installation is complete, the files will have been installed in the selected location and will be accessible within a Command Prompt window.

27.4 **Installing Node.js on Linux**

The steps to install Node.js on Linux will vary depending on the Linux distribution. On Red Hat and CentOS systems, take the following steps:

```
yum install epel-release
yum install nodejs npm --enablerepo=epel
```

On systems running Ubuntu, Node.js may be installed using the following command:

```
sudo apt-get install nodejs nodejs-legacy npm
```

27.5 **Initializing and Configuring Node.js**

Regardless of the platform on which Node.js has been installed, the same configuration steps need to be performed before Node.js is ready to send Firebase cloud messages.

Open a terminal or command prompt window and execute the following command to verify that the package was successfully installed:

```
node -v
```

Assuming that this command outputs the version of Node.js installed on the system, the next step is to create a *package.json* file. To achieve this, create and change to a new directory in which to work with Node.js and run the npm command as follows:

```
npm init
```

When prompted, enter information at each prompt. Since this is simply a test package, the exact information entered is not of paramount importance. The following lists some suitable options:

- name: firebasefcm
- version: 1.0.0
- description: An example package for testing Firebase FCM
- entry point: index.js
- test command: (leave blank)
- git repository: (leave blank)
- keywords: (leave blank)
- author: (your name or company)
- license: ISC

The remainder of this chapter assumes that all actions are being performed within the directory containing the *package.json* file.

27.6 Running a Test

Perform one final installation check by creating a new file named *index.js* containing the following code using an editor of your choice:

```
var sys = require("util");
console.log("Hello World");
```

These lines of code indicate that the *util* module is to be imported before using the *console.log* function to output a message to the console. Once the file has been created, execute it using the node command-line tool:

```
node index.js
```

When the code is executed, output reading "Hello World" will appear.

27.7 Installing the Firebase Admin SDK

Since the Node.js code written in the remainder of this chapter is going to make extensive use of the Firebase Admin SDK the next step is to install this module using the npm command. Remaining in the directory containing the *package.json* file, install the module library as follows:

```
npm install firebase-admin --save
```

A sub-directory named *node_modules* containing the firebase-admin module will have been created and a review of the *package.json* file will show that the firebase-admin module is now listed as a dependency for the current project:

```
.
.
  "dependencies": {
    "firebase-admin": "^5.0.0"
.
```

27.8 Generating the Service Account Credentials

Before any Firebase cloud messages can be sent using Node.js, an additional JSON file needs to be generated and installed on the server. This file contains a private key that allows Node.js code to communicate through the SDK to the Firebase messaging service and is generated from within the Firebase console.

Open the Firebase console in a browser window, select the *Firebase Examples* project and select the Settings option as highlighted in Figure 27-1:

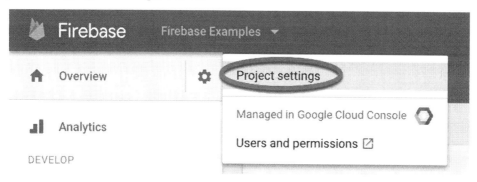

Figure 27-1

On the settings page, select the *Service Accounts* tab followed by the *Firebase Admin SDK* option:

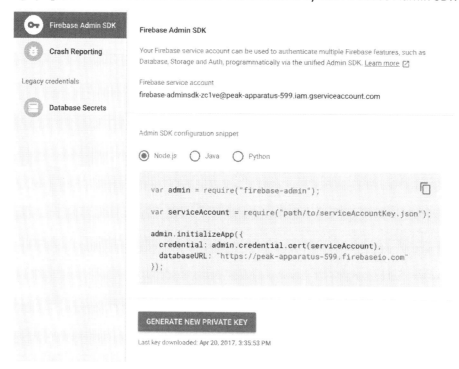

Figure 27-2

Click on the *Generate New Private Key* button, download the generated file and place it in a suitable directory on the system on which Node.js has been installed. This can be in the directory containing the *package.json* file or any other directory where it can be referenced within Node.js code. Regardless of where the file is placed, it is important to keep this file secure to prevent others from using your account to send Firebase cloud messages. If the key security is compromised, return to the Firebase console and generate a new one.

The Firebase Admin SDK page also includes a useful Node.js snippet that will be used in the next section to perform some initialization tasks so keep this page open in the browser for now.

27.9 Initializing the Admin SDK

With Node.js installed and configured, work can begin writing code to send a message to a device. Once again using the editor of your choice, create a new file named *send.js* and copy and paste the Node.js snippet from the Firebase console web page into the file:

```
var admin = require("firebase-admin");

var serviceAccount = require("path/to/serviceAccountKey.json");

admin.initializeApp({
    credential: admin.credential.cert(serviceAccount),
    databaseURL: "<your database URL here>"
});
```

The code imports the firebase-admin module and then declares a variable referencing the location of the JSON file containing the private key generated earlier in the chapter. Modify the placeholder path to reference the actual name and location of the file, for example:

```
var serviceAccount = require("/home/neil/nodejs/firebase-adminsdk.json");
```

Wrapping the path in a *require* statement ensures that an error will be thrown if the file does not exist at the specified location.

Note also that the databaseURL for the Firebase project is included in the arguments passed to the *initializeApp* method. This is the URL for the realtime database associated with the project. If the initialization snippet was copied from the Firebase console this should already be set to the correct URL.

27.10 Adding the Destination Registration Token

For the purposes of this example, a message will be sent only to a specific device. Locate the registration token for the device and app combination tested in the previous chapter and assign it to a variable in the *send.js* file beneath the SDK initialization code:

```
.

.

var registrationToken = "<registration token goes here>";
```

27.11 **Understanding Message Payloads**

The content of a message is referred to as the *payload*. Firebase messaging supports *notification, data* and *combined* messages.

- **Notification Messages** - Consist of a title and a message body and trigger the notification system on arrival at the device. In other words, an icon will appear in the status bar and an entry will appear in the notification shade. Such notifications should be used when sending an informational message that you want the user to see.
- **Data Messages** - Contain data in the form of key/value pairs and are delivered directly to the app without triggering the notification system. Data messages are used when sending data silently to the app.
- **Combined Messages** – Contain a payload comprising both notification and data. The notification is shown to the user and the data is delivered to the app.

The following example declares a notification payload consisting of a title and a message body:

```
var payload = {
  notification: {
    title: "Account Deposit",
    body: "A deposit to your savings account has just cleared."
  }
};
```

A data message, on the other hand, uses the data keyword together with one or more key/value pairs:

```
var payload = {
  data: {
    account: "Savings",
    balance: "$3020.25"
  }
};
```

A combined message payload contains both notification and data elements as follows:

```
var payload = {
  notification: {
    title: "Account Deposit",
    body: "A deposit to your savings account has just cleared."
  },
  data: {
    account: "Savings",
    balance: "$3020.25"
  }
};
```

The payload may also have options associated with it. The main option keys are as follows:

- **collapseKey** – Used to identify a group of messages where only the most recent message is sent if multiple messages are waiting to be delivered to the device.
- **contentAvailable** – Used when sending messages to iOS devices. When set to true, the app is woken on message receipt. This is the default behavior for messages received on Android devices.
- **dryRun** – When set to true the message is not actually sent. Useful for testing purposes during development.
- **mutableContent** – Applies only to iOS client apps and when set to true allows the app to modify the message content before it is presented to the user as a notification.
- **priority** – A string value that may be set to "high" or "normal". By default notifications are high priority while data messages default to normal priority. Normal priority messages may be delayed but impose a lower burden on the device battery. High priority messages, on the other hand, are sent immediately, wake sleeping devices and open a network connection to the corresponding server.
- **timeToLive** – A numeric value indicating the amount of time in seconds that the message should be held if the destination device is offline. This can be set to any duration up to four weeks (2419200 seconds). If no TTL is specified the default is four weeks.

The following is an example option declaration that sets the priority to normal with a time to live duration of one hour:

```
var options = {
  priority: "normal",
  timeToLive: 60 * 60
};
```

27.12 Defining the Payload and Sending the Message

Edit the *send.js* file and add the following payload and options declaration beneath the registration token variable:

```
var payload = {
  notification: {
    title: "This is a Notification",
    body: "This is the body of the notification message."
  }
};

 var options = {
  priority: "high",
  timeToLive: 60 * 60 *24
};
```

All that remains is to send the message. This involves a call to the *sendToDevice()* method of the Firebase Admin SDK, passing through the registration token, payload and options and then checking the response to find out if the message was sent successfully:

```
admin.messaging().sendToDevice(registrationToken, payload, options)
  .then(function(response) {
    console.log("Successfully sent message:", response);
  })
  .catch(function(error) {
    console.log("Error sending message:", error);
  });
```

27.13 Testing the Code

Run the Messaging app created in the previous chapter on the device or emulator session that matches the reference token included in the message and place it in the background. Within the terminal or command prompt window, run the following command:

```
node send.js
```

After a short delay, output similar to the following should appear indicating that the message was send successfully:

```
Successfully sent message: { results: [ { messageId:
'0:1493066541057227%00ae8e2b00ae8e2b' } ],
  canonicalRegistrationTokenCount: 0,
  failureCount: 0,
  successCount: 1,
  multicastId: 7678894013550453000 }
```

Refer to the device or emulator and note the appearance of the notification icon in the status bar. Drag down from the status bar to reveal the notification shade and tap on the notification sent from the Node.js server. The notification body text should now appear in the TextView in the main activity.

Next, change the payload in the *send.js* file to a data message:

```
var payload = {
  data: {
    MyKey1: "Hello"
  }
};
```

Send the message again with the app in the foreground and note that the data is output to the Android Studio logcat panel. Send the message once more, this time with the app in the background. Note that no notification is triggered but that the value is once again displayed in the logcat output. Clearly the message was still received even though no notification was triggered on the device.

27.14 Topics

Firebase FCM topics offer developers a publish and subscribe system that allows apps to opt-in to receiving messages within certain categories. A news app might, for example, provide the user with the option of subscribing to notifications for different categories of news headlines such as business, local and international news.

A client app can be subscribed to a topic either from within the app itself, or on the server using the app's registration token.

A client app subscribes itself to a topic by making a call to the *subscribeToTopic()* method of the FirebaseMessaging instance. If the topic does not already exist, the method call creates the topic. The following code, for example, subscribes an app to a topic named "finance":

```
FirebaseMessaging.getInstance().subscribeToTopic("finance");
```

A call to the *unsubscribeFromTopic()* method of the FirebaseMessaging instance (passing through the topic string as an argument) will opt the app instance out of receiving further messages for that topic.

```
FirebaseMessaging.getInstance().unsubscribeFromTopic("finance");
```

To subscribe an app instance from the server using Node.js, a call must be made to the Admin SDK *subscribeToTopic()* method passing through the registration token of the app/device combination and the name of the topic:

```
var registrationToken = "<registration token here>";

var topic = "finance";

admin.messaging().subscribeToTopic(registrationToken, topic)
  .then(function(response) {
    console.log("Successfully subscribed to topic:", response);
  })
  .catch(function(error) {
    console.log("Error subscribing to topic:", error);
  });
```

Multiple app instances may be subscribed to a topic by passing through an array of registration tokens as follows:

```
var registrationTokens = [ "<registration token one>",
                           "<registration token two>", … ];
var topic = "finance";

admin.messaging().subscribeToTopic(registrationTokens, topic)
  .then(function(response) {
    console.log("Successfully subscribed to topic:", response);
  })
  .catch(function(error) {
    console.log("Error subscribing to topic:", error);
  });
```

Sending Firebase Cloud Messages from a Node.js Server

To opt client apps out from a topic using Node.js on the server, simply call the *unsubscribeFromTopic()* method passing through a registration token (or array of tokens) together with the topic name string.

Messages may be sent to subscribed devices either from a server, or using the Notifications panel of the Firebase console. To send a notification to topic subscribers within the Firebase console, compose a new notification message and select the Topic option within the Target section of the message composition screen. With the Topic option selected, type the first few letters of the topic name into the text field to see a list of matching topics to which the message is to be sent:

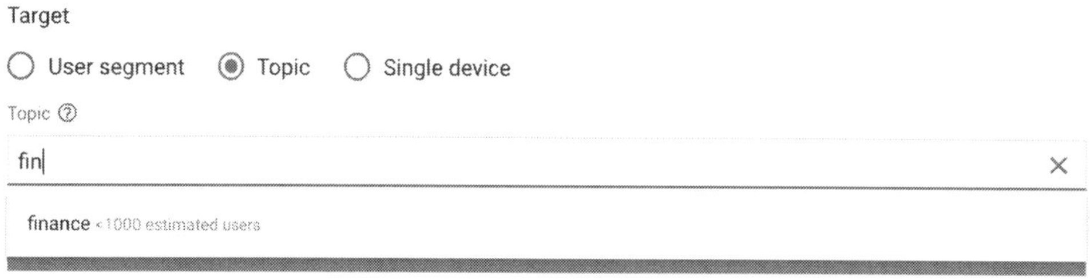

Figure 27-3

Note when using the Firebase console to send notifications to topic subscribers that it can take up to 24 hours for a newly created topic to appear within the topic list.

To send a message to subscribed client apps from a server using Node.js, the *sendToTopic()* Admin SDK method is called passing through the payload and topic string. In the following code fragment, a notification message is sent to all "finance" topic subscribers:

```
var payload = {
  notification: {
    title: "NASDAQ News",
    body: "The NASDAQ climbs for the second day. Closes up 0.60%."
  }
};

var topic = "finance";

admin.messaging().sendToTopic(topic, payload)
  .then(function(response) {
    console.log("Successfully sent message:", response);
  })
  .catch(function(error) {
    console.log("Error sending message:", error);
  });
```

When sending messages to a topic, Firebase supports the use of regular expressions ([a-zA-Z0-9-_.~%]+) to target multiple topics based on matching criteria. Assuming three topics named news_local, news_business and news_politics, for example, the following expression would send a message to all three topics:

268

```
var topic = "news_*";

admin.messaging().sendToTopic(topic, payload)
.
.
```

27.15 Using Topic Conditions

Topic conditions may also be used when sending messages to topics. Conditions allow the sender to define the terms under which a subscriber is eligible to receive a message. This is defined based on the topics to which the app is subscribed.

Topic conditional expressions support both the AND (&&) and OR (||) operators and are used with the *sendToCondition()* Admin SDK method. In the following code, for example, the message will be received by an app only if it has subscribed to the *news* topic while also being subscribed to either the *finance* or *politics* topics:

```
var condition = "'news' in topics && ('finance' in topics || 'politics' in
topics')";

admin.messaging().sendToCondition(condition, payload)
  .then(function(response) {
    console.log("Successfully sent message:", response);
  })
  .catch(function(error) {
    console.log("Error sending message:", error);
  });
```

When working with topic conditions, the conditional expressions are limited to two conditional statements.

27.16 Summary

This chapter has outlined and demonstrated the use of Node.js and the Firebase Admin Node.js SDK to send and manage Firebase cloud messages from a server environment. This involves the installation of the Node.js environment and Admin SDK configured with the appropriate Firebase account credentials. When an app is installed on a device it is assigned a registration token which uniquely identifies that combination of device and app. Using this token, messages can be targeted to specific devices from the server. Messages may also be targeted to devices where the app has subscribed to specific topics. As will be outlined in the next chapter, messages may also be sent to multiple devices through the use of device groups.

Chapter 28

28. Managing Firebase Cloud Messaging Device Groups with Node.js

Firebase cloud messaging device groups allow messages to be sent to groups of devices. While there are no restrictions on which devices can belong to a group, the feature is intended primarily for sending messages to multiple devices owned by the same user. Device groups may be created either on the server or within the client app. This chapter will introduce the concepts of creating, managing and sending messages to device groups on the server using Node.js before working through some practical examples. Working with device groups in a client Android app will be covered in the next chapter.

28.1 Understanding Device Groups

Device groups work by collecting the registration tokens for all of the app clients that are to be included and assigning this group a *notification key*. This key is then used when sending messages to the group in much the same way that messages are sent to topic subscribers. Once created, registration tokens may be added to or removed from the group as needed.

A device group can be created on the server (for example using Node.js) or within the client app. In both cases, the process essentially involves using HTTP to post a request to the Google cloud messaging servers containing information relating to the device group.

28.2 Requirements for Creating a Device Group

Before a device group can be created the following information will need to be gathered:

• Registration tokens for all device group members
• The cloud messaging server key for the Firebase project
• The cloud messaging sender ID for the Firebase project
• A notification key name for the device group

Both the cloud messaging server key and sender ID for the project are available within the Firebase console. Within the console, select the *Firebase Examples* project, click on the gear icon next to the Overview heading (Figure 28-1) and select the *Project settings* menu option:

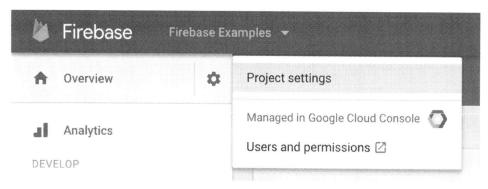

Figure 28-1

On the Settings screen, select the *Cloud Messaging* tab and locate the *Server key* and *Sender ID* fields in the Project credentials section as highlighted in Figure 28-2 below:

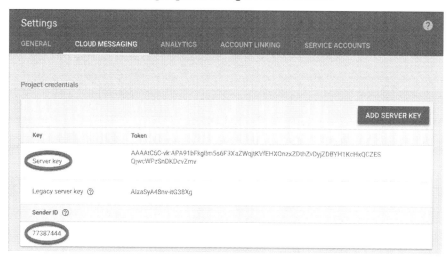

Figure 28-2

This information will be required later in this chapter so keep this page open in the browser window for convenience.

28.3 Creating a Device Group using HTTP

As previously mentioned, much of the interaction with the Firebase cloud messaging servers relating to device groups involves the use of HTTP post requests. The format for a request to create a new device group is as follows:

```
https://android.googleapis.com/gcm/notification
Content-Type:application/json
Authorization:key=<your server key here>
project_id:<your sender id here>

{
   "operation": "create",
```

```
    "notification_key_name": "<notification key name here>",
    "registration_ids": ["token 1", "token 2", "token 3", …]
}
```

The *notification_key_name* value can be any string value that uniquely identifies the group within the context of the Firebase project. Given that device groups are intended for targeting the devices owned by a single user this is often set to the user's email address.

28.4 **Creating a Device Group using Node.js**

To see device groups in action, begin by obtaining the registration IDs for two app/device instances by running the Messaging app (created in the chapter entitled *Integrating Firebase Cloud Messaging Support to an Android App*) on any combination of devices or emulator sessions. After the registration tokens have been recorded, place both apps in the background ready for message testing later in the chapter.

Next, change directory to the filesystem location containing the Node.js examples from the previous chapter. In order to post an HTTP request, the code is going to make use of the Node.js *request* module which will need to be installed using the following command:

```
npm install request --save
```

With the Node.js request module installed, create a new file named *group.js* and add the following code to it, substituting your sender ID and server ID where indicated and your email address for the notification name key. Also replace the token 1 and token 2 registration IDs with the two registration tokens obtained above:

```
var request = require('request');

var token1 = '<token one here>';
var token2 = '<token two here>';

var headers = {
    'Authorization': 'key=<your server key here>',
    'project_id': '<your sender id here>',
    'Content-Type':    'application/json'
        }

var options = {
    url: 'https://android.googleapis.com/gcm/notification',
    method: 'POST',
    headers: headers,
    json: {'operation': 'create',
            'notification_key_name': 'you@example.com',
            'registration_ids': ['token 1 here', 'token 2 here']}
}
```

```
request(options, function (error, response, body) {
                console.log(body)
})
```

The above code imports the *request* module and declares the header information for the HTTP post. Options are then defined indicating the URL of the Google cloud messaging server and that this is a POST request. Next, the previously declared headers are included and a set of key/value pairs declared as a JSON object.

Finally the *request()* method is called passing through the options and the response displayed to the console.

Review the code to make sure all of the IDs, keys and tokens are correct before running the code:

```
node group.js
```

Assuming the successful creation of the group, the response will contain the notification key for the group with output similar to the following:

```
{ notification_key: 'WPX91bFxpiCMFe5p6JjypsOSgXn2lCVHMrX5Q1d-fjYqFoHMMc-
DjE8S97GJiCsOlwODPGnckSGe_AQhhOViV5MF67Rodb9bNlCPmYt2UUi2-
vPmrwncYJs7NqdZE7DyuO3sZ0e_b98c' }
```

This is the key that will be used to send a message to the device group in the next section of this chapter, so be sure to keep a copy of it.

28.5 Sending a Message to a Device Group

To send a message from a server using Node.js, a call needs to be made to the *sendToDeviceGroup()* method of the Admin SDK, passing through both the notification key for the destination group and the message payload. To send a message to the newly created group, edit the *send.js* file and modify it to use the *sendToDeviceGroup()* method:

```
var admin = require("firebase-admin");

var serviceAccount = require("path/to/serviceAccountKey.json");

admin.initializeApp({
  credential: admin.credential.cert(serviceAccount),
  databaseURL: "<your database URL>"
});

var notificationKey = "<YOUR NOTIFICATION KEY HERE>";

var payload = {
  notification: {
    title: "NASDAQ News",
    body: "The NASDAQ climbs for the second day. Closes up 0.60%."
```

```
  }
};

admin.messaging().sendToDeviceGroup(notificationKey, payload)
  .then(function(response) {
    console.log("Successfully sent message:", response);
  })
  .catch(function(error) {
    console.log("Error sending message:", error);
  });
```

Make sure that both instances of the app launched earlier in the chapter are still running and in the background then run the *send.js* script as follows:

```
node send.js
```

Check the devices and/or emulators on which the apps are running and note that the notification has been delivered to both.

28.6 **Managing Device Group Members in Node.js**

Once a device group has been created, devices may be added or removed via HTTP POST requests. When the group was created, the *operation* value was set to *create*. To add one or more devices, send the same request, replacing *create* with *add*, including the notification key and referencing the registration tokens of the devices to be added:

```
.
.
    json: {'operation': 'add',
           'notification_key_name': 'you@example.com',
           'notification_key': '<notification key here>',
           'registration_ids': ['token 1 here', 'token 2 here']}
.
.
```

To remove devices from a group, repeat the above step, this time specifying *remove* as the operation value. When all devices have been deleted from a group, the group itself is also deleted.

28.7 **Summary**

Firebase Cloud Messaging device groups allow multiple devices to be grouped together and assigned a registration token. This token can then be used to send messages targeted only to those device/app combinations that are group members. Before a device group can be created, the Sender ID and Server ID for the project must be obtained from the Firebase console.

A device group may be created either on the server or from within the client app. This chapter has demonstrated the creation and targeting of device groups from a server using Node.js code.

29. Managing Firebase Messaging Device Groups from an Android App

Having covered server-side creation and management of device groups in the previous chapter, the next step is to explain how to perform the same operations from within a client app. Many of the concepts are largely the same in that the operations are performed using HTTP POST requests, though there are some additional steps and restrictions that need to be taken into consideration when taking this approach to device group management.

29.1 Managing Device Groups from a Client App

Working with Firebase device groups from within a client app is primarily a case of constructing appropriately configured HTTP POST requests and submitting them to the Firebase cloud server. In common with server-side implementation, the client app also makes use of the sender ID when creating and managing a device group. Unlike the server, however, the client app uses an *ID token* instead of the server key when posting device group requests. Obtaining an ID token is a multistep process which will be outlined in this chapter.

A key limitation of client-side device group management is that the user must be authenticated with a Google account within the app before the ID token can be obtained and any device group requests are posted. A further limitation is that the only notification name key permitted for the device group is the email address associated with the Google account.

29.2 Generating the Client ID

The first step toward getting the ID token is to create a client ID for the Firebase project in the Google Developer Console. To access the console, open a browser window and navigate to the following URL:

https://console.cloud.google.com

Sign into the console if necessary and, using the drop-down menu highlighted in Figure 29-1, make sure that *Firebase Examples* is the currently selected project. With the project loaded into the console, select the *API Manager -> Credentials* option from the left-hand navigation panel (also highlighted in Figure 29-1):

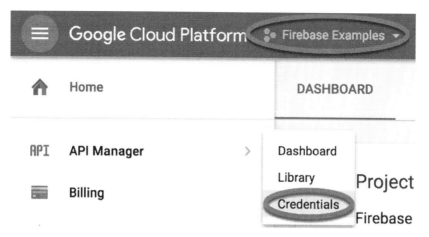

Figure 29-1

On the resulting credentials page, click on the *Create credentials* button and select the *OAuth client ID* option:

Credentials

Credentials   OAuth consent screen   Domain verification

Create credentials ▾   Delete

> API key
> Identifies your project using a simple API key to check quota and access   ition for details.
>
> OAuth client ID
> Requests user consent so your app can access the user's data
>
> Service account key   estriction
> Enables server-to-server, app-level authentication using robot accounts   lone
>
> Help me choose
> Asks a few questions to help you decide which type of credential to use   lone

Figure 29-2

On the next page, select the *Web application* option and name the credentials "Firebase Device Group Example". Although this ID is being used in an Android app, the web application option is selected here because the requests are still made using HTTP posts. Leave the remaining fields unchanged and click on the *Create* button.

A dialog will appear containing both the client ID and secret. This client ID may be copied now or located later within the list of OAuth Client IDs within the Credentials page of the developer console.

29.3 **Creating the Client App Project**

As already mentioned, the app must be authenticated with a Google account before any device group actions can be performed. Rather that repeat steps already taken in earlier chapters, this example will repurpose the GoogleAuth project created in the chapter entitled *Google Authentication using the Firebase SDK*. Locate this project on your filesystem if you have already completed the chapter, or download a copy along with the other book code examples from the following URL:

http://www.ebookfrenzy.com/print/firebase_android

Make a copy of the GoogleAuth project folder, name it *GoogleAuth_FCM* and then open the renamed project in Android Studio.

29.4 **Adding the Group Button**

Load the *activity_google_auth.xml* file into the layout editor, enable Autoconnect mode and add a new button view to the layout so that it is positioned against the bottom and left-hand margin lines as illustrated in Figure 29-3. Change the text on the Button to read "Create Group" and assign an onClick handler method named *createGroup()*:

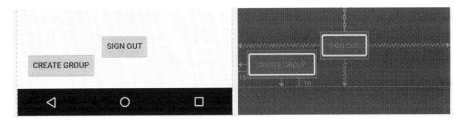

Figure 29-3

29.5 **Obtaining the ID Token**

Code now needs to be added to the main activity to obtain the ID token associated with the user's Google account. To obtain the ID token, the client ID generated above needs to be referenced when building the GoogleSignInOptions object that will be used during the authentication process. Within the *GoogleAuthActivity.java* file, locate the following code in the *onCreate()* method:

```
GoogleSignInOptions signInOptions = new
        GoogleSignInOptions.Builder(GoogleSignInOptions.DEFAULT_SIGN_IN)
        .requestIdToken(getString(R.string.default_web_client_id))
        .requestEmail()
        .requestProfile()
        .build();
```

Modify the *requestIdToken()* method call to pass through your client ID instead of the default web client ID used previously (note also the removal of the *getString()* method call):

```
.requestIdToken("<your project client id goes here>")
```

When the user successfully authenticates, the ID token will be available within the resulting Account object which is available within the *onActivityResult()* method. The Account object will also contain the email address for the user's Google account which must be used as the notification key name when creating the device group.

Add two new variables to the class and modify the *onActivityResult()* method to extract both the email address and ID token. Also import the Log package and declare a tag string so that diagnostic output can be included for testing purposes:

```
.
.
import android.util.Log;

.
.
private static final String TAG = "GoogleAuth";
private String idToken = null;
private String userEmail = null;

.
.
@Override
public void onActivityResult(int requestCode, int resultCode, Intent data) {
    super.onActivityResult(requestCode, resultCode, data);

    if (requestCode == RC_SIGN_IN) {
        GoogleSignInResult result =
            Auth.GoogleSignInApi.getSignInResultFromIntent(data);
        if (result.isSuccess()) {
            GoogleSignInAccount account = result.getSignInAccount();
            idToken = account.getIdToken();
            userEmail = account.getEmail();
            Log.i(TAG, "Token = " + idToken);
            Log.i(TAG, "Email = " + userEmail);
            authWithFirebase(account);
        } else {
            this.notifyUser("onActivityResult: failed");
        }
    }
}
```

Compile and run the app and sign in using a Google account. Refer to the logcat output in the Android Studio Android Monitor tool window and verify that both the idToken and email address values have been displayed. If the idToken variable is set to null, double check that the client ID was generated for the correct Firebase project and that it has been entered correctly into the code.

Tap the Sign Out button to sign out of the app before continuing.

29.6 Declaring the Sender ID

When the request is sent to the Google cloud messaging server, it will need to include the sender ID for the project. As outlined in the previous chapter, the sender ID for the project is available within the Firebase console. Within the console, select the *Firebase Examples* project, click on the gear icon next to the Overview heading and select the *Project settings* menu option.

On the Settings screen, select the *Cloud Messaging* tab and locate the *Sender ID* field in the Project credentials section. Copy the ID and include it when adding the following variable declaration beneath the *userEmail* variable added in the previous section:

```
private static final String sender_id = "<your sender id here>";
```

29.7 Creating an Asynchronous Task

The HTTP POST request to create the device group will be performed using the HttpURLConnection class. Since the amount of time required to complete this operation will depend on the speed of the internet connection of the device, it is generally recommended that such actions be performed outside of the main thread of the application. Running the operation on a separate thread will avoid the app locking up while awaiting a response from the server.

For this example, AsyncTask will be used to asynchronously communicate with the cloud messaging server. Within the *GoogleAuthActivity.java* file, begin the initial implementation of the AsyncTask class as follows:

```
public class CreateDeviceGroup extends AsyncTask<String, Void, String> {

    @Override
    protected String doInBackground(String... params) {
        return "Failed to create device group";
    }

    @Override
    protected void onPostExecute(String result) {
        Log.i(TAG, "Notification key: " + result);
    }
}
```

The *doInBackground()* method contains the code that will be executed asynchronously from the main thread and is configured to accept an array of String objects assigned to a variable named params. The *onPostExecute()* method, on the other hand, is called when the *doInBackground()* method returns and outputs the result (either the failure message or the notification key assigned to the new device group) to the logcat panel.

29.8 **Creating the Device Group**

The work to create the device group will be performed asynchronously by the *doInBackground()* method of the CreateDeviceGroup AsyncTask class. Implement the code within this method now as follows:

```
.
.
import org.json.JSONArray;
import org.json.JSONObject;

import java.io.InputStream;
import java.io.OutputStream;
import java.net.HttpURLConnection;
import java.net.URL;
import java.util.Arrays;
import java.util.Scanner;

.
.
public class CreateDeviceGroup extends AsyncTask<String, Void, String> {

@Override
protected String doInBackground(String... params) {

    try {

        URL url =
            new URL("https://android.googleapis.com/gcm/googlenotification");
        HttpURLConnection con = (HttpURLConnection) url.openConnection();
        con.setDoOutput(true);

        con.setRequestProperty("project_id", sender_id);
        con.setRequestProperty("Content-Type", "application/json");
        con.setRequestProperty("Accept", "application/json");
        con.setRequestMethod("POST");
        con.connect();

        JSONObject data = new JSONObject();
        data.put("operation", "add");
        data.put("notification_key_name", userEmail);
        data.put("registration_ids",
                new JSONArray(Arrays.asList(params)));
        data.put("id_token", idToken);
```

```
        OutputStream os = con.getOutputStream();
        os.write(data.toString().getBytes("UTF-8"));
        os.close();

        InputStream is = con.getInputStream();
        String responseString =
                new Scanner(is, "UTF-8").useDelimiter("\\A").next();
        is.close();

        JSONObject response = new JSONObject(responseString);
        return response.getString("notification_key");

    } catch (Exception e) {
        Log.i(TAG, "FAILED " + e);
    }
    return "Failed to create device group";
}
```

Before moving on to the next step, it is worth taking time to explain what is happening in the above method. First, much of the code in the method has the potential to throw an exception, hence the enclosure of the code in a try/catch structure:

```
try {
.
.
} catch (Exception e) {
    Log.i(TAG, "FAILED " + e);
}
```

The first task performed configures an HttpURLConnection object for connection to the Google cloud messaging server:

```
URL url = new URL("https://android.googleapis.com/gcm/googlenotification");
HttpURLConnection con = (HttpURLConnection) url.openConnection();
con.setDoOutput(true);
```

Once the connection has been configured, the header for the HTTP request is constructed. This consists of the sender ID, the content type (JSON) and a declaration that this is a POST request. The connection to the server is then established via a call to the *connect()* method of the HttpURLConnection object:

```
con.setRequestProperty("project_id", sender_id);
        con.setRequestProperty("Content-Type", "application/json");
        con.setRequestProperty("Accept", "application/json");
        con.setRequestMethod("POST");
        con.connect();
```

Next, the HTTP request JSON data is constructed as a JSON object consisting of key/value pairs using the format outlined in the previous chapter, including the *add* operation value, the notification key name (in this case the user's email address), and the array of device registration tokens that will be passed to the task when it is executed:

```
JSONObject data = new JSONObject();
        data.put("operation", "add");
        data.put("notification_key_name", userEmail);
        data.put("registration_ids",
                new JSONArray(Arrays.asList(params)));
        data.put("id_token", idToken);
```

After the JSON object has been initialized, the code obtains a reference to the output stream of the HttpURLConnection object and writes the JSON object to it before closing the stream:

```
OutputStream os = con.getOutputStream();
os.write(data.toString().getBytes("UTF-8"));
os.close();
```

After closing the output stream, the input stream of the HTTP connection is opened and used to read the response string from the Google cloud server. The response is converted into a JSON object, from which the value assigned to the notification key is extracted and returned:

```
InputStream is = con.getInputStream();
String responseString = new Scanner(is, "UTF-8").useDelimiter("\\A").next();
is.close();

JSONObject response = new JSONObject(responseString);
return response.getString("notification_key");
```

When the method returns, the *onPostExecute()* method is called and passed the response string.

29.9 Executing the AsyncTask

All that remains is to create an instance of the AsyncTask and execute it, passing through an array containing the registration tokens of the devices to be included in the group.

When the user interface layout was modified earlier in the chapter, the Create Group button was configured to call a method named *createGroup()* when clicked. Edit the *GoogleAuthActivity.java* file and add this method, substituting registration tokens where appropriate (for convenience, consider using those from the previous chapter since these devices are already configured to run the example Messaging app):

```
public void createGroup(View view) {

    String token1 = "<registration token one here>";
    String token2 = "<registration token two here>";
```

```
   CreateDeviceGroup task = new CreateDeviceGroup();
   task.execute(new String[] { token1, token2 });
}
```

29.10 Testing the App

Compile and run the app and, if the user is already signed into a Google account, sign out and then back in again (as implemented in this example, the ID token is only obtained during the sign-in process). Check the logcat output to ensure that the userEmail and idToken variables are initialized, then click on the Create Group button. If the group has been successfully created, the notification key will appear in the logcat output.

Copy the notification key, edit the *send.js* file created in the previous chapter and replace the previous key with the new one.

Make sure that the example Messaging app is running and placed in the background on the two devices from which the registration tokens were taken and then run the *send.js* script as follows:

```
node send.js
```

Once the message has been sent, it should appear within the status bar of both devices, the Node.js output should read as follows:

```
Successfully sent message: { successCount: 2,
  failureCount: 0,
  failedRegistrationTokens: [] }
```

Edit the *remove.js* file, and replace the existing notification key with the new key before running the script to remove the device group from the server.

29.11 Removing Devices from a Device Group

If devices need to be removed from a device group from the client app, an HTTP Post request similar to that created for creating a device group may be used. The only section of the *doInBackground()* method that would need to be changed is the code responsible for constructing the JSON object. In order to perform the deletion, the request must contain the *remove* operation value, the notification key name (in other words the user's email address), the registration tokens of the devices to be removed and the ID token:

```
JSONObject data = new JSONObject();
data.put("operation", "remove");
data.put("notification_key_name", userEmail);
data.put("registration_ids", new JSONArray(Arrays.asList(params)));
data.put("id_token", idToken);
```

29.12 Summary

In addition to creating and managing device groups from the server, many of these tasks may also be performed from the client app. As with the server, the client app uses HTTP POST requests to perform device group operations such as creating a group and adding and removing devices. Device group management features are only available within apps where the user has authenticated using a Google account. This account is used to obtain an ID token which is used to authenticate the client when sending the HTTP requests. Unlike server side device group management, the notification key name can only be set to the email address associated with the user's Google account.

30. Firebase Cloud Upstream Messaging

Up until this point, all of the chapters covering Firebase Cloud Messaging have focused on so called downstream messaging (in other words the transmission of messages from either the Firebase console or a server to device-based client apps). Starting with this chapter, the concept of upstream messaging will be covered in detail. As the name suggests, upstream messaging involves sending a message from the app client. The reason for sending upstream messages depends on the requirements of the specific app, but can be used as a way either for a client app to communicate with the server, or for sending messages between clients.

This chapter will provide a relatively high level overview of upstream messaging in terms of the architecture, data formats and API calls. Subsequent chapters will present a functional client-to-client upstream messaging example including both client and server implementations.

30.1 Firebase Cloud Upstream Messaging Architecture

The preceding chapters have covered the concept of sending downstream messages to a device-based client app, using either the Firebase console, or a Node.js based server to send messages to the client. The situation changes considerably when upstream messaging is introduced. The diagram illustrated in Figure 30-1 outlines the basic architecture necessary to implement upstream messaging using Firebase Cloud Messaging:

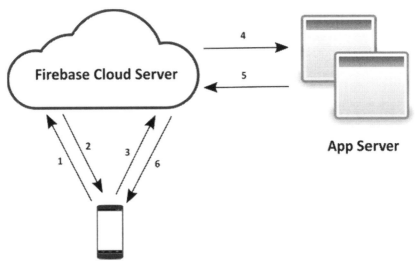

Figure 30-1

Upstream messaging involves client apps, the Firebase Cloud Connection Server (CCS) and an application server. The sequence of events that occur when sending upstream messages can be broken down as follows (where the step numbers correlate to the arrows in the above architecture diagram):

1. The client app registers itself via the Firebase Cloud Messaging API using the same approach as that outlined in previous chapters.
2. Firebase provides the client app with a registration token that uniquely identifies that device/app combination within the Firebase messaging environment.
3. The client app sends an upstream message to the Firebase CCS. In addition to any message the payload also includes, by default, the registration token.
4. The Firebase CCS sends the request to the app server. The app server sends an acknowledgement to the CCS on receipt of the message and implements application specific logic to interpret the message and take appropriate action.
5. If the action involves the transmission of a message (for example sending a response to the original device or passing a message to a different device), this is sent from the app server to the CCS.
6. The CCS delivers the message to the client app on the device.

In this scenario, all communication between the clients and the app server is handled entirely by the CCS. This has the advantage that issues such as message delivery, error handling and message retries are all performed automatically and do not need to be addressed in either the client or app server code. From the point of view of the client, the transmission of an upstream message can be achieved with a single API call.

The connection between the CCS and the app server is a permanent connection and the app server must acknowledge (ACK) every message received from the CCS. In the absence of an acknowledgement, the CCS will assume that the app server is offline and will continue to resend the message until an acknowledgement is received. Similarly, the CCS will send acknowledgements in response to any messages received from the app server. In the event that the data received is in any way invalid, the CCS will typically respond with a negative-acknowledgement (NACK) indicating the nature of the problem.

The CCS and app server communicate with each other using the Extensible Messaging and Presence Protocol (XMPP). XMPP (originally named Jabber) is a protocol designed specifically as a foundation on which to build instant messaging services and allows for the exchange of structured data in near real-time over network connections. XMPP is an open standard and a range of open source libraries and frameworks exist to ease the implementation of XMPP-based communication.

When the app server first starts up, it is responsible for establishing the connection to the CCS. During this connection process, the app server uses the Firebase project server key and sender ID used in previous examples to authenticate with the Firebase messaging system. Once authenticated and connected, the app server simply waits to process incoming messages.

30.2 **Implementing the App Server**

As long as it is able to engage in a meaningful XMPP-based dialog with the CCS, the app server can be written using just about any programming language. Most programming languages have more than one open source library available for handling the XMPP communication protocol from which to choose.

The app server can also run on just about any platform, ranging from a simple Java program running on just about any operating system, to a vast enterprise system running on a cloud-based server farm.

The logic within the app server is, of course, entirely dependent on the requirements of the client app. That being said, a typical app server will need to be able to interpret the content of incoming message packets and respond appropriately with outbound messages. It will also be a common requirement for the app server to maintain some form of database that maps user identities (such as usernames or email addresses) to device registration tokens. It is unlikely, for example, that the user of a chat app will know the 174-digit registration token of a friend's device when sending a message. The app server will, therefore, need to be able to extract the registration token associated with the friend's username from a database in order to be able to deliver the message.

30.3 **Sending an Upstream Message from the Client**

Once a client has registered and received a registration token, an upstream message is sent via a call to the *send()* method of the FirebaseMessaging object instance. The message is encapsulated within a Google Play services library RemoteMessage class instance. For convenience, RemoteMessage.Builder may be used when constructing the message.

In addition to a message payload consisting of key/value pairs, the message must also contain a unique message ID and a string that reads @gcm.googleapis.com prefixed with the sender ID associated with the Firebase project. The unique message ID takes the form of a string and can be any sequence of characters that uniquely identifies the message within the Firebase project.

The following code fragment demonstrates the use of RemoteMessage.Builder to create and send an upstream message from within an Android app:

```
FirebaseMessaging fm = FirebaseMessaging.getInstance();

fm.send(new RemoteMessage.Builder(SenderID + "@gcm.googleapis.com")
        .setMessageId(getMsgId())
        .addData("key1", "a value")
        .addData("key2", "another value")
        .build());
```

In addition to the *setMessageId()* and *addData()* methods, the *setTtl()* method may be used to specify the amount of time that the message should be queued if the device is not currently connected. This can be set to any duration up to four weeks (2419200 seconds). If this value is not specified the default is four weeks. If, on the other hand, the time to live value is set to 0 the message is discarded after the first attempt.

Similarly, the *setCollapseKey()* method may be used to identify a group of messages where only the most recent message is sent if multiple messages with the same key are waiting to be sent.

Once the message is sent it will arrive at the CCS where it will be passed to the app server. Any downstream messages sent to the client app will need to be handled within the *onMessageReceived()* method of the FirebaseMessagingService subclass as documented in the chapter entitled *Firebase Cloud Messaging*.

If the *onMessageSent()* and *onMessageError()* callback methods are also overridden in the FirebaseMessagingService subclass, these will be called to notify the app of the status of the message transmission:

```
@Override
public void onMessageSent(String msgID) {
    Log.d(TAG, "onMessageSent: " + msgID );
}

@Override
public void onSendError(String msgID, Exception exception) {
    Log.d(TAG, "onSendError: " + exception.getMessage() );
}
```

30.4 **Summary**

An upstream message is a message that originates on the client app and is passed up through to the Firebase messaging cloud. Upstream messaging requires the presence of an app server connected directly to the Firebase Cloud Connection Server (CCS) using the XMPP protocol. The CCS passes upstream messages to the app server where the data is processed and appropriate actions taken. Any downstream messages sent by the app server are transmitted via the CCS.

31. A Firebase Cloud Messaging Upstream XMPP App Server

Having established the importance of the role that an app server plays when working with upstream Firebase Cloud messages, it is now time to take a look at an example server. The server outlined in this chapter will be used in the next chapter in the implementation of a simple instant messaging app designed to allow users to exchange messages.

This chapter will explain how to load the app server project into Android Studio before providing a guided tour of the key elements of the code that enable the server to communicate with the Firebase Cloud Connection Server (CCS) and to receive and send messages.

31.1 About the FCM App Server Project

The app server covered in this project is written in Java and is based on code examples provided by Google for the Google Cloud Messaging service (the precursor to Firebase Cloud Messaging). The code examples were used by Wolfram Rittmeyer as the basis for a simple app server which was subsequently updated for Firebase Cloud Messaging by Nimrod Dayan. For the purposes of this book, the server has been further modified to include persistent storage of user identities and registration IDs and to support the sending of messages between devices.

The project code is contained within the *fcm-app-server* folder of the sample code download that accompanies this book which may be downloaded from the following URL:

http://www.ebookfrenzy.com/print/firebase_android

Launch Android Studio, select the Open an Existing Android Studio Project option and locate and open the *fcm-app-server* project.

31.2 Project Dependencies

As previously mentioned, the app server is written entirely in Java. The server code also makes use of the following open source libraries which can be found listed under the libs folder in the Android Studio project tool window:

- **Smack** – Smack is an open source Java library providing an API for communicating with XMPP servers. This API is used to communicate between the app server and the CCS.
- **Smackx** – The Smack Extensions library. Although the app server code does not make direct use of this library, it is a requirement for the main Smack library.

- **Moshi** – JSON library for Android and Java. This library is used by the app server to parse JSON to and from Java objects. The app server implements custom Moshi-based type adaptors to work with both upstream and downstream messages.
- **Okio** – A library used to process input and output data. While it is not used directly by the app server it is a requirement for other libraries.
- **XML Pull** – Used by the Smack library to parse streaming XML.

31.3 CcsClient.java

The CcsClient class implements a simple client for communicating with the Firebase CCS. It is responsible for reading the configuration settings from a property file, establishing the connection to the CCS using the Smack API and then handling incoming messages. The class also includes a send method which takes as an argument a JSON request and sends it to the CCS.

The key methods of the class are as follows:

- **main()** – The entry point into the app server when it is started from the command-line. This method reads server key and sender ID values from a properties file and initiates the connection to the CCS.
- **connect()** – Called by the *main()* method to establish the CCS connection. Once the connection has been established, the method also adds a listener to the connection to report the loss of a connection and attempt to reconnect. The method also adds a packet listener to detect the arrival of new messages from the CCS. This listener converts the incoming packet to JSON and passes it to the *handleMessage()* method.
- **handleMessage()** – This method examines the incoming JSON message and identifies the message type. If the message is an ACK or NACK from the CCS output is sent to the logger identifying the corresponding message ID. If the message is determined to be an upstream message from a client app, an ACK message is sent to the CCS and the message passed to the *handleIncomingDataMessage()* method.
- **handleIncomingDataMessage()** – This app server is designed to handle two types of upstream message. A registration message contains the registration ID from the client and the email address of the user. These need to be stored for reference later when sending messages to specific users. The second message type contains the email address of a recipient and the message to be sent to that user. The task of determining how the message is to be treated is handled by the *getProcessor()* method of the ProcessorFactory class.

31.4 PayloadProcessor.java

The PayloadProcessor class is responsible for deciding which type of processor is needed to handle an upstream message. When upstream messages are sent from the client app, the data payload contains an action key set to a value of either "REGISTER" or "MESSAGE". The CcsClient *handleIncomingDataMessage()* method extracts the value assigned to the action key and passes it to the *getProcessor()* method a PayloadProcessor object which, in turn, returns an instance of either the PayloadProcessor or RegisterProcessor class to handle the message.

31.5 **RegisterProcessor.java**

When the client app is launched it sends a registration type upstream message containing the user's email address. By default an upstream message also contains the app's registration token. The RegisterProcessor *handleMessage()* method uses an instance of the AccountStore class to store this data in a HashMap which is saved to a file.

31.6 **AccountStore.java**

A rudimentary storage class designed to store user email and registration token data as properties in a data file:

- **readFile()** – Checks whether or not the properties file exists. If it exists, the data is read into a HashMap.
- **addRegistration()** – Called when a client sends a registration upstream message. The email address and corresponding registration token are added to the HashMap and the *writeFile()* method called.
- **writeFile()** – Converts the HashMap to a Properties object and writes it to the properties file.
- **getRegistrationIdForAccount()** – When passed an email address, this method returns the corresponding registration token.
- **getUniqueMessageId()** – Returns a string based on a random long number to act as a message ID when sending outbound messages.

31.7 **MessageProcessor.java**

When the client app sends an upstream message containing a message to be sent to another user, the *handleMessage()* method of this class is called. This method extracts the email address of the destination user from the message payload and uses it to obtain the corresponding registration token from the account store together with a unique message ID. A JSON message is then constructed and the *send()* method of the CcsClient instance called to send it to the CCS for delivery to the recipient's device.

31.8 **Building and Running the Server**

The server can be built and run on any system that supports Java and has access to the internet via port 5236. In this example, the server can be executed from within the Android Studio environment and the log output viewed within the Run tool window. Before starting the server, however, the *fcm-app-server.properties* file needs to be configured with the server key and sender ID associated with the *Firebase Examples* project.

As previously outlined, both the cloud messaging server key and sender ID for the project are available within the Firebase console. Within the console, select the *Firebase Examples* project, click on the gear icon next to the Overview heading and select the *Project settings* menu option. On the Settings screen, select the *Cloud Messaging* tab and locate the *Server key* and *Sender ID* fields in the Project credentials section.

Edit the *fcm-app-server.properties* file which is located in the top level directory of the *fcm-app-server* project folder and enter the credentials into the appropriate fields.

Build the project by selecting the *Build -> Make Module 'fcm-app-server'* menu option. If the menu provides two options to build the module, be sure to select the second one as highlighted in Figure 31-1:

Figure 31-1

After the server has built, click on the toolbar run button to start the server. Refer to the Run tool window and verify that the server has started without any errors:

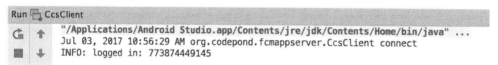

Figure 31-2

Assuming that no errors occurred, the server is now connected to the CCS and is listening for incoming messages.

The Smack library also includes a debugging user interface window (Figure 31-3) that displays all of the packets sent and received over the XMPP connection.

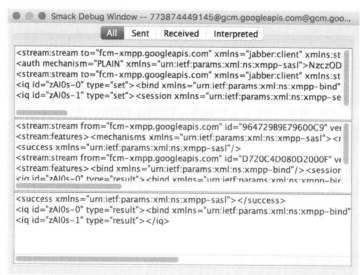

Figure 31-3

By default, the window shows three panels listing sent, received and interpreted packets (the latter being messages that have been parsed by the Smack library as opposed to raw messages passed directly to the server). Tabs along the top of the window can be used to focus solely on one category of packet. At this point the interpreted panel should show the successful authentication of the app server with the CCS. If an error occurred (such as an invalid server key), the panel will include details of the failure.

The debug window is useful for monitoring the packets travelling between the CCS and app server, both to aid in resolving problems and as a way to learn how the XMPP protocol works. To disable the debug window (an important step if the app server is to be run on a headless server), edit the *CcsClient.java* file and modify the following variable declaration so that it reads as follows:

```
private boolean mDebuggable = false;
```

With the app server now running, the next step is to develop a client app so that it can be put to use.

31.9 Summary

Upstream Firebase cloud messaging requires the presence of an app server continuously connected to the Firebase CCS. The app server contains the logic that defines what happens when upstream messages are sent from client devices. This chapter has outlined the structure and basic logic of a simple app server that will be used in the next chapter to implement an example instant messaging app.

32. An Example Firebase Upstream Cloud Messaging Client App

With the app server running and communicating with the Firebase CCS, the next step is to build a client Android app that will make use of upstream messaging and the features built into the app server.

The purpose of the app created in this chapter is to allow users to send instant messages to each other.

32.1 Creating the Project

Launch Android Studio and select the *Start a new Android Studio project* quick start option from the welcome screen.

Within the new project dialog, enter *UpstreamDemo* into the Application name field and your domain as the Company Domain setting before clicking on the *Next* button.

On the form factors screen, enable the *Phone and Tablet* option and set the minimum SDK to API 16: Android 4.1 (Jellybean). Proceed through the screens, requesting the creation of an Empty Activity named *UpstreamDemoActivity* with a corresponding layout named *activity_upstream_demo*.

32.2 Adding Firebase Messaging Support to the Project

Select the *Tools -> Firebase* menu option and click on the Cloud Messaging entry in the Firebase assistant panel. Once selected, click on the *Set up Firebase Cloud Messaging* link. In the next panel, connect the project to Firebase using the provided connection button and select the *Firebase Examples* project from the list of existing projects. Once the project has been connected, click on the *Add FCM to your app* button.

A dialog will appear listing the changes that will be made to the project build files to add cloud messaging support to the project. Review these changes before clicking on the *Accept Changes* button.

32.3 Designing the User Interface

Select the *activity_upstream_demo.xml* user interface layout file, load it into the layout editor and delete the default "Hello World" TextView object.

Turn off Autoconnect mode and, from the Text category of the palette, drag a Plain EditText object and drop it so that it is positioned near the top of the layout and centered horizontally. With the object selected, use the Properties panel to delete the default "Name" string from the *text* property, enter text which reads "Your username" into the *hint* property field and change the ID to *usernameText*. Drag and drop a Button widget so that it is positioned beneath the username EditText object. Change the text property to read "Register", specify an onClick method of *registerUser* and change the ID property to *registerButton*.

Add two more EditText widgets and a Button so that they are centered horizontally and positioned beneath the Register button as illustrated in Figure 32-1 below:

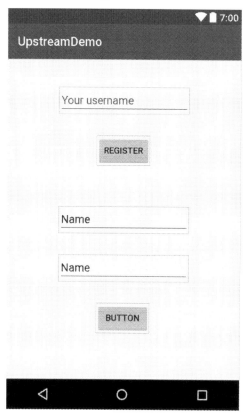

Figure 32-1

Delete the "Name" text from both EditText views and change the hint properties to read "To username" and "Message text" respectively. Change the text on the button to read "Send" and configure an onClick method named *sendMessage*. Change the IDs of the two EditText widgets to *recipientText* and *messageText*.

Either shift-click on each widget, or click and drag on the layout canvas to select all six widgets. Right-click on the top widget and select the *Center Horizontally* menu option to add horizontal constraints to all of the widgets. Select all of the widgets once again, and repeat this step, this time selecting the *Center Vertically* menu option.

On completion of these steps, the layout should match that of Figure 32-2:

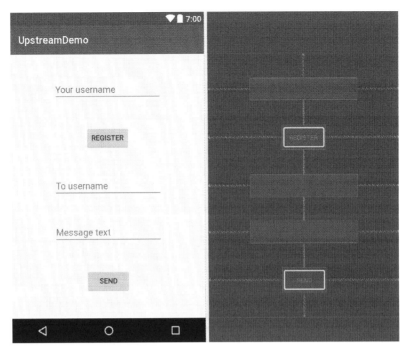

Figure 32-2

32.4 **Obtaining the Registration Token**

Revisiting the techniques covered in the chapter entitled *Integrating Firebase Cloud Messaging Support to an Android App*, add a new FirebaseInstanceIdService subclass to the project by right-clicking on the *app -> java -> <package name>* entry in the project tool window and selecting the *New -> Java Class...* menu option. In the New Java Class dialog, enter *FirebaseIDService* into the Class Name field and select the FirebaseInstanceIdService class as the superclass before clicking on the OK button.

Edit the newly created *FirebaseIDService.java* file and modify it so that it reads as follows:

```
.
.
import com.google.firebase.iid.FirebaseInstanceId;
import com.google.firebase.iid.FirebaseInstanceIdService;

import android.util.Log;

public class FirebaseIDService extends FirebaseInstanceIdService {

    private static final String TAG = "FirebaseIDService";

    @Override
    public void onTokenRefresh() {
```

```
            String token = FirebaseInstanceId.getInstance().getToken();
            Log.d(TAG, "Registration Token: = " + token);

            sendRegistrationToServer(token);
    }

    private void sendRegistrationToServer(String token) {

    }
}
```

Now that the service has been added to the project, it needs to be declared within the project manifest file so that it will be triggered in the event of a change to the token. Within the project tool window, locate the *AndroidManifest.xml* file, load it into the editor and add the service entry:

```
<?xml version="1.0" encoding="utf-8"?>
<manifest xmlns:android="http://schemas.android.com/apk/res/android"
    package="com.ebookfrenzy.messaging">

    <application
        android:allowBackup="true"
        android:icon="@mipmap/ic_launcher"
        android:label="@string/app_name"
        android:roundIcon="@mipmap/ic_launcher_round"
        android:supportsRtl="true"
        android:theme="@style/AppTheme">
        <activity android:name=".MessagingActivity">
            <intent-filter>
                <action android:name="android.intent.action.MAIN" />

                <category android:name="android.intent.category.LAUNCHER" />
            </intent-filter>
        </activity>

        <service
            android:name=".FirebaseIDService">
            <intent-filter>
                <action
                    android:name="com.google.firebase.INSTANCE_ID_EVENT"/>
            </intent-filter>
        </service>
    </application>
</manifest>
```

With the code and manifest changes completed, compile and run the app on a device or emulator and review the output in the logcat panel of the Android Monitor tool window to locate the registration token string. The output will resemble the following (though the token will, of course, be different):

```
Registration Token: =
cxpKdykhQeY:APA91bEl3LnBTnEzaWTUoW7aGARytp2KeOMuE_1Z496msWhQ5EjRRH75WYFO4Fwq91
Dp7_KGcK8B9mnwAJ2E2sF5QcoXTl5eQ7PCspfYkHSgWlEFQr91t2PxXMwgOyGdPQlFPa65dCIu
```

32.5 Handling Incoming Messages

Clearly, the app will need a FirebaseMessagingService service to handle downstream messages arriving from the app server. Add a new service to the project for this purpose by right-clicking on the *app -> java -> <package name>* entry in the project tool window and selecting the *New -> Java Class...* menu option. In the New Class dialog, enter *FirebaseMsgService* into the Class Name field and select the FirebaseMessagingService class as the superclass before clicking on the OK button.

Edit the newly created *FirebaseMsgService.java* file and modify it so that it reads as follows:

```java
.
.
import android.content.Context;
import android.os.Handler;
import android.os.Looper;
import android.widget.Toast;

import com.google.firebase.messaging.FirebaseMessagingService;
import com.google.firebase.messaging.RemoteMessage;

public class FirebaseMsgService extends FirebaseMessagingService {

    private static final String TAG = "FirebaseMsgService";

    public FirebaseMsgService() {
    }

    @Override
    public void onMessageReceived(RemoteMessage remoteMessage) {

        if (remoteMessage.getData().size() > 0) {
            final String message = remoteMessage.getData().get("message");
            showMessage(message);
        }
    }

    public void showMessage(final String message)
    {
```

```
        final Context context = this;
        new Handler(Looper.getMainLooper()).post(new Runnable() {
          @Override public void run() {
              Toast toast = Toast.makeText(context, message,
                            Toast.LENGTH_LONG);
              toast.show();
          }
        });
    };
}
```

When the *onMessageReceived()* method is called, it is passed as an argument a RemoteMessage object containing the details of a Firebase cloud message. The only kind of message the client app expects to receive contains message text from another user. This value is contained within the data payload assigned to the "message" key. The code in the *onMessageReceived()* method verifies that the payload contains data, extracts the message text and then passes it to a method named *showMessage()* which displays the message text in a Toast popup. Since displaying a toast message is a UI operation and this service is not running on the main UI thread a reference to the main UI thread is obtained and the Toast message displayed using that thread.

The final task before testing the code is to add an entry within the *AndroidManifest.xml* file for the service:

```
<service android:name=".FirebaseMsgService">
    <intent-filter>
        <action android:name="com.google.firebase.MESSAGING_EVENT"/>
    </intent-filter>
</service>
```

32.6 Registering the User

When the user enters a username and clicks the Register button, an upstream message needs to be sent to the app server containing a key-value pair consisting of the REGISTER action and the username string.

When the user interface was designed, the onClick method of the Register button was configured to call a method named *registerUser()*. Edit the *UpstreamDemoActivity.java* file to add a variable containing the Sender ID for your project, a method to generate a random string to act as the message ID and to implement the *registerUser()* method:

```
.

.

import android.view.View;
import android.widget.EditText;


import com.google.firebase.iid.FirebaseInstanceId;
import com.google.firebase.messaging.FirebaseMessaging;
```

```
import com.google.firebase.messaging.RemoteMessage;

import java.util.Random;

public class UpstreamDemoActivity extends AppCompatActivity {

    static final String SenderID = "<your sender id here>";

    .
    .

    public void registerUser(View view) {

        EditText username = (EditText) findViewById(R.id.usernameText);

        FirebaseMessaging fm = FirebaseMessaging.getInstance();
        fm.send(new RemoteMessage.Builder(SenderID + "@gcm.googleapis.com")
                .setMessageId(getRandomMessageId())
                .addData("action", "REGISTER")
                .addData("account", username.getText().toString())
                .build());
    }

    static Random random = new Random();

    public String getRandomMessageId() {
        return "m-" + Long.toString(random.nextLong());
    }
}
```

32.7 Sending the Upstream Message

The final task before testing can commence is to add the *sendMessage()* method to the *UpstreamDemoActivity.java* file. This method needs to extract the username of the recipient and the message text from the EditText views in the user interface layout and then include them in a message configured for the MESSAGE action type. Add this method now so that it reads as follows:

```
public void sendMessage(View view) {
    EditText recipient = (EditText) findViewById(R.id.recipientText);
    EditText message = (EditText) findViewById(R.id.messageText);

    FirebaseMessaging fm = FirebaseMessaging.getInstance();
    fm.send(new RemoteMessage.Builder(SenderID + "@gcm.googleapis.com")
            .setMessageId(getRandomMessageId())
            .addData("action", "MESSAGE")
            .addData("recipient", recipient.getText().toString())
            .addData("message", message.getText().toString())
```

```
                    .build());
}
```

32.8 **Testing the Upstream Project**

Begin the testing phase by starting the fcm-app-server server and making sure than no errors are displayed in the Run tool window. Also refer to the Smack Debug window and make sure that the interpreted packets panel shows a successful authentication between the app server and the CCS.

Build and run the UpstreamDemo client so that it is running on two different devices (or a suitable combination of devices and emulator sessions).

With the Smack debug window and the Android Studio Run tool window for the fcm-app-server project visible, enter a user name and tap the Register button on one of the app instances. As soon as the button is clicked, both the debug and run tool windows should update to show the effect of the upstream message transmission.

Repeat the above step on the second instance of the app, this time entering a different user name before tapping the Register button.

Using a text editor, open the *account.properties* file located in the top level directory of the fcm-app-server project and verify that entries for both user names are present and associated with registration tokens.

All being well, select one of the app instances, enter the username registered on the other device into the recipient field and some text into the message field. Click on the Send button and verify that the message appears on the other device in the form of a Toast message. Check the Smack Debug window and review the packets that were sent and received during the message transaction to gain an understanding of the protocol.

Repeat this step, this time sending a message from the second app instance using the username associated with the first instance.

If the messages fail to arrive, check both the Smack Debug window and fcm-app-server Android Studio Run tool window for errors and exceptions. Also check that you have access to port 5236 through your firewall. Problems may also occur if you are behind a proxy server.

32.9 **Summary**

This chapter has worked through the implementation of upstream messaging from an Android client app using the CCS and the example app server described in the previous chapter. Once completed, the client app was able to register a user via the app server, associating a user name to a registration token. Once two or more users are registered, text messages can be send between devices.

Chapter 33

33. Firebase Cloud Storage

Firebase Cloud Storage provides a secure and reliable way for client apps to store and retrieve files located on the Google Cloud Storage servers using just a few lines of code. This chapter will introduce Firebase Cloud Storage covering storage references, metadata and the uploading and downloading of files. Security of the stored files will be the topic of the next chapter.

33.1 An Overview of Firebase Cloud Storage

Firebase Cloud Storage allows files of any type to be stored using the Google Cloud Storage platform. Uploaded files are contained within Google Cloud Storage *buckets*. These storage buckets are also available to servers running within the Google Cloud ecosystem, providing the option to process the uploaded files via a server backend. By default the files for a client will be stored in a single bucket, though it is also possible to use multiple buckets.

Behind the scenes, Firebase automatically handles all aspects of the transfer process, including retrying and resuming in the event of a loss of connectivity. In addition to the files themselves, Firebase also provides support for custom metadata to be stored along with the files.

Security is implemented using a set of rules that are declared for the Firebase project in conjunction with Firebase Authentication. This ensures that the only users granted access to stored files are those who have been authorized to do so. The topic of cloud storage security rules is covered in the next chapter entitled *A Guide to Firebase Cloud Storage Security Rules*.

Just like any other operating system filesystem, cloud-based files are stored using a hierarchical structure of *nodes*. These nodes equate to the files, directories and sub-directories of a traditional filesystem and are accessed using *storage references*.

33.2 Storage References

Files are accessed from within a client app using a storage reference. Storage references are instances of the StorageReference class and are obtained by calling the *getReference()* method of the FirebaseStorage instance:

```
StorageReference storageRef = FirebaseStorage.getInstance().getReference();
```

By default, a newly obtained storage reference instance points to the root node of the project's default storage bucket (/). The *child()* method of the reference object is used to navigate deeper into the storage node hierarchy. The following code, for example, configures a reference to point to the /images/photos node of the storage bucket:

```
photoRef = storageRef.child("/images/photos");
```

A storage reference may also be configured to reference a specific file:

```
photoRef = storageRef.child("/images/photos/myPhoto.png");
```

In addition to the *child()* method, navigation is also possible using the *getParent()* and *getRoot()* methods of the storage reference instance. As the names suggest, the *getRoot()* method navigates to the top level of the storage node hierarchy, while the *getParent()* method returns the parent of the current node. Assuming a storage reference pointing at /images/photos, the following code would navigate to the /images/drawings node:

```
photoRef = storageRef.child("/images/photos");

StorageReference secondRef =
                photoRef.getParent().child("drawings");
```

When working with the *getParent()* method, it is important to be aware that a filename in a path counts as a node level (referred to as the *name node*) when navigating in this way. Had the original reference been pointing to /images/photos/myPhoto.png, for example, it would have been necessary to call the *getParent()* method twice to navigate back as far as the /images node:

```
photoRef = storageRef.child("/images/photos/myPhoto.png");

StorageReference secondRef =
                photoRef.getParent().getParent().child("drawings");
```

Though a client app may create as many storage reference objects as required, an existing storage reference may be reused as many times as needed. Once created and configured, references are used to upload, download, delete and update files stored using Firebase Cloud Storage. A range of methods is also available for obtaining information about a storage reference.

33.3 **Storage Reference Properties**

The StorageReference class includes three additional methods that provide access to the properties of a reference. The *getBucket()* method returns the bucket within which the reference is pointing. This is returned as a string and will typically read as follows:

```
<firebase-project-id>.appspot.com
```

The *getPath()* method returns a string containing the full path to which the reference is pointing, for example:

```
/images/drawings/houseplans.svg
```

Finally, the *getName()* method returns the last component of the path. Assuming the above path, the method would return the filename as follows:

```
houseplans.svg
```

If the final component of the path is not a filename, the name of the last node is returned instead (in the case of the above example this would return *drawings*).

33.4 **Uploading a File to Firebase Cloud Storage**

Firebase Cloud Storage provides three ways in which a file may be uploaded. The most basic involves the upload of an existing file located on the local device storage. To achieve this, the *putFile()* method of the storage reference instance is called, passing through as an argument the Uri of the file to be uploaded, for example:

```
Uri fileUri = Uri.fromFile(new File("/path/to/local/file"));

photoRef = storageRef.child("/images/photos/myPhoto.png");

UploadTask uploadTask = photoRef.putFile(fileUri);
```

When executed, the above code will upload the local file to the project's cloud storage bucket and store it as myPhoto.png in the /images/photos node.

33.5 **Uploading a File as a Stream**

An alternative upload option involves uploading the content of a file as an input stream. This involves the use of the *putStream()* method of the storage reference which also returns an UploadTask object:

```
InputStream stream = new FileInputStream(new File("/path/to/local/file"));

photoRef = storageRef.child("/images/photos/myPhoto.png");

UploadTask uploadTask = photoRef.putStream(stream);
```

33.6 **Uploading a File From Memory Data**

If the data to be contained in the file is currently stored in device memory, the *putBytes()* method of the storage reference will upload that data to a file in the cloud storage bucket. The *putBytes()* method takes as an argument a *byte* array (byte[]).

The most likely use for this approach will be to upload an image that is currently residing in memory, perhaps within an ImageView object in a user interface. This image can be extracted from the ImageView object as a bitmap and then converted via byte stream to a byte array suitable for uploading to a cloud storage file:

```
imageView.setDrawingCacheEnabled(true);
imageView.buildDrawingCache();
Bitmap bmap = imageView.getDrawingCache();
ByteArrayOutputStream stream = new ByteArrayOutputStream();
bmap.compress(Bitmap.CompressFormat.JPEG, 100, stream);
byte[] uploadData = stream.toByteArray();
photoRef = storageRef.child("/images/photos/myPhoto.png");
UploadTask uploadTask = photoRef.putBytes(data);
```

33.7 **Monitoring and Managing the Upload**

When called, the *putFile()* method begins the upload process in the background and returns an UploadTask instance which can be used to monitor and manage the upload progress. The success or otherwise of the upload can be monitored by adding onSuccess and onFailure listeners to the UploadTask instance with corresponding callback methods as follows:

```
uploadTask.addOnFailureListener(new OnFailureListener() {
    @Override
    public void onFailure(@NonNull Exception exception) {
        // Upload failed
    }
}).addOnSuccessListener(new OnSuccessListener<UploadTask.TaskSnapshot>() {
    @Override
    public void onSuccess(UploadTask.TaskSnapshot taskSnapshot) {
        // Upload succeeded
    }
});
```

The UploadTask object may also be used to pause, resume and cancel the upload via the *pause()*, *resume()*, and *cancel()* methods respectively.

An onPaused listener may be added to receive notification when the upload is paused. Similarly, the callback method assigned to the onProgress listener will, if added, be called at regular intervals during the upload process. This can be useful for displaying the upload progress to the user.

```
uploadTask.addOnProgressListener(
            new OnProgressListener<UploadTask.TaskSnapshot>() {
    @Override
    public void onProgress(UploadTask.TaskSnapshot taskSnapshot) {
        // Called at regular interval during upload
    }
}).addOnPausedListener(
            new OnPausedListener<UploadTask.TaskSnapshot>() {
    @Override
    public void onPaused(UploadTask.TaskSnapshot taskSnapshot) {
        // The upload has been paused.
    }
});
```

33.8 **Accessing Upload Task Snapshot Properties**

With the exception of the onFailure listener, each of these listener callback methods is passed an UploadTask.Snapshot object when called. This object contains the following methods which can be called to get information about the status of the upload:

- **getDownloadUrl()** - If the upload was successful, this returns a URL string that can be used to download the file.
- **getError()** - Returns an Exception object if the upload failed.
- **getBytesTransferred()** - When called, this method returns the total number of bytes that had been transferred at the time the snapshot was created.
- **getTotalByteCount()** - Returns the total number of bytes that will have been uploaded by the time the operation is complete.
- **getUploadSessionUri()** - Returns a URI that can be used to continue the upload if a previous attempt was stopped before completion. The upload can be continued by making another *putFile()* method call, passing through this session Uri as the final argument.
- **getMetadata()** - When called before the upload completes, this method returns the Metadata being uploaded along with the file. After the upload completes. The method returns the metadata held on the server. In both cases the metadata is returned in the form of a StorageMetadata object.
- **getTask()** - Returns the UploadTask instance that was used to initiate the upload.
- **getStorage()** - The StorageReference used to create the UploadTask.

33.9 **Reading Metadata from an Uploaded File**

When a file is uploaded to cloud storage, a default set of metadata is included with the file. As mentioned above, the metadata for a stored file may be accessed by making a call to the *getMetadata()* method of an UploadTask.Snapshot object. The metadata for an uploaded file may also be accessed at any time via a call to the *getMetadata()* method of a storage reference object associated with the file. The following code, for example, requests the metadata for a stored file and adds two listeners to receive notification of the success or failure of the request:

```
photoRef = storageRef.child("/images/photos/myPhoto.png");


photoRef.getMetadata().addOnSuccessListener(
                    new OnSuccessListener<StorageMetadata>() {
        @Override
        public void onSuccess(StorageMetadata storageMetadata) {
            // Metadata request succeeded
        }
    }).addOnFailureListener(new OnFailureListener() {
        @Override
        public void onFailure(@NonNull Exception exception) {
            // Metadata request failed
        }
    });
```

If the request is successful, the metadata is passed to the *onSuccess()* callback method of the success listener in the form of a StorageMetadata object. The methods listed in Table 33-1 may then be called on this object to access specific property values:

Method	Return Type	Description
getBucket()	String	The identifier of the Google Cloud Storage bucket in which the file resides.
getCacheControl()	String	Provides control over the amount of time for which browsers are allowed to cache the stored file object. For example "max-age=2400", "no-cache" etc.
getContentDisposition()	String	Used to specify the information on how the file should be displayed when it is downloaded. Details on valid settings can be found at: https://tools.ietf.org/html/rfc6266
getContentEncoding()	String	The file encoding (for example 'gzip').
getContentLanguage()	String	The language of the file content (for example 'en' or 'ja').
getContentType()	String	The type of the file content (e.g. image/png).
getCreationTimeMillis()	long	The date and time in milliseconds that the file was originally stored.
getCustomMetadata(String key)	String	The metadata value associated with the specified key if custom metadata has been included with the file.
getCustomMetadataKeys()	<Set>String	The keys for all custom metadata values assigned to the file.
getDownloadUrl()	Uri	The URL by which the file can be downloaded.
getDownloadUrls()	<List>Uri	A list containing the internal path Uris by which the file may be referenced. Unlike the *getDownloadUrl()* method, these are not HTTP URLs suitable for sharing with third parties.

getGeneration()	String	An automatically generated string value indicating the current version of the saved file.
getMd5Hash()	String	The MD5 hash of the stored file.
getMetadataGeneration()	String	An automatically generated string value indicating the current version of the metadata associated with the file.
getName()	String	The filename of the stored file.
getPath()	String	The full path to the file within the cloud storage bucket.
getReference()	StorageReference	The storage reference object associated with the stored file.
getSizeBytes()	long	The size in bytes of the stored file
getUpdatedTimeMillis()	long	The date and time in milliseconds that the stored file was last updated.

Table 33-1

The following *onSuccess()* callback method, for example, outputs the creation date and time, content type and size of an uploaded file:

```
photoRef.getMetadata().addOnSuccessListener(
            new OnSuccessListener<StorageMetadata>() {
    @Override
    public void onSuccess(StorageMetadata storageMetadata) {

        long milliseconds = storageMetadata.getCreationTimeMillis();
        SimpleDateFormat formatter =
            new SimpleDateFormat("dd/MM/yyyy hh:mm:ss");

        String dateString = formatter.format(new Date(milliseconds));
        Log.i(TAG, "Created = " + dateString);
        Log.i(TAG, "Content type = " + storageMetadata.getContentType());
        Log.i(TAG, "File size = " + storageMetadata.getSizeBytes());
    }
```

```
});
```

33.10 Customizing the File Metadata

The previous section explored the metadata properties that are included by default when a file is uploaded to the storage bucket. Firebase also offers the ability to change a subset of these default values using the StorageMetadata.Builder before the upload is performed. Once the StorageMetadata object has been created and configured, it is passed through as an argument to the appropriate put method when the upload is initiated. In the following code, the language and content type properties are changed within the StorageMetadata object before the file is uploaded:

```
StorageMetadata metadata = new StorageMetadata.Builder()
                .setContentType("image/jpg")
                .setContentLanguage("en")
                .build();


uploadTask = photoRef.putFile(fromUri, metadata);
```

The following methods are available for changing a metadata property before performing an upload using the above technique, all other StorageMetadata properties are read-only:

- setCacheControl()
- setContentType()
- setContentLanguage()
- setContentDisposition()
- setContentEncoding()
- setCustomMetadata()

The *setCustomMetadata()* method allows custom key-value pairs to be added to the file's metadata as follows:

```
StorageMetadata metadata = new StorageMetadata.Builder()
                .setCustomMetadata("myKey1", "My Value One")
                .setCustomMetadata("myKey2", "My Value Two")
                .build();
```

As outlined in Table 33-1, a list of custom keys within the metadata of a stored file may be obtained via a called to the *getCustomMetadataKeys()* method:

```
photoRef.getMetadata().addOnSuccessListener(
                new OnSuccessListener<StorageMetadata>() {
    @Override
    public void onSuccess(StorageMetadata storageMetadata) {

        Set<String> customKeys = storageMetadata.getCustomMetadataKeys();

        for (String s : customKeys) {
```

```
            Log.i(TAG, "key = " + s);
        }
}
```

Similarly, the value assigned to a custom key can be accessed by passing the key through to the *getCustomMetadata()* method of the StorageMetadata object:

```
String customValue = storageMetadata.getCustomMetadata("myKey1");
```

33.11 **Updating File Metadata**

The metadata assigned to an uploaded file can be changed by creating a new StorageMetadata object, customizing it with the values to be changed and then passing it to the *updateMetadata()* method of the storage reference object. This allows existing custom metadata properties to be changed and new custom metadata to be added. In addition, updates may be made to any standard properties that are not read-only:

```
StorageMetadata metadata = new StorageMetadata.Builder()
        .setContentType("image/png")
        .setContentLanguage("ja")
        .setCustomMetadata("myKey1", "A New Value")
        .setCustomMetadata("myKey3", "A New Key/Value")
        .build();

photoRef.updateMetadata(metadata)
        .addOnSuccessListener(new OnSuccessListener<StorageMetadata>() {
            @Override
            public void onSuccess(StorageMetadata storageMetadata) {
            }
        })
        .addOnFailureListener(new OnFailureListener() {
            @Override
            public void onFailure(@NonNull Exception exception) {
            }
        });
```

33.12 **Deleting an Uploaded File**

In addition to uploading and downloading files, it is also important to be able to delete files contained in a storage bucket. This involves a call to the *delete()* method of the storage reference object associated with the file to be deleted. Once again, the addition of listeners allows the success or otherwise of the deletion to be tracked:

```
photoRef.delete().addOnSuccessListener(new OnSuccessListener<Void>() {
    @Override
    public void onSuccess(Void aVoid) {
        // File deleted
```

```
    }
}).addOnFailureListener(new OnFailureListener() {
    @Override
    public void onFailure(@NonNull Exception exception) {
        // File deletion failed
    }
});
```

33.13 Resuming an Interrupted Upload

It is important to be prepared for the possibility that an upload process may get shutdown before the upload has completed. One option in this situation is to simply restart the upload from the beginning. A more efficient approach, however, is to resume the upload from the point at which the interruption occurred. This involves saving the current session Uri for the upload in persistent storage. In the event that the upload is interrupted, this session Uri can be retrieved and used to resume the upload.

Since this session Uri needs to be saved after the upload has started, the *onProgress()* callback method of the *onProgress()* listener method is the ideal location for this to take place. Each time the *onProgress()* method is called, it is passed an UploadTask.TaskSnapshot object. A call to the *getUploadSessionUri()* method of this object will return a String object containing the current session Uri. In the following example the session Uri is saved using shared preferences:

```
Context context = CurrentActivity.this;
SharedPreferences pref = getApplicationContext().getSharedPreferences(
                        "StoragePrefs", context.MODE_PRIVATE);
SharedPreferences.Editor editor = pref.edit();
boolean saved = false;
.
.
.
uploadTask = photoRef.putFile(fromFile);

uploadTask.addOnProgressListener(new
            OnProgressListener<UploadTask.TaskSnapshot>() {
    @Override
    public void onProgress(UploadTask.TaskSnapshot taskSnapshot) {
        Uri sessionUri = taskSnapshot.getUploadSessionUri();
        if (sessionUri != null && !saved) {
            saved = true;
            // Save Session Uri to persistent storage
            editor.putString("sessionUri", sessionUri.toString()).commit();
        }
    }
});
```

When the client app is ready to resume the upload, the *putFile()* method is called, passing through the saved session Uri as the last argument as shown in the following code. Note that the session Uri does not retain any custom metadata from the original upload attempt so this needs to be reconstructed and included in the resumed upload:

```
// Restore saved session Uri from persistent storage
Uri sessionUri = Uri.parse(pref.getString("sessionUri", null));

StorageMetadata metadata = new StorageMetadata.Builder()
                .setContentType("image/jpg")
                .setContentLanguage("en")
                .build();

uploadTask = photoRef.putFile(fromFile, metadata, sessionUri);
```

33.14 Managing Cloud Storage in the Firebase Console

The Firebase console provides a screen where the files stored using cloud storage can be managed. Navigate to the console in a browser and select a Firebase project followed by the *Storage* option in the left-hand navigation panel. Within the Storage screen, select the Files tab as illustrated in Figure 33-1:

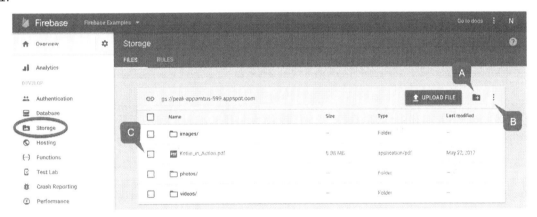

Figure 33-1

To navigate through the folders in the bucket simply click on the links in the list. Clicking on the Upload File button allows a file to be uploaded into the currently selected folder. The folder button (marked A) to the right of the upload button allows a new folder be created in the current bucket.

To add or delete a storage bucket, click on the menu button (B) and select the Add bucket option from the menu. Note that it will be necessary to upgrade from the basic Spark Firebase plan to be able to add buckets.

To delete or download one or more items, select those items using the check boxes (C) and then click on the appropriate button in the toolbar:

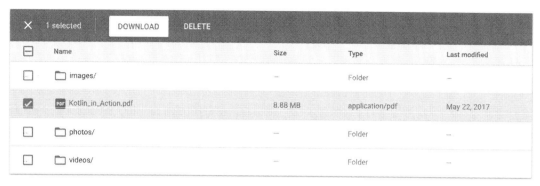

Figure 33-2

33.15 **Summary**

Firebase Cloud Storage allows files of any type to be stored in the cloud. Files are stored in cloud buckets and uploaded and downloaded using the FirebaseStorage instance. This instance is used to obtain a StorageReference object which is used to define the location of a file within cloud storage. In addition to the file, metadata is also included with the stored file providing information about the file such as file type, size and creation time. Custom metadata may also be included for storing app specific data relating to the file. In addition to working with stored files from within app code the Firebase console also provides an interface for navigating and managing the storage filesystem for a project.

Chapter 34

34. A Guide to Firebase Cloud Storage Security Rules

Security is of paramount importance when storing a user's files and data in the cloud. In recognition of this, Firebase Cloud Storage provides an system of security rules that provide a flexible way to control access to stored files.

When a client makes a cloud storage request (in the form of a file upload, download or deletion) the request is passed through the rules defined for the Firebase project to which the client belongs. Based on these rules, the request will either be fulfilled or denied. Understanding how to write these rules is a key part of working with Firebase Cloud Storage.

34.1 Understanding Cloud Storage Security Rules

Security for Firebase Cloud Storage is configured using rules that are declared within the Firebase console. Each Firebase project has its own set of rules which can be viewed and edited by selecting the project within the console and navigating to the Rules page of the Storage screen as shown in Figure 34-1 below:

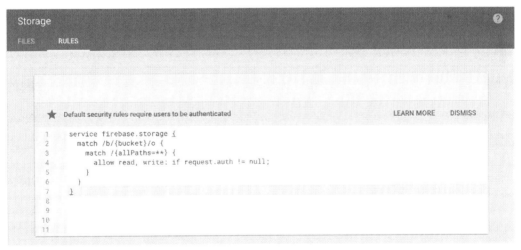

Figure 34-1

Rules can be defined to meet a wide range of requirements. Examples of the types of rules that may be specified include restricting access to specific users on a per file basis, allowing only files of a certain content type to be uploaded, or files of a certain size to be deleted. A rule could be declared, for example, that only allows image files to be stored in a particular folder.

By default, the following rules are configured allowing only authenticated users to read and write to the bucket:

```
service firebase.storage {
  match /b/{bucket}/o {
    match /{allPaths=**} {
      allow read, write: if request.auth != null;
    }
  }
}
```

In the above example, the rule uses a standard reference /b/{bucket}/o which indicates that the rules are to apply to all Google Cloud buckets belonging to the Firebase project (the use of braces indicates a wildcard, a topic which will be covered later in this chapter). The reason for the /b/ and /o is that the internal path to a file stored in a cloud bucket will typically be structured as follows:

```
/b/<cloud storage bucket id>/o/path/to/file/myfile.jpg
```

Alternatively, the rule to allow read and write access to all files and sub-directories to all users (authenticated or otherwise) would read as follows:

```
service firebase.storage {
  match /b/{bucket}/o {
    match /{allPaths=**} {
      allow read, write;
    }
  }
}
```

34.2 Security Rules Structure

As with Firebase Realtime Database rules, cloud storage rules are structured hierarchically. In the above examples, the read and write permissions applied to all files and folders within the project's Google Cloud bucket.

It helps to think of the rules in terms of "what, how and when". The rules control what is accessible within the cloud storage bucket, how those items are protected and, finally, the circumstances when access is permitted. These three requirements are declared using the *match*, *allows* and *if* keywords. A typical rule element will, therefore, be structured as follows:

```
match /file/path/pattern {
    allow read, write: if <condition>;
}
```

A single match declaration may also contain multiple *allow* statements. The following rule declares separate permissions for reading and writing:

```
match /file/path/pattern {
    allow read: if <condition 1>;
```

```
    allow write: if <condition 2>;
}
```

34.3 The match Keyword

The match keyword is used to define the path or paths within the storage filesystem to which a rule is to apply. In the above examples, the rule applied to all files and directories contained within the bucket. Matches can also be declared to target specific files. The following rule, for example, provides read-only access for authenticated users to a file with a path that matches /profiles/photos/userphoto.png:

```
service firebase.storage {
  match /b/{bucket}/o {
    match /profiles/photos/userphoto.png {
      allow write: if request.auth != null;
    }
  }
}
```

Match statements may also be nested as in the following example:

```
service firebase.storage {
  match /b/{bucket}/o {
    match /calendar {
        match /uservideo.3gp {
            allow write: if request.auth != null;
        }
      }
    }
}
```

As will be covered in a later section, matching also supports the use of wildcards.

34.4 The allow Keyword

Having defined the paths for which rules are to apply using the match keyword, the allow keyword controls the kind of access permitted for any matching paths. Acceptable options are read, write or both read and write permissions.

Each match rule element will contain at least one allow statement. In the absence of an *if* statement, the allow permissions are applied unconditionally to matched paths, regardless of the storage request being made by the client.

34.5 The if Statement

The allow keyword transforms from a blunt instrument into a precision tool when used in conjunction with the if conditional statement. In the above examples, the if statement has been used repeatedly to allow access only to authenticated users with statements similar to the following:

```
allow read, write: if request.auth != null;
```

In this case, read and write access is only permitted when the current user has been authenticated. The authentication status is obtained by accessing the *auth* property of the *request* object.

When a client attempts to upload, download or delete a cloud storage based file, it arrives at the cloud server in the form of a *request* object. This object, which contains a number of properties, is available for use within the if statement as the basis on which to create rule conditions.

The *auth* property, for example, will be null if the user making the request has not signed in using a Firebase Authentication provider. In the event the user has been authenticated, the *auth* property contains the user's uid (request.auth.uid) and the Firebase authentication token (request.auth.token).

A full list of the properties provided by the request object is contained in Table 34-1:

Property	Description
auth	Contains the uid and Firebase authentication token for the current user. If the user is not authenticated, this property is set to null.
path	Contains the path at which the request is being made by the client. This is provided in the form of an array allowing individual path components to be accessed in an if statement. For example, request.path[1].
resource	An object containing the metadata of the file associated with the storage request. This allows information such as the file size, type, creation time and name to be accessed and used in an if statement.
time	The current time on the server. Typically used to compare against the creation time of a file to avoid uploading of outdated files or to restrict upload and download operations at certain dates and times.

Table 34-1

The resource property of the request object also contains a number of properties specific to the file associated with the request. Table 34-2 outlines the most commonly used resource properties:

Property	Description
name	The name of the file associated with the request including the full path.
bucket	The name of the Google Cloud Storage bucket in which the file is stored.
size	The size in bytes of the file.
timeCreated	The time and date when the file was first created.
updated	The time at which the file was last updated.
contentEncoding	A string identifying the encoding of the file (for example 'gzip').
contentLangauge	A string identifying the language of the file content (for example 'en' or 'ja').
contentType	A string identifying the type of the file content (for example 'image/jpg').
metadata	A string map containing developer specific metadata (if provided) included with the file.

Table 34-2

Clearly, there are quite a few options for inclusion in an if statement so it would be beneficial to work through some example rules that make use of some of the properties outlined above. The following allow statement, for example, prevents files being uploaded that exceed 15Mb in size:

```
allow write: if resource.size < 15 * 1024 * 1024;
```

A rule to allow reading only if the content of the file is English would read as follows:

```
allow read: if resource.contentLanguage == 'en';
```

Conditions may also be combined using AND and OR operators. The following rule, for example, only allows a file to be written if the user is authenticated, the file contains a PNG image, does not exceed 25Mb in size and was created less than two hours ago:

```
allow write: if request.resource.size < 25 * 1024 * 1024
        && request.auth != null
        && request.resource.contentType.matches('image/png')
        && resource.timeCreated < request.time + duration.value(120, "m");
```

321

34.6 **Wildcard Matching**

When specifying matching criteria for a rule it is often useful to use wildcards to match multiple paths. Consider, for example, the following match statement:

```
match /calendar/january/scenicphoto.jpg {
.
.
}
```

Clearly any allow statement associated with this match will apply only to a file named scenicphoto.jpg residing in the /calendar/january directory. If the match was intended to apply to all files located in the /calendar/january directory, the match statement could read as follows:

```
match /calendar/january/{imageName} {
.
.
}
```

The {imageName} section of the match path represents a wildcard. The expression syntax for a wildcard is as follows:

```
{variable name}
```

When included in a match path, this syntax essentially tells cloud storage to accept any value as a match and to assign that current value to a variable with the specified name. That variable can then be used within an if statement to add conditions to the rule. The following rule allows any file to be written to the /calendar/january directory as long as the name of the file being written does not exceed 10 characters in length:

```
match /calendar/january/{imageName} {
    allow write: if imageName.size() > 10;
}
```

Wildcards may be used to replace any section of a path. Consider, for example, the following rule which allows any file to be written to any path that matches /calendar/*:

```
match /calendar/{monthName} {
    allow write: if request.auth != null;
}
```

With the above rule applied, a client will be permitted, for example, to upload a file with any filename to directories such as /calendar/january, /calendar/february, /calendar/2017 and so on.

When working with rules it should be noted that rules do not, by default, cascade to the sub-directories of a matched directory. In other words, while the above rule would apply to directory path /calendar/2017, it would not apply to directory /calendar/2017/january. To declare a cascading wildcard it is necessary to use the multiple segment wildcard syntax (represented by =**) as follows:

```
match /calendar/{monthName=**} {
    allow write: if request.auth != null;
}
```

The declared write permission will now cascade down through all levels of sub-directories beneath /calendar in the storage bucket. Note that the multiple segment wildcard may only be used to replace the last segment in a path. The following, therefore, is not a valid wildcard:

```
match /calendar/{monthName=**}/photos { // <---- Invalid wildcard
.
.
}
```

34.7 **Protecting User Files**

An important part of implementing cloud storage security rules involves ensuring that files that are private to a user are not accessible to any other users. The key to this involves the use of Firebase Authentication together with the *auth* property of the storage request object.

As previously outlined, the auth property contains the Firebase Auth ID token and the user's unique ID (uid). This allows rules to be defined which, when applied to an appropriately structured storage filesystem, restrict access to stored files based on user identity.

As with Firebase Realtime Databases, the uid information can be used to separate one user's files from another. Consider a client app that allows each user to record and upload an introductory video about themselves. While anyone is allowed to view the video, only the owner of the video is allowed to upload and update the video file. The cloud storage filesystem structure for this app might be implemented as follows where <uid> is replaced by each user's id:

```
/videos/<uid>/userIntro.3gp
```

Since the uids are contained within the filename path, the storage security rules can be configured to compare the uid in the path against the auth.uid property (in other words the uid of the user making the request) of the of the request object:

```
service firebase.storage {
  match /b/{bucket}/o {
    match /videos/{userId}/userIntro.3gp {
        allow read;
        allow write: if request.auth.uid == userId;
    }
  }
}
```

The above example establishes a rule that uses a wildcard to assign the uid segment of the request path to a variable named userId. If the uid segment of the path does not match the uid of the current user write access is denied.

34.8 **Summary**

Firebase Cloud Storage rules provide a mechanism for controlling the circumstances under which files may be stored and accessed. Storage rules are declared using the match, allow and if statements to define sets of rules and the files to which those rules are to apply. As with the Firebase Realtime Database, user files can be protected by making use of Firebase Authentication.

35. A Firebase Cloud Storage Tutorial

The two preceding chapters have covered the theoretical aspects of Firebase Cloud Storage and the rules that need to be implemented to protect user data. In this chapter, this theory will be put into practice through the creation of an Android app that makes use of cloud storage to store and retrieve video files.

35.1 About the Firebase Cloud Storage Example

The app project created in this chapter will make use of the Android video capture intent to allow the user to record a video using the device camera. Once recorded, the user will be given the option to upload the video file to the Firebase cloud and, once uploaded, subsequently download and play the video. Firebase Authentication will be used to keep the videos belonging to different users separate from one another. Storage security rules will also be applied so that only the owner of a video is able to download and view it.

35.2 Creating the Project

Launch Android Studio and select the *Start a new Android Studio project* quick start option from the welcome screen.

Within the new project dialog, enter *CloudStorage* into the Application name field and your domain as the Company Domain setting before clicking on the *Next* button.

On the form factors screen, enable the *Phone and Tablet* option and set the minimum SDK to API 16: Android 4.1 (Jellybean). Continue working through the screens, requesting the creation of an Empty Activity named *CloudStorageActivity* with a corresponding layout named *activity_cloud_storage*.

35.3 Adding Authentication to the Project

As with most projects where user data is to be protected, Firebase Authentication will be used as the foundation of the security implemented in this chapter. For the purposes of this tutorial, only email/password authentication will be used.

Begin by opening the Firebase console in a browser window and selecting the *Firebase Examples* project. Navigate to the Authentication screen, select the *Sign-In Method* tab and enable the Email/Password provider if it is currently disabled.

Return to the project in Android Studio and select the *Tools -> Firebase* menu option. When the Firebase assistant panel appears, locate and select the *Authentication* section and click on the *Email and password authentication* link.

A Firebase Cloud Storage Tutorial

In the resulting panel, click on the *Connect to Firebase* button to display the Firebase connection dialog.

Choose the option to store the app in an existing Firebase project and select the *Firebase Examples* project before clicking on the *Connect to Firebase* button.

With the project's Firebase connection established, refer to the Firebase assistant panel once again, this time clicking on the *Add Firebase Authentication to your app* button. A dialog will appear outlining the changes that will be made to the project build configuration to enable Firebase Authentication. Click on the *Accept Changes* button to implement the changes to the project configuration.

Within the Project tool window, locate and double-click on the *build.gradle (Module: app)* file so that it loads into the editor and modify the dependencies section to include the *firebase-ui* and *firebase-ui-auth* libraries (note that more recent versions of these libraries may have been released since this book was published):

```
dependencies {
    compile fileTree(dir: 'libs', include: ['*.jar'])
    androidTestCompile('com.android.support.test.espresso:espresso-core:2.2.2', {
        exclude group: 'com.android.support', module: 'support-annotations'
    })
    compile 'com.android.support:appcompat-v7:25.3.1'
    compile 'com.android.support.constraint:constraint-layout:1.0.2'
    compile 'com.google.firebase:firebase-auth:11.0.1'
    compile 'com.firebaseui:firebase-ui:2.0.1'
    compile 'com.firebaseui:firebase-ui-auth:2.0.1'
    testCompile 'junit:junit:4.12'
}
```

In addition to the FirebaseUI dependencies, the build system will also need to download some additional Twitter library dependencies for the Firebase UI library. These libraries are available via Twitter's fabric.io project and can be integrated into the Gradle build process for the project by adding a repository entry to the module level *build.gradle* file as follows:

```
.
.
.
    compile 'com.firebaseui:firebase-ui-auth:1.0.1'
    compile 'com.google.firebase:firebase-auth:10.0.1'
    testCompile 'junit:junit:4.12'
}

repositories {
    maven { url 'https://maven.fabric.io/public' }
```

}
.
.

Once the build file changes have been made, click on the Sync Now button located in the yellow bar above the editor window to commit the changes.

35.4 **Adding the Signed In Activity**

The CloudStorageActivity class will be used to authenticate the user. Once the user has signed in to the app, a second activity will be launched within which the user will record, store and playback video.

Add this second activity to the project now by locating the *app -> java -> <yourdomain>.cloudstorage* entry in the Project tool window and right-clicking on it. When the menu appears, select the *New -> Activity -> Empty Activity* menu option. In the *New Android Activity* dialog, name the activity *SignedInActivity*.

Before clicking on the *Finish* button, make sure that the *Generate Layout File* option is enabled and the *Launcher Activity* option disabled.

35.5 **Designing the SignedInActivity User Interface**

The user interface for the second activity is going to consist of three Buttons, a ProgressBar and a VideoView. Locate the *activity_signed_in.xml* file, load it into the layout editor and turn off Autoconnect mode using the button located in the toolbar.

Drag and drop three Button widgets from the palette and position them so that they are located along the bottom of the layout as shown in Figure 35-1. Change the text properties on the three buttons so that they read "Record", "Upload" and "Download" and configure the onClick property to call methods named *record*, *upload* and *download* respectively:

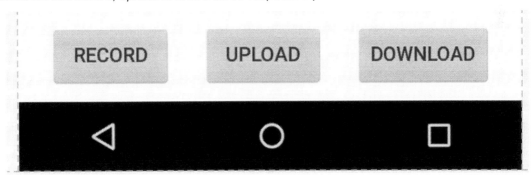

Figure 35-1

A constraint layout chain will be used to ensure that the buttons are distributed evenly across the width of the screen, regardless of screen size and device orientation. Add the chain by selecting all three button widgets, right-clicking on the left-most widget and selecting the *Center Horizontally* option from the resulting menu. With the widgets chained, attach the bottom anchor of each button to the bottom of the parent layout by clicking on the anchor and dragging to the bottom edge of the layout. On completion of these steps, the button layout should match that shown in Figure 35-2:

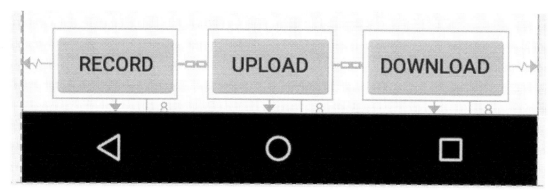

Figure 35-2

The next component to add is the ProgressBar view which will be positioned directly above the row of buttons. From the palette, locate and select the ProgressBar (Horizontal) widget and drag it so that it is positioned above the buttons. Resize the bar so that it extends to cover most of the width of the layout. Using the anchor points, anchor the left and right sides of the bar to the corresponding sides of the parent layout. Using the bottom anchor, constrain the bottom of the bar to the top of the center button. With the ProgressBar widget selected, use the Properties tool window to change the ID to *pbar*. Also change the *layout_width* property to 0dp. This switches the width to *match constraints* mode, causing the view to resize based on the applied constraints.

The progress bar will be used to display the progress of the file upload as a percentage. Before proceeding, therefore, change the *max* property to 100.

On completion of these steps, the layout should resemble Figure 35-3:

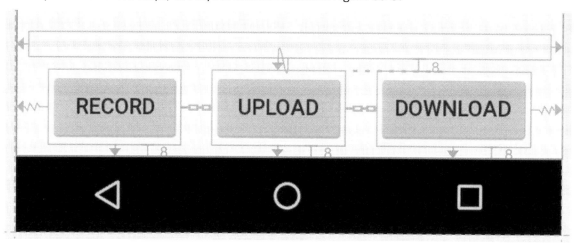

Figure 35-3

From the Images category of the palette, drag and drop a VideoView object onto the layout canvas and position and resize the view to match the layout in Figure 35-4:

Figure 35-4

With the VideoView selected use the anchor points to constrain the top, left and right sides of the view to the corresponding sides of the parent layout, then connect the bottom anchor point to the top of the ProgressBar widget.

Referring to the Properties tool window, change both the *layout_height* and *layout_width* properties to 0dp so that the view is sized to match the constraints set on it.

As the final step in the design of the user interface layout, change the ID property of the VideoView to *videoView*.

35.6 Performing the Authentication

With the user interface designed, code can now be added to the project to perform the user authentication. Edit the *CloudStorageActivity.java* file and modify it as follows to initiate the authentication process:

```
package com.ebookfrenzy.cloudstorage;

import android.content.Intent;
import android.support.v7.app.AppCompatActivity;
import android.os.Bundle;
```

```
import com.firebase.ui.auth.AuthUI;
import com.google.firebase.auth.FirebaseAuth;
import com.firebase.ui.auth.ErrorCodes;
import com.firebase.ui.auth.IdpResponse;
import com.firebase.ui.auth.ResultCodes;

import java.util.ArrayList;
import java.util.List;

public class CloudStorageActivity extends AppCompatActivity {

    FirebaseAuth auth;
    private static final int REQUEST_CODE = 101;

    @Override
    protected void onCreate(Bundle savedInstanceState) {
        super.onCreate(savedInstanceState);
        setContentView(R.layout.activity_signed_in);

        auth = FirebaseAuth.getInstance();

        if (auth.getCurrentUser() != null) {
            startActivity(new Intent(this, SignedInActivity.class));
            finish();
        } else {
            authenticateUser();
        }

    }
.
.
.
}
```

The code added above will call a method named *authenticateUser()* if the current user is not already signed in. The next step is to add this method:

```
private void authenticateUser() {

    List<AuthUI.IdpConfig> providers = new ArrayList<>();

    providers.add(
            new AuthUI.IdpConfig.Builder(AuthUI.EMAIL_PROVIDER).build());
```

```
    startActivityForResult(
            AuthUI.getInstance().createSignInIntentBuilder()
                    .setAvailableProviders(providers)
                    .setIsSmartLockEnabled(false)
                    .build(),
            REQUEST_CODE);
}
```

When the authentication activity is completed, the *onActivityResult()* method will be called. Implement this method now to launch the SignedInActivity on a successful authentication:

```
@Override
protected void onActivityResult(int requestCode, int resultCode, Intent data)
{
    super.onActivityResult(requestCode, resultCode, data);

    IdpResponse response = IdpResponse.fromResultIntent(data);

    if (requestCode == REQUEST_CODE) {

        if (resultCode == ResultCodes.OK) {
            startActivity(new Intent(this, SignedInActivity.class));
            return;
        }
    } else {
        if (response == null) {
            // User cancelled Sign-in
            return;
        }

        if (response.getErrorCode() == ErrorCodes.NO_NETWORK) {
            // Device has no network connection
            return;
        }

        if (response.getErrorCode() == ErrorCodes.UNKNOWN_ERROR) {
            // Unknown error occurred
            return;
        }
    }
}
```

After making the code changes, compile and run the app, sign in using either a new or existing Firebase user account and verify that the SignedInActivity appears.

35.7 **Recording Video**

Video recording will begin when the user taps the Record button in the SignedInActivity screen. This button is configured to call a method named *record()* which now needs to be implemented within the *SignedInActivity.java* file. Video recording will be performed by making use of the built-in Android video capture intent. Before this code is added, some libraries need to be imported and a constant added to act as the request code for the video capture intent and a variable in which to store the Uri of the locally saved video file. Edit the *SignedInActivity.java* file and modify it as follows:

```
package com.ebookfrenzy.cloudstorage;

import android.content.Intent;
import android.provider.MediaStore;
import android.net.Uri;
import android.support.v7.app.AppCompatActivity;
import android.os.Bundle;
import android.view.View;
import android.widget.Toast;
import android.widget.ProgressBar;

public class CloudStorageActivity extends AppCompatActivity {

    private Uri videoUri;
    private static final int REQUEST_CODE = 101;
.

.
}
```

Next, add the code for the *record()* method:

```
public void record(View view) {
    Intent intent = new Intent(MediaStore.ACTION_VIDEO_CAPTURE);
    startActivityForResult(intent, REQUEST_CODE);
}
```

When the video capture intent returns, a method named *onActivityResult()* will be called and passed a request code and an Intent object containing the Uri of the file containing the video footage. This method now needs to be added to the class:

```
protected void onActivityResult(int requestCode,
                                int resultCode, Intent data) {
    videoUri = data.getData();
    if (requestCode == REQUEST_CODE) {
        if (resultCode == RESULT_OK) {
            Toast.makeText(this, "Video saved to:\n" +
                    videoUri, Toast.LENGTH_LONG).show();
```

```
        } else if (resultCode == RESULT_CANCELED) {
            Toast.makeText(this, "Video recording cancelled.",
                    Toast.LENGTH_LONG).show();
        } else {
            Toast.makeText(this, "Failed to record video",
                    Toast.LENGTH_LONG).show();
        }
    }
}
```

Compile and run the app and make sure that the Record button successfully launches the video capture intent. Within the video capture screen, tap the record button and record some video. After recording a few seconds of video, tap the stop button followed by the confirmation button (usually a blue button displaying a white check mark). The intent should return to the SignedInActivity screen where a Toast message will appear displaying the path to the video file on the local device storage.

Now that video is being captured it is now time to add code to upload the file to cloud storage. Before adding this code, however, Firebase Cloud Storage support first needs to be added to the project.

35.8 Adding Firebase Cloud Storage Support

Within Android Studio, select the *Tools -> Firebase* menu option and, in the Firebase assistant panel, unfold the *Storage* option and click on the *Upload and download a file with Firebase Storage* link. On the resulting page, click on the *Add Firebase Storage to your app* button. In the confirmation dialog, review and then accept the changes:

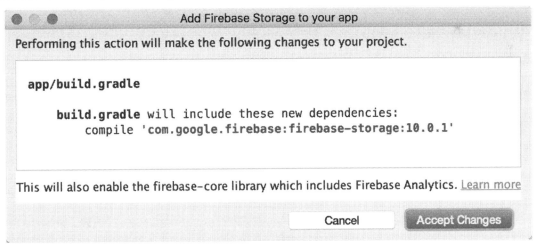

Figure 35-5

35.9 Uploading the Video File to the Cloud

The video file is to be uploaded when the user clicks the *Upload* button within the SignedInActivity screen. Before the upload can be performed, however, a storage reference needs to be created. In creating the storage reference, the current user's ID will be included as a component in the path as a way to separate user files. The storage reference path used in this app will read as follows:

```
/videos/<uid>/userIntro.3gp
```

Modify the *SignedInActivity.java* file to add some imports and variables, then add code to the *onCreate()* method to initialize a storage reference object:

```java
import android.support.annotation.NonNull;
import android.widget.VideoView;
import android.provider.MediaStore;
.
.
import com.google.android.gms.tasks.OnFailureListener;
import com.google.android.gms.tasks.OnSuccessListener;
import com.google.firebase.storage.FirebaseStorage;
import com.google.firebase.storage.OnProgressListener;
import com.google.firebase.storage.StorageReference;
import com.google.firebase.storage.FileDownloadTask;

import com.google.firebase.auth.FirebaseAuth;
import com.google.firebase.storage.UploadTask;

import java.io.File;
.
.
public class SignedInActivity extends AppCompatActivity {

    private Uri videoUri;
    private static final int REQUEST_CODE = 101;
    private StorageReference videoRef;

    @Override
    protected void onCreate(Bundle savedInstanceState) {
        super.onCreate(savedInstanceState);
        setContentView(R.layout.activity_signed_in);

        String uid = FirebaseAuth.getInstance().getCurrentUser().getUid();

        StorageReference storageRef =
                FirebaseStorage.getInstance().getReference();
        videoRef = storageRef.child("/videos/" + uid + "/userIntro.3gp");
    }
.
.
```

```
}
```

With the storage reference initialized, add the *upload()* method to the class as follows:

```
public void upload(View view) {
    if (videoUri != null) {
        UploadTask uploadTask = videoRef.putFile(videoUri);

        uploadTask.addOnFailureListener(new OnFailureListener() {
            @Override
            public void onFailure(@NonNull Exception e) {
                Toast.makeText(SignedInActivity.this,
                        "Upload failed: " + e.getLocalizedMessage(),
                        Toast.LENGTH_LONG).show();

            }
        }).addOnSuccessListener(
                new OnSuccessListener<UploadTask.TaskSnapshot>() {
            @Override
            public void onSuccess(UploadTask.TaskSnapshot taskSnapshot) {
                Toast.makeText(SignedInActivity.this, "Upload complete",
                        Toast.LENGTH_LONG).show();
            }
        }).addOnProgressListener(
                new OnProgressListener<UploadTask.TaskSnapshot>() {
            @Override
            public void onProgress(UploadTask.TaskSnapshot taskSnapshot) {

            }
        });
    } else {
        Toast.makeText(SignedInActivity.this, "Nothing to upload",
                Toast.LENGTH_LONG).show();

    }
}
```

The code uses the *putFile()* method of the storage reference object to initiate the file upload and then uses listener methods to receive updates on the upload progress. A Toast message is displayed to notify the user of the success or failure of the upload.

35.10 Updating the Progress Bar

As the file is uploaded, the progress bar needs to be updated to visually convey to the user the progress being made. Clearly the code to track progress needs to be placed within the *onProgress()* listener callback method which will be called at regular intervals during the upload process. To calculate this value, the number of bytes uploaded so far needs to be compared to the total size of the file and the resulting value used as the current setting for the ProgressBar. As described in earlier chapters, each time the *onProgress()* method is called it is passed an UploadTask.TaskSnapshot object from which a variety of properties can be extracted, including the file size and current number of bytes transferred.

When the user interface layout was designed, the ProgressBar was configured with a range of 0 to 100, allowing the current position to be specified as a percentage. With this in mind, create a new method named *updateProgress()* which takes as an argument a task snapshot object:

```
public void updateProgress(UploadTask.TaskSnapshot taskSnapshot) {

    @SuppressWarnings("VisibleForTests") long fileSize =
            taskSnapshot.getTotalByteCount();

    @SuppressWarnings("VisibleForTests")
            long uploadBytes = taskSnapshot.getBytesTransferred();

    long progress = (100 * uploadBytes) / fileSize;

    ProgressBar progressBar = (ProgressBar) findViewById(R.id.pbar);
    progressBar.setProgress((int) progress);
}
```

Next, edit the *onProgress()* callback method to call this method, passing through the current task snapshot:

```
.
.
@Override
public void onProgress(UploadTask.TaskSnapshot taskSnapshot) {
    updateProgress(taskSnapshot);
}
.
.
```

35.11 Downloading the Video File

The final coding task is to implement the *download()* method, the purpose of which is to download the video file from cloud storage using the storage reference and play it back to the user on the VideoView object. The download is started via a call to the *getFile()* method of the storage reference object, passing through a File instance initialized with a temporary local file. Listeners are also used to monitor the status of the download:

```
public void download(View view) {

    try {
        final File localFile = File.createTempFile("userIntro", "3gp");
```

```
            videoRef.getFile(localFile).addOnSuccessListener(
                    new OnSuccessListener<FileDownloadTask.TaskSnapshot>() {
                @Override
                public void onSuccess(
                    FileDownloadTask.TaskSnapshot taskSnapshot) {

                    Toast.makeText(SignedInActivity.this, "Download complete",
                            Toast.LENGTH_LONG).show();

                    final VideoView videoView =
                                    (VideoView) findViewById(R.id.videoView);
                    videoView.setVideoURI(Uri.fromFile(localFile));
                    videoView.start();

                }
            }).addOnFailureListener(new OnFailureListener() {
                @Override
                public void onFailure(@NonNull Exception e) {
                    Toast.makeText(SignedInActivity.this,
                            "Download failed: " + e.getLocalizedMessage(),
                            Toast.LENGTH_LONG).show();
                }
            });
        } catch (Exception e) {
            Toast.makeText(SignedInActivity.this,
                    "Failed to create temp file: " + e.getLocalizedMessage(),
                    Toast.LENGTH_LONG).show();
        }
    }
}
```

35.12 Setting the Storage Security Rules

The final task before testing the project is to configure the security rules. Since the storage path includes the user's authentication ID, this can be used to ensure that the ID of the user seeking access matches that contained in the storage reference path. Access will also be further restricted to enable reading and writing only when the filename matches *userIntro.3gp*.

Open the Firebase console in a browser window, open the *Firebase Examples* project and navigate to the Storage screen. Select the Rules tab and enter the following rules:

```
service firebase.storage {
  match /b/{bucket}/o {
    match /videos/{userId}/userIntro.3gp {
        allow read;
```

```
          allow write: if request.auth.uid == userId;
     }
  }
}
```

Click on the Publish button to commit the rules for the project ready for testing.

35.13 Testing the Project

Compile and run the app and sign in if prompted to do so. Record some video and tap the button to accept the recording. Upload the video to cloud storage and verify that the progress bar is updated regularly until the upload completes. Tap the download button and wait for the video file to download and begin playing in the video view.

Within the Storage section of the Firebase console, select the Files tab and navigate to the /videos/<uid> folder where the *userIntro.3gp* video file should now be listed:

Figure 35-6

35.14 Summary

This chapter has created an Android app that makes use of Firebase Cloud Storage to store a video file. The example has demonstrated the use of storage references, file uploading and downloading, the use of listeners to track file transfer progress and the implementation of storage rules to restrict storage file access.

36. Firebase Remote Config

Firebase Remote Config allows changes to the behavior of apps already installed and running on user devices to be made without the need to perform an upgrade or re-installation. This chapter will explain how, by making use of Remote Config, dynamic app changes can be controlled via the Firebase console and pushed out either to all app users, or to different user segments.

36.1 An Overview of Firebase Remote Config

Prior to the introduction of Firebase Remote Config, there was no easy way to make dynamic changes to the way an app looks and functions without issuing an upgrade to existing users. There was also no way to control which users received the update, making it all but impossible to gradually roll out changes, perform A/B testing to gauge the success of the changes, or to target specific groups of users based on demographics such as device type or geographical location.

Firebase Remote Config addresses this problem by providing a simple way to make remote configuration changes to an app and then target specific groups of users to receive those changes.

As with most other Firebase features, Remote Config begins with integration of a library into the app project. Within the app, a set of parameters are then defined either in a Map object or an XML resource file. These parameters take the form of key-value pairs that are used to control the default configuration of the app. The code of the app is implemented such that these parameters are checked at predefined intervals and used in the logic of the running app. An in-app parameter could, for example, be declared with a default setting to configure a blue background or to display a particular welcome message.

These default in-app parameters may then be overridden on a per-parameter basis using a set of matching *server-side parameters*, the values of which are controlled from within the Firebase console. The decision as to whether or not a server-side parameter overrides the corresponding in-app parameter may also be made conditionally based on factors such as user location, device operating system and the user's language and locale settings. Parameters may also be targeted to randomized percentages of the user base, or in conjunction with audiences defined using Firebase Analytics.

Once a server-side parameter has been configured, it is published and ready to be fetched by the app. Once fetched, the parameters must then be activated before they can be used to override the corresponding in-app parameters.

36.2 **The FirebaseRemoteConfig Object**

The main object responsible for providing Remote Config support within an Android app is the FirebaseRemoteConfig object. The first step in implementing Remote Config support within an app is to obtain a reference to this object as follows:

```
FirebaseRemoteConfig fbRemoteConfig = FirebaseRemoteConfig.getInstance();
```

The FirebaseRemoteConfig object is responsible for storing the local in-app parameters, fetching the server-side parameters and controlling when those parameters are activated for use within the app.

36.3 **Declaring and Setting In-App Parameters**

The default in-app parameters may be declared within an XML resources bundled with the app, or contained within a Java Map object. When using an XML resources, the file must be located within the res/xml folder of the app. The listing below contains a basic Remote Config parameter file containing background color and welcome message values:

```xml
<?xml version="1.0" encoding="utf-8"?>
<defaultsMap>
    <entry>
        <key>welcome_text</key>
        <value>Welcome to Remote Config</value>
    </entry>
    <entry>
        <key>main_background_color</key>
        <value>#42f486</value>
    </entry>
</defaultsMap>
```

Once the in-app parameters have been declared, they need to be loaded into the FirebaseRemoteConfig object. This is achieved by passing the reference to the resource file to the *setDefaults()* method of the FirebaseRemoteConfig object. Assuming the above XML resource file was named *remote_config_params.xml*, the code to set the defaults would read as follows:

```
firebaseRemoteConfig.setDefaults(R.xml.remote_config_params);
```

As an alternative to using an XML resource file, the same result can be achieved using a HashMap. For example:

```
HashMap<String, Object> config_params = new HashMap<>();

config_params.put("welcome_text", "Welcome to Remote Config");
config_params.put("main_background_color", "#42f486");

fbRemoteConfig.setDefaults(config_params);
```

36.4 Accessing Remote Config Parameters

Once the in-app parameters have been applied to the FirebaseRemoteConfig object, the code will need to be able to access the values in order to make use of them in configuring the app's appearance and behavior. This is achieved by calling one of a number of *get* methods on the FirebaseRemoteConfig object passing through as an argument the key for which the corresponding value is required. The correct get method to call will depend on the type of the value associated with the parameter. The following is the current list of available methods:

- getBoolean()
- getByteArray()
- getDouble()
- getLong()
- getString()

The *main_background_color* parameter contained within the example resource file would, for example, be obtained from the FirebaseRemoteConfig object as follows and used to set the background color of a layout accordingly:

```
String bg_color = fbRemoteConfig.getString("main_background_color");
layout.setBackgroundColor(Color.parseColor(bg_color));
```

36.5 Setting Server Side Parameters

Once the app is set up to make use of Remote Config parameters, the next step is to learn how to override the in-app parameters with remote server side parameters. As outlined earlier in the chapter, server-side parameters are declared using the Firebase console. To configure these parameters, open the Firebase console in a browser window, select the appropriate Firebase project and click on the Remote Config link in the left-hand navigation panel to display the screen shown in Figure 36-1:

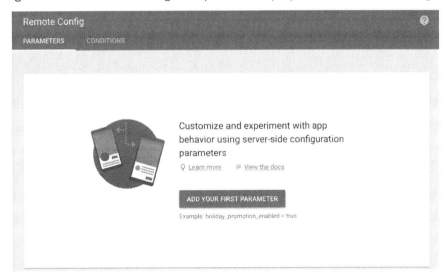

Figure 36-1

Clicking on the *Add Your First Parameter* button will display a popup dialog within which the key and value for the parameter may be entered. When adding server-side parameters, the key must match that of the in-app parameter being overridden. In Figure 36-2, a server-side parameter for the background color parameter is being added:

Figure 36-2

Once the parameter has been added, it will appear in the parameter list where it may be edited by clicking the button highlighted in Figure 36-3. Although the parameter has been added, it is not available to be fetched by the app until the *Publish Changes* button (also highlighted) at the top of the list is clicked:

Figure 36-3

Additional parameters may be added using the *Add Parameters* button.

36.6 Fetching the Parameters

Although server-side parameters may have been declared and published, nothing will change on the client app unless steps are taken to fetch and then activate the parameters. The fetching operation is initiated via a call to the *fetch()* method of the FirebaseRemoteConfig object.

When the parameters are fetched, they are stored within the cache of the FirebaseRemoteConfig object. By default, the cache will consider these parameters to be valid for 12 hours after being fetched. Any subsequent fetch calls within that time period will simply continue to use the cached parameters. After 12 hours have expired, the next fetch method call will once again download the parameters from the server. The following code demonstrates the use of the *fetch()* method with the default 12 hour expiration:

```
fbRemoteConfig.fetch();
```

A shorter cache expiration duration may specified by passing through the number of seconds as an argument to the *fetch()* method. In the following line of code, the cache is set to expire after one hour:

```
fbRemoteConfig.fetch(3600);
```

In practice, the expiration time should not be set too low. Remote Config fetch requests are subject to throttling by the Firebase server. In the event that an app makes too many fetch requests, future requests will be denied until a timeout period has elapsed.

When testing Remote Config during development, it makes sense to set the cache timeout to zero so that configuration changes can be tested instantly. To avoid encountering throttling during testing, the *setConfigSettings()* method of the FirebaseRemoteConfig object should be used to enable developer mode:

```
fbRemoteConfig.setConfigSettings(new FirebaseRemoteConfigSettings.Builder()
        .setDeveloperModeEnabled(true)
        .build());


fbRemoteConfig.fetch(0);
```

This developer mode must be disabled before the app is distributed to users.

The fetch operation is performed asynchronously so a completion listener should be added to receive notification that the fetch completed:

```
fbRemoteConfig.fetch(0).addOnCompleteListener(this,
                        new OnCompleteListener<Void>() {
    @Override
    public void onComplete(@NonNull Task<Void> task) {
        if (task.isSuccessful()) {
            // Fetch succeeded
        } else {
            // Fetch failed
        }


    }
});
```

36.7 Activating Fetched Parameters

Once a successful fetch operation has been performed the parameters must be activated before they will be accessible via the various get methods. To activate the most recently fetched parameters, a call needs to be made to the *activateFetched()* method of the FirebaseRemoteConfig object. Since it only makes sense to activate the parameters when a successful fetch has completed, this call is best made within the *onComplete()* method of the completion listener:

```
.
.
public void onComplete(@NonNull Task<Void> task) {
    if (task.isSuccessful()) {
        fbRemoteConfig.activateFetched();
```

343

```
    } else {
        // Fetch failed
    }
}
.
.
```

36.8 **Working with Conditions**

The Remote Config section of the Firebase console allows the conditions under which a server-side parameter will be passed to the client during a fetch request to be specified. Conditions are defined using rules which are selected either when adding or editing a parameter within the console. When adding a parameter, conditions are declared by clicking on the *Add value for condition* menu as highlighted in Figure 36-4:

Parameter key	Default value	Add value for condition ▾
main_background_color	#42b6f4	

CANCEL   **ADD PARAMETER**

Figure 36-4

The menu will provide the option to create a new condition or to select a previously added condition. The condition definition dialog (Figure 36-5) requires that the condition be given a name and assigned a color by which to identify the condition within the Remote Config Conditions screen.

Define a new condition

Use conditions to provide different parameter values if a condition is met

Name

All German Users

Color

Applies if...

Select...   AND

CANCEL   CREATE CONDITION

Figure 36-5

Clicking on the *Select...* menu in the *Applies if...* section of the dialog provides the following list of options from which to begin building the rule:

- **App ID** – The Android package name for the app.
- **App version** – The value assigned to the android:versionName property in the app's manifest file.
- **OS type** – The operating system running on the device (iOS or Android).
- **User in random percentile** – Targets a random sampling of users up to a specified percentage of the overall user base. This option is particularly useful for implementing A/B testing to judge how users react to different app behavior or appearance.
- **User in audience** – Allows for the selection of user groups defined using the Analytics features of Firebase.
- **Device in country/region** – Users in one or more specific geographic regions.
- **Device language** – The locale and language configured on the user's device.
- **User property** – Targets users based on user properties configured using Firebase Analytics.

Once a selection has been made, the corresponding criteria must be selected. If the random percentile option is selected, for example, an operator and percentage value will need to be selected as shown in Figure 36-6:

Figure 36-6

Similarly, the device region requires that one or more countries or territories be selected:

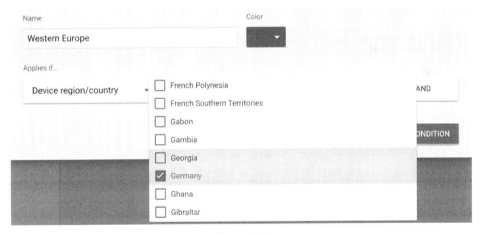

Figure 36-7

Once a condition has been defined, the AND button may be used to add additional rules to the condition, all of which must resolve to be true in order for the condition to the met.

Once the condition is complete, clicking on the *Create Condition* button returns to the parameter creation dialog where a parameter value must be entered to be used when the condition rules are met. In Figure 36-8, for example, a different background color is defined for users matching a condition named Western Europe:

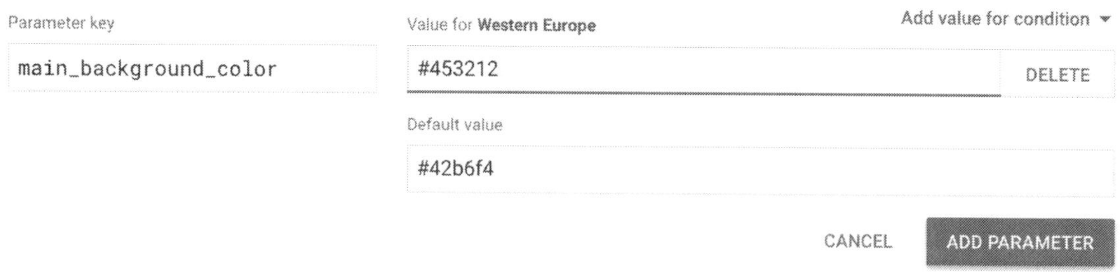

Figure 36-8

Note that the above dialog contains a field titled *Default value*. While the condition in the above example dictates the background color that will be used for users in western Europe, the default setting defines the background color that will be provided for the remaining users. If no value is to be provided for other users (in other words the app will use the in-app parameter in other geographic regions) this field can be left as an empty value.

If conditions overlap to the extent that more than one condition might be true under certain circumstances, the system needs to know which should take priority. Condition priorities may be altered by selecting the Conditions tab within the Remote Config screen of the Firebase console. This will list all of the conditions currently configured for the Firebase project in the order in which they will be evaluated. Once a condition in the list evaluates to true no other conditions beneath that point in the list will be evaluated. To change the position of a condition in the evaluation order, simply click on the handle and drag the item to the appropriate position in the list:

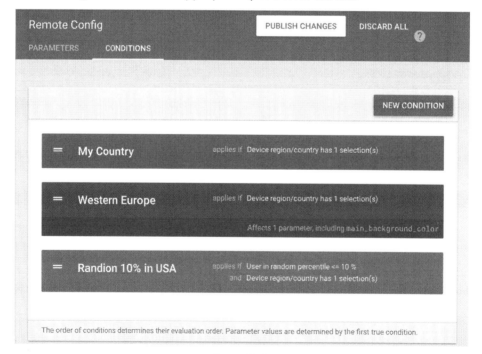

Figure 36-9

Once the conditions are configured, the *Publish Changes* button must be clicked before the new settings take effect.

36.9 **Parameter Fetching Strategies**

The timing and frequency of fetch requests is largely at the discretion of the app. The app controls the expiration duration for the cache and when calls are made to the *fetch()* method. That being said, there are some recommended guidelines that should be followed when using Remote Config.

In general, performing significant configuration changes while the user is interacting with the app should be avoided. If such changes are necessary, they should be made the next time the user interface for an activity loads, rather than dynamically while the user is interacting with the screen.

Whenever possible, updated configuration parameters should ideally be activated the next time the user launches the app. When taking this approach, however, the user should not be made to wait for the fetch process to complete before being able to begin using the app. To avoid delaying the start of the app while the fetch operation completes, Google recommends fetching new parameters while the app is running, but not activating them until the user next launches the app. This way the new parameters are already downloaded and ready to be used instantly when the app next starts. This technique will be demonstrated in the tutorial contained in the next chapter.

To allow for the possibility that certain configuration changes may need to take effect immediately, also consider using Firebase Notifications to trigger a fetch operation within the app using a zero caching expiration value. Care should be taken when using this approach for large user bases to avoid throttling when all running app instances attempt to fetch parameters simultaneously.

36.10 **Getting Status Information**

Status information is available from the FirebaseRemoteConfig object via a call to the *getInfo()* method. This method returns a FirebasebaseRemoteConfigInfo object on which the *getLastFetchStatus()* method may be called. A call to this method will return one of the following status values:

- **LAST_FETCH_STATUS_NO_FETCH_YET** – A fetch attempt has yet to be made by the app.
- **LAST_FETCH_STATUS_SUCCESS** – The last fetch was performed successfully.
- **LAST_FETCH_STATUS_FAILURE** – The last fetch failed.
- **LAST_FETCH_STATUS_THROTTLED** – The last fetch attempt was throttled indicating that the app has made too many fetch requests.

Code to check for throttling might, for example, read as follows:

```
FirebaseRemoteConfigInfo info = fbRemoteConfig.getInfo();
int status = info.getLastFetchStatus());

if (status == FirebaseRemoteConfig.LAST_FETCH_STATUS_THROTTLED) {
        // Last fetch was throttled
}
```

In addition to the *getInfo()* method, the timestamp of the last successful fetch (in milliseconds since January 1st, 1970) is available via a call to the *getFetchTimeMillis()* method.

Access to the current settings of the FirebaseRemoteConfig object is available via the *getConfigSettings()* method which returns a FirebaseRemoteConfigSettings object. The only method currently provided by this object is the *isDeveloperModeEnabled()* method which, as the name suggests, returns a Boolean value indicating whether developer mode is enabled.

36.11 Summary

Firebase Remote Config provides a way to make configuration changes to an app after it has been installed on user devices without the need to issue upgrades. The service is based on the concept of sets of parameters in the form of key-value pairs that are used internally by the app logic to control the look and behavior of the app. Local parameters provide the default values for the app which are then overridden on a per-parameter basis from within the Firebase console. Conditions provide control over which groups of users receive modified parameters based on criteria such as geographical location, app version, language or device operating system.

37. A Firebase Remote Config Tutorial

In this chapter of Firebase Essentials, an example Android Studio project will be created with the objective of demonstrating the use of Firebase Remote Config to remotely change a number of configuration options within an Android app.

37.1 Creating the Project

The app created in this chapter will use Firebase Remote Config to allow the background color, text and font size of components within a user interface to be modified via the Firebase console.

Begin by starting Android Studio and selecting the *Start a new Android Studio project* quick start option from the welcome screen.

Within the new project dialog, enter *RemoteConfig* into the Application name field and your domain as the Company Domain setting before clicking on the *Next* button.

On the form factors screen, enable the *Phone and Tablet* option and set the minimum SDK to API 16: Android 4.1 (Jellybean). Continue through the screens, requesting the creation of an Empty Activity named *RemoteConfigActivity* with a corresponding layout named *activity_remote_config*.

37.2 Adding Remote Config Support to the Project

In order to make use of Remote Config the project needs to be registered with a Firebase project and configured with the appropriate Remote Config libraries. Within the Android Studio main window, select the *Tools -> Firebase* menu option to display the Firebase assistant panel. Within the panel locate and unfold the Remote Config section and click on the *Set up Firebase Remote Config* link. On the Remote Config setup screen, click on the *Connect to Firebase* button and, in the resulting dialog, select the *Firebase Examples* project from the list of existing projects before clicking on the *Connect to Firebase* button.

After the project has been connected to Firebase, click on the *Add Remote Config to your app* button in the Firebase assistant panel followed by the *Accept Changes* button in the configuration dialog.

37.3 Designing the User Interface

Once the project has been created, open the *activity_remote_config.xml* layout file in the layout editor tool and drag and drop a Button widget onto the layout so that it is positioned beneath the existing "Hello World" TextView as shown in Figure 37-1 below:

Figure 37-1

Select the Button widget and, using the Properties tool window, set the text property to "Update Config" and configure the onClick property to call a method named *updateConfig*. Select the TextView widget and change the ID property to *welcomeText*.

Select the ConstraintLayout entry in the Component Tree tool window (Figure 37-2) and change the ID of the layout in the properties panel to *layout*.

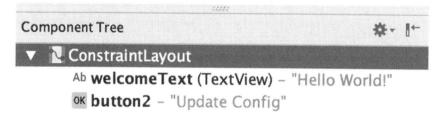

Figure 37-2

Finally, click on the Infer Constraints button (Figure 37-3) in the toolbar to add appropriate constraints to the layout.

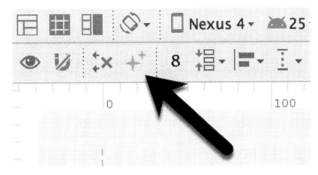

Figure 37-3

37.4 Declaring the Default In-App Parameters

The in-app parameters for the project will be contained within an XML resource file which now needs to be added to the project. Within the Project tool window, locate and right-click on the *app -> res* folder and select the *New -> Android Resource Directory* menu option. In the resulting dialog, enter *xml* into the directory name field and select *xml* for the resource type before clicking on the OK button:

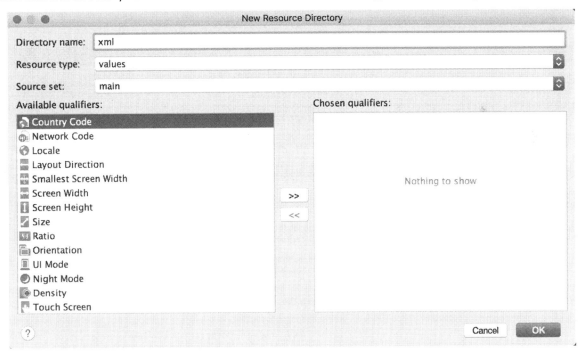

Figure 37-4

After the xml directory has been created it will appear in the Project tool window. Right-click on the new directory, this time selecting the *New –> File* menu option. In the new file dialog, specify *remote_config_params.xml* as the filename before clicking on the OK button to create the file.

Load the new XML resource file into the editor and modify it to declare the default in-app parameters as follows:

```xml
<?xml version="1.0" encoding="utf-8"?>
<defaultsMap>
    <entry>
        <key>welcome_text</key>
        <value>Welcome to Firebase</value>
    </entry>
    <entry>
        <key>welcome_font_size</key>
        <value>16</value>
    </entry>
    <entry>
        <key>main_background_color</key>
        <value>#42f486</value>
    </entry>
</defaultsMap>
```

37.5 Loading the Config Parameters

Code now needs to be added to the main activity class to obtain a FirebaseRemoteConfig object reference and to load into it the default in-app parameters from the XML resource file. Open the *RemoteConfigActivity.java* file and modify the code so that it reads as follows. Note that a number of import directives are also added in preparation for later additions to the class:

```java
package com.ebookfrenzy.remoteconfig;

import android.support.v7.app.AppCompatActivity;
import android.os.Bundle;
import android.graphics.Color;
import android.support.annotation.NonNull;
import android.support.constraint.ConstraintLayout;
import android.view.View;
import android.widget.TextView;

import com.google.android.gms.tasks.OnCompleteListener;
import com.google.android.gms.tasks.Task;
import com.google.firebase.remoteconfig.FirebaseRemoteConfig;
import com.google.firebase.remoteconfig.FirebaseRemoteConfigSettings;

public class RemoteConfigActivity extends AppCompatActivity {

    private FirebaseRemoteConfig fbRemoteConfig;
```

```
    @Override
    protected void onCreate(Bundle savedInstanceState) {
        super.onCreate(savedInstanceState);
        setContentView(R.layout.activity_remote_config);

        fbRemoteConfig = FirebaseRemoteConfig.getInstance();
        fbRemoteConfig.setDefaults(R.xml.remote_config_params);

        fbRemoteConfig.setConfigSettings(
            new FirebaseRemoteConfigSettings.Builder()
                .setDeveloperModeEnabled(true)
                .build());
    }
}
```

Note that for testing purposes, code has also been added to the method to enable developer mode.

Next, some code needs to be added to apply the parameter values to the user interface. For the purposes of this example, a method named *applyConfig()* will be added and called from within the *onCreate()* method:

```
@Override
protected void onCreate(Bundle savedInstanceState) {
    super.onCreate(savedInstanceState);
    setContentView(R.layout.activity_remote_config);

    fbRemoteConfig = FirebaseRemoteConfig.getInstance();
    fbRemoteConfig.setDefaults(R.xml.remote_config_params);
.
.
    applyConfig();
}

protected void applyConfig() {

    ConstraintLayout layout = (ConstraintLayout) findViewById(R.id.layout);
    TextView textView = (TextView) findViewById(R.id.welcomeText);

    String bg_color = fbRemoteConfig.getString("main_background_color");
    layout.setBackgroundColor(Color.parseColor(bg_color));
    textView.setTextSize(fbRemoteConfig.getLong("welcome_font_size"));
    textView.setText(fbRemoteConfig.getString("welcome_text"));
}
```

Compile and run the app and make sure that the in-app parameters are being used to set the background color, text and font size. Assuming the code is working, the next step is to add server-side parameters within the Firebase console.

37.6 Adding the Server-side Parameters

Open a browser window, navigate to the Firebase console and select the Firebase Example project. Once the project has loaded, click on the Remote Config option in the navigation panel followed by the *Add your first parameter* button:

Figure 37-5

The first parameter to be added is the welcome text. Within the new parameter dialog (shown in Figure 37-6), enter *welcome_text* into the *Parameter key* field and *Welcome to Remote Config* into the *Default value* field before clicking on the *Add Parameter* button.

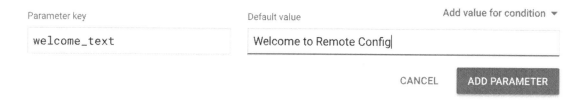

Figure 37-6

Repeat this step to add the *main_background_color* and *welcome_font_size* parameters set to #f4419d and 35 respectively. On completion of these steps the list of parameters within the console should match that shown in Figure 37-7:

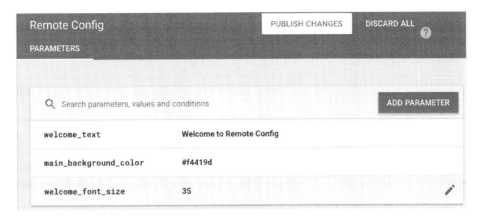

Figure 37-7

Having verified that the entries are correct, click on the *Publish Changes* button to make the configuration changes available to the app.

37.7 Fetching and Activating the Remote Parameters

Now that parameters have been added within the console, the app needs to be modified to fetch and activate the changes. Later in this chapter we will look at fetching and activating parameters at app startup. For now though, the callback method on the *Update Config* button will be used to demonstrate instantly applying configuration changes.

Edit the *RemoteConfigActivity.java* file and add the *updateConfig()* callback method as follows:

```
public void updateConfig(View view) {
    fbRemoteConfig.fetch(0).addOnCompleteListener(this,
                    new OnCompleteListener<Void>() {

        @Override
        public void onComplete(@NonNull Task<Void> task) {
            if (task.isSuccessful()) {
                fbRemoteConfig.activateFetched();
                applyConfig();
            } else {
                // Fetch failed
            }
        }
    });
}
```

The above code calls the *fetch()* method of the FirebaseRemoteConfig instance with a cache timeout value of 0. A listener is also added which activates the fetched parameters and calls the *applyConfig()* method so that the changes are immediately visible within the user interface.

Run the app once again, click on the *Update Config* button and confirm that the changes configured in the console are reflected in the user interface. If any of the changes fail to take effect, check that the parameter keys declared in the Firebase console match those in the in-app parameter resource file. Also add some logging output within the completion listener callback to verify that the fetch operation completes successfully.

37.8 Handling Changes at Startup

As outlined in the previous chapter, a recommended strategy for dealing with Remote Config changes is to fetch changes while the app is running and then activate them on the next app launch. To implement this behavior, edit the *onCreate()* method to first activate any parameters that may have been fetched during the previous session and then perform a new fetch ready for the next time the app is started by the user:

```
.

.
@Override
protected void onCreate(Bundle savedInstanceState) {
    super.onCreate(savedInstanceState);
    setContentView(R.layout.activity_remote_config);

    fbRemoteConfig = FirebaseRemoteConfig.getInstance();
    fbRemoteConfig.setDefaults(R.xml.remote_config_params);

    fbRemoteConfig.activateFetched();
    applyConfig();
    fbRemoteConfig.fetch(0);
}
.

.
```

Note that a completion listener is not added to the *fetch()* method call this time. This is intentional since no action needs to be taken yet after the fetch operation completes. By design, the updated configuration will not be activated until the next time the app starts up.

To test this behavior perform the following steps:

1. Change the values assigned to the parameter keys in the Firebase console.
2. Run the app and note that, while the changes are fetched in the background they are not activated and visible in the user interface.
3. Stop and restart the app. Note that the cached changes are now activated and visible.

37.9 Creating a Conditional Parameter Change

As a final step, a simple condition rule will be added for the background color parameter. Within the Remote Config Firebase console screen, edit the *main_background_color* parameter and click on the *Add value for condition* menu as highlighted in Figure 37-8:

Figure 37-8

From the condition menu, select the *Define new condition* option. Within the new condition dialog (Figure 37-9) name the condition *My Country*, select the *Device region/country* option and then choose the country in which you are currently residing from the *Select countries* menu:

Figure 37-9

Click on the *Create Condition* button to return to the parameter editing dialog. An entry will now be shown for the My Country condition with a field ready to accept a new color settings for all users in your country. Enter a new color setting into this field:

Figure 37-10

357

Note that the previous color value is now listed as the default and will be used in all countries except the one specified in the condition.

Click on the Publish Changes button before returning to the running app and clicking on the *Update Config* button at which point the background color should change indicating the condition is working.

37.10 **Summary**

This chapter has provided a tutorial designed to demonstrate the key features of Firebase Remote Config. This has included the addition of Remote Config support to an Android Studio project, accessing the FirebaseRemoteConfig object and the implementation of in-app parameters using a resource file. The chapter then covered the creation of server-side parameters using the Firebase console and the fetching and activating of those parameters. Finally, a condition was used to target a specific parameter change based on geographical location.

38. Firebase Analytics

Firebase Analytics provides a way to learn about the user base of an app and to analyze and track the way in which those users engage and interact with the app.

This chapter and the chapters that follow are intended to provide an overview of Firebase Analytics and to introduce the features that are provided by this service.

The chapter will begin by providing an overview of the different features provided by Firebase Analytics including events, user parameters and audiences. Subsequent chapters will explore the various screens that make up the Analytics section of the Firebase console before working through a tutorial involving events, user properties and audiences.

38.1 An Overview of Firebase Analytics

Using Firebase Analytics, app developers can capture and analyze data about users and the way in which they interact with an app. Firebase Analytics consists of a library that integrates with the app combined with a set screens within the Firebase console designed to provide easily understandable visual representations of the collected data in the form of graphs, charts and tables.

Without the need to add a single line of code to an app project, Firebase Analytics will provide demographic data about an app user base including the age, gender and geographical location. A number of events are also captured automatically including the first time users open the app, Google Play in-app purchases, user engagement with the app, app crashes and the receipt and opening of Firebase Notification messages.

With the addition of a few lines of code, app developers can add custom events to track just about any type of user interaction within an app, allowing analytics data capture to be adapted to the specific requirements of the app.

Firebase Analytics also allows custom audiences to be defined, allowing users to be grouped together based on behavior patterns. Once created, audiences can be used within other Firebase features such as Notifications and Remote Config.

The four key elements of Firebase Analytics are the FirebaseAnalytics object, events, user properties and audiences, each of which will be covered in detail in the remainder of this chapter.

38.2 The FirebaseAnalytics Object

The object responsible for providing Firebase Analytics support within an Android app is the FirebaseAnalytics object. The first step in implementing Analytics support within an app is to obtain a reference to this object instance as follows:

```
FirebaseRemoteConfig fbAnalytics = FirebaseAnalytics.getInstance(this);
```

38.3 **Events**

Event logging provides a way to track user behavior within an app. Events are categorized by type, with each app allowed to define up to 500 different types of event. Although the number of event types is limited, there is no limit to the number of events that can be logged using Firebase Analytics.

Events may also include parameters which provide additional information relevant to the event. A flight booking app might, for example, log an event each time a user books a ticket and include the departure and destination airports as event parameters. These parameters can then be used when filtering results within the Firebase console.

Firebase Analytics allows the use of predefined, suggested and custom events types, each of which requires some explanation:

38.3.1 Predefined Events Types

Firebase Analytics automatically captures a set of predefined events without the need to add any additional code to the app. A full listing of events and event parameters that are captured automatically is available online at:

https://support.google.com/firebase/answer/6317485?hl=en&ref_topic=6317484

38.3.2 Suggested Event Types

In addition to the predefined events that are captured automatically, Firebase Analytics includes a set of suggested event types with predefined names and parameter sets. These event types are grouped into different categories such as retail, ecommerce, travel and games. A full listing of suggested events and corresponding parameters can be found at the following URL:

https://support.google.com/firebase/topic/6317484?hl=en

Suggested events are not logged automatically and must be triggered from within code using the *logEvent()* method of the FirebaseAnalytics object. Consider, for example, a requirement to log an event each time a user signs up for an app. A review of the suggested events list will identify that the *sign_up* event would be a suitable candidate. According to the documentation, this particular event type is designed to include the sign up method (email, Google, Facebook etc.) as a parameter. The code to log a sign up event within an app would, therefore, read as follows:

```
Bundle event = new Bundle();
event.putString(FirebaseAnalytics.Param.SIGN_UP_METHOD, "Google");
fbAnalytics.logEvent(FirebaseAnalytics.Event.SIGN_UP, event);
```

38.3.3 Custom Event Types

In addition to predefined and suggested events, it is also possible to configure custom events. This is useful if none of the suggested events are a good match for the event type. Neither the predefined nor suggested events, for example, include an event for tracking when a user logs out of an app. Such an event would, therefore, need to be created as a custom event. The code to log a custom event of this type, including parameters for the authentication provider and the number of seconds the user was logged in would read as follows:

```
Bundle custom = new Bundle();
custom.putString("logout", "Facebook");
custom.putLong("duration", 1200);
fbAnalytics.logEvent("user_logout", custom);
```

When the above event is triggered, an event named *user_logout* will be logged within Firebase Analytics containing the two parameters.

38.4 Viewing Events in the LogCat Window

When implementing events within a project, it can be useful to enable logcat debugging. This causes events to appear in the Android Studio logcat panel as they are logged. To enable this mode, connect a device or start an emulator and execute the following adb commands within a terminal or command-prompt window:

```
adb shell setprop log.tag.FA VERBOSE
adb shell setprop log.tag.FA-SVC VERBOSE
```

In addition to the logcat panel, debugging output may also be viewed within the command-prompt or terminal window using the following command:

```
adb logcat -v time -s FA FA-SVC
```

Realtime event tracking during development is also available in the Analytics DebugView screen, a topic which is covered in the chapter entitled *An Overview of the Firebase Analytics Screens*.

38.5 User Properties

User properties are key-value pairs that are created within an app which, once defined, are sent with every event that is subsequently logged. The purpose of user properties is to store information about the user.

Once declared, user properties can be used to filter the results in the Firebase Analytics console screens, and also to create audiences.

A food delivery app might, for example, set a user property to indicate each user's most frequently ordered item. That property could then be used to create an audience consisting of all users who frequently order pizza. The resulting audience could then be targeted with Firebase Notification messages or Remote Config app changes to promote a special offer on pizza deliveries.

User properties are created using the *setUserProperty()* method of the FirebaseAnalytics object, for example:

```
fbAnalytics.setUserProperty("most_ordered", "pizza");
```

Each app can declare up to 25 different user properties. When working with user properties it is important to be aware that it can take up to 24 hours before the properties start appearing in the Firebase Analytics results.

38.6 **Audiences**

Google Analytics essentially uses event logging, event parameters and user properties to gather and store detailed information about the user base of an app. With access to all of this information it becomes possible to segment users into groups referred to as audiences. The data associated with these audiences can then be analyzed independently from the rest of the user base, or used to target those users via Firebase services like Notifications and Remote Config.

The possible combinations of ways to create audiences is limited only by the different types of events and user properties captured for an app. Assuming appropriate use of events and user properties, it would, for example, be entirely possible for a flight booking app to create an audience of 39-45 year-old men living in Germany who have made a purchase within the app in the last two weeks of a ticket to fly from Berlin to London Heathrow Airport.

Audiences are created within the Firebase console using the steps covered in the chapter entitled *An Overview of the Firebase Analytics Screens*.

38.7 **Summary**

Firebase Analytics is a service that allows app developers to gain an understanding of the users of an app including user demographics and app engagement. Firebase Analytics consists of a series of screens within the Firebase console and a library integrated into app projects. The key elements of Firebase Analytics are events, user properties and audiences each of which has been described in this chapter and will be covered in greater detail in the following chapters.

39. A Guided Tour of the Firebase Analytics Dashboard

Google Analytics for Firebase provides a vast array of charts, tables and graphs containing information covering not only the way in which users interact with the app, but also details about the users themselves.

An important part of getting up to speed using Firebase Analytics involves gaining a familiarity with the various screens that make up the Analytics section of the Firebase console. This chapter will provide a tour of the Analytics Dashboard provided by the Firebase console together with an outline of the types of information you can expect to find within each chart and graph. The next chapter, entitled *An Overview of the Firebase Analytics Screens*, will provide details of the other screens available within Firebase Analytics.

39.1 The Firebase Analytics Dashboard

Firebase Analytics data is accessed by opening the Firebase console in a browser window, selecting a project and then clicking on the Analytics option located at the top of the navigation panel. The first screen to appear is always the Dashboard which is shown in reduced size in Figure 39-1:

Figure 39-1

The purpose of the Dashboard is to provide an overview of the key metrics in a single screen. Before exploring these metrics, it is important to be aware of the filtering options that are available to tailor the results being displayed.

39.2 Filtering the Data

A single Firebase project can contain multiple apps. The menu (marked A in Figure 39-2) allows the app for which data is being shown to be selected. The Add Filter (B) button is also provided to allow the data to be filtered based on audiences, user properties, and demographic data.

The area marked C allows configurable date ranges to be specified. The top entry represents the date range for which data is to be displayed. The bottom date range represents a data range against which the current data will be compared within certain sets of data (for example comparing whether user engagement for the currently selected data range has increased since a previous time period).

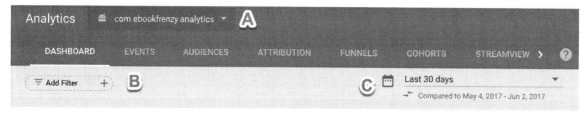

Figure 39-2

The rest of the Dashboard contains a collection of cards, each of which shows specific metrics related to the currently selected app and any prevailing filtering options. Some of these cards provide a summary of information which is available in greater detail on other Analytics screens.

These cards can be summarized as follows:

39.2.1 Active users

The Active Users card contains a graph tracking the number of users that were actively using the app over 1-day, 7-day and 30-day periods.

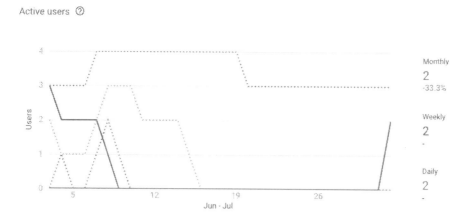

Figure 39-3

39.2.2 Average revenue

The Average Revenue card reports the average revenue per user (ARPU) and average revenue per paying user (ARPPU). The ARPU is calculated by dividing the revenue earned during the specified period by the total number of users. The ARPPU, on the other hand, divides the revenue by the number of users that made a purchase.

Average revenue ⑦

ARPU	ARPPU
Monthly	Monthly
$0.00	$0.00
-	-
Weekly	Weekly
$0.00	$0.00
-	-
Daily	Daily
$0.00	$0.00
-	-

Figure 39-4

The data is captured for this report via the *ecommerce_purchase* and *in_app_purchase* events. Note that while *in_app_purchase* events are recorded automatically, the *ecommerce_purchase* event must be triggered within the app.

39.2.3 first_open attribution

The term *first_open attribution* refers to the tracking of the number times the app has been opened for the first time. This essentially tracks users who not only install the app, but also launch it. This card also contains the *lifetime value*, an indicator of the total amount of revenue earned during the first 120 days of app use. A more detailed breakdown of the first open events and revenue sources (such as advertising) is available in the main attributions screen which may be accessed using either the tab located in the console toolbar, or by clicking on the link located at the bottom of the card.

Figure 39-5

39.2.4 Retention cohorts

A cohort in this context refers to a group of users who all started using the app within the same time period. This card shows the retention for each cohort, in other words the percentage of users within each cohort who continued to use the app within subsequent weeks. Each row in the table represents a cohort and each block in the row a percentage value indicating the retention rate for that group of users. The darker the shading of the block, the higher the retention rate.

Figure 39-6

A decline on retention as weeks progress is a warning sign that users tend to lose interest with the app over time.

39.2.5 User engagement

As illustrated in Figure 39-2 above, the Dashboard allows a date range for which metrics are to be provided to be specified. A comparison date range is also selected for the purposes of comparing metrics for different date ranges. The user engagement card compares the following engagement statistics between the specified date ranges.

- **Daily engagement** – The total amount of time spent by users engaging with the app.
- **Daily engagement per user** – The average duration of engagement per user.
- **Sessions per user** – The total number of sessions divided by the total number of active users.
- **User engagement per screen** – An analysis of the user engagement time on a per screen basis within the app.

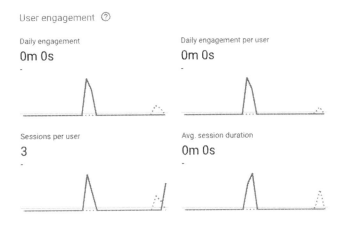

Figure 39-7

In each graph in the above figure, the solid line represents the currently selected date range and the dotted line the comparison date range. The percentage value indicates the amount by which each of the engagement metrics has changed between the two ranges.

39.2.6 In-app purchases

In order to track in-app purchases, the Firebase project must be linked to the app entry in the Google Play account through which in-app purchases are being processed. If the account is not yet linked, click on the Link to Google Play button and complete the linking process:

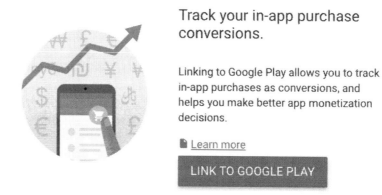

Figure 39-8

Once linked, the In-app Purchase card will report comparison data for the selected date ranges for the number of users who have completed a purchase, the percentage of those users relative to the entire user base and the total number and value of the purchase transactions. In-app purchases are recorded automatically via the *in_app_purchase* event.

39.2.7 App version

The app version card displays the number of users currently using each of the top three versions of the app.

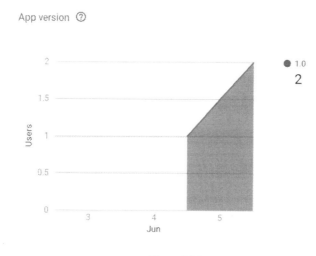

Figure 39-9

39.2.8 Devices

The Devices card presents a percentage breakdown of the top three device and operating system versions on which the app is running together with a fourth category representing all other device types and operating system versions:

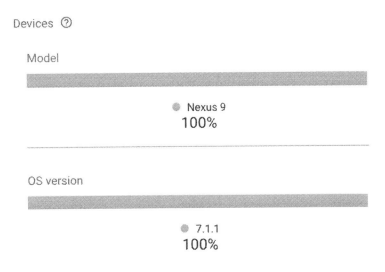

Figure 39-10

39.3 Location

The Location card simply reports the breakdown of app sessions listed by country.

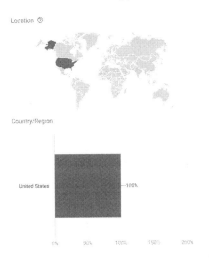

Figure 39-11

39.3.1 Demographics

The demographics card reports app usage categorized by user gender and age group. Firebase Analytics gathers this information using the Google Play Android Advertising ID which is used by Google to create anonymous user profiles for each Android device for advertising targeting purposes.

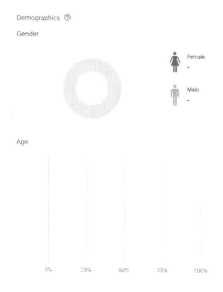

Figure 39-12

39.3.2 Interests

Reports the number of users in specific interest groups. Interest groups are created by Google using the Android Advertising ID and include topics such as finance, health, education, real estate, shopping and sports.

Figure 39-13

39.4 **Summary**

Firebase Analytics involves the collection and analysis of data relating to the users of an app. The Firebase Analytics Dashboard provides a single location in which all of the key metrics gathered by the analytics system can be reviewed. The dashboard is comprised of a collection of cards containing visual summaries of data logged for the currently selected app during a specified date range. A filter option is also provided to customize the data using a range of demographic and event based criteria.

As will be outlined in the next chapter, additional detail beyond that provided by the dashboard is available using dedicated Firebase console analytics screens.

Chapter 40

40. An Overview of the Firebase Analytics Screens

The previous chapter provided an overview of the Firebase Analytics Dashboard screen. In addition to the dashboard, the Firebase console also provides other screens that provide more detail on each metric. This chapter will provide an overview of these screens and explain how each fits into the Firebase Analytics system.

Note that many of these screens provide the same filtering and date range options available within the dashboard screen for the purpose of reviewing different time periods or for comparing one date range against another.

40.1 The Events Screen

Clicking on the Events tab located in the analytics toolbar will display the screen shown in Figure 40-1:

Event name ↑	Count		Value		Users		Mark as conversion	
app_exception	0	-100%	-		0	-100%		
app_remove	1	0%	-		1	0%		
first_open	2	+100%	-		2	+100%		
notification_dismiss	0	-100%	-		0	-100%		
notification_foreground	2	0%	-		1	-50%		
notification_open	1		-		1			
notification_receive	4	+33.3%	-		1	-50%		
session_start	3	-66.4%	-		2	-33.3%		

Figure 40-1

The table presented on the Events screen lists all of the events that have been triggered by the app in the designated date range. This will include both those events that are automatically recorded by Firebase Analytics and any custom events configured for the app.

The table includes columns for the event name, the number of times the event triggered and the number of users who triggered the event together with comparison percentages.

If an event has a value parameter, the value column will list the total accumulated value amount for the corresponding event.

The switches in the *Mark as conversion* column indicate whether the event is to count as a conversion, a topic which will be covered when discussing attributions later in this chapter.

Clicking on the menu icon in the far right column allows any parameters assigned to the event to be edited.

Selecting an event from the list will display a detail screen showing additional information about the event statistics including an event timeline, location information, user demographics and events per session.

40.2 **The Audiences Screen**

The Audiences screen allows audiences to be viewed, created and managed. Firebase Analytics audiences are groups of users with something in common. Audiences can be created based on user properties (such as geographical location, age, device type or language) or on events. An audience could, for example, be created to contain all users that have made in in-app purchase, or triggered a custom event with a specific value.

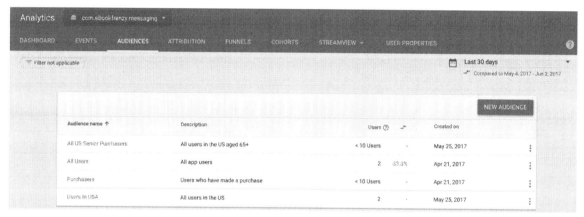

Figure 40-2

By default, only the built-in All Users and Purchaser audiences will be available. To add an audience, click on the *New Audience* button. In the resulting dialog (Figure 40-3), enter a name and description for the audience, then select the events or user properties by which the audience is to be identified.

Figure 40-3

Within the new audience dialog, the AND and OR buttons can be used to create audiences based on multiple conditions. An audience could, for example, be created to contain all male French users who have made an in-app purchase greater than a specified value *and* are either in the 25-34 age range, *or* over the age of 65.

Clicking on an audience name in the table will display a detail screen containing the standard analytics metrics for that audience. Clicking on the menu button in the far right column provides the option to add the metrics for that audience to the Analytics Dashboard screen.

Once an audience has been created it can be used in a variety of ways, for example both Firebase Notifications and Remote Config updates can be targeted to audiences created on this screen.

40.3 **The Attribution Screen**

The Attribution screen provides a way to track the effectiveness of marketing campaigns (typically advertising) designed to acquire new users and encourage them to engage with the app. When a user takes an action as a result of a marketing campaign (such as installing the app or making an in-app purchase), this is referred to as a *conversion*. By default, Firebase considers a *first_open* event to be a conversion if it can be associated as having come from an advertising network. To make other events count as conversions, switch to the Events screen, locate the event in the list and turn on the switch in the *Mark as conversion* column.

To associate advertising campaigns with conversion tracking, click on the *Network Settings* tab shown in Figure 40-4:

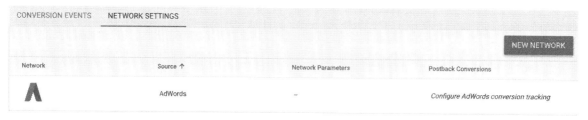

Figure 40-4

Within this screen, clicking on the *Campaign source* menu will provide a list of ad networks from which a selection can be made. Once the ad network on which the advertisements are going to run has been selected, copy the campaign URL and paste it into the campaign settings within the ad network's own portal.

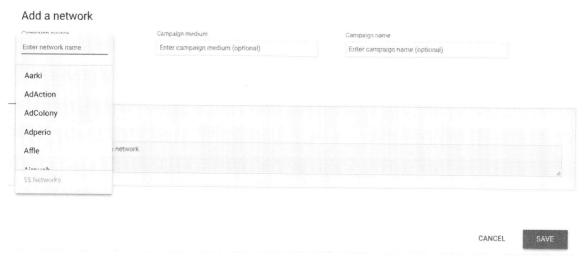

Figure 40-5

When a conversion event is triggered via a campaign URL, it will be recorded within the Attribution metrics and attributed to the ad network.

In addition to the ad networks listed in the Network Setting screen, a Google AdWords account may be linked with Firebase Analytics for tracking conversions. To link the account, scroll down within the Network Settings screen and click on the *Configure AdWords conversion tracking* link.

Once linked, conversion tracking can be configured for AdWords campaigns by clicking on the *Configure AdWords conversion tracking* link within the Network Settings screen.

40.4 **The Funnels Screen**

The term funnel refers to a series of steps taken by a user within a website or app. A user might, for example, browse through a list of items within an app, select an item of interest, click on an add to cart button and then proceed through the process of entering shipping and payment info before finally making the purchase. If each of these steps is associated with an event, a funnel can be defined within Firebase Analytics and then used to track how users progress through the funnel. This can be particularly useful for identifying the point at which users frequently stop progressing through the steps so that corrective action can be taken or app design changes made (for example making a particular screen more user friendly or by requiring less information from the user to complete the step).

To create a funnel, go to the Funnels screen and click in the *Add your first funnel* button. In the new funnel dialog, enter a name and description for the funnel, then add two or more events to make up the funnel.

Figure 40-6

The funnels screen will list all configured funnels. Clicking on a funnel will display stats for each step of the funnel providing insight into user behavior and highlighting steps where users appear to stop and give up:

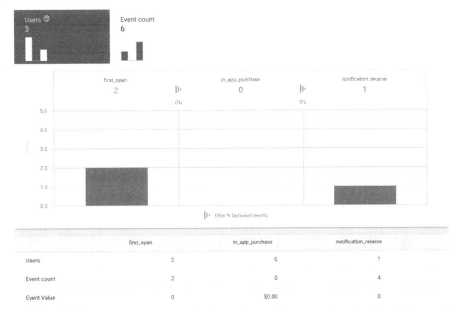

Figure 40-7

40.5 **The Cohorts Screen**

The cohorts screen essentially displays the same information as the Retention cohorts card located in the Firebase Analytics Dashboard with the addition of an extra line graph. As with the dashboard, this screen shows the level of retention for groups of users that began using the app at the same time.

Figure 40-8

40.6 **The StreamView Screen**

The StreamView screen provides a live view of the events that are taking place within the installed app base.

The live view consists of a map on which either users or events are displayed. The display can be switched between event and user modes by clicking on one of the two buttons shown in Figure 40-9:

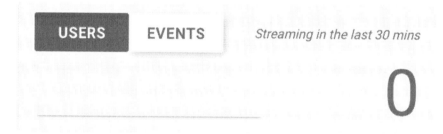

Figure 40-9

Timeline details and a trending table are also available by hovering the mouse pointer above the toggle buttons and clicking on one of the two thumbnail panels that appear:

Figure 40-10

40.7 **The DebugView Screen**

In the real world, Firebase Analytics only gathers data from user devices approximately once an hour. Clearly this would make testing a slow process during development since every code change will require a wait of up to an hour to see the results. In recognition of this issue, Google provides the DebugView screen.

DebugView is accessed by clicking on the StreamView tab and selecting DebugView from the drop-down menu as shown in Figure 40-11:

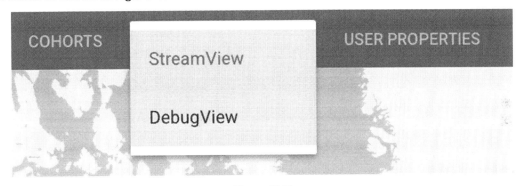

Figure 40-11

Before events will appear within the DebugView, the device on which testing is to be performed must be switched into Analytics Debug mode. This involves attaching the device to, or running an emulator on a development system on which the adb tool is available and then running the following command in a command-prompt or terminal window (where <package name> is replaced by the package name of the app being tested):

```
adb shell setprop debug.firebase.analytics.app <package_name>
```

Analytics Debug mode should be disabled after testing is complete by running the following command:

```
adb shell setprop debug.firebase.analytics.app .none.
```

An Overview of the Firebase Analytics Screens

Once enabled, the events will begin appearing a short time after they occur within the app. If multiple devices are being used to generate app analytics events, the device selector in the top left-hand corner of the screen can be used to select the device for which stats are to be displayed within the DebugView:

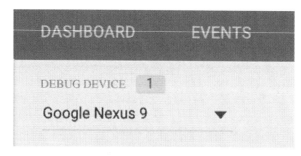

Figure 40-12

The main panel of the DebugView provides two streams of data. In the *minutes stream* (marked A in Figure 40-13), each circle represents a minute of time over a 30 minute time period. The number displayed within the circle indicates the number of events that occurred during that minute and clicking on the circle reveals the timeline of events during that 60 second time period within the seconds stream (B):

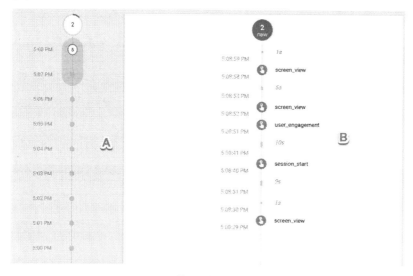

Figure 40-13

Clicking on an event in the seconds stream will display information about the event including parameters associated with the event:

380

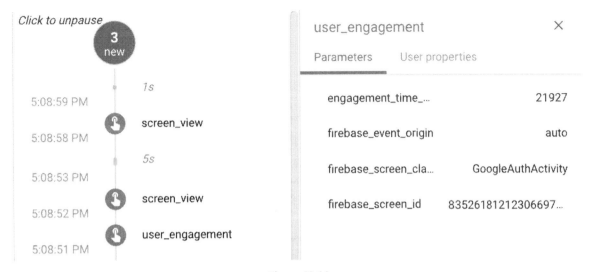

Figure 40-14

The screen also contains a Top Events card (Figure 40-15) listing the most frequent events captured during the current 30 minute period. Clicking on an event from the list will display a detailed analysis of all instances of that event over a 30 minute time window:

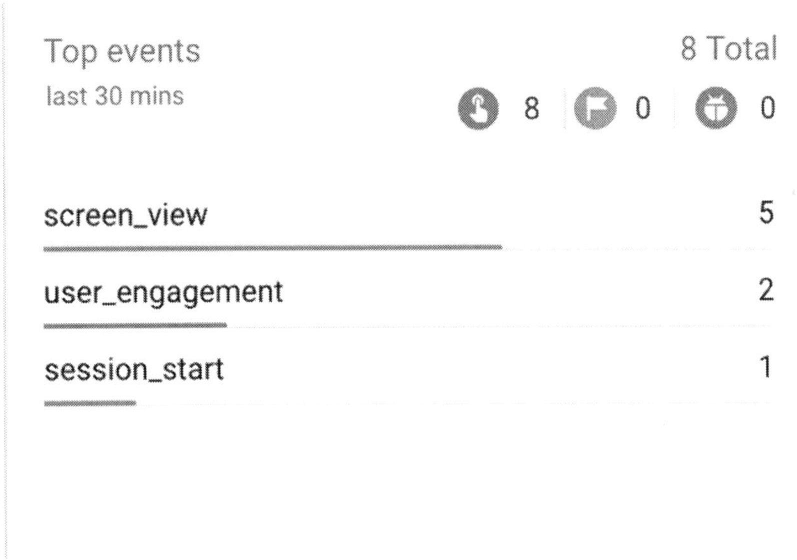

Figure 40-15

Finally, the current user properties panel lists the current set of user properties as configured by the app on the test device.

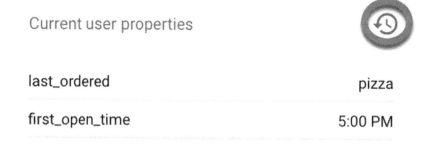

Figure 40-16

Clicking on the time button (highlighted in Figure 40-16 above) will display a history of the changes to the values of the listed properties over the preceding 30 minutes:

User properties		from 4:49 PM - 5:19 PM ✕
last_ordered	pizza	4:53:52 PM
last_ordered	pizza	4:53:43 PM
last_ordered	coffee	4:53:10 PM
last_ordered	coffee	4:52:54 PM
last_ordered	pizza	4:52:32 PM
last_ordered	pizza	4:52:10 PM
last_ordered	pizza	4:51:46 PM
last_ordered	pizza	4:51:39 PM

Figure 40-17

40.8 User Properties Screen

As described in the previous chapters, user properties provide a way for an app to provide user specific information along with each event that is logged. Once configured, user properties are then used when filtering results or building audiences within the Firebase console.

User properties are created and updated in code but are not available for filtering within Firebase Analytics until they have been registered within the User Properties screen. To register a user property click on the User Properties tab and click on the *New User Property* button:

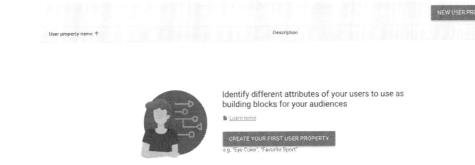

Figure 40-18

In the resulting dialog, simply enter the property name as implemented in the app code together with a description and click on the Create button.

40.9 Summary

In addition to the Analytics Dashboard, the Firebase console also includes eight other screens containing detailed information relating to metrics such as events, audiences, user retention and user engagement. Screens are also provided for creating audiences and building funnels to track user progress through predefined sequences of steps within an app.

41. A Firebase Analytics Tutorial

Now that the basics of Firebase Analytics have been covered in some detail in the preceding chapters, this chapter will step through the creation of a simple Android application project that demonstrates some of the key features of both the Firebase Analytics library and the screens within the Firebase console. The tutorial will also make use of both the logcat and DebugView debug modes for viewing events and user parameter changes in real-time.

41.1 Creating the Firebase Analytics Project

The app created in this chapter will use Firebase Analytics to demonstrate the use of events, user properties and audiences.

Begin by starting Android Studio and selecting the *Start a new Android Studio project* quick start option from the welcome screen.

Within the new project dialog, enter *Analytics* into the Application name field and your domain as the Company Domain setting before clicking on the *Next* button.

On the form factors screen, enable the *Phone and Tablet* option and set the minimum SDK to API 16: Android 4.1 (Jellybean). Proceed through the screens, requesting the creation of an Empty Activity named *AnalyticsActivity* with a corresponding layout named *activity_analytics.*

41.2 Designing the User Interface

The user interfaced for the app consists of a simple layout containing an EditText view, two buttons and a RadioGroup containing two RadioButtons as illustrated in Figure 41-1 below:

Figure 41-1

Open the *activity_analytics.xml* file in the layout editor and select and delete the default TextView. From the Containers section of the widget palette, locate the RadioGroup object and drag and drop it into position on the layout canvas. Switch the palette to the Widgets category, then drag and drop two RadioButton instances onto the RadioGroup entry in the Component Tree panel as outlined in Figure 41-2:

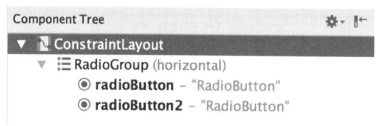

Figure 41-2

Using the Properties panel, change the text displayed on the two RadioButtons to read "Cash" and "Credit" with IDs set to *cashRadio* and *creditRadio* respectively.

Next, drag and drop the EditText and Button views onto the layout. Delete the text property for the EditText view, set the hint property to "Item" and change the ID to *itemText*. Change the text property of the Button to "Order" and configure an onClick method named *orderItem*.

Finally, select all of the widgets in the layout, right-click on the Button and select the *Center Horizontally* menu option. Repeat this a second time, this time selecting the *Center Vertically* option.

41.3 Adding Firebase Analytics Support to the Project

Within Android Studio, select the *Tools -> Firebase* menu option to display the Firebase assistant panel. Within the assistant, unfold the Analytics section, click on the *Log an Analytics event* link and connect the project to Firebase using the existing *Firebase Examples* project.

Once the project has connected to Firebase, click on the *Add Analytics to your app* button and accept the proposed changes in the resulting dialog.

41.4 Performing the App Initialization

Before adding the code to log Analytics events, some steps must first be taken to obtain a reference to the FirebaseAnalytics instance and to add a listener to the RadioGroup container to detect changes to the user's payment method selection. Edit the *AnalyticsActivity.java* file and make the following modifications to add import directives, declare variables and perform initialization tasks in the *onCreate()* method:

```java
package com.ebookfrenzy.analytics;

import android.support.v7.app.AppCompatActivity;
import android.os.Bundle;
import android.view.View;
import android.widget.EditText;
import android.widget.RadioButton;
import android.widget.RadioGroup;

import com.google.firebase.analytics.FirebaseAnalytics;

public class AnalyticsActivity extends AppCompatActivity {

    private String paymentMethod = "Cash";
    private FirebaseAnalytics fbAnalytics;

    @Override
    protected void onCreate(Bundle savedInstanceState) {
        super.onCreate(savedInstanceState);
        setContentView(R.layout.activity_analytics);

        fbAnalytics = FirebaseAnalytics.getInstance(this);

        RadioGroup radioGroup = (RadioGroup) findViewById(R.id.radioGroup);
        radioGroup.check(R.id.cashRadio);
```

```
            radioGroup.setOnCheckedChangeListener(
                        new RadioGroup.OnCheckedChangeListener() {
            @Override
            public void onCheckedChanged(RadioGroup group, int checkedId) {
                RadioButton radioButton =
                        (RadioButton) group.findViewById(checkedId);
                if (radioButton != null && checkedId > -1) {
                    paymentMethod = radioButton.getText().toString();
                }
            }
        });
    }
.
.
.
}
```

41.5 Adding the orderItem() Method

The Button widget within the user interface layout is configured to call a method named *orderItem()* when clicked by the user. The code within the method will identify whether the customer is paying by cash or credit card and extract the ordered item from the EditText widget. An event named *item_ordered* will then be logged with parameters containing the ordered item and the user's payment method. A user property named *last_ordered* will then be used to record the last item ordered by the user.

Edit the *AnalyticsActivity.java* file and add code for the *orderItem()* method as follows:

```
public void orderItem(View view) {

    EditText itemText = (EditText) findViewById(R.id.itemText);

    String item = itemText.getText().toString();
    fbAnalytics.setUserProperty("last_ordered", item);

    Bundle event = new Bundle();
    event.putString("item", item);
    event.putString("payment_method", paymentMethod);

    fbAnalytics.logEvent("item_ordered", event);
}
```

41.6 Enabling Debugging Modes

Before testing the app built in this chapter, both the logcat and DebugView debugging modes need to be enabled so that the event logging can be viewed in realtime.

Connect a device to the system on which Android Studio is running or launch an emulator. In a command prompt or terminal window, enable logcat debug mode by running the following command:

```
adb shell setprop log.tag.FA VERBOSE
adb shell setprop log.tag.FA-SVC VERBOSE
```

Next, enable DebugView mode using the following command, where <package name> is replaced by the package name used when the project was created:

```
adb shell setprop debug.firebase.analytics.app <package_name>
```

41.7 Adding the User Property in the Firebase Console

User properties are only visible within the Firebase console if they are first declared within the *User Properties* screen. Navigate to the Firebase console in a browser window, select the *Firebase Examples* project and, within that project, the Analytics app created in this chapter. If the app is not yet listed, it may be necessary to wait for a few hours before it appears.

Once the app has been selected, click on the Analytics link in the left-hand navigation panel so that the Analytics Dashboard screen appears. Click on the *User Properties* tab in the toolbar at the top of the dashboard screen followed by the *New User Property* button. In the new property panel, enter *last_ordered* into the user property name field and a brief description into the description field before clicking on the *Create* button. The property should then be listed as illustrated in Figure 41-3:

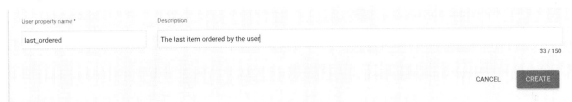

Figure 41-3

41.8 Testing the App

Compile and run the app on the device or emulator on which the two event debugging modes were enabled. Navigate to the DebugView within the Firebase console Analytics screens and display the logcat panel within the Android Monitor tool window within Android Studio. Once both are visible, enter an item name (for example pizza) into the EditText view and tap the *Order* button.

Within the logcat panel, both the event log and the user property creation should appear in the output as follows:

```
Logging event (FE): item_ordered, Bundle[{payment_method=Cash, _o=app,
_sc=AnalyticsActivity, _si=3794813512415499826, item=}]
```

After logging the event, the setting of the user property will be reported:

```
Setting user property (FE): last_ordered, pizza
```

Assuming that the events are appearing in the log output, refer to the DebugView on the browser window and make sure the device or emulator is selected from the menu in the top left-hand corner and that the current *Analytics* app project is selected. Each time the *Order* button is clicked, both the event and the change to the user property should appear in the seconds stream as shown in Figure 41-4:

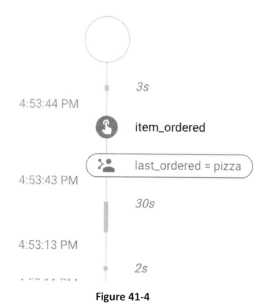

Figure 41-4

Clicking on the *item_ordered* event in the stream will display additional information about the event, including the payment method and item parameters:

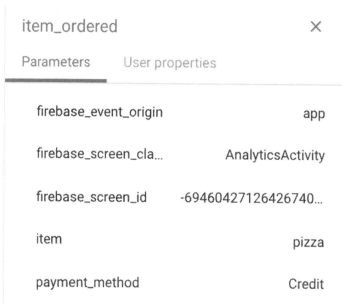

Figure 41-5

Spend some time interacting with the app, for example moving it between background and foreground and entering different text into the text field. Note that within the DebugView the stream begins to register *user_engagement* events. This is one of the event types recorded automatically by Firebase Analytics.

It can take up to 24 hours for the other screens to begin displaying event information. It should be possible, however, to create an audience using the user property.

41.9 Creating an Audience

Within the Firebase console, select the Audiences tab and click on the New Audience button when the audiences screen is displayed. The objective here is to create an audience of users who have previously ordered pizza. Within the audience creation panel, enter a name for the audience (for example pizza buyers) and a brief description of the audience. Next, click on the *Select Event or User Property* menu and choose *User Property* followed by the *last_ordered* property as shown in Figure 41-6:

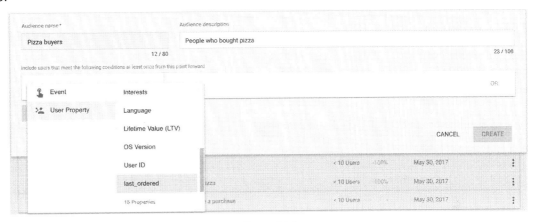

Figure 41-6

In the next column select the *exactly matches* condition listed under the *For Text* category:

Figure 41-7

Finally, enter *pizza* into the last field and press the Enter key. The completed condition should now read as shown in Figure 41-8:

Figure 41-8

Once created, the audience is available for use when filtering results within the Firebase Analytics screens, and also when targeting users using the Firebase Notifications and Remote Config services.

It is also possible to create audiences based on events and parameters (for example an audience could be created containing all users who logged an *item_ordered* event with the payment method set to cash). Although user properties are available for use with audience creation, it can take up to 24 hours for a custom event type to appear as an option in the audience creation menus.

41.10 **Summary**

This chapter has demonstrated the use of Firebase Analytics to track events within an Android app. This included the use of custom events and user parameters. The chapter also created an example audience based on a combination of events and user parameters.

Chapter 42

42. Firebase Test Lab

Throughout programming history testing has been an integral part of the development process. With numerous combinations of device types and operating system versions, Android presents unique challenges in terms of app testing. It is no longer possible to test an app on a single device and Android version and assume that it will run with equal reliability on all other potential hardware and operating system combinations. Firebase Test Lab takes a large step towards addressing this problem by providing a testing platform that allows apps to be tested using many hundreds of device configurations simultaneously.

This chapter will introduce Firebase Test Lab and explain how it can be used to perform different types of testing. Subsequent chapters will cover the two main testing options, namely Robo testing and instrumentation testing, in greater detail.

42.1 An Overview of Firebase Test Lab

Firebase Test Lab allows you to define a collection of different device configurations (called a test matrix) on which a test is to be performed. Each individual device configuration (referred to as a *test execution*) is created by selecting from a range of device type, operating system version, language and orientation configuration options known as *test dimensions*.

All of the testing is performed using physical and virtual devices located at a Google data center allowing a wide range of device platforms to be tested without the need to purchase devices or configure multiple emulator sessions.

Once a test matrix has been defined, the APK file for the app is uploaded and testing started with a single button click. Once started, the tests in the matrix are performed simultaneously (up to a maximum of 200 device combinations). Once testing has completed, results of the test are provided including logcat output, screenshots, video playback and performance data.

Firebase currently supports Robo, instrumentation and game loop testing.

42.2 Robo Testing

Robo testing allows apps to be tested without having to write any tests. To perform a Robo test, simply upload the APK file for the app and define the maximum duration of the tests and the depth within the app to which the test should be performed. Robo testing works by identifying the hierarchy of the user interface and then performing a sequence of simulated user actions (such as button presses, user input and screen navigation) intended to exercise as much of the app as possible. This testing will continue until either the app crashes or the maximum time is reached.

393

The main purpose of Robo testing is to quickly and easily find bugs that cause an app to crash. Robo test has no knowledge of the way the app is intended to work, so consequently has no way to verify that any response from the app to a particular action (aside from a crash) was the expected response. This level of testing requires the use of instrumentation testing. Robo testing with Firebase Test Lab is covered in the chapter entitled *A Firebase Test Lab Robo Testing Example*.

42.3 **Instrumentation Testing**

Instrumentation testing involves the creation of tests designed specifically to test an app and validate that the app behaves as expected in response to actions. A test could, for example, be written to click on a Button widget and then verify that the action caused specific text to appear on a TextView object elsewhere in the user interface layout.

Firebase Test Lab currently supports instrumentation tests created using the Espresso, Robotium and UI Automator Android testing frameworks.

Instrumentation testing with Firebase Test Lab is covered in detail in the chapter entitled *A Firebase Test Lab Instrumentation Testing Example*.

42.4 **Game Loop Testing**

Game loop testing is a new Firebase Lab Test feature that allows user actions to be simulated within game apps that use third-party user interface frameworks. Game loop testing involves the addition of code to the app being tested to simulate user interaction.

Test implementation is highly app specific in that test implementation beyond the basic setup steps will vary depending on the frameworks used and the game design and logic. More information on game loop testing can be found at:

https://firebase.google.com/docs/test-lab/game-loop

42.5 **Test Lab Pricing**

Firebase currently provides a choice of three Firebase plans named Spark, Flame and Blaze. At the Spark level testing is free but limited to 10 virtual device and 5 physical device test executions per day. When working through the tutorials in this book and experimenting with Test Lab, the Spark level should be more than adequate. Even though the Flame plan is a paid tier, it is subject to the same daily restrictions as the free Spark plan.

Unlimited testing is only available with the Blaze plan on which testing is charged at an hourly rate on a per device basis.

42.6 **Summary**

Firebase Test Lab allows Android apps to be tested on a wide range of device types and operating system versions simply by uploading an APK file to the Google cloud and designating the tests to be performed. Test Lab currently supports Robo, instrumentation and game loop testing.

Chapter 43

43. A Firebase Test Lab Robo Testing Example

Clearly, Firebase provides a number of different options when it comes to testing Android apps. In this chapter a sample app will be tested using Firebase Test Lab Robo testing. As will become clear in this chapter, while Robo testing provides a quick and easy way to perform very basic tests, complete and thorough testing is only possible using instrumentation testing.

43.1 Getting the Test App

For the purposes of this chapter, an example app named *Database* will be used as the test subject. The Android Studio project for this app can be downloaded as part of the code sample download available from the following web page:

http://www.ebookfrenzy.com/print/firebase_android

After opening the project in Android Studio, select the *Tools -> Firebase* menu option to display the Firebase assistant. Within the assistant panel, unfold the section and click on the *Run Firebase Test Lab for Android from Android Studio* link followed by the *Connect to Firebase* button. In the resulting dialog, connect the project to the *Firebase Examples* project.

Verify that the app is ready for testing by compiling and running it on a device or emulator session and adding, finding and then deleting a database record.

43.2 Running a Robo Test

To initiate a Robo test of the app, open a browser window and navigate to the Firebase console. Select the *Firebase Examples* project followed by the Test Lab link in the navigation panel.

Within the Test Lab screen, click on the Run a Test button and select *Run a Robo test* from the drop-down menu:

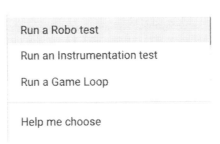

Figure 43-1

A Firebase Test Lab Robo Testing Example

The first item needed by Firebase Test Lab is the APK file for the app to be tested. To upload the APK file, click on the Browse button in the configuration panel (Figure 43-2) and traverse the local filesystem to the folder containing the Database project. Once located, navigate within the folder to the *app/build/outputs/apk* subfolder where a file named *app-debug.apk* should reside. Select this file and click on the Open button.

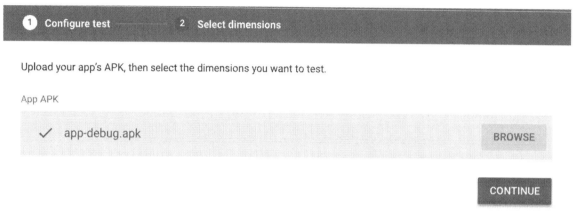

Figure 43-2

Once the APK file upload is complete, click on the *Continue* button to configure the test dimensions. It is, of course, possible to select multiple test devices (both physical and virtual) and combinations of API level, language and orientations to meet the testing needs of the app. Since this will likely exceed the limits of the free Spark plan level the default Nexus 5 API Level 23 will be suitable for this example:

Figure 43-3

Since the user interface for the app contains EditText widgets it would be useful to be able to have text entered into these fields during the test execution. This is possible using the Robo testing advanced options.

Turn on the Advanced switch and note that options are available to change the depth within the app and the maximum amount of time for which testing is to be performed. For this example, leave these values unchanged:

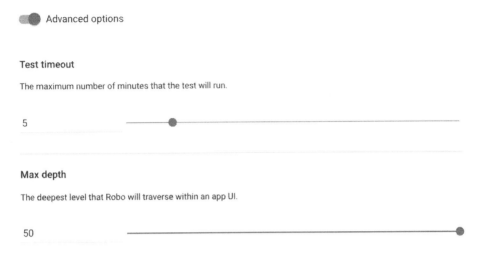

Figure 43-4

If an app requires user authentication, fields are also provided for entering user name and password information for a test account during the testing process. This consists of the resource names of the login and password EditText fields within the user interface of the app together with the values to be entered:

Test account credentials (Optional)

If your app requires custom login, enter the resource names of the login elements and the login credentials.

| Enter username resource | Enter username |
| Enter password resource | Enter password |

Figure 43-5

If the app uses Google Authentication it is not necessary to use these fields. Robo test will automatically create a temporary Google account and use it to sign into the app during testing.

An option is also available to specify the resource ID of any other input fields within the user interface together with a value to be entered. This is the option that will be used in this test. When the Database app was designed, the product name EditText widget was assigned an ID of *productName* which now needs to be referenced along with a product name to be entered during the test execution as illustrated in Figure 43-6:

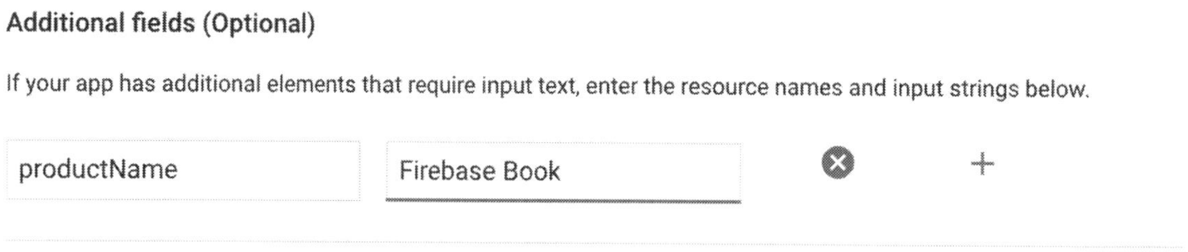

Additional fields (Optional)

If your app has additional elements that require input text, enter the resource names and input strings below.

| productName | Firebase Book | ⊗ | + |

Figure 43-6

Leave the remaining default settings unchanged and enable the *Save template* option. Name the template "Nexus 5 Test" before clicking on the *Start 1 Test* button.

Figure 43-7

After starting the test, a new screen will appear (Figure 43-8) indicating that the test is running at which point there is very little option, aside from cancelling the test, but to wait for the test to complete.

Figure 43-8

43.3 Reviewing Robo Test Results

Once the test has completed, the Firebase Test Lab screen will update to indicate whether the test passed, failed or returned an inconclusive result. A successful test run will look similar to the screen shown in Figure 43-9 below:

		Failed	Passed	Skipped	Inconclusive
✓ Robo test, 6/2/17, 1:29 PM ⓘ		0	1	0	0

Test execution	Duration	Locale	Orientation	Issues
✓ Nexus 5, API Level 23	57 sec	English, United States	Portrait	–

Figure 43-9

To begin reviewing the tests results, click on the *Nexus 5, API Level 23* entry in the results list.

The results screen contains a range of different screens containing information about the test execution. If issues were encountered during the test run, the Test Issues screen will provide a description of the issue.

The Logs screen will display logcat output captured during the testing process and is useful for identifying the cause of crashes or other failures. The log output is presented on multiple pages which can be navigated using the left and right arrows in the bottom right-hand corner of the screen. To access the entire log, click on the *View Source Files* button and select the *logcat* entry.

The output may also be filtered by level of severity using the menu located in the top left-hand corner of the screen:

| ✓ Passed | 📅 6/2/17, 1:29 PM | ⏱ 3 min 23 sec | 🌐 English, United States | ◇ Portrait | **VIEW SOURCE FILES** ↗ |

LOGS   SCREENSHOTS   ACTIVITY MAP   VIDEOS   PERFORMANCE

≡ Warning and higher ▼   ● Styled

| Ⓦ | 10:29:40.166 | **PackageParser** | Unknown element under <manifest>: meta-data at /data/app/vmdl397226823.tmp/base.apk Binary XML file line #14 |
| Ⓦ | 10:29:40.540 | **dex2oat** | Before Android 4.1, method int android.support.v7.widget.ListViewCompat.lookForSelectablePosition(int, boolean) would have incorrectly overridden the package-private method in android.widget.ListView |

Figure 43-10

The Screenshot screen contains screenshots of the app taken at various times during the test run. An inspection of these screenshots will probably show that Test Lab added a number of empty entries into the database during execution.

The Activity Map screen shows a visual representation of the path taken through the app during testing. Following the arrows on the map it will become clear that Robo test simply clicked on the buttons and selected items as they were added to the list.

To view a video of the test run, select the Videos tab and play back the video. In some cases the text may have been added to the database, while in others the Add button may have been clicked while the text field was empty. Robo testing is not a precision testing tool so this is to be expected. The system is simply trying out multiple combinations of actions in an attempt to make the app crash. A more controlled approach to testing will be performed in the chapter entitled *A Firebase Test Lab Instrumentation Testing Example*.

Finally, the Performance tab will provide information about the performance metrics of the app during the test execution including CPU, memory and Network usage (Figure 43-11). Note that these metrics are only available when testing on a physical device:

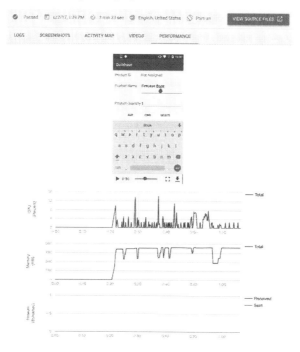

Figure 43-11

43.4 Introducing a Bug

The final step in this example is to introduce a bug into the app to see if it is detected by Robo test. Return to the app in Android Studio, edit the *DatabaseActivity.java* file and comment out the *newProduct()* method as follows:

```
/*
public void newProduct (View view) {

    if ((quantityBox.getText().toString().isEmpty()) &&
            (productBox.getText().toString().isEmpty())) {
.
.
.
}
```

```
}
*/
```

Compile and run the app on a device or simulator and check that a click on the Add button now causes the app to crash with an exception due to the missing method.

Within the Firebase console run another test, uploading the newly built APK file and using the Nexus 5 Test template saved earlier in the chapter. The Test Lab will report that the test has failed, and clicking on the test execution line item (Nexus 5, API Level 23) will display the Test Issues screen containing the exception message:

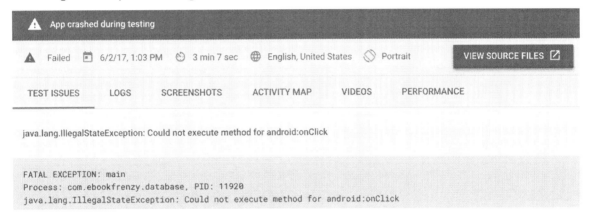

Figure 43-12

A review of the Activity Map screen will show that the last action performed was a click on the Add button.

Before continuing, be sure to uncomment the *addProduct()* method and rebuild the app so that the APK file no longer includes the bug.

43.5 Summary

This chapter demonstrated the use of Robo testing to perform automated testing of an Android app without the need to create specific tests. Robo testing performs a wide range of actions within an app by interacting with the user interface in as many ways as possible in an effort to identify areas where the app crashes. Running a Robo test involves uploading the APK file for the app, specifying the test dimensions and then running the tests. After the test completes a comprehensive set of results are available including log output, screenshots, video playback and performance metrics.

Chapter 44

44. A Firebase Test Lab Instrumentation Testing Example

The previous chapters have introduced Firebase Test Lab and worked through an example focused on testing using Robo test. This chapter contains an example of instrumentation testing using the Espresso testing framework in conjunction with Android Studio. Topics covered include the creation of a test using Espresso and execution of that test from within both the Firebase console and remotely via Android Studio.

Since full coverage of Espresso testing is outside the scope of this book, this chapter will provide an introductory knowledge base from which to begin exploring other capabilities and features of the framework.

44.1 Getting the Test App

As with the previous chapter, the *Database* app will be used as the test subject in this tutorial. Follow the steps at the beginning of the previous chapter if you do not have a copy of this app already set up within Android Studio.

44.2 An Overview of Espresso

Espresso is a testing framework that allows automated instrumentation tests to be created that simulate user interaction within an Android app.

As described previously, Robo testing works by analyzing the user interface view hierarchy of an app and devising tests that exercise as much of the user interface as possible given time and depth restrictions selected by the user. Although Robo testing is ideal for quickly finding bugs within an app, it knows nothing about the logic of the app. Robo testing does not know, for example, that text needed to be added to a text field before a button is clicked. Nor does is it able to check an action caused the expected change elsewhere within the user interface. Robo test cannot, for example, check whether a click on a specific button caused the text displayed on a TextView widget to change.

Instrumentation testing frameworks such as Espresso define the actions that are to be simulated within the app, including the order in which they are to be performed. Instrumentation testing also allows the results of an action to be verified ensuring, for example, that the correct text appears on the correct TextView in response to a click on a specific button. Since the tests are themselves programs, testing can include logic allowing different actions to be taken based on the results of individual test actions.

The tests are contained within an Espresso test class which is essentially a Java class containing the sequence of tests that are to be performed. The test class is bundled in a separate APK file and executed in the same process alongside the running app. The actions contained within the app are performed automatically and any discrepancies from the expected behavior reported to the tester.

Espresso test classes can be written by hand, or generated automatically using the Espresso Test Recorder built into Android Studio. A combination of these approaches is also common, involving a process of recording a test and then enhancing it by modifying the code.

44.3 **Enabling Test Lab in the Project**

Before implementing instrumentation testing within Android Studio, the app project must first be connected to a Firebase project. If the project is not yet connected, display the Firebase assistant panel within Android Studio using the *Tools -> Firebase* menu option and, within the assistant panel, unfold the *Test Lab* section and click on the *Run Firebase Test Lab from Android Studio* link. On the next screen, click on the Connect to Firebase button and select the *Firebase Examples* project.

44.4 **Creating the Espresso Test Class**

For this example, the Espresso test class will be created using the Espresso Test Recorder. From within Android Studio, select *Run -> Record Espresso Test* menu option and select a physical device or emulator session on which to run the app. The app will launch on the chosen deployment target and connect to the debugger. A window will also appear on the development system in which events will be displayed as they are recorded within the app.

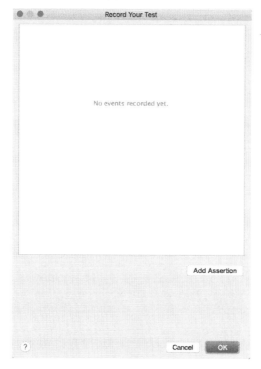

Figure 44-1

44.5 **Recording the Test**

The objective of the test is to verify that a database record can be added, found and deleted within the app. To verify that these actions have been performed, assertions will be added to the test at key points to verify that expected information is displayed within the text fields of the user interface.

With recording started, perform the following steps within the app:

1. Select the Product Name field and enter text which reads *Firebase Book*.
2. Select the Product Quantity field and enter 10.
3. Click on the Add button to add the record to the database.
4. Select the Product Name field and enter text which reads *Firebase Book*.
5. Click on the Find button.

At this stage a record has been added and then located using the Find button. Before moving to the next step, an assertion needs to be added to verify that the record was successfully found. This can be achieved by verifying that the value 10 is present in the quantity text field.

Assertions can be added during recording by clicking on the *Add Assertion* button located in the Android Studio Espresso recording dialog. Once clicked a screenshot of the app user interface will appear as shown in Figure 44-2:

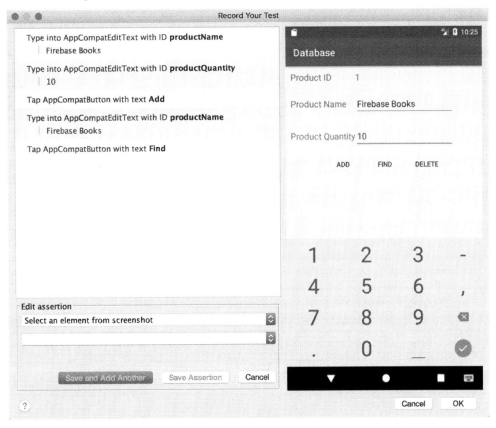

Figure 44-2

A Firebase Test Lab Instrumentation Testing Example

The first step in adding an assertion is to choose an element from the user interface. This can be achieved either by selecting the element within the screenshot, or using the *Select an element from screenshot* drop down menu. Select the quantity TextView object by clicking on it in the screenshot, then refer to the *Edit assertion* section of the dialog and verify that it is configured with a *text is* comparison with a value of 10:

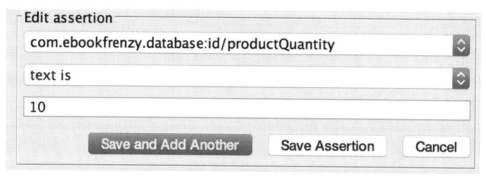

Figure 44-3

Click on the *Save Assertion* button to add the assertion to the test class, then return to the running app and perform the following steps to verify that record deletion also works:

1. Click on the Delete button to remove the Firebase Books record from the database.
2. Select the Product ID field and enter text which reads *Firebase Book*.
3. Click on the Find button.

Assuming that the deletion was successful, the Product ID field should read *No Match Found*. Return to the recording dialog in Android Studio, click on the *Add Assertion* button and select the text view element to the right of Product ID in the screenshot. Verify that a *test is* assertion comparing against text that reads "No Match Found" has been configured before clicking on the *Save Assertion* button:

Figure 44-4

Complete the recording by clicking on the OK button in the recording dialog. When recording has finished a dialog will appear requesting a name for the Espresso test class file. Enter *DatabaseActivityTest* into the name field and click on OK.

44.6 Reviewing the Test Class

Once the test class has been saved it will be listed in the Project tool window under *app -> java -> com.ebookfrenzy.database (androidTest)* as shown in Figure 44-5:

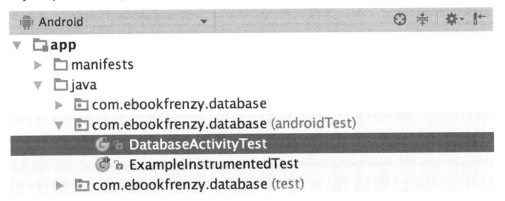

Figure 44-5

Locate this file, double-click on it to load it into the editor and review the code that makes up the test. The code for each action takes a similar format. The code to enter the book name into the product name field, for example, reads as follows:

```
ViewInteraction appCompatEditText = onView(
        allOf(withId(R.id.productName), isDisplayed()));
appCompatEditText.perform(replaceText("Firebase Book"), closeSoftKeyboard());
```

Similarly, the assertions also follow a standard pattern. The code fragment below, for example, checks that the quantity text field contains a string which reads "10":

```
ViewInteraction editText = onView(
        allOf(withId(R.id.productQuantity), withText("10"),
            childAtPosition(
                childAtPosition(
                    IsInstanceOf.<View>instanceOf(
                        android.widget.TableLayout.class), 2), 1),
                isDisplayed()));

editText.check(matches(withText("10")));
```

Take some time to review the code to gain a familiarity with the way in which the Espresso framework API works.

44.7 Running the Test Locally

Before making use of Firebase Test Lab, it is worth taking time to make sure the test works correctly locally. To run the test on a local device or emulator session, right-click on the *DatabaseActivityTest* entry within the Project tool window and select the *Run DatabaseActivityTest* menu option. In the deployment target dialog, select a suitable device or emulator and click on the *Ok* button. The app will launch and run through the sequence of actions and assertion verifications. When the test completes, the results will appear in the Android Studio Run window (Figure 44-6). Assuming the tests were recorded correctly, the window should indicate a successful test run.

Figure 44-6

44.8 Firebase Console Testing

Once the Espresso test class has been created it can be used to perform tests within the Firebase Test Lab. This can be initiated either using the Firebase console or from within Android Studio.

To run tests from within the Firebase console, open the console in a browser window, select the *Firebase Examples* project then click on *Test Lab*. In the Test Lab screen click on the *Run a Test* button and choose the *Run an instrumentation test* option.

An instrumentation test within the Test Lab requires both the standard and test APKs to be uploaded. In the *Configure test* screen (Figure 44-7) click on the Browse button for the App APK to display the file selection dialog. Locate the folder containing the Database project, then navigate to the *app/build/outputs/apk* subfolder. Within the apk folder, select and open the *app-debug.apk* file.

Next, click on the Browse button for the Test APK, this time selecting the *app-debug-androidTest.apk* file.

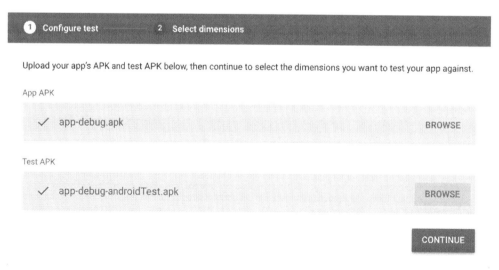

Figure 44-7

When the files have uploaded, click on the *Continue* button and configure the test dimensions. For this example, deselect the default physical device and select the Nexus 9, API level 25 configuration from the Virtual devices section of the screen.

Initiate the test by clicking on the *Start 1 Test* button located at the bottom of the dimension configuration screen.

Wait for the test to complete, then click on the Nexus 9, Virtual, API Level 25 link in the matrix screen to view the results. Results screens are available for log output, video recording of the test and performance data. Playing back the video, you may find that the actual test actions occur too quickly to see if correct tests were performed. Ideally, some screenshots at key points during the test execution would be useful. While screenshots are taken automatically during Robo testing, code must be added to the test class file to initiate screenshots during instrumentation testing.

44.9 Adding the Screenshotter Library to the Project

Adding support for screenshots during instrumentation test runs is a multistep process that begins with the installation of a special library into the project. Begin by downloading this library from the following URL:

https://dl.google.com/firebase/testlab/cloudtestingscreenshotter_lib.aar

Once the library has been downloaded, it needs to be placed in a directory named *aars* located at the top level of the project file structure. Within Android Studio, switch the Project tool window into Project mode using the toolbar menu:

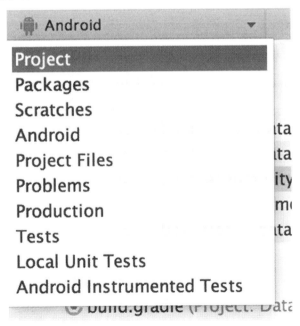

Figure 44-8

A Firebase Test Lab Instrumentation Testing Example

Within the project hierarchy, right-click on the *Database* entry and select the *New -> Directory* menu option. When prompted, name the new directory *aars*.

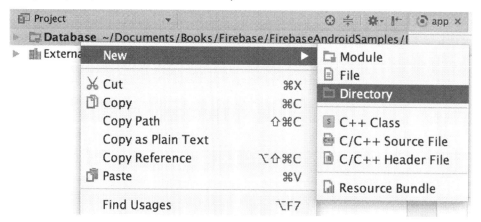

Using the file system browser for your operating system, locate the downloaded *cloudtestingscreenshotter_lib.aar* file and copy it. Return to Android Studio, right-click on the new *aars* directory in select the *Paste* menu option. With the library added, return the Project tool window to Android mode before proceeding.

Locate the *build.gradle (Project: Database)* file listed under *Gradle Scripts* in the Project tool window and edit it to add the *aars* directory to the repository declarations:

```
buildscript {
    repositories {
        jcenter()
        flatDir {
            dirs '../aars'
        }
    }
    dependencies {
        classpath 'com.android.tools.build:gradle:2.3.2'
    }
}

allprojects {
    repositories {
        flatDir {
            dirs '../aars'
        }
        jcenter()
    }
}
```

```
repositories {
    jcenter()
    flatDir {
        dirs '../aars'
    }
}
task clean(type: Delete) {
    delete rootProject.buildDir
}
```

Next, edit the *build.gradle (Module: app)* file and add an entry for the library to the dependencies section:

```
dependencies {
    compile fileTree(dir: 'libs', include: ['*.jar'])
    .
    .
    androidTestCompile (name:'cloudtestingscreenshotter_lib', ext:'aar')
    .
    .
}
```

The library will need access to external storage and the internet in order to function. The final task in adding the library to the project, therefore, is to add the following lines to the *app -> manifests -> AndroidManifest.xml* file as follows:

```
<?xml version="1.0" encoding="utf-8"?>
<manifest xmlns:android="http://schemas.android.com/apk/res/android"
    package="com.ebookfrenzy.database">

    <uses-permission
        android:name="android.permission.WRITE_EXTERNAL_STORAGE"/>
    <uses-permission android:name="android.permission.INTERNET"/>

    <application
    .
    .
</manifest>
```

44.10 Adding the Screenshotter Code

The next step is to add code within the test class at the points where a screenshot is needed. Edit the *DatabaseActivityTest.java* file and add screenshot code after the Add button and Delete buttons are clicked:

```
import com.google.android.libraries.cloudtesting.screenshots.ScreenShotter;
.
```

```
.
ViewInteraction appCompatButton = onView(
        allOf(withId(R.id.button3), withText("Add"), isDisplayed()));
appCompatButton.perform(click());

ScreenShotter.takeScreenshot("after_add", mActivityTestRule.getActivity());
.

.
ViewInteraction appCompatButton2 = onView(
        allOf(withId(R.id.button2), withText("Find"), isDisplayed()));
appCompatButton2.perform(click());
ScreenShotter.takeScreenshot("after_find", mActivityTestRule.getActivity());
```

Compile and run the test on a local device or emulator to verify that the test still runs, then execute another instrumentation test run within the Firebase console. When the tests are complete, the Screenshots tab will be present in the results and should contain the two screenshots taken during the test.

44.11 Running the Test from Android Studio

To start a Test Lab instrumentation test from within Android Studio, run DatabaseActivityTest once again. When the deployment target selection dialog appears, select the *Cloud Testing* tab as shown in Figure 44-10:

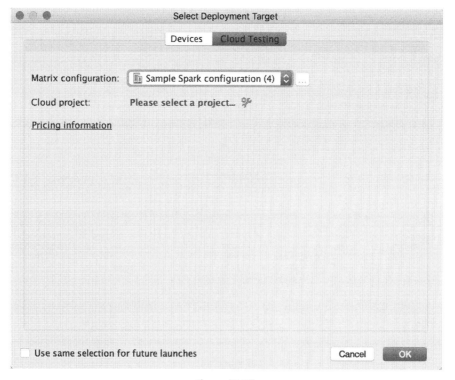

Figure 44-10

The first step is to either choose or create a matrix configuration for the testing. Click on the button displaying the three dots to the right of the configuration selection menu to display the matrix configurations dialog:

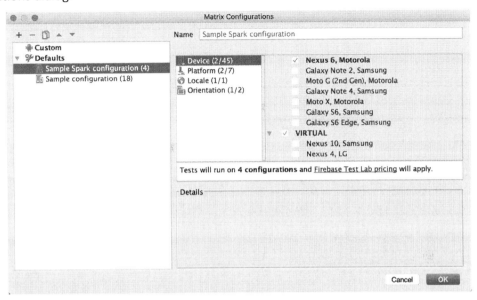

Figure 44-11

To create a new configuration matrix, click on the plus button located above the list of configurations. A new unnamed configuration will appear beneath the Custom heading in the list (marked A in Figure 44-12). Begin by entering *Database App Test Configuration* into the name field before working through the list of categories (B), in each case selecting one or more options from the selection panel (C).

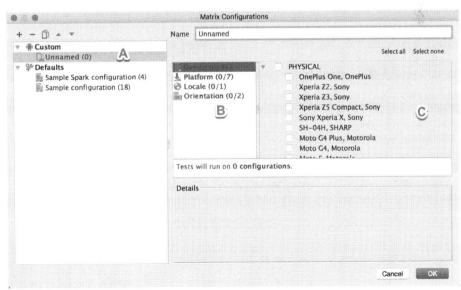

Figure 44-12

For this example, make the following selections from the corresponding categories:

- **Device** – Virtual Nexus 9, HTC
- **Platform** – Android 7.1.x API Level 25 (Nougat)
- **Locale** – Select the default value for your Android Studio configuration
- **Orientation** – Portrait

Once the configuration is complete, click on the *OK* button to return to the Cloud Testing dialog. Before testing can begin, the test needs to be associated with a Firebase project. Within the Cloud Testing panel, click on the button to the right of the *Please select a project...* text and select the *Firebase Examples* project within the project selection dialog.

Verify that the matrix configuration and project settings are correct before clicking on the *OK* button to start the test execution. Android Studio will build the app and test APK files, upload them to the Test Lab and start the test. The status of the test will appear within the Android Studio Run tool window (Figure 44-13) and may also be viewed within the Firebase console by clicking on the link provided in the Run window.

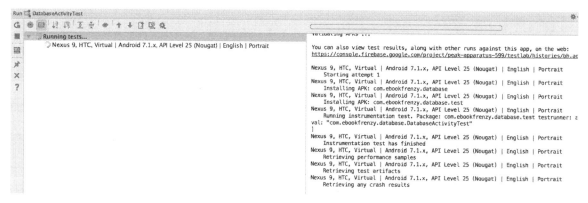

Figure 44-13

44.12 **Summary**

This chapter has provided an example of instrumentation testing using Firebase Test Lab and the Espresso Android testing framework. Espresso tests are contained in Java class files that run alongside the app during testing. These test classes can be written by hand or generated automatically using the Espresso Test Recorder built into Android Studio. Once the test has been created the APK files for both the app and the test class are uploaded to the Firebase Test Lab and used to run tests on selected device configurations. Firebase uploading and test initiation can be performed either within Android Studio or via the Firebase console. Unlike Robo testing, screenshots are not taken automatically when performing instrumentation testing. As demonstrated in this chapter, screenshots can be taken using an additional library and some extra code within the test class.

45. Firebase Dynamic Links

Firebase Dynamic links are URL links used both to drive new users to install your app, and as a way to link directly to a particular place in your app from an external source such as a website or app.

In this chapter, a basic overview of dynamic links will be covered outlining the ways in which dynamic links are used, created and handled within the receiving app.

45.1 An Overview of Firebase Dynamic Links

The primary purpose of dynamic links is to allow app developers to generate a URL that, when clicked, will either take the user to a specific location in an app or, if the app is not yet installed, load the Google Play store page for the app so that it can be installed and launched. A website might, for example, include a "Download our App in the Google Play Store" button which uses a dynamic link. Alternatively, dynamic links can be used to share references to content within the app. An app might, for example, allow users to recommend to other users particular content within the app. When the user follows the link, the app will open and use the dynamic link to present the screen and content that needs to be displayed.

Dynamic links may also be configured with a *fallback URL* which will open a designated web page if clicked on a platform on which launching or opening the app is not a possibility. Dynamic links are also cross-platform and can be implemented on Android and iOS apps, or used exclusively for web based content.

45.2 The Anatomy of a Dynamic Link

Dynamic links are available in both long and short form. A short URL, which can be useful for obfuscating the content of the link, is simply a long URL that has been processed by a URL shortener.

The format of a typical long form dynamic link URL is as follows:

*http://<**appCode**>.app.goo.gl/?apn=<**packageName**>&link=<**deeplinkUrl**>&ad=<**value**>&afl=<**fallba ckUrl**>&amv=<**version**>&utm_source=<**utmSource**>&utm_medium=<**utmMedium**>&utm_campaign =<**utmCampaign**>&utm_term=<**utmTerm**>&utm_content=<**utmContent**>?st=<**title**>?sd=<**descriptio n**>?si=<**imageink**>*

The bold values in the above URL are replaced by values as follows:

- **<appCode>** - The unique code which identifies the Firebase project to which the app belongs. Steps to find this code within the Firebase console are covered later in this chapter.
- **<packageName>** - The full package name of the app, as defined when the app project was created in Android Studio (for example com.example.myapp).

- **<deeplinkUrl>** - This is the URL that is passed to the app when it is launched as the result of a link click. This can be any valid URL and will typically contain path and parameter information that is used by the app to identify the content or screen that is to be presented to the user.
- **<ad>** - (Optional) Setting this value to 1 indicates that the link is being used in an advertising campaign.
- **<fallbackURL>** - (Optional) The URL for the webpage to be displayed when the link is clicked in an environment in which the app cannot be installed and launched.
- **<version>** - (Optional) The minimum version of the app which is able to handle the receipt of a dynamic link.
- **<utmSource>** - (Optional) When the dynamic link is being used within an advertising campaign, this property may be set to the name of the advertising source for tracking purposes. Results are shown in the Google Play console analytics.
- **<utmMedium>** - (Optional) Useful when using the dynamic link in advertising campaigns to record the type of ad which generated the click (for example a mobile interstitial, email campaign or website banner ad). Results are shown in the Google Play console analytics.
- **<utmContent>** - (Optional) The name by which the advertising campaign associated with the dynamic link can be identified within the Google Play console analytics.
- **<st>** - (Optional) The title to be used for the link when it is shared within a social media post.
- **<sd>** - (Optional) The description to be used for the link when shared within a social media post.
- **<si>** - (Optional) The URL of an image to be used when the link is shared within a social media post.

A basic Dynamic Link URL without any of the optional parameters might read as follows:

```
https://jhyt1.app.goo.gl/?link=http://example.com&apn=com.ebookfrenzy.dynamicl
ink&afl=http://www.example.com
```

The same dynamic URL might be presented by the following short form link:

```
https://jhyt1.app.goo.gl/CTXh
```

45.3 Creating Dynamic Links in the Firebase Console

Dynamic links may be created either from within the Firebase console, or within the code of a running app. To create a dynamic link within the Firebase console, open the console in a browser window, select the project with which the app is associated and click on the *Dynamic Links* option in the navigation panel. Before a dynamic link can be created for the first time, Firebase will request that you accept the terms of service by clicking on the *Get Started* button.

Once the terms of service have been accepted, click on the *New Dynamic Link* button to display the creation dialog as shown in Figure 45-1:

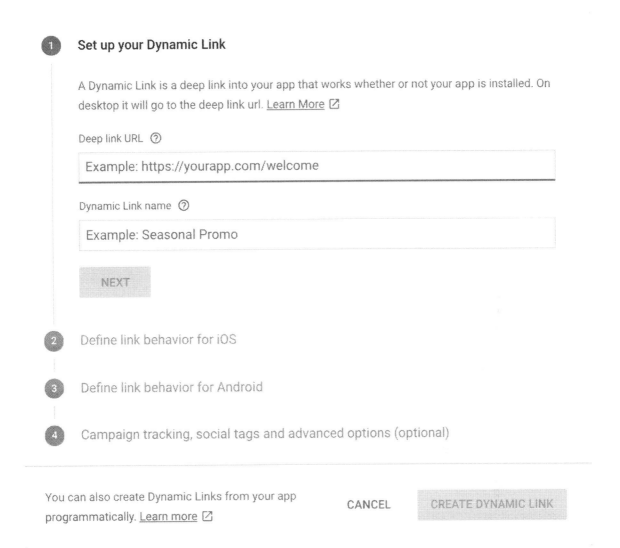

Figure 45-1

Creation of the link simply involves stepping through the different stages and filling in fields where required. Within the Android behavior section, the *Open the deep link in your Android App* option should be selected and the app chosen from the menu. Selections also need to be made to configure what should happen if the user does not already have the app installed:

3
Define link behavior for Android
Open the deep link URL in a browser
Open the deep link in your Android App
com.ebookfrenzy.dynamiclinks
If your app is not installed, send the user to
Google Play page for your app
Deep link URL
Custom URL
Advanced Settings (optional)
Open Google Play for versions lower than

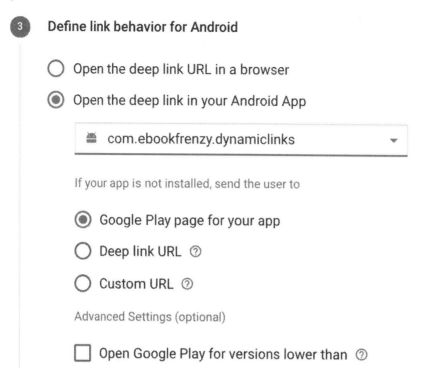

Figure 45-2

After completing the configuration steps, simply click on the *Create Dynamic Link* button to generate the link.

45.4 Reviewing a Link in the Console

Once the link has been configured and created it will appear in the list of previously generated links:

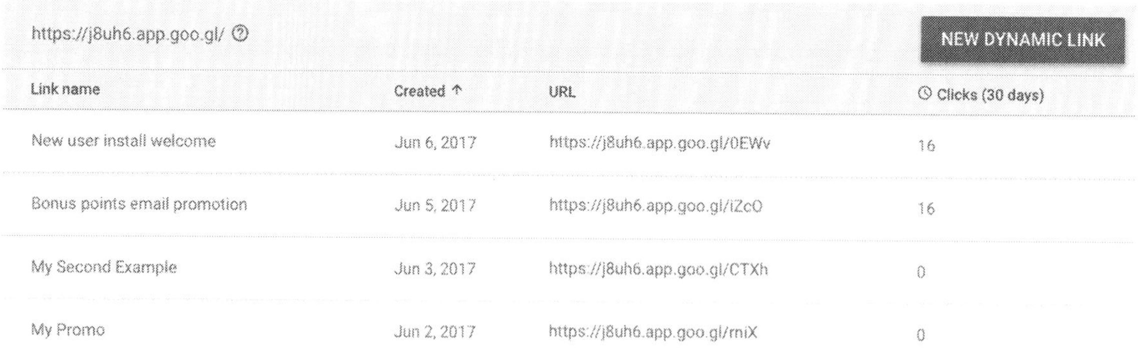

https://j8uh6.app.goo.gl/
NEW DYNAMIC LINK
Link name
Created ↑
URL
Clicks (30 days)
New user install welcome
Jun 6, 2017
https://j8uh6.app.goo.gl/0EWv
16
Bonus points email promotion
Jun 5, 2017
https://j8uh6.app.goo.gl/iZcO
16
My Second Example
Jun 3, 2017
https://j8uh6.app.goo.gl/CTXh
0
My Promo
Jun 2, 2017
https://j8uh6.app.goo.gl/rniX
0

Figure 45-3

To review the dynamic link, hover the mouse pointer over the row in the table, click on the menu button that appears (Figure 45-4) and select an option from the menu.

Figure 45-4

Selecting the Link details menu option will display information about the link, including both the long and short forms of the URL:

Figure 45-5

The *Link analytics* button will display a graph showing the number of clicks performed on the link over specified periods of time:

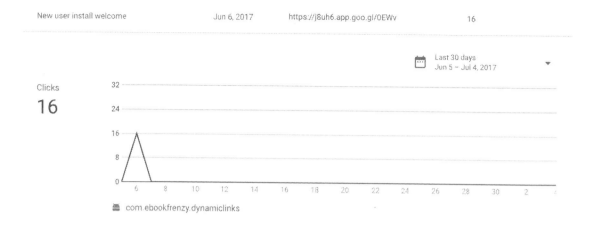

New user install welcome   Jun 6, 2017   https://j8uh6.app.goo.gl/0EWv   16

Clicks
16

com.ebookfrenzy.dynamiclinks

Figure 45-6

The Link flow screen is of particular use for identifying how the link will perform under different conditions, for example the circumstances under which the app will be launched or installed depending on the platform on which the link was clicked:

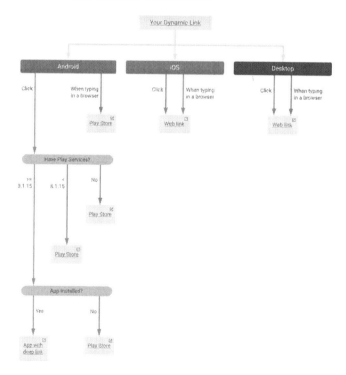

Figure 45-7

45.5 Creating a Dynamic Link in Code

A dynamic link can be generated in code either manually by constructing the URL using the format outlined earlier in this chapter, or using the standard Java Uri Builder. The components needed to build the URL begin with the Firebase app code for the Firebase project within which the app is contained. In fact, each project is given its own domain by Firebase which is used when generating and handling dynamic links, the format of which is https://<appcode>.app.goo.gl. The app code for a project can be found in the Dynamic Links screen within the Firebase console as highlighted in Figure 45-8:

Figure 45-8

The Uri will also require, at a minimum, the app package name and the deep link URL to be passed to the app. The following code fragment shows the creation of an example dynamic link URL from within the code of an Android app:

```
String appCode = "j8uh6";
final Uri deepLink = Uri.parse("http://example.com/welcome");

String packageName = getApplicationContext().getPackageName();

Uri.Builder builder = new Uri.Builder()
        .scheme("https")
        .authority(appCode + ".app.goo.gl")
        .path("/")
        .appendQueryParameter("link", deepLink.toString())
        .appendQueryParameter("apn", packageName);

Uri dynamicLink = builder.build();
```

45.6 Sharing a Dynamic Link

A dynamic link is not of much use unless it can be made available to other users. A quick and easy way to do this is to use the Android ACTION_SEND Intent. This allows the user to send the link to others using options that include email, SMS message and social media. The code to share the dynamic link created above reads as follows:

```
try {
    URL rl = new URL(URLDecoder.decode(dynamicLink.toString(), "UTF-8"));
    Intent intent = new Intent(Intent.ACTION_SEND);
    intent.setType("text/plain");
```

```
    intent.putExtra(Intent.EXTRA_SUBJECT, "Firebase Deep Link");
    intent.putExtra(Intent.EXTRA_TEXT, url.toString());
    startActivity(intent);
} catch (Exception e) {
    Log.i(TAG, "Could not decode Uri: " + e.getLocalizedMessage());
}
```

When the share intent activity is started, a panel will appear giving the user a choice of apps via which the message may be sent:

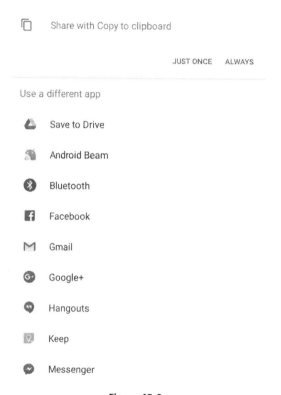

Figure 45-9

When a selection has been made, the chosen app will launch ready for the link to be sent.

45.7 Receiving a Dynamic Link

The next step in working with dynamic links involves modifying the target app to receive and handle the link. This involves adding one or more intent filters to the manifest file of the app project and the addition of some initialization code within the main activity.

There are two ways in which an incoming deep link can be handled. One option is to modify the app startup code to detect that a dynamic link caused the app to launch and, if so, obtain and interpret the incoming deep link URL. Based on the content of the deep link, the app can then decide on the appropriate action to be performed (for example launching a second activity).

Another option is to configure the app so that an activity is automatically launched when a specific dynamic link is used (referred to as *auto loading*).

For either option, an intent filter element needs to be added to the entry for the main activity within the *AndroidManifest.xml* file as follows:

```
<activity android:name=".ExampleActivity">
.

.

.
    <intent-filter>
        <action android:name="android.intent.action.VIEW"/>
        <category android:name="android.intent.category.DEFAULT"/>
        <category android:name="android.intent.category.BROWSABLE"/>
        <data android:host="example.com" android:scheme="http"/>
        <data android:host="example.com" android:scheme="https"/>
    </intent-filter>
.

.

.
</activity>
```

If auto loading of an intent is to be used for a deep link, an additional intent filter needs to be assigned to the activity that is to be launched when that deep link is detected by the system. In the following example, the intent filter configures an activity named WelcomeActivity to be launched when a deep link URL of *http://www.example.com/welcome* is detected by the system:

```
<activity
    android:name=".WelcomeActivity"
    android:label="@string/title_activity_second"
    android:theme="@style/AppTheme.NoActionBar">
    <intent-filter>
        <action android:name="android.intent.action.VIEW" />
        <category android:name="android.intent.category.DEFAULT" />
        <category android:name="android.intent.category.BROWSABLE" />
        <data android:scheme="http"
            android:host="www.example.com"
            android:pathPrefix="/welcome" />
    </intent-filter>
</activity>
```

The code to detect an incoming deep link can be added to the *onCreate()* method of the launcher activity of the app (in other words the first activity that is started when the app is launched).

The code needs to create an instance of the GoogleApiClient class configured to use the AppInvite API:

```
private GoogleApiClient googleApiClient;

googleApiClient = new GoogleApiClient.Builder(this)
                .enableAutoManage(this, this)
                .addApi(AppInvite.API)
                .build();
```

Next, the *getInvitation()* method of the AppInvite class must be called to identify if an incoming deep link is waiting for the app. A callback is also assigned to the method call to handle the results:

```
boolean launchDeepLink = false;

AppInvite.AppInviteApi.getInvitation(googleApiClient, this, launchDeepLink)
        .setResultCallback(
            new ResultCallback<AppInviteInvitationResult>() {
                @Override
                public void onResult(
                    @NonNull AppInviteInvitationResult result) {

                    if (result.getStatus().isSuccess()) {
                        // A deep link was found
                    } else {
                        // No deep link found.");
                    }
                }
            });
```

Note that a Boolean variable named *launchDeepLink* is assigned a false value and passed through as an argument to the *getInvitation()* method. When set to true, the app will auto load an activity if it has an intent filter that matches the deep link.

In the event that a deep link was received and auto launching is disabled, code needs to be implemented to obtain the invitation intent and to extract from it the deep link URL:

```
.
.
public void onResult(@NonNull AppInviteInvitationResult result) {

    Intent intent = result.getInvitationIntent();
    String deepLink = AppInviteReferral.getDeepLink(intent);

    // Parse URL here to identify action to be taken within the app
}
```

The *onResult()* method is passed an AppInvitationResult object on which the *getInvitationIntent()* method is called which, in turn, returns the intent used to deliver the link. The intent object is then passed to the *getDeepLink()* method of the AppInviteReferral class to get the deep link URL that was embedded in the dynamic link.

The deep link URL can then be parsed and used to interpret the actions that are to be taken within the app (for example navigating to a screen associated with the dynamic link or displaying specific app content). Though the way in which an app interprets and acts on the content of the deep link URL will be app specific, a common example will be provided in the next chapter *Creating, Receiving and Testing a Firebase Dynamic Link*.

45.8 Summary

Dynamic links provide so called *deep links* into an app via a URL. Dynamic links can be used to direct new users to the appropriate entry in the Google Play store where they can install an app, or as a way to direct an existing user to a specific screen or content area within the app. Dynamic links may be created using the Firebase console or from within the code of a running app or web page. In addition to providing a way to generate dynamic links, the Firebase console also provides analysis of the number of times the link has been clicked. Dynamic links can be created in either long or short form. The short form is simply a long URL that has been processed by a URL shortener. By default, the Firebase console provides the link in both long and short forms.

A clicked dynamic link can be handled in one of two ways within the destination app. The app can be modified to receive and manually interpret the link, deciding what action needs to be taken. Alternatively, an app can be implemented such that it automatically loads a specific activity when the deep link URL matches an intent filter specified within the manifest file.

46. Creating, Receiving and Testing a Firebase Dynamic Link

This chapter will provide a practical example of Dynamic Links in the context of an Android app. The topics that will be covered in this chapter include the creation of dynamic links using both the Firebase console and within the app together with both approaches to handling a link within the app. Finally, the chapter will explore some of the ways in which dynamic links can be tested without the app being published in the Google Play store.

46.1 About the Dynamic Links Example App

The example project created in this chapter is intentionally simple. The only features the app will include are the ability to generate and share a dynamic link and to implement custom behavior as a result of being launched by a dynamic link click.

46.2 Creating the Dynamic Links Project

Begin by starting Android Studio and selecting the *Start a new Android Studio project* quick start option from the welcome screen.

Within the new project dialog, enter *DynamicLinks* into the Application name field and your domain as the Company Domain setting before clicking on the *Next* button.

On the form factors screen, enable the *Phone and Tablet* option and set the minimum SDK to API 16: Android 4.1 (Jellybean). Continue to proceed through the screens, requesting the creation of an Empty Activity named *DynamicLinksActivity* with a corresponding layout named *activity_dynamic_links.*

46.3 Designing the User Interface

The user interface for the main activity will consist of two Button objects in addition to the default "Hello World" TextView. Within Android Studio open the *activity_dynamic_links.xml* file in the layout editor and use the toolbar buttons to remove all constraints from the layout and to disable the Autoconnect feature.

Move the default TextView object so that it is positioned nearer to the top of the layout before dragging and dropping two Button objects from the palette onto the layout canvas so that they are centered beneath the TextView. Set the text property on the buttons to read *Get Link* and *Share* as shown in Figure 46-1:

Figure 46-1

Select all three widgets in the layout, then right-click on the TextView widget. From the resulting menu, select the *Center Horizontally* option. With all three widgets still selected, repeat this step and choose the *Center Vertically* menu option to constrain the widgets using a chain.

Before proceeding to the next step, assign onClick methods named *getLink* and *shareLink* to the buttons. Also, change the IDs on the TextView and Share button to *statusText* and *shareButton* respectively.

46.4 Connecting the Project to Firebase

Connect the project to Firebase by selecting the *Tools -> Firebase* menu option and unfolding the Dynamic Links section within the Firebase assistant panel. Click on the *Add a dynamic link* option and use the buttons on the Dynamic Links page to connect the app to the *Firebase Examples* project and to add the project dependencies.

46.5 Performing Basic Initialization

Before starting work on generating dynamic links, some basic initialization tasks need to be performed. Within Android Studio, edit the *DynamicLinksActivity.java* file as follows:

```
import android.support.v7.app.AppCompatActivity;
import android.os.Bundle;
```

```
import android.widget.Button;
import android.widget.TextView;

public class DynamicLinksActivity extends AppCompatActivity {

    private TextView statusText;
    private Button shareButton;

    @Override
    protected void onCreate(Bundle savedInstanceState) {
        super.onCreate(savedInstanceState);
        setContentView(R.layout.activity_dynamic_links);

        statusText = (TextView) findViewById(R.id.statusText);
        shareButton = (Button) findViewById(R.id.shareButton);

        shareButton.setEnabled(false);
    }
    .
    .
}
```

46.6 Adding the Link Generation Code

The app needs to generate a dynamic link when the user taps the *Get Link* button. Before adding the method, use the steps outlined in the previous chapter to find the app code for your Firebase project.

Within the *DynamicLinksActivity.java* file, add the *getLink()* method so that it reads as follows (where *<app_code>* is replaced by your app code):

```
import android.support.v7.app.AppCompatActivity;
import android.os.Bundle;
import android.widget.Button;
import android.widget.TextView;
import android.net.Uri;
import android.util.Log;
import android.view.View;

public class DynamicLinksActivity extends AppCompatActivity {

    private Uri dynamicLink = null;
    private static final String TAG = "DynamicLinks";
    .
    .
    .
```

```
public void getLink(View view) {
    String appCode = "<app_code>";
    final Uri deepLink = Uri.parse("http://example.com/promo?discount");

    String packageName = getApplicationContext().getPackageName();

    // Build the link with all required parameters
    Uri.Builder builder = new Uri.Builder()
            .scheme("https")
            .authority(appCode + ".app.goo.gl")
            .path("/")
            .appendQueryParameter("link", deepLink.toString())
            .appendQueryParameter("apn", packageName);

    dynamicLink = builder.build();
    shareButton.setEnabled(true);
}
.
.
}
```

The code builds a dynamic link containing a deep link URL of *http://www.example.com/promo* with a query value of *discount*. Once the link has been generated, it is assigned to a variable named *dynamicLink* and the Share button is enabled.

46.7 Sharing the Dynamic Link

Now that a dynamic link has been generated the code for the *shareLink()* method can be added to the project so that users can share links. This will be achieved using the standard Android ACTION_SEND intent. Remaining within the *DynamicLinksActivity.java* file, add the *shareLink()* method:

```
.
.
.
import android.content.Intent;

import java.net.URL;
import java.net.URLDecoder;

public class DynamicLinksActivity extends AppCompatActivity {
.
.
.
    public void shareLink(View view) {
        try {
```

```
            URL url = new URL(URLDecoder.decode(dynamicLink.toString(),
                                                  "UTF-8"));
            Log.i(TAG, "URL = " + url.toString());
            Intent intent = new Intent(Intent.ACTION_SEND);
            intent.setType("text/plain");
            intent.putExtra(Intent.EXTRA_SUBJECT, "Firebase Deep Link");
            intent.putExtra(Intent.EXTRA_TEXT, url.toString());
            startActivity(intent);
        } catch (Exception e) {
            Log.i(TAG, "Could not decode Uri: " + e.getLocalizedMessage());
        }
    }
.
.
.
}
```

Run the app (for a greater range of sharing options a physical device is recommended) and tap the *Get Link* button. When the Share button enables, click on it and select a way to send the link to someone else (or even to yourself for testing purposes). Within the body of the message, the dynamic link should have already been inserted and should resemble the following URL:

```
https://<app_code>.app.goo.gl/?link=http://example.com&apn=com.ebookfrenzy.dyn
amiclinks
```

46.8 Adding the Main Activity Intent Filter

The next task is to add the intent filter for the main activity within the app project. This filter will ensure that the main activity is launched when a dynamic link with an example.com deep link is received by the system. Edit the *AndroidManifest.xml* file and modify the DynamicLinksActivity entry to add this additional intent filter:

```
<?xml version="1.0" encoding="utf-8"?>
<manifest xmlns:android="http://schemas.android.com/apk/res/android"
    package="com.ebookfrenzy.dynamiclink_work">

    <application
.
.
.
        <activity android:name=".DynamicLinkActivity">
            <intent-filter>
                <action android:name="android.intent.action.MAIN" />

                <category android:name="android.intent.category.LAUNCHER" />
            </intent-filter>
            <intent-filter>
```

```
            <action android:name="android.intent.action.VIEW" />

            <category android:name="android.intent.category.DEFAULT" />
            <category android:name="android.intent.category.BROWSABLE" />

            <data
                android:host="example.com"
                android:scheme="http" />
            <data
                android:host="example.com"
                android:scheme="https" />
        </intent-filter>
    </activity>

.

.

</application>
```

46.9 **Detecting a Dynamic Link Launch**

With the intent filter configured, code now needs to be added to detect when the app has been launched as the result of a dynamic link. Edit the *DynamicLinkActivity.java* file and add some import directives. The class will also need to be declared as implementing the OnConnectionFailedListener interface of the GoogleApiClient. A variable will also be needed in which to store a reference to the GoogleApiClient instance:

```
.

.

.

import android.widget.Toast;
import android.support.annotation.NonNull;

import com.google.android.gms.appinvite.AppInvite;
import com.google.android.gms.appinvite.AppInviteInvitationResult;
import com.google.android.gms.appinvite.AppInviteReferral;
import com.google.android.gms.common.ConnectionResult;
import com.google.android.gms.common.api.GoogleApiClient;
import com.google.android.gms.common.api.ResultCallback;

public class DynamicLinksActivity extends AppCompatActivity implements
                GoogleApiClient.OnConnectionFailedListener {

.

.

    private GoogleApiClient googleApiClient;

.

.
```

The OnConnectionFailedListener interface requires that the OnConnectionFailed method be overridden within the class so add this method now:

```
@Override
public void onConnectionFailed(@NonNull ConnectionResult connectionResult) {
    Log.w(TAG, "onConnectionFailed:" + connectionResult);
    Toast.makeText(this, "Google Play Services Error: "
                        + connectionResult.getErrorCode(),
            Toast.LENGTH_SHORT).show();
}
```

Finally, modify the *onCreate()* method to handle a dynamic link app launch:

```
@Override
protected void onCreate(Bundle savedInstanceState) {
    super.onCreate(savedInstanceState);
    setContentView(R.layout.activity_dynamic_links);

    statusText = (TextView) findViewById(R.id.statusText);
    shareButton = (Button) findViewById(R.id.shareButton);
    shareButton.setEnabled(false);

    googleApiClient = new GoogleApiClient.Builder(this)
            .enableAutoManage(this, this)
            .addApi(AppInvite.API)
            .build();

    boolean launchDeepLink = false;

    AppInvite.AppInviteApi.getInvitation(googleApiClient, this,
                launchDeepLink).setResultCallback(

                new ResultCallback<AppInviteInvitationResult>() {
                    @Override
                    public void onResult(
                        @NonNull AppInviteInvitationResult result) {

                        if (result.getStatus().isSuccess()) {

                            Intent intent = result.getInvitationIntent();
                            String deepLink =
                                AppInviteReferral.getDeepLink(intent);

                            handleDeeplink(deepLink);
                        } else {
```

433

```
                                   Log.i(TAG, "Deeplink not found");
                    }
               }
          });
}
```

Note that in the event that a dynamic link is detected, the deep link URL is extracted from the intent and passed through to a method named *handleDeepLink()* for handling. This method now needs to be added to the class.

46.10 **Parsing the Deep Link URL**

Now that we have a deep link, the app needs to decide what to do with it. Typically, an app will take different actions depending on the content of the deep link URL. In this case, the app dynamic link is being used as part of a promotional email sent to existing users to encourage them to use the app. When the user clicks on the dynamic link the app will load and credit the user's account with extra points.

The code within the *handleDeepLink()* method will need to check for a */credit* path within the deep link URL together with a query parameter representing the number of points to be credited. If a match is found, a message will be displayed within the TextView object confirming that the points have been applied to the user's account:

```
public void handleDeeplink(String deepLink) {

    Uri deepUri = Uri.parse(deepLink);

    if (deepUri.getPath().equals("/credit")) {
        statusText.setText(deepUri.getQuery() +
                    " points have been applied to your account");
    }
}
```

Although for the sake of simplicity such steps are not being taken in this example, code should be added in a real world situation to record that the user has claimed the offer to ensure that the user cannot use the link more than once.

46.11 **Generating the Dynamic Link**

The dynamic link to test the app will be generated using the Firebase console. Open the Firebase console in a browser window, select the *Firebase Examples* project and click on the *Dynamic Links* option. Within the Dynamic Links screen, click on the *New Dynamic Link* button and configure the link as follows:

- **Deep link URL** – *http://www.example.com/credit?200*
- **Dynamic Link name** – Bonus points email promotion
- **iOS behavior** – Open the deep link URL in a browser

- **Android behavior** – Open the deep link in your Android app (select the app from the menu).
- **UTM parameters** – None
- **Social media tags** – None

Once the link has been configured, click on the *Create Dynamic Link* button to generate the link. After the link has been generated, hover the mouse pointer over the link row, click on the menu dots when they appear and select *Link details* from the menu.

When using dynamic links in scenarios such as this it is important to use the short form of the URL. In this example, the user could easily reverse engineer the long form URL to increase the number of bonus points awarded.

Copy the short dynamic link to the clipboard before moving to the next step.

46.12 **Testing a Dynamic Link**

There are a few different ways to test that a dynamic link is working. The simplest way is to edit the run configuration of the app within Android Studio to launch the app using the dynamic link URL.

To modify the run configuration, click on the *app* entry in the Android Studio toolbar and select the *Edit Configurations...* menu option:

Figure 46-2

When the Run/Debug Configurations dialog appears, locate the Launch Options section of the General screen and change the Launch menu from Default Activity to URL:

Figure 46-3

Paste the dynamic link into the URL: text field before clicking on the *Apply* button followed by the *OK* button to commit the change and close the dialog.

When the app is run using the new configuration the deep link should be detected and the text view updated within the main activity to show that the points have been credited to the user's account.

Another option is to use the adb command-line tool together with the Chrome browser running on the device or emulator on which the test app is installed. On the device or emulator, open the Chrome browser and enter the shortened dynamic link into the search bar and attempt to load the URL. After a short delay, the DynamicLinks app should launch and display the message indicating that bonus points have been earned.

Typing the URL into the browser can be time consuming and prone to error (particularly when using a long form URL). A useful trick to avoid having to type the URL is to use the adb tool. On the device or emulator, open Chrome once again and select the search bar so that the keyboard appears ready to receive input and remove any previous URL within the search field. Open a command-prompt or terminal window on the development system and run the following command where *<dynamic url here>* is replaced by the dynamic link URL copied from the Firebase console:

```
adb shell input text "<dynamic url here>"
```

When the command is executed, the text will appear within the Chrome search bar. Tapping the search button on the virtual keyboard will then load the URL and launch the app.

46.13 Adding a Second Activity

The final step of this tutorial is to add a second activity to the app which will be launched automatically in response to a dynamic link click. This second activity is intended to display a welcome message to users after they have installed the app for the first time.

Within the Android Studio Project tool window, right click on the package name (*app -> java -> <your domain>.dynamiclinks*) and select the *New -> Activity -> Empty Activity* menu option. In the New Android Activity dialog, name the activity *WelcomeActivity*, verify that the *Generate Layout File* and *Backwards Compatibility* options are enabled, and that *Launcher Activity* is disabled before clicking on the *Finish* button.

Load the *activity_welcome.xml* file into the layout editor, position a TextView widget in the center of the layout and use the *Infer constraints* button in the layout editor toolbar to constrain the widget appropriately. Using the Properties tool window, change the text on the view to "Thank you for installing our app":

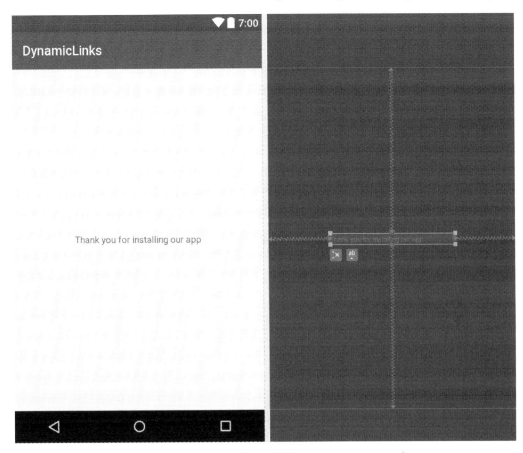

Figure 46-4

46.14 Configuring Automatic Activity Launching

The goal for the Welcome Activity is to have it launch automatically when a dynamic link containing the following deep link URL is clicked:

http://www.example.com/welcome

This involves the addition of an intent filter to the manifest entry for the activity. Edit the *AndroidManifest.xml* file, locate the WelcomeActivity entry and modify it to read as follows:

```
<activity android:name=".WelcomeActivity">
    <intent-filter>
        <action android:name="android.intent.action.VIEW" />
        <category android:name="android.intent.category.DEFAULT" />
        <category android:name="android.intent.category.BROWSABLE" />
        <data android:scheme="http"
            android:host="www.example.com"
            android:pathPrefix="/welcome" />
    </intent-filter>
```

```
</activity>
```

Next, edit the *DynamicLinksActivity.java* file and change the code to assign a true value to the *launchDeepLink* variable:

```
boolean launchDeepLink = true;
```

Compile and run the app so that the latest version is installed ready for testing.

46.15 Testing Automatic Launching

Return to the Firebase console and generate a new dynamic link containing a deep link URL of *http://www.example.com/welcome* configured to launch the DynamicLinks Android app.

Edit the run configuration for the app once more within Android Studio and paste the dynamic link URL into the settings dialog before clicking on the *Apply* and *Ok* buttons.

When the app is run the Welcome activity should appear instead of the main activity.

As a final test, attempt to launch the app with the original bonus credit dynamic URL and verify that the dynamic link works as before with the main activity launching and the TextView displaying the credited points.

46.16 Dynamic Link Analytics

Although basic statistics relating to dynamic link clicks are available within the Dynamic Links screen of the Firebase console, a greater level of detail is provided within Firebase Analytics. In fact, dynamic link clicks are one of the event types captured automatically by Firebase Analytics.

To view dynamic link analytics, select the Analytics screen within the Firebase console followed by the *Events* tab and, using the app selection menu at the top of the page, select the DynamicLinks app. In the event table, dynamic link events will be listed on the *dynamic_link_app_open* line:

Figure 46-5

To view dynamic link stats in greater detail, select the event to display the graphs, charts and demographic data.

Event parameters are also available to gather additional information about dynamic link clicks. To configure event parameters display the menu for the event as shown in Figure 46-6 and select the *Edit parameter reporting* menu option:

Figure 46-6

In the parameter configuration dialog, select the parameters to be added to the event. In Figure 46-7, the accept time and link ID parameters have been selected for inclusion in the dynamic links analytics data:

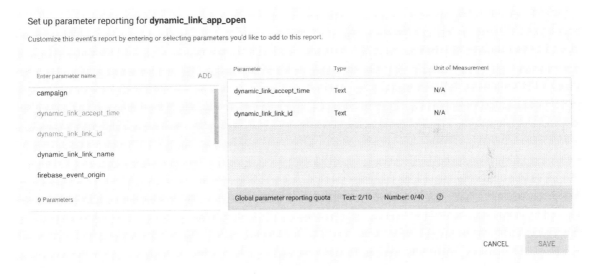

Figure 46-7

Each added event parameter will be represented by a graph within the detail event view.

46.17 **Summary**

This chapter provided a practical example of creating and handling Dynamic Links. The topics covered included the creation of dynamic links using both the Firebase console and within an Android app together with both manual and auto loading approaches to handling a link within the app. The chapter also outlined ways to test dynamic links before an app is published in the Google Play store.

47. Firebase Invites

Firebase Invites provide a way for users to recommend your app to other potential users. From the point of view of the developer, invite support can be added to an app with just a few lines of code. When the user chooses to refer your app to someone else, Firebase handles all aspects of the invitation process, including presenting an invitation dialog from which recipients may be selected and transmitting the messages to the chosen recipients.

The invitation takes the form of an email or SMS message containing a Firebase Dynamic Link URL which, when clicked, takes the user to the page within the Google Play store from which the app can be installed. Once the app has been installed, the dynamic link is passed to the app when it is launched, allowing custom behavior to be implemented using the steps outlined in the previous chapters.

47.1 Creating a Firebase Invite Intent

Firebase Invites are sent using the AppInviteInvitation intent which is used to launch the app invitation activity containing the invitation dialog.

The AppInviteInvitation intent is created and configured using the AppInviteInvitation intent builder and then launched using the *startActivityForResult()* method. In the following example, a basic intent consisting of a message and a deep link is created and then used to launch the invitation activity:

```
public void sendInvite(View view) {
    Intent intent = new AppInviteInvitation.IntentBuilder("My Invitation")
            .setMessage("Try out this amazing app!")
            .setDeepLink(Uri.parse("http://www.example.com/invite"))
            .build();
    startActivityForResult(intent, INVITE_REQUEST);
}
```

A number of methods are available for customizing the intent including the following:

- **setMessage()** – Used to declare a default message to be included with the invitation. This default text can be modified by the user within the invitation dialog before the message is sent.
- **setDeepLink()** – The deep link URL which is to be embedded into the dynamic link sent with the message. This can be used to pass information to the app when it is installed and launched by the message recipient.
- **setCustomImage()** – Allows an image to be included within the message. The image can be up to 4000x4000 pixels in size, though 600x600 pixels is the recommended size.

- **setCallToActionText()** – The text that is to appear on the Install button included within email messages. Text is limited to 32 characters.
- **setEmailHtmlContent()** – Allows HTML content to be defined for email based invitations. The dynamic link URL should be substituted by the %%APPINVITE_LINK_PLACEHOLDER%% string. This method must be used in conjunction with the *setEmailSubject()* method. When using HTML content, the *setMessage()*, *setCustomImage()* and *setCallToActionText()* methods are redundant.
- **setEmailSubject()** – Used to set the email subject line when using HTML content.
- **setGoogleAnalyticsTrackingId()** – Allows a Google Analytics tracking ID to be specified to track the performance of the invitation.

The following code fragment shows an example invitation that makes use of HTML content:

```
public void sendInvite(View view) {
    Intent intent = new AppInviteInvitation.IntentBuilder("My Invitation")
            .setDeepLink(Uri.parse("http://www.example.com/invite"))
            .setEmailSubject("I recommend this app")
            .setEmailHtmlContent("<body><p>I've been using this app." +
                    ".<p>You should try it. " +
                    "You can use this " +
                    "<a href=\"%%APPINVITE_LINK_PLACEHOLDER%%\">link</a>" +
                    " to install it on your Android device.</p></body>")
            .build();
    startActivityForResult(intent, INVITE_REQUEST);
}
```

47.2 Sending the Invitation

When the intent activity starts, the invitation dialog will appear populated with any settings configured in the intent together with a list of known contacts from which to select recipients. Additional contacts may be added by clicking on the *Add recipients* link and entering additional email addresses or phone numbers.

If the invitation is HTML based, the message can be previewed using the *Preview Email* button. Once the message is ready to send, the user simply taps on the send button in the top right-hand corner:

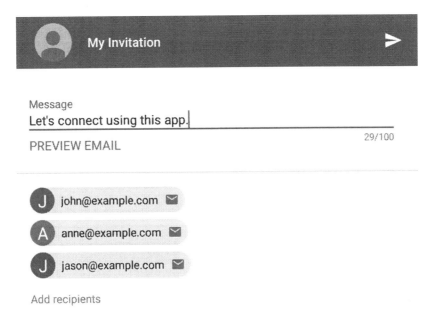

Message
Let's connect using this app.|

                                                                29/100
PREVIEW EMAIL

J john@example.com ✉

A anne@example.com ✉

J jason@example.com ✉

Add recipients

Figure 47-1

47.3 Handling the Activity Result

Since the app invitation intent is launched using the *startActivityForResult()* method, clearly some code needs to be added to handle the result. This is handled in the usual way by implementing an *onActivityResult()* method.

When invitations have been sent each one is automatically assigned an *invitation ID* which can be extracted from the results data as shown in the following method:

```
@Override
protected void onActivityResult(int requestCode, int resultCode, Intent data)
{
    super.onActivityResult(requestCode, resultCode, data);

    if (requestCode == INVITE_REQUEST) {
        if (resultCode == RESULT_OK) {
            String[] ids = AppInviteInvitation.getInvitationIds(
                            resultCode, data);
            for (String id : ids) {
                Log.d(TAG, "id of sent invitation: " + id);
            }
        } else {
            // Failed to send invitations
        }
    }
}
```

47.4 **Testing Invitations**

If invitations are being added to an app that is not yet in the Google Play store, it is only possible to test the implementation up until the point that the invitation link is clicked. At this point the Google Play store will report that the URL is not valid. If the app is already available on the store, invitations can be tested fully, including installing and launching the app and handling the deep link during app initialization using the techniques outlined in the previous chapters.

47.5 **Summary**

App Referrals are built on Firebase Dynamic Links and provide a way for users to invite others to download and install an app with minimal coding effort on the part of the developer. All that is required is that the app configures and launches an AppInviteInvitation Intent. The Intent then handles all aspects of building the link and allowing the user to select recipients and sending method (email or SMS). If required, standard dynamic link handling can be built into the app to perform specific actions in response to a new user installing and signing into an app from an app referral.

48. Firebase App Indexing

Firebase App Indexing makes the content contained within an app discoverable to app users within both web and device-based Google search results, thereby increasing user engagement with the app. App Indexing also provides an effective way to drive new users to an app by including an app install button next to the search results.

This chapter will provide an introduction to Firebase App Indexing while explaining the different indexing features available and how to implement them within an Android app.

48.1 An Overview of Firebase App Indexing

One of the challenges facing app developers today is finding a way to encourage users to use an app once it has been installed on a device. While some apps such as news or social network apps tend to experience frequent use, many apps will remain unused after being installed on the user's device. One solution to this involves presenting the user with notifications that attempt to provide a reason for opening the app. Another option is to make use of App Indexing.

With app indexing, when a user has an app installed and performs a relevant search either on the web or device, the matching content within the app will appear within the search results. When the result is clicked, the app will launch and present the content to the user.

App Indexing may also be used to log the actions performed by users within the app in relation to the content. These actions are then used to improve the ranking of your content when the user performs content related Google searches and also to provide autocomplete suggestions while the user is entering a search query.

Firebase App Indexing categorizes app content as either public or personal. Public content is content associated with the app that is visible to all app users. This can take the form of content provided by the app, or content added by users with the understanding that it will be made visible to all other users. Personal content, on the other hand, is content that is added by users solely for their own personal use. When implementing app indexing, it is important to differentiate between public and personal content and actions so that a user's personal data is protected.

48.2 Public Content Indexing

Public content indexing includes links to app content within Google search results, regardless of whether the search is performed on the Google search website or using the Google app on the device. If the user has the app installed and app indexing has been implemented, the user can click the link to launch the app and access the content. As will be demonstrated in a later chapter, the search results on the device appear within the *In Apps* page of the Google search page.

Public content indexing involves indexing content that is considered to be accessible to all users and can only be implemented if the content within the app directly corresponds to the content structure of a web site. In other words, the deep link URLs that launch the correct content within the app must match the URL to reach the same content within the web site.

Consider, for example, a website that contains descriptions of vintage computer systems. The URLs for some web pages might be structured as follows:

http://www.example.com/computers/commodore64

http://www.example.com/computers/trs80

http://www.example.com/computers/amiga500

Clearly, entering one of the above URLs into a browser search bar would load the web page for the corresponding computer system.

Now assume that the web site also has a companion Android app containing the same content. In order to be able to support app indexing, the app must be able to accept the same URLs in the form of deep links and display the same content.

In a typical scenario, the user might install the app and view information about the Amiga 500 before closing the app. At some point in the future the same user may perform a Google search for the Amiga 500 using the Chrome browser or Google app. Firebase App Indexing will recognize that the search relates to content that the user previously viewed within the app and provide a link to the app based content within the search results. Selecting the link will launch the app and present the Amiga 500 content to the user.

Once content has been publicly indexed, it has the potential to also appear in search results for users that have yet to install the app. In this situation, an install button will appear next to the search result, providing a convenient installation path for new users.

48.3 Personal Content Indexing

Personal content is user generated content that is not intended to be viewed by other users. The example vintage computer app might, for example, provide the option for users to add notes about the price and condition of computer systems they are considering purchasing. Notes such as these would be indexed as personal content.

Personal content indexes are stored locally on the device and appear only within searches performed using the Google app and only when the content owner is signed into the device.

Unlike public content indexing, personal indexing does not require that the content also exist on a companion web site.

48.4 User Action Logging

App Indexing allows apps to log the actions taken by a user within an app. As with content, actions can be categorized as public or private. When actions are logged, Google uses this information when ranking content within a search query and to offer autocompletion suggestions when users enter queries into the Google search bar.

Typical actions to consider logging include viewing of specific content, watching a video, adding new content, listening to a song or sharing content with another user.

48.5 Summary

App Indexing provides a way to drive increased user engagement with an app by presenting the app content within search results both on the device and within Google web based searches. App Indexing can be used to index both app content and user activity, the latter being used to rank content and as the basis for autocomplete suggestions within the Google search bar. When using app indexing it is important to differentiate between public and personal content. Public content can only be indexed if the same content is also available on a web site and accessible via the same URL structure.

49. Implementing Firebase App Indexing

While the previous chapter took a high level approach to explaining Firebase App Indexing, this chapter will begin to outline in practical terms how the various app indexing features are implemented for an Android app.

49.1 Public Content Indexing

As discussed in the previous chapter, public content indexing requires matching website and app content, both accessible using the same URL structure. Assuming that this requirement has been met, public content indexing is primarily a matter of linking the website with the app. This is achieved by placing a JSON configuration file on the web site containing information about the companion app in the form of a *digital asset link*. The JSON file must be named *assetlinks.json* and located in the *.well-known* directory of the web site.

A digital asset link comprises a *relation* statement granting permission for a target app to be launched using the web site's link URLs and a target statement declaring the companion app package name and SHA-256 certificate fingerprint. A typical asset link file might, for example, read as follows:

```
[{
    "relation": ["delegate_permission/common.handle_all_urls"],
    "target" : { "namespace": "android_app",
      "package_name": "<app package name here>",
                "sha256_cert_fingerprints": ["<app certificate here>"] }
}]
```

The *assetlinks.json* file can contain multiple digital asset links, potentially allowing a single web site to be associated with more than one companion app.

When the app is launched as the result of a link click, the Android *app link* mechanism is used to launch the app and pass through the URL. Much like Firebase Dynamic Links, the target app must be prepared to handle the app link intent. The first step involves adding an intent filter for the target activity within the project *AndroidManifest.xml* file:

```
<activity android:name=".LandmarkActivity">
    <intent-filter>
        <action android:name="android.intent.action.MAIN" />
        <action android:name="android.intent.action.VIEW" />

        <category android:name="android.intent.category.DEFAULT" />
        <category android:name="android.intent.category.BROWSABLE" />
```

```
        <data
            android:host="example.com"
            android:pathPrefix="/computers"
            android:scheme="http" />
    </intent-filter>
</activity>
```

When the app is launched, the intent needs to be handled and the URL parsed to ensure that the correct content is presented to the user. The URL is delivered as a string stored in the data payload of the intent and can be extracted using code similar to the following:

```
@Override
    protected void onCreate(Bundle savedInstanceState) {
        super.onCreate(savedInstanceState);
        setContentView(R.layout.activity_computers);

        Intent intent = getIntent();
        String action = intent.getAction();
        String data = intent.getDataString(); // Get the URL

        if (Intent.ACTION_VIEW.equals(action) && data != null) {
                // Code here to parse URL and display content
        }
    }
}
```

49.2 Personal Content Indexing

Personal content indexing is performed by making calls to the Firebase Indexing API. Content items are added to the index on the device in the form of Indexable objects which are created using either Indexable.Builder or one of the preconfigured Builders provided by the Indexables class. The following code creates an Indexable object for a content entry for a vintage computer system using the standard builder:

```
Indexable indexableComputer = new Indexable.Builder()
        .setName("Atari ST")
        .setUrl("http://www.example.com/computers/atarist")
        .setDescription("Developed after Jack Tramiel bought Atari")
        .build();
```

Alternatively, one of the many convenience methods provided by the Indexables class can be used. Preconfigured Builder methods are available for creating Indexable objects for content such as documents, messages and notes. Regardless of the convenience builder used, the Indexable object must include name and URL properties. The full list of convenience methods can be found online at:

https://firebase.google.com/docs/reference/android/com/google/firebase/appindexing/builders/Indexables

The following code fragment uses the noteDigitalDocumentBuilder convenience method to create an Indexable object for a user note within the app:

```
Indexable indexableNote = Indexables.noteDigitalDocumentBuilder()
        .setUrl("http://www.example.com/computers/atarist/comment")
        .setName("Atari ST Personal Notes")
        .setText("Three in good condition on eBay")
        .setImage("http://www.excample.com/images/atariST.png")
        .setDateCreated(creationDate)
        .build();
```

Once an Indexable object has been created for the content item, it needs to be added to the app index on the device. This involves obtaining a reference to the FirebaseAppIndex instance and a call to its *update()* method passing through one or more Indexable objects. Since the update is performed asynchronously, the method call returns a Task object onto which listeners may be attached to track the success of the request:

```
Task<Void> task = FirebaseAppIndex.getInstance().update(indexableComputer);

task.addOnSuccessListener(new OnSuccessListener<Void>() {
    @Override
    public void onSuccess(Void aVoid) {
        // Content added to index
    }
});

task.addOnFailureListener(new OnFailureListener() {
    @Override
    public void onFailure(@NonNull Exception exception) {
        // Failed to add content to index
    }
});
```

49.3 App Indexing Service

Indexable objects can, of course, be created and added to the index at any time in the app lifecycle. A useful option, however, is to implement an app indexing intent service within the app to automatically add new content to the index and to rebuild the index in the event of an app upgrade or a corruption of the index. The app indexing service takes the form of an Intent Service which has been assigned app indexing permission and is configured to respond to UPDATE_INDEX intents. When implemented, Google Play services will call the app indexing service under the following conditions:

- After the app is installed on the device.
- If a version of the app that does not make use of app indexing is upgraded to a version that does.
- At periodic intervals to ensure that the index is kept up to date.

When called, it is the responsibility of the app indexing service to create Indexable objects for all of the personal content associated with the app and to perform an update operation using the FirebaseAppIndex instance. The steps to implementing an app indexing service are included in the next chapter entitled *A Firebase App Indexing Tutorial*.

49.4 Logging User Actions

Logging of user actions is, once again, divided into public and personal actions. User actions are represented by instances of the Action class built using Action.Builder and specifying an appropriate action type. A wide range of types are available for actions including commenting, sending, sharing viewing, liking, adding and bookmarking. For a full list of types, refer to the following web page:

https://firebase.google.com/docs/reference/android/com/google/firebase/appindexing/Action.Build er

The following code, for example, creates a view Action object when a user views specific content within the app:

```
Action action = new Action.Builder(Action.Builder.VIEW_ACTION)
    .setObject("Amiga 500", "http://www.example.com/computers/amiga500")
    .build();
```

Alternatively, the same Action object can be created using the *newView()* convenience method of the Actions class:

```
Action action = Actions.newView("Amiga 500",
            "http://www.example.com/computers/amiga500")
```

When the action being logged is associated with personal content, metadata must be included within the action to indicate that the action should not be uploaded to Google:

```
Action action = new Action.Builder(Action.Builder.VIEW_ACTION)
    .setObject("Amiga 500", "http://www.example.com/computers/amiga500")
    .setMetadata(new Action.Metadata.Builder().setUpload(false))
    .build();
```

Once the Action object has been built, it needs to be logged using the FirebaseUserActions instance. For actions that take time the *start()* and *end()* methods of the FirebaseUserActions instance should be called at the beginning and end of the action respectively, passing through the Action object in each call:

```
FirebaseUserActions.getInstance().start(action); // User action starts

FirebaseUserActions.getInstance().end(action); // User action ends
```

If the action does not take place over a period of time, simply call the *end()* method:

```
FirebaseUserActions.getInstance().end(action); // User action ends
```

Note that before an action can be logged, the content must already be indexed. When indexing content and logging an action at the same time, therefore, it is important to complete the indexing operation before logging the action.

As previously mentioned, user action logging is used in part to allow the Google app to provide autocomplete suggestions when entering a search query. To include public content in the autocomplete list, index the public content as though it is personal content before logging the public action.

49.5 Removing Index Entries

When a user removes personal content from within an app, the matching index entry must also be removed from the index. Individual index entries are deleted by calling the *remove()* method of the FirebaseAppIndex instance, passing through as an argument the URL associated with the content, for example:

```
FirebaseAppIndex.remove("http://www.example.com/computers/atarist/comment");
```

To remove all the index entries on the device, make a call to the *removeAll()* method:

```
FirebaseAppIndex.removeAll();
```

This can be useful if the index entries need to be removed when the user logs out of the app. Assuming that the app indexing service has been implemented, the app index entries belonging to the user will be re-instated next time the user accesses the app.

49.6 Summary

Implementation of public content app indexing is a multi-step process that involves the structuring of content within the app to match that of the corresponding web site and then notifying Google through a digital assets link file that the app and web site content are related. The indexing of personal content involves the creation of Indexable objects in conjunction with the *update()* method of the FirebaseAppIndex instance. Actions are logged by building Action objects and logging them via the *start()* and *end()* methods of the FirebaseUserActions instance. The personal content index should also be kept up to date through the implementation of an App Indexing intent service.

Chapter 50

50. A Firebase App Indexing Tutorial

The previous chapters have covered a considerable amount of information relating to App Indexing. As is often the case, the best way to gain familiarity with the concepts of an area of this level of complexity is to put the information to practical use and to see it in action. With these goals in mind, this chapter will create an example Android app which makes use of many of the features offered by Firebase App Indexing.

50.1 About the Example App

In this chapter app indexing support will be added to an existing project. The project, named AppIndexing, is a basic app designed to allow users to find out information about landmarks in London. The app uses a SQLite database accessed through a standard Android content provider class. The app is provided with an existing database containing a set of records for some popular tourist attractions in London. In addition to the existing database entries, the app also lets the user add and delete personal landmark descriptions.

In its current form, the app allows records to be searched and new records to be added and deleted. The app also makes use of deep links to allow landmark descriptions to be loaded and viewed within the app via URL link clicks.

The goal of this chapter is to enhance the app to add support for app indexing including public and personal content indexing and user action logging.

50.2 The Database Schema

The data for the example app is contained within a file named *landmarks.db* located in the *app -> assets –> databases* folder of the project hierarchy. The database contains a single table named *locations*, the structure of which is outlined in Table 50-1:

Column	Type	Description
_id	String	The primary index, this column contains string values that uniquely identify the landmarks in the database.
Title	String	The name of the landmark (e.g. London Bridge).
description	String	A description of the landmark.

personal	Boolean	Indicates whether the record is personal or public. This value is set to true for all records added by the user. Existing records provided with the database are set to false.

Table 50-1

50.3 **Loading and Running the Project**

The project is contained within the *AppIndexing* folder of the sample source code download archive located at the following URL:

http://www.ebookfrenzy.com/print/firebase_android

Having located the folder, open it within Android Studio and run the app on an device or emulator. Once the app is launched, the screen illustrated in Figure 50-1 below will appear:

Figure 50-1

As currently implemented, landmarks are located using the ID for the location. The default database configuration currently contains two records referenced by the IDs "londonbridge" and "toweroflondon". Test the search feature by entering the ID for London Bridge into the ID field and clicking the *Find* button. When a matching record is found, a second activity (named *LandmarkActivity*) is launched and passed information about the record to be displayed. This information takes the form of a deep link URL which is then used by *LandmarkActivity* to extract the record from the database and display it to the user using the screen shown in Figure 50-2. The first time the second activity is launched, Android may ask you to select which app to use to handle the intent. If so, select the *AppIndexing* option followed by the *Always* button.

Figure 50-2

Finally, verify that deep links work by opening a terminal or command-prompt window and executing the following adb command:

```
adb shell am start -a android.intent.action.VIEW -d
  "http://example.com/landmarks/toweroflondon" com.ebookfrenzy.appindexing
```

After the command has executed, the app should display information about the Tower of London.

50.4 Adding Firebase App Indexing Support

Using the Firebase assistant panel, locate the App Indexing entry and take the necessary steps to connect the project to Firebase and to add the App Indexing libraries.

50.5 **Logging User Actions**

When a user performs a search or views information about a landmark using a deep link, that action needs to be recorded so that it appears as an auto-completion option when performing a search within the Google app on the device. When logging these actions, it will be important to differentiate between personal and public database records to ensure that only public actions are uploaded to Google.

Landmark information is displayed by the *displayLandmark()* method located in the *LandmarkActivity.java* file. This method is passed a Landmark object containing the information extracted from the database. From this information we can identify whether a public or personal record is being viewed and log the action accordingly. Edit the *LandmarkActivity.java* file and add two new methods to perform the logging:

```
import com.google.firebase.appindexing.Action;
import com.google.firebase.appindexing.FirebaseUserActions;
import com.google.firebase.appindexing.builders.Actions;

private void logPublicAction() {
    Action action = Actions.newView(landmark.getTitle(),
                        landmark.getLandmarkURL());
    FirebaseUserActions.getInstance().end(action);
}
.
.
.
private void logPersonalAction() {
    Action action = new Action.Builder(Action.Builder.VIEW_ACTION)
            .setObject(landmark.getTitle(),landmark.getLandmarkURL())
            .setMetadata(new Action.Metadata.Builder().setUpload(false))
            .build();

    FirebaseUserActions.getInstance().end(action);
}
```

Next, locate the *displayLandmark()* method and modify it to call the appropriate logging method depending on whether the landmark is public or personal:

```
private void displayLandmark(String landmarkId) {
    MyDBHandler dbHandler = new MyDBHandler(this, null, null, 1);

    landmark =
            dbHandler.findLandmark(landmarkId);

    if (landmark != null) {
```

```
    if (landmark.getPersonal() == 0) {
        logPublicAction();
        deleteButton.setEnabled(false);
    } else {
        logPersonalAction();
        deleteButton.setEnabled(true);
    }

    titleText.setText(landmark.getTitle());
    descriptionText.setText(landmark.getDescription());
} else {
    titleText.setText("No Match Found");
}
}
}
```

50.6 Adding Content Indexing

Now that actions are being logged, the next step is to begin indexing both public and personal content. The code to perform the content indexing will be implemented in a method named *indexLandmark()* which now needs to be added to the *LandmarkActivity.java* file:

```
.
.
import android.support.annotation.NonNull;
import com.google.android.gms.tasks.OnFailureListener;
import com.google.android.gms.tasks.OnSuccessListener;
import com.google.android.gms.tasks.Task;
import com.google.firebase.appindexing.FirebaseAppIndex;
import com.google.firebase.appindexing.Indexable;
.
.
private void indexLandmark() {

    Indexable indexableLandmark = new Indexable.Builder()
            .setName(landmark.getTitle())
            .setUrl(landmark.getLandmarkURL())
            .setDescription(landmark.getDescription())
            .build();

    Task<Void> task =
        FirebaseAppIndex.getInstance().update(indexableLandmark);

    task.addOnSuccessListener(new OnSuccessListener<Void>() {
        @Override
        public void onSuccess(Void aVoid) {
```

```
                Log.d(TAG, "App Indexing added "
                    + landmark.getTitle() + " to " +
                        "index");
        }
    });

    task.addOnFailureListener(new OnFailureListener() {
        @Override
        public void onFailure(@NonNull Exception exception) {
            Log.e(TAG, "App Indexing failed to add " +
                        landmark.getTitle() + " to index. " +
                    "" + exception.getMessage());
        }
    });
}
```

The method builds an Indexable object containing the landmark title, URL and description before passing it through to the *update()* method of the FirebaseAppIndex instance as a background task. Success and failure listeners are then added to the task to report on the status of the update once the task completes.

The objective is to index the content when the user views it within the app. To ensure that this happens, a call to the *indexLandmark()* method will be added to the activity's *onStart()* method:

```
@Override
protected void onStart() {
    super.onStart();

    if (landmark != null) {
        indexLandmark();
    }
}
```

50.7 Testing Content Indexing

With content indexing added to the app, compile and run the app on a device or emulator and enter "londonbridge" into the ID field before clicking on the *Find* button. When the Landmark activity loads with the London Bridge information, check the logcat output to verify that the content was successfully indexed.

Display the device home screen and swipe right to display the Google screen (Figure 50-3).

Figure 50-3

Enter London Bridge into the search bar and initiate the search. When the search results screen appears, scroll sideways through the list of search categories and select the *In Apps* option (the option may be displayed as *Tablet* or *Phone* if testing is being performed on a physical device). The results should now include the London Bridge content from the AppIndexing app:

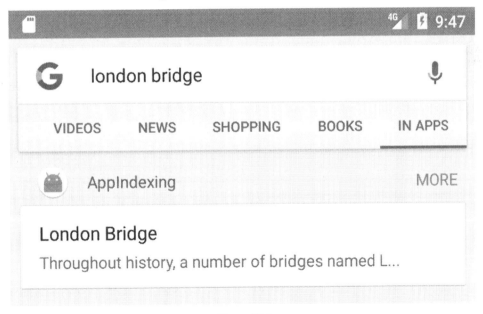

Figure 50-4

Selecting the London Bridge entry from the search results should launch the app and load the London Bridge content into the Landmark activity view.

If the app is running on a physical device, the index information can be reviewed within the Settings app. After opening Settings, select the *Google* entry, scroll down to the Developer section and click on the *Firebase App Indexing* option:

Figure 50-5

Within the list of applications, select the *AppIndexing* entry to display index information captured for the app:

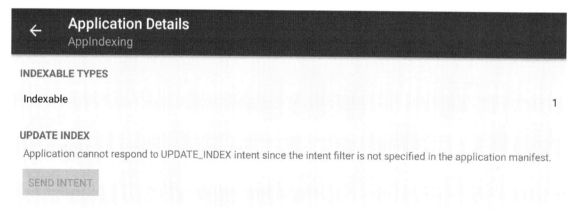

Figure 50-6

Note that the screen includes a Send Intent button. This is provided to force the app to update the index entries for personal content. This button is currently disabled because index updating support has not yet been added to the project. This feature will be implemented later in the chapter.

The above figure shows that one Indexable item has been stored for the app. Selecting this entry will display the index list including the title and URL:

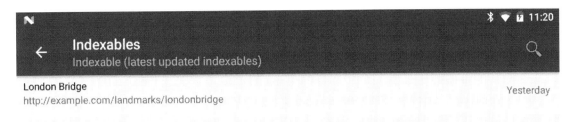

London Bridge
http://example.com/landmarks/londonbridge

Yesterday

Figure 50-7

Selecting the London Bridge item will display all of the data that has been included for that index entry:

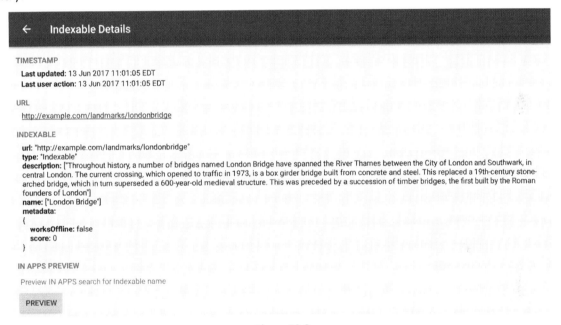

Figure 50-8

Clicking the Preview button in the Indexable Details screen will launch the AppIndexing app and load the London Bridge content within the Landmark Activity.

50.8 Indexing User Added Content

The final task is to make sure that any new personal content added by the user is indexed at regular intervals. New landmarks are added to the database using the main activity screen. As currently configured, a newly added landmark will not be indexed until the user views the details in the Landmark activity. One possible solution to this problem might be to add code to index each new landmark as it is added. Another option, and the one that will be used in this instance, is to add an App Indexing Service to the app. This intent service is called when the app is installed or updated, each time it is launched and intermitantly over time.

A Firebase App Indexing Tutorial

The purpose of the service is to identify the personal content within the app and to add it to the on-device index. To add an app indexing service to the project, locate and right-click on the package name (com.ebookfrenzy.appindexing) within the Android Studio project tool window and select the *New -> Service -> Service (IntentService)* menu option. In the resulting dialog, name the class AppIndexingService, turn off the option to include helper start methods and click on the Finish button.

Edit the *AppIndexingService.java* file, delete the current content and implement the class as follows:

```java
package com.ebookfrenzy.appindexing;

import android.app.IntentService;
import android.content.Intent;
import android.support.annotation.NonNull;
import android.util.Log;

import com.google.android.gms.tasks.OnFailureListener;
import com.google.android.gms.tasks.OnSuccessListener;
import com.google.android.gms.tasks.Task;
import com.google.firebase.appindexing.FirebaseAppIndex;
import com.google.firebase.appindexing.Indexable;
import com.google.firebase.appindexing.builders.Indexables;

import java.util.ArrayList;
import java.util.List;
public class AppIndexingService extends IntentService {

    public static final String TAG = "AppIndexingService";

    public AppIndexingService() {
        super("AppIndexingService");
    }

    @Override
    protected void onHandleIntent(Intent intent) {

    }

}
```

The first method that needs to be added to the class will be used to return an array of personal landmark records contained within the database. Remaining within the *AppIndexingService.java* file, add this method as follows:

```java
private List<Landmark> getPersonalLandmarks() {
```

```
        ArrayList<Landmark> landmarks = new ArrayList();

        MyDBHandler dbHandler = new MyDBHandler(this, null, null, 1);

        landmarks = dbHandler.findAllLandmarks();

        for (Landmark landmark : landmarks) {
            if (landmark.getPersonal() == 1) {
                landmarks.add(landmark);
            }
        }
        return landmarks;
}
```

The code calls a method on a MyDBHandler instance that returns all of the landmarks in the database. The code then iterates through all of the landmarks, adding only those with the personal flag set to the array list. Once all the landmarks have been checked, the array list is returned.

Each time the intent service is launched, the method named *onHandleIntent()* will be called. The following code now needs to be added to this method to call the *getPersonalLandmarks()* method and add each landmark to the index:

```
@Override
protected void onHandleIntent(Intent intent) {

    ArrayList<Indexable> indexableLandmarks = new ArrayList<>();

    for (Landmark landmark : getPersonalLandmarks()) {

        if (landmark != null) {

            Indexable personalLandmark = Indexables.digitalDocumentBuilder()
                    .setName(landmark.getTitle())
                    .setText(landmark.getDescription())
                    .setUrl(landmark.getLandmarkURL())
                    .build();

            Task<Void> task =
                FirebaseAppIndex.getInstance().update(personalLandmark);

            task.addOnSuccessListener(new OnSuccessListener<Void>() {
                @Override
                public void onSuccess(Void aVoid) {
                    Log.d(TAG, "AppIndexService: Successfully added
landmark");
```

```
            }
        });


        task.addOnFailureListener(new OnFailureListener() {
            @Override
            public void onFailure(@NonNull Exception exception) {
                Log.e(TAG, "AppIndexService: Failed to add landmark " +
                        "" + exception.getMessage());
            }
        });


    }
  }
}
```

The intent will be called at regular intervals by Google Play services. In order for this to happen, the intent needs an UPDATE_INDEX intent filter and app indexing permission. Edit the *AndroidManifest.xml* file, locate the *.AppIndexingService* element and modify it so that it matches the entry below:

```
<service android:name=".AppIndexingService"
    android:exported="true"
    android:permission="com.google.android.gms.permission.APPINDEXING">
    <intent-filter>
      <action android:name="com.google.firebase.appindexing.UPDATE_INDEX" />
    </intent-filter>
</service>
```

50.9 Testing Index Updates

Compile and run the app (ideally on a physical Android device) and add a new landmark to the database. Before viewing the landmark, open the Google app and perform a search for the newly added landmark. The In Apps screen of the search results should indicate that the content has not yet been indexed.

Using the App Indexing screen of the Settings app, select the AppIndexing app and click on the *Send Intent* button shown in Figure 50-8 above. This will launch the AppIndexingService intent causing the new landmark to be indexed. Remaining within the Settings app, navigate to the index details for new index entry and click on the Preview button.

This should launch the Google app and show the new content in the In App search results.

50.10 Deleting Index Entries

The final task is to make sure that when a personal landmark is deleted, the corresponding index entry is also removed. When a personal landmark is displayed in the Landmark activity screen, the Delete button is enabled allowing the record to be removed from the database. The code to perform this task is contained in the *deleteLandmark()* method located in the *LandmarkActivity.java* file. Edit this file, locate the method and modify it to remove the index entry for the landmark:

```
public void deleteLandmark(View view) {

    MyDBHandler dbHandler = new MyDBHandler(this, null, null, 1);

    if (landmark != null) {
        dbHandler.deleteLandmark(landmark.getID());
        titleText.setText("");
        descriptionText.setText("");
        deleteButton.setEnabled(false);
        FirebaseAppIndex.getInstance().remove(landmark.getLandmarkURL());
    }
}
```

Run the app one last time, find the personal landmark added in the previous section and delete it from the database. Using either the Google app or App Indexing Settings screens, verify that the landmark is no longer indexed.

50.11 Summary

The objective of this chapter has been to demonstrate in practical terms the indexing of personal content and logging of user actions using Firebase App Indexing within an Android app. This included the implementation of an app indexing service and use of the Android Settings app to test app indexing functionality.

51. Firebase Performance Monitoring

As the name suggests, Firebase Performance Monitoring is a service that allows app developers to review and monitor the performance of an app. In this chapter of Firebase Essentials, the key features of Performance Monitoring will be covered, including a short tutorial that demonstrates some of these monitoring features in action.

51.1 An Overview of Firebase Performance Monitoring

Performance monitoring is enabled by adding the Performance Monitoring SDK to an app project but without adding any additional code to the app. The SDK will automatically measure a range of performance metrics for the app, including startup time, foreground and background activity and HTTP/S network requests.

Performance monitoring is based on traces. A trace is the capture of performance data that occurs between two different points within the execution cycle of an app.

In addition to the automatic traces, Performance Monitoring also allows custom performance traces to be implemented within the app code. This allows monitoring to be started and stopped at different points in the app lifecycle to gain an insight into the performance of specific areas of app functionality. Custom traces may also be added to specific methods simply by adding a single annotation to method declarations within the source code of the app. Counters may also be created to monitor the frequency with which events occur within the scope of a custom trace (for example a counter could be incremented each time the app encounters a problem writing to a remote storage file).

In terms of the data included in performance monitoring, this includes app version, country, device, operating system, radio and carrier information. For HTTP/S network requests, the response time, payload size and success rate are also captured.

The results of performance monitoring are viewed within the Performance Monitoring section of the Firebase console.

51.2 Adding Performance Monitoring to a Project

For the purposes of demonstrating Firebase Performance Monitoring, the RealtimeDBList app created earlier in this book will be used. If you have already completed this project, open it in Android Studio now. Alternatively, the completed project can be found in the code sample download for the book available from the following URL:

http://www.ebookfrenzy.com/print/firebase_android

Firebase Performance Monitoring

If the app has not yet been connected to Firebase, begin by selecting the Android Studio *Tools -> Firebase* menu option. When the Firebase assistant panel appears, check to see if you are using a version of Android Studio that includes the option for Performance Monitoring, select it and follow the steps to connect to Firebase and add the Performance Monitoring SDK before proceeding to the next section of this chapter.

If, on the other hand, you are using a version of Android Studio that does not provide a Performance Monitoring option, select the Analytics option and use that option to connect to Firebase. Once connected, edit the project level *build.gradle (Project: RealtimeDBList)* file and modify the buildscript dependencies section to include a reference to the Firebase plugins package as follows:

```
buildscript {
    repositories {
        jcenter()
    }
    dependencies {
        classpath 'com.android.tools.build:gradle:2.3.3'
        classpath 'com.google.firebase:firebase-plugins:1.1.0'
        classpath 'com.google.gms:google-services:3.0.0'
    }
}
```

Next, edit the module level *build.gradle (Module: app)* file to apply the performance plugin and to add a dependency for the Firebase Performance SDK:

```
apply plugin: 'com.android.application'
apply plugin: 'com.google.firebase.firebase-perf'

.

.

.

dependencies {
    compile fileTree(dir: 'libs', include: ['*.jar'])
    androidTestCompile('com.android.support.test.espresso:espresso-
core:2.2.2', {
        exclude group: 'com.android.support', module: 'support-annotations'
    })
    compile 'com.google.firebase:firebase-perf:11.0.1'
    compile 'com.android.support:appcompat-v7:25.3.1'

.

.

.

}
```

Once these changes have been made and the app rebuilt, Firebase will automatically monitor the following traces:

- **App Startup** – Traces startup performance from the point that the app is launched until it becomes responsive to the user. This essentially covers the period of time from the app being opened up until the *onResume()* method is called in the launcher activity.
- **App Background** – Traces performance of the app while it is in the background. Trace monitoring begins from the point that the *onStop()* method of the last activity to enter the background is called. Monitoring ends when the *onResume()* method of the first activity to reenter the foreground is called.
- **App Foreground** – Traces performance of the app while it is in the foreground. Monitoring begins when the *onResume()* method of the first activity to enter the foreground is called and ends when the *onStop()* method is called on the last activity to enter the background.
- **HTTP/S Network Requests** – Traces the performance of an HTTP/S network request from the point that the request is made until the response is received. Data gathered includes the response time, the size of the request payload and the percentage of successful requests.

51.3 Defining Custom Traces

Custom traces are added to an app by specifying the trace start and end points within the code. Before custom traces can be added, the following libraries must first be imported. Begin, therefore by adding the following import directives to the *RealtimeDBListActivity.java* class file:

```
import com.google.firebase.perf.FirebasePerformance;
import com.google.firebase.perf.metrics.AddTrace;
import com.google.firebase.perf.metrics.Trace;
```

To start a trace, an instance of the Trace class needs to be created via a call to the *newTrace()* method of the FirebasePerformance instance, passing through the name by which the trace is to be identified. The trace is then started via a call to the *start()* method of the Trace object:

```
Trace trace = FirebasePerformance.getInstance().newTrace("file_save");
myTrace.start();
```

To end the trace, a call must be made to the *stop()* method of the same Trace object used to start the trace:

```
trace.stop();
```

Within the *RealtimeDBListActivity.java* class, add a custom trace within the *addItem()* method as follows:

```
public void addItem(View view) {

    String item = itemText.getText().toString();
    String key = dbRef.push().getKey();
    Trace trace = FirebasePerformance.getInstance().newTrace("add_item");
    trace.start();
    itemText.setText("");
    dbRef.child(key).child("description").setValue(item);
```

```
    adapter.notifyDataSetChanged();
    trace.stop();
}
```

If a trace needs to cover a method from beginning to end, this can be added using the @AddTrace annotation above the method declaration. Remaining within the *RealtimeDBListActivity.java* class file, add a trace to the *deleteItem()* method as follows:

```
@AddTrace(name = "deleteItemTrace", enabled = true)
public void deleteItem(View view) {
    dataListView.setItemChecked(selectedPosition, false);
    dbRef.child(listKeys.get(selectedPosition)).removeValue();
}
```

To implement a trace counter, simply call the *incrementCounter()* method of the Trace object, passing through the name by with the counter is to be referenced. For example, the following code change to the *addItem()* method will record every time that an item is added to the database list:

```
public void addItem(View view) {

    String item = itemText.getText().toString();
    String key = dbRef.push().getKey();
    Trace trace = FirebasePerformance.getInstance().newTrace("add_item");
    trace.start();
    trace.incrementCounter("item_add_counter");
    itemText.setText("");
    dbRef.child(key).child("description").setValue(item);

    adapter.notifyDataSetChanged();
    trace.stop();
}
```

If the counter needs to incremented by a value greater than 1, the value by which the count is to be increased is passed through as a second argument to the method:

```
trace.incrementCounter("item_add_counter", 10);
```

51.4 Enabling Logcat Output

Unfortunately, it can take up to 12 hours before performance monitoring results begin to appear within the Firebase console. To check that performance monitoring is working without having to wait for the Firebase console to catch up, it is possible to configure the app to report performance events within the logcat output. This involves the addition of an element within the <application> element of the project's *AndroidManifest.xml* file as follows:

```
<application...>
```

```
        <meta-data android:name="firebase_performance_logcat_enabled"
android:value="true" />
        <activity android:name=".RealtimeDBListActivity">
.
.
</application>
```

Compile and run the app and display logcat within the Android Studio Android Monitor tool window. When monitoring events are logged, they will be prefixed with FirebasePerformance. To view only the performance logging, enter FirebasePerformance into the logcat filter field as highlighted in Figure 51-1:

Figure 51-1

As long as the performance events are being logged performance monitoring is working. Take some time to interact with the app by adding, finding and deleting database entries. Also move the app between background and foreground modes. Once some data has been recorded, all that remains is to review the data in the Firebase console.

51.5 Reviewing Performance Data in the Firebase Console

After sufficient time has elapsed for the Firebase console to begin displaying performance data, open the Firebase console in a browser window and select the *Firebase Examples* project followed by the *Performance Monitoring* entry in the left-hand navigation panel. Within the Performance Monitoring screen, select the RealtimeDBList app from the dropdown menu as shown in Figure 51-2:

Figure 51-2

If the Performance Monitoring page for the app provides instructions to install the SDK, it may be necessary to wait longer for the data to be ready for analysis.

Once Firebase has begun presenting data, the performance dashboard (Figure 51-3) will appear providing a summary of the performance data collected for the app:

Firebase Performance Monitoring

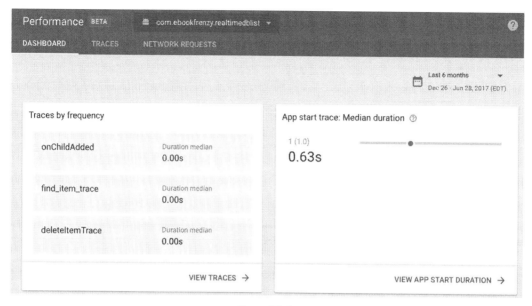

Figure 51-3

The screen also includes tabs to access detailed information on traces (Figure 51-4) and network requests. Each screen provides options to filter the results and to specify different date ranges:

Figure 51-4

To view additional performance details for a trace, select it from the list to display the trace detail screen. Figure 51-5, for example, shows data for the *add_item* trace including the trace counter. Clicking on the *View More* link will display information based on the device type, app version, operating system and network characteristics:

Figure 51-5

Metrics can be displayed in either Aggregate or Over Time mode by selecting the corresponding buttons. Aggregate mode displays the median value for the current metric together with a percentile distribution slider. Hovering the mouse pointer over the slider and moving it left or right changes the percentile value and displays the corresponding metric value. Figure 51-6, for example, shows the duration metric for the 25th percentile:

Figure 51-6

The Over Time view shows the trace metrics and the median value indicating the amount by which the metric changed over the currently selected period of time.

51.6 **Turning Off Performance Monitoring**

To disable automatic trace monitoring at build time, simply add the following line to the project's *gradle.properties* file (located under Gradle Scripts within the Android Studio tool window).

```
firebasePerformanceInstrumentationEnabled=false
```

Note this setting only disables automatic traces and that custom traces will continue to be monitored. Performance monitoring (both automatic and custom) may be disabled by placing the following entry within the application element of the *AndroidManifest.xml* file:

```
<application ...>
.
.
<meta-data android:name="firebase_performance_collection_enabled"
        android:value="false" />
.
.
</application>
```

When disabled in this way, performance monitoring may be re-enabled from within the app by making a call to the *setPerformanceCollectionEnabled()* method of the FirebasePerformance instance, passing through a *true* value:

```
FirebasePerformance.getInstance().setPerformanceCollectionEnabled(true);
```

Performance monitoring can be disabled using the same method call, passing through a false value. Combining this feature with Firebase Remote Config (a topic covered in the chapter entitled *An Overview of Firebase Remote Config*) provides an easy way to enable and disable performance monitoring after the app is live within the Google Play Store.

To deactivate performance monitoring such that it cannot be reactivated via the app code, add the following element to the *AndroidManifest.xml* file:

```
<application ...>
.
.
<meta-data android:name="firebase_performance_collection_deactivated"
        android:value="true" />
.
.
</application>
```

51.7 **Summary**

Firebase Performance Monitoring offers an easy way to monitor the performance of an app. Performance is monitored using traces that measure app performance at certain periods of execution. Once the performance monitoring library has been added to an app a number of trace metrics are monitored automatically. Custom traces may also be implemented by making trace start and stop method calls within the app. Once performance information has been gathered, the data is analyzed within the Performance Monitoring section of the Firebase console.

52. Firebase Cloud Functions

Firebase Cloud Functions are essentially JavaScript functions hosted on the Google cloud. These functions are triggered in response to Firebase related events such as data being written to a Firebase realtime database or the creation of a user account using Firebase authentication.

This chapter will introduce the key concepts of Firebase Cloud Functions.

52.1 A Cloud Functions Overview

Cloud Functions can be thought of server side code that is executed in response to events triggered by other Firebase services. A Cloud Function could, for example, be used to send a welcome email message to new users in response to user account creation events, or to send a Firebase Notification message when a particular value is written to a node in a realtime database.

Cloud Functions are written in JavaScript using Node.js and the Firebase Cloud Functions SDK and, once written, are deployed to the Google Cloud Platform using a command-line tool known as the Firebase CLI.

Once the functions have been deployed, Google Cloud performs all of the management tasks to ensure that the functions are triggered in response to events occurring on the Firebase and Google Cloud platforms. Each cloud function runs within a virtual server managed by Google Cloud which automatically adjusts the number of virtual servers for each function in response to changes in demand.

Deployed functions may be updated at any time using the Firebase CLI and detailed logging information is available both from the command line and within the Firebase console.

Firebase Cloud Functions can be triggered by events from any of the following triggers:

- **Authentication** – User account creation and deletion.
- **Realtime Database** - Database write operations.
- **Cloud Storage** – Uploading, deleting and updating of files.
- **Google Analytics for Firebase** – Conversion events such as an in-app purchase.
- **Google Cloud Pub/Sub** – Transmission of a new Pub/Sub message.
- **HTTP** – HTTP request to a specified URL (includes GET, POST, PUT, DELETE and OPTIONS).

52.2 Firebase Authentication Functions

A cloud function can be triggered in response to the creation or deletion of Firebase Authentication based user accounts. Authentication cloud functions are implemented using the *functions.auth.user().onCreate()* and *functions.auth.user().onDelete()* event handlers.

The event data passed to the JavaScript function when it is called contains all of the attributes relating to the new user including email, display name, photo URL, authentication provider and whether or not the email address has been verified. The following is an example function designed to be triggered by account creation events:

```
exports.newUserAdded = functions.auth.user().onCreate(event => {

        const user = event.data;
        const email = user.email;
        const displayname = user.displayName;
        const photoUrl = user.photoURL;
    .
    .
});
```

A function to handle account deletion events is similarly structured:

```
exports.userDeleted = functions.auth.user().onCreate(event => {
    .
    .
});
```

52.3 Realtime Database Functions

Realtime database cloud functions are triggered by write operations performed on a database tree at any point beneath a specified reference point and are implemented using the *functions.database.ref().onWrite()* event handler. The database path for which write operations are to trigger the function is specified via a *ref()* call, for example:

```
exports.userStatusChange = functions.database.ref('/users/profile')
        .onWrite(event => {
    .
    .
};
```

The function will then be triggered by a write operation that occurs at the */users/profile* path in the database tree including all child nodes (for example data written to */user/profile/email* will also trigger the function call).

The reference path may also include wildcards by placing the path component in braces ({}):

```
exports.userStatusChange = functions.database.ref('/users/{userId}/email')
        .onWrite(event => {
```

When the function is called, it is passed event data in the form of a DeltaSnapshot object. This contains both the new value being written and the previous value that is being overwritten:

```
exports.userStatusChange = functions.database.ref('/users/profile')
        .onWrite(event => {
```

```
        const newValue = event.data.val();
        const previousValue = event.data.previous();
.

.
};
```

Much like the DataSnapshot objects used when working with Realtime Databases in Android Java code, the DeltaSnapshot can be navigated to access specific nodes of the tree:

```
var snapshot = event.data.child('email');
```

To detect the removal of data from the database, simply call the *exists()* method of the event data. If no data exists, the cloud function is being called in response to a data deletion event within the Firebase database:

```
if (event.data.exists()) {
        // New data is being written to the database
else {
        // Data was deleted from the database
}
```

52.4 **Google Analytics Functions**

Any Firebase Analytics event that has been configured as a conversion can be used to trigger a cloud function. As outlined in the earlier chapters covering analytics, events can be marked as conversions using the switch highlighted in Figure 52-1 within the Events screen of the Firebase console Analytics screen:

Figure 52-1

This allows functions to be triggered based on just about any type of activity taking place within an app as long as that activity is associated with an analytics conversion event. Analytics cloud functions are implemented using the *functions.analytics.event()* event handler, for example:

```
exports.userUpgraded = functions.analytics.event('customEvent')
        .onWrite(event => {
```

.

.

Included with the event data passed to the function when it is called are all of the parameters and user properties associated with the analytics event.

52.5 HTTP Functions

HTTP cloud functions are triggered in response to an HTTP request and are implemented using the *functions.https.onRequest()* event handler. When called, the function is passed *request* and *response* objects from which information such as the request method (POST, GET etc.) and query values may be extracted.

HTTP cloud functions should self-terminate via a call to either *send()*, *redirect()* or *end()*:

```
exports.httpFunction = functions.https.onRequest((request, response) => {
    const name = request.query.name;
    console.log("Name = " + name);
    response.send("Hello from Firebase, " + name);
});
```

Once an HTTP cloud function has been deployed, it is assigned a unique URL via which it can be triggered. An example HTTP cloud function will be implemented in the next chapter (*Installing the Firebase CLI*).

52.6 Cloud Storage Functions

Cloud Storage functions are triggered when a file is uploaded using Cloud Storage, or when an existing file is updated or deleted. Once triggered, the function is also able to download a copy of the file, modify it and upload the new version back to cloud storage. Cloud Functions also have access to the ImageMagick utility which can be used to transform downloaded image files.

Cloud Storage Functions are implemented using the *functions.storage.object* and *functions.storage.bucket().object()* event handlers, the latter being used to reference a specific storage bucket, for example:

```
exports.makeMonochrome =
    functions.storage.bucket('images').object().onChange(event => {
        .
        .
        .
});
```

The event data passed through to the function includes all of the properties of the file, including bucket name, file path, content type, resource state, download link, file size and timestamp:

```
exports.makeMonochrome =
    functions.storage.bucket('images').object().onChange(event => {
```

```
    const fileObject = event.data;

    const filePath = fileObject.name;
    const bucket = fileObject.bucket;
    const contentType = fileObject.contentType;
    const resourceState = fileObject.resourceState;
    const size = fileObject.size;
    const timeCreated = fileObject.timeCreated;
    const mediaLink = fileObject.mediaLink;
    .
    .
    .
});
```

For performing file downloads and uploads from within a cloud function, the Google Cloud Storage package is recommended. This can be installed using npm as follows:

```
install --save @google-cloud/storage
```

This package should then be imported at the top of the *.js* file containing the cloud function:

```
const gcs = require('@google-cloud/storage')();
```

Clearly, a storage cloud function is triggered in response to a change being made to a specific file in cloud storage. This file can be downloaded to the virtual server containing the cloud function using the following code:

```
const object = event.data;
const fileBucket = object.bucket;
const filePath = object.name;
const bucket = gcs.bucket(fileBucket);
const tempFilePath = `/tmp/mypic.png`;

return bucket.file(filePath).download({destination: tempFilePath
            }).then(() => {

    // Code to be executed when the download finishes

});
```

The *then()* call in the above example is part of the handling mechanism for a JavaScript *Promise*. Promises are often used when a task is performed asynchronously and may not be completed immediately. The *download()* method used above, for example, returns a Promise object when it is called. By calling *then()* method on that Promise object, we are able to specify the code that is to be executed when the download either completes or fails. A promise can be thought of as an alternative to the listeners or completion handlers that typically have to be implemented to handle the result of an asynchronous operation. All Firebase JavaScript functions that perform an asynchronous task now support both promises and the traditional completion handler methods.

483

Note also that the Promise from the above download operation is returned. This returns the Promise from the download call to the code that originally invoked the cloud function. The calling code may then also call the *then()* method on the Promise object to define the actions to be performed on completion. This technique also ensures that the cloud function is kept alive until the asynchronous task is complete. Failing to do this runs the risk of the function exiting and the virtual machine shutting down before the asynchronous task finishes.

To upload a file, simply call the upload function:

```
return bucket.upload(tempFilePath, {destination: newFilePath
            }).then(() => {
      // Code to be executed when the upload finishes
});
```

When uploading files to cloud storage from within a cloud function it is important to remember that the upload will trigger another call to the cloud function (since it counts as a change to a file). To avoid a recursive loop, be sure to add some defensive code to exit from the cloud function in the event that the file change was caused by the function itself. An example of how to achieve this will be covered in the chapter entitled *A Cloud Functions and Firebase Cloud Storage Example*.

It is also important to distinguish file update events from file deletions. If an event is being triggered due to a file being deleted from cloud storage, the *resourceState* property of the event data will be set to "not_exists" allowing defensive code similar to the following to be written to return from the function if the file has been deleted:

```
const object = event.data;
const resourceState = object.resourceState;

if (resourceState === 'not_exists') {
    // This is a file deletion event
    return;
}
```

52.7 Performing External Operations

Any external file operations performed within a cloud function (such as running the ImageMagick *convert* utility) should be spawned as a child object and returned as a Promise from within the function. This makes use of the Child Process Promise package which must be installed as follows:

```
install -save child-process-promise
```

Once installed, the package must also be imported within the cloud function *.js* file within which the spawn operation is to be performed:

```
const spawn = require('child-process-promise').spawn;
```

The following code fragment demonstrates the use of child process spawning to perform an image conversion using the ImageMagick *convert* utility:

```
return spawn('convert', [tempFilePath, '-monochrome', tempFilePath])
            .then(() => {
        // Code to be executed after the conversion completes
});
```

As with many functions, the spawn function returns a Promise, allowing code to be specified which will be called when the task completes.

52.8 **Modifying Cloud Function Settings**

Once a cloud function has been deployed the Firebase console provides a list of deployed functions and access to the logs generated during execution. Additional information about deployed cloud functions is available within the Google Cloud Platform Console (*https://console.cloud.google.com*).

In addition to greater detail of metrics such as memory usage, quota usage and execution time, this console also provides the ability to edit properties relating to the function such as the amount of memory allocated to the virtual machines within which the function executes (a topic which will be covered in the chapter entitled *A Cloud Functions and Firebase Cloud Storage Example*).

52.9 **Summary**

Cloud functions are JavaScript functions that reside in small virtual machines hosted in the Google Cloud. These functions are triggered in response to certain Firebase related events that take place within an app. Cloud functions are written using Node.js and deployed to the Google Cloud Platform using the Firebase CLI tool. Once deployed, all of the work involved in detecting events, triggering the functions and provisioning virtual machines is handled by the Google cloud.

53. Installing the Firebase CLI

The Firebase CLI is a utility used to administer Firebase projects and perform tasks such as Realtime Database management tasks from the command-line of a terminal or command-prompt window. The Firebase CLI is also the method by which Firebase Cloud Functions are deployed and managed.

This chapter covers the installation of the Firebase CLI before creating and testing a simple Firebase Cloud Functions project.

53.1 Installing Node.js

The Firebase CLI is built on Node.js and, as such, the first step in installing the CLI is to set up the Node.js environment. If you do not already have Node.js installed, refer to the steps outlined in the chapter entitled *Sending Firebase Cloud Messages from a Node.js Server*.

53.2 Installing the Firebase Tools Package

With Node.js installed, the next step is to install the Firebase Tools package using the following npm command within a terminal or command-prompt window:

```
npm install -g firebase-tools
```

Note that on some platforms such as macOS and Linux it may be necessary to execute the above command with super user privileges:

```
sudo npm install -g firebase-tools
```

53.3 Logging into Firebase

Before a new Cloud Functions project can be created it is necessary to sign into Firebase using the same account credentials used for access to the Firebase console. Installed as part of the Firebase Tools package is the Firebase CLI tool which can now be used to log into Firebase:

```
firebase login
```

The command will prompt for permission to gather anonymous usage data before displaying a browser window within which to select the Google account associated with your Firebase development projects. Select an account and agree to the terms and conditions. Once the login is complete the panel shown in Figure 53-1 will appear in the browser window:

> **Woohoo!**
>
> Firebase CLI Login Successful
>
> You are logged in to the Firebase Command-Line interface. You can immediately close this window and continue using the CLI.

Figure 53-1

Close the browser window and return to the terminal window. To logout at any point in the future, simply execute the following Firebase CLI command:

```
firebase logout
```

53.4 Creating a Cloud Functions Project

The Firebase CLI is also used to create new Firebase Cloud Functions projects. For this example a project named MyCloudFunctions will be created. Begin by creating a subdirectory named MyCloudFunctions in a suitable filesystem location in which to store the project. Change directory into the new project folder and run the following command to create the project:

```
firebase init functions
```

When executed, the initialization command will generate the following output:

```
Neils-iMac:Work neilsmyth$ firebase init functions
```

```
You're about to initialize a Firebase project in this directory:

    /Users/neilsmyth/Documents/Books/Firebase/WORK


=== Project Setup

First, let's associate this project directory with a Firebase project.
You can create multiple project aliases by running firebase use --add,
but for now we'll just set up a default project.

? Select a default Firebase project for this directory:
  [don't setup a default project]
  Notification Demo (notification-demo-45c88)
  Notifications (notifications-ec42e)
  Firebase Demo Project (fir-demo-project)
> Firebase Examples (peak-apparatus-599)
  [create a new project]
```

Figure 53-2

Using the up and down arrow keys on the keyboard, select the *Firebase Examples* project and press Enter. Select the option to install dependencies and wait for the initialization to complete.

53.5 **Reviewing the Project**

When the project creation is complete the project folder will contain the following files and directories:

- **.firebaserc** – A script file used by the *firebase use* command to switch between projects.
- **firebase.json** – The properties configuration file.
- **functions/package.json** – The JSON configuration file for the project containing version number and dependency information.
- **functions/index.js** – The source code file within which the Cloud Functions will be written.
- **functions/node_modules** – Contains the dependency packages defined in the package.json file.

53.6 **Deploying a Simple HTTP Cloud Function**

Using your preferred editor, edit the *index.js* file located in the *functions* folder. By default, the first line of the file imports the firebase-functions package. This is a standard requirement for all cloud function source files:

```
const functions = require('firebase-functions');
```

The remainder of the file contains a commented out example HTTP cloud function. Remove the comment markers so that the function reads as follows:

```
// Create and Deploy Your First Cloud Functions
// https://firebase.google.com/docs/functions/write-firebase-functions

exports.helloWorld = functions.https.onRequest((request, response) => {
    response.send("Hello from Firebase!");
});
```

Save the file and deploy it using the following Firebase CLI command:

```
firebase deploy --only functions:helloWorld
```

This command will deploy only the helloWorld function. To deploy all of the functions in the *index.js* file, use the following command:

```
firebase deploy --only functions
```

Deployment of cloud functions can take a few minutes, but once the deployment is finished, the full output should read as follows:

```
=== Deploying to 'peak-apparatus-599'...

i  deploying functions
i  functions: ensuring necessary APIs are enabled...
i  runtimeconfig: ensuring necessary APIs are enabled...
✔  functions: all necessary APIs are enabled
✔  runtimeconfig: all necessary APIs are enabled
i  functions: preparing functions directory for uploading...
i  functions: packaged functions (2.29 KB) for uploading
✔  functions: functions folder uploaded successfully
i  starting release process (may take several minutes)...
i  functions: current functions in project: imageConverter, newUserAdded, userStatusChange
i  functions: uploading functions in project: helloWorld
i  functions: creating function helloWorld...
✔  functions[helloWorld]: Successful create operation.
✔  functions: all functions deployed successfully!

✔  Deploy complete!

Project Console: https://console.firebase.google.com/project/peak-apparatus-599/overview
Function URL (helloWorld): https://us-central1-peak-apparatus-599.cloudfunctions.net/helloWorld
```

Figure 53-3

The final line of output contains the URL by which the cloud function will be triggered. Copy and paste this URL into a browser window and verify that the "Hello from Firebase!" message appears.

Edit the *index.js* file and modify the function to accept a query value as part of the URL and to output diagnostics to the log:

```
exports.helloWorld = functions.https.onRequest((request, response) => {
    const name = request.query.name;
    console.log("Name = " + name);
    response.send("Hello from Firebase, " + name);
});
```

Redeploy the app using the Firebase CLI then open the same URL, this time adding a query value:

```
https://<your server here>.cloudfunctions.net/helloWorld?name=John
```

When the web page now loads, the new message containing the name value should appear.

53.7 Reviewing the Logs

Cloud function logs can be accessed either using the Firebase CLI, or from within the Firebase console. To view log output using the CLI, simply run the following command:

```
firebase functions:log
```

Alternatively, select the *Firebase Examples* project in the Firebase console and click on the Functions link in the navigation panel. The Functions Dashboard screen will list the functions currently deployed for the project together with basic runtime and execution metrics:

Function	Event	Executions	Median run time
helloWorld	**HTTP** Request https://us-central1-peak-apparatus-599.cloudfunctions.net/helloWorld	10	18.40ms

Figure 53-4

Hovering over the function will display the menu dots (highlighted in the figure above). Open this menu and select the *View logs* option to view the log output for the function:

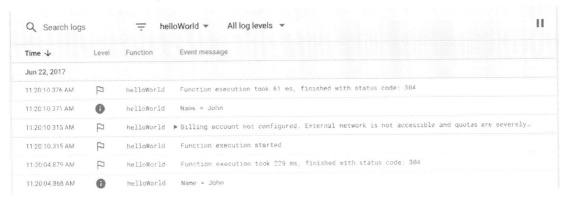

Figure 53-5

53.8 Removing a Deployed Function

To withdraw a cloud function from deployment, remove it from the *index.js* file (or comment it out) and then run the Firebase CLI deployment command:

```
firebase deploy —only functions
```

Firebase will detect the absence of the previously deployed function and delete it from the cloud.

53.9 Summary

Firebase Cloud Functions are deployed and managed using the Firebase CLI tool. This tool is built on Node.js and is installed using the npm command. Once installed, the Firebase CLI is used to sign into Firebase and create new Firebase Cloud Function projects. Once the project has been created, cloud functions are added to the *index.js* file and deployed to the cloud. In addition to outlining the installation process for Firebase CLI, this chapter also created, deployed and tested a simple HTTP cloud function.

54. A Firebase Cloud Functions Tutorial

This chapter will demonstrate the creation of Firebase Cloud Functions designed to be triggered in response to Realtime Database and Authentication related events.

54.1 About the Example Project

Practical implementation of Firebase Cloud Functions will be demonstrated using a pre-existing Android Studio app project named *CloudFunctions*. This project is a simple app that uses Firebase Authentication to allow users to create accounts and sign into and out of the app. In addition to these features, the app also uses a Firebase Realtime Database to keep track of the users that are currently logged in. When a user signs into the app, an entry is added to the realtime database. The database entry is then removed when the user signs out.

When the app is launched it makes a call to the *subscribeToTopic()* method of the FirebaseMessaging instance to subscribe the app to a topic named "OnlineUsers". This topic will be used to send out notifications later in the chapter.

The app has also been configured to handle incoming Firebase messages both when in the foreground and background. When the app is in the foreground, a Firebase Messaging Service instance is used to display the incoming notification to the user in the form of a Toast message.

The objective of the tutorial in this chapter is to implement cloud functions that will perform the following tasks:

- Detect when a new user account has been created and notify all users of this via a Firebase notification.
- Detect changes to the Realtime Database and notify all users when a user signs in or out of the app.

For the purposes of this tutorial, the app is considered to be functionally complete. All of the above requirements, therefore, will be implemented entirely using Firebase Cloud Functions without making any changes to the project code.

54.2 Loading and Configuring the App

The Android Studio project files for the app can be found in the *CloudFunctions* folder of the sample code download available from the following URL:

http://www.ebookfrenzy.com/print/firebase_android

Once the project has been located, load it into Android Studio. Although the app in its current form has all of the necessary Firebase library dependencies configured, the project will need to be connected to your Firebase account before it can be run. Within Android Studio, select the *Tools ->* *Firebase* menu option and, within the resulting Firebase assistant panel, select the Authentication option and click on the *Email and password authentication* link. In the Authentication panel click on the *Connect to Firebase* button and select the *Firebase Examples* project from the list of existing projects before clicking on the *Connect to Firebase* button.

Before running the app, open the Firebase console in a browser window, select the *Firebase Examples* project and click on the Database option in the navigation panel. Within the Database screen, select the Rules tab and modify the rules to allow access only to authenticated users:

```
{
  "rules": {
    ".read": "auth != null",
    ".write": "auth != null"
  }
}
```

54.3 Trying out the App

With the project configured, it is worth taking a few minutes to check that it works correctly by running the app on a device or emulator. Once the app has loaded, return to the Firebase console, this time selecting the Data tab of the Realtime Database screen. To avoid confusion, delete any previous test data contained within the database.

Keeping the Database screen visible in the browser window, create a new account within the running app. Note that once the account has been created, a second screen appears displaying the email address for the account and a button for logging out:

Figure 54-1

Refer to the Firebase console and verify that an entry has been added indicating that the new user is signed into the app:

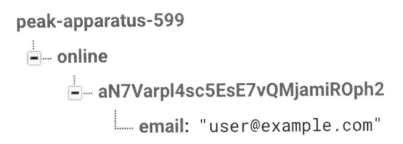

Figure 54-2

Sign out of the app by clicking the Sign Out button and confirm that the database entry for the user has been deleted from the database.

Having made sure that the app works as expected, the next step is to write and deploy some cloud functions to be triggered when a new user account is created and when users sign in and out of the app.

54.4 Writing the Authentication Cloud Function

A cloud function now needs to be written to detect when a new user account is created. Within a terminal or command-prompt window, log into Firebase using the Firebase CLI as follows:

```
firebase login
```

After logging in, change directory to the *MyCloudFunctions/functions* folder created in the previous chapter, edit the *index.js* file and remove the example HTTP cloud function so that the file only contains the following lines:

```
const functions = require('firebase-functions');
const admin = require('firebase-admin');
admin.initializeApp(functions.config().firebase);
```

The first cloud function will need to be triggered whenever a new user account is created within the app. This will involve the use of the *functions.auth.user().onCreate* event handler. Within the *index.js* file, add the code for this function:

```
exports.newUserAdded = functions.auth.user().onCreate(event => {

    const user = event.data;
    const email = user.email;

    var payload = {
      notification: {
        title: "New User",
```

```
            body: "New user " + email + " just joined."
        }
    };

    var topic = "OnlineUsers";

    return admin.messaging().sendToTopic(topic, payload)
        .then(function(response) {
            console.log("Successfully sent message:", response);
        })
        .catch(function(error) {
            console.log("Error sending message:", error);
        });
});
```

The code begins by extracting the user data from the event object and then accessing the email address. A message payload is then created consisting of a title and a body, where the body is constructed to include the new user's email address. The function then calls the messaging *sendToTopic()* function to send the message to the OnlineUsers topic. Since this action will be performed asynchronously, the function returns a Promise in the form of the result from the *sendToTopic()* call. This ensures that the send operation will continue to run asynchronously until completion.

54.5 **Writing the Realtime Database Function**

The Cloud Function Authentication event handlers do not provide a way to trigger a function when a user signs in or out of an account. To get around this limitation, the app maintains realtime database entries for users that are currently signed in. The following cloud function designed to trigger when changes are made to the database reference now needs to be added to the *index.js* file:

```
exports.userStatusChange = functions.database.ref('/online/{userId}/email')
    .onWrite(event => {

        const original = event.data.val();
        const previous = event.data.previous.val();

        if (!event.data.exists()) {
            var title = "User Signed Out";
            var body = "User " + previous + " signed out";
        } else {
            title = "User Signed In";
            body = "User " + original + " signed in";
        }

        var payload = {
```

```
      notification: {
        title: title,
        body: body
      }
    };

    var topic = "OnlineUsers";

    return admin.messaging().sendToTopic(topic, payload)
      .then(function(response) {
        console.log("Successfully sent message:", response);
      })
      .catch(function(error) {
        console.log("Error sending message:", error);
      });
});
```

Since this function is slightly more complicated, it is worthwhile reviewing the code in more detail. The code makes use of the *functions.database.ref* event handler to detect when a write operation is performed at the database location referenced by */online/<userId>/email*:

```
exports.userStatusChange = functions.database.ref('/online/{userId}/email')
    .onWrite(event => {
```

Next, the event data is accessed to obtain both the new data being written (original) and the value of the data prior to the write operation (previous):

```
const original = event.data.val();
const previous = event.data.previous.val();
```

If the new data is empty then it can be safely assumed that the entry is being deleted and that the user is signing out. Otherwise, the user is clearly signing into the app. Based on this information, custom strings are built and included in the message payload:

```
if (!event.data.exists()) {
        var title = "User Signed Out";
        var body = "User " + previous + " signed out";
} else {
        title = "User Signed In";
        body = "User " + original + " signed in";
}
```

Finally, the payload is sent to all users subscribed to the OnlineUsers topic:

```
var topic = "OnlineUsers";

return admin.messaging().sendToTopic(topic, payload)
```

```
    .then(function(response) {
        console.log("Successfully sent message:", response);
    })
    .catch(function(error) {
        console.log("Error sending message:", error);
    });
```

54.6 Deploying the Cloud Functions

All that remains before testing the app again is to deploy the functions to the cloud. Using the Firebase CLI, run the following command to deploy the functions:

```
firebase deploy --only functions
```

Assuming that the functions deploy without error they are ready to be tested.

54.7 Testing the Cloud Functions

Return to the running app and experiment with adding new accounts and signing in and out of the app. On completion of each action, a Toast message should appear containing the message text from the corresponding cloud function:

Figure 54-3

Open the Firebase console in a browser window and select the *Firebase Examples* project followed by the Cloud Functions link. Within the Functions screen, the two new functions should now be listed within the dashboard:

Function	Event		Executions	Median run time
newUserAdded	user.create		18	422.14ms
userStatusChange	ref.write /online/{userid}/email		31	638.53ms

Figure 54-4

Clicking on the Logs tab will display the full log details for the functions:

Figure 54-5

When selected, the Usage tab will display statistics on the number of function invocations over a given period of time. This is useful for tracking function usage and in calculating potential costs:

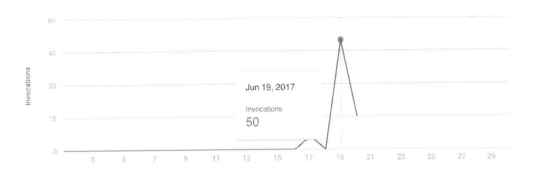

Figure 54-6

As an alternative to viewing the logs within the Firebase console, run the following Firebase CLI command to view the log output within the terminal or command-prompt window:

```
firebase functions:log
```

54.8 Summary

This chapter has combined a number of different Firebase services to add functionality to an app using Firebase Cloud Functions. Without having to make any changes to the Android project code, cloud functions have been used to detect when user's create, login into and out of accounts and to trigger when changes are made to a branch of a realtime database. The example also demonstrated the use of Firebase Messaging within cloud functions.

Chapter 55

55. A Cloud Functions and Firebase Cloud Storage Example

The chapter entitled *Firebase Cloud Functions* introduced the basic concepts of working with Cloud Functions and Firebase Cloud Storage, including uploading and downloading files from within a cloud function. This chapter will work through the implementation of a cloud function intended to be triggered whenever an image file is uploaded to a storage bucket. The function will download the image file, convert it to monochrome then upload the converted file.

55.1 The CloudStorage App

The cloud function created in this chapter is intended to be used in conjunction with an example Android Studio project named CloudStorage_Functions which is included in the sample code download available from the following web page:

http://www.ebookfrenzy.com/print/firebase_android

Load the project into Android Studio and connect the project to Firebase by selecting the *Tools -> Firebase* menu option, selecting the Authentication option and clicking on the *Email and Password authentication* link. In the resulting panel, click on the *Connect to Firebase* button and follow the usual steps to connect to the *Firebase Examples* project.

Run the app on a suitable device or emulator and, when the app is running, either create a new email-based user account or sign in using an existing account.

The app has bundled with it an image file which is displayed within the ImageView object as shown in Figure 55-1:

Figure 55-1

When the upload button is clicked, the image file is uploaded to Firebase Cloud Storage. The objective of this tutorial is to implement a cloud function to be triggered when the file is uploaded. This cloud function will download the file, convert it to monochrome then upload the converted file. Selecting the Download button within the app will download the converted image and display it to the user.

Leave the app running in preparation for testing the cloud function later in the chapter.

55.2 Setting Cloud Storage Rules

The app will upload the image file as a file named *mountain.jpg* in the */photos/<userid>* path. To ensure that the app has permission to write to this location the Cloud Storage rules need to be modified. Open the Firebase console in a browser window and select the *Storage* option. Within the Storage screen, click on the Rules tab and change the rules to the following:

```
service firebase.storage {
  match /b/{bucket}/o {
    match /photos/{userId}/mountain.jpg {
        allow read;
        allow write: if request.auth.uid == userId;
    }
    match /photos/{userId}/mono_mountain.jpg {
        allow read;
```

```
        allow write: if request.auth.uid == userId;
    }
  }
}
```

When the changes have been made, commit them by clicking on the Publish button.

55.3 Installing Dependencies

The cloud function will make use of the *child-process-promise* and Google Cloud Storage Node.js packages, both of which need to be installed before writing the code for the function:

```
npm install --save child-process-promise
npm install --save @google-cloud/storage
```

55.4 Writing the Cloud Function

The cloud function will be added to the same *index.js* file as used in the previous chapters. Open a terminal or command-prompt window and change directory to the *MyCloudFunctions/functions* project folder. If you have not yet created the project used in earlier chapters, refer to the steps in the chapter entitled *Installing the Firebase CLI*.

Edit the *index.js* file and modify it to declare the two package dependencies:

```
const functions = require('firebase-functions');
const admin = require('firebase-admin');
const gcs = require('@google-cloud/storage')();
const spawn = require('child-process-promise').spawn;


admin.initializeApp(functions.config().firebase);
```

Remaining within the *index.js* file, add the imageConverter cloud function as follows:

```
exports.imageConverter = functions.storage.object().onChange(event => {

    const object = event.data;
    const fileBucket = object.bucket;
    const filePath = object.name;
    const bucket = gcs.bucket(fileBucket);
    const contentType = object.contentType;
    const resourceState = object.resourceState;
    const tempFilePath = `/tmp/mountain.jpg`;

    const fileName = filePath.split('/').pop();

    if (fileName.startsWith('mono_')) {
        return;
    }
```

```
    if (!contentType.startsWith('image/')) {
        console.log('Not an image file.');
      return;
    }

    if (resourceState === 'not_exists') {
      console.log('File is being deleted.');
      return;
    }

    return bucket.file(filePath).download({
      destination: tempFilePath
    }).then(() => {
      console.log('Image downloaded locally to', tempFilePath);
      return spawn('convert', [tempFilePath, '-monochrome',
              tempFilePath]).then(() => {
        console.log('Thumbnail created at', tempFilePath);
        const monoFilePath =
              filePath.replace(/(\/)?([^\/]*)$/, '$1mono_$2');
        console.log('Uploading file ' + monoFilePath);
        return bucket.upload(tempFilePath, {
            destination: monoFilePath
          });
        });
      });
    });
});
```

The function begins by extracting some properties from the event data and assigning them to constants. A constant is also declared containing the path to the temporary file that will be used during the image conversion:

```
const object = event.data;
const fileBucket = object.bucket;
const filePath = object.name;
const bucket = gcs.bucket(fileBucket);
const contentType = object.contentType;
const resourceState = object.resourceState;
const tempFilePath = `/tmp/mountain.jpg`;
```

Next, the filename component is extracted from the path and a test performed to identify if the filename begins with *mono_*. When the file is converted and uploaded the filename is prefixed with *mono_* to differentiate it from the original file. If the filename has this prefix, it means that this event has been triggered by the function itself uploading the converted file. To avoid the function being called recursively, it simply returns to avoid another conversion upload taking place:

```
const fileName = filePath.split('/').pop();

if (fileName.startsWith('mono_')) {
    return;
}
```

The code then checks the file's content type to verify that it is an image file and returns if it is not. A check is also made to make sure that this is not a file deletion event:

```
if (!contentType.startsWith('image/')) {
    console.log('Not an image file.');
    return;
}

if (resourceState === 'not_exists') {
    console.log('File is being deleted.');
    return;
}
```

Having verified that it makes sense to proceed with the conversion, the file is downloaded:

```
return bucket.file(filePath).download({
        destination: tempFilePath
    }).then(() => {
```

Since this download function returns a Promise, a *then()* call is made on the Promise object to provide the image conversion code to be executed when the download completes:

```
console.log('Image downloaded locally to', tempFilePath);
        return spawn('convert', [tempFilePath, '-monochrome',
                tempFilePath]).then(() => {
```

Since the spawn function also returns a Promise, another *then()* call is made containing the code to prefix the filename with *mono_* and to upload the file to Cloud Storage after the conversion completes:

```
const monoFilePath =
        filePath.replace(/(\/)?([^\/]*)$/, '$1mono_$2');
        console.log('Uploading file ' + monoFilePath);
        return bucket.upload(tempFilePath, {
            destination: monoFilePath
        });
```

After making the changes, save the *index.js* file and deploy it using the following command:

```
firebase --only functions:imageConverter
```

55.5 **Testing the Cloud Function**

Return to the device or emulator on which the Android app is running and tap the *Upload* button to upload the file to cloud storage. After the upload completes, navigate to the Storage section of the Firebase console, select the *Files* tab and navigate to the *photos/<userId>* folder where both the original and monochrome versions of the file should be listed as shown in Figure 55-2:

Figure 55-2

If the monochrome file is not listed, check the cloud function logs either in the Functions screen of the Firebase console or by running the following Firebase CLI command:

```
firebase functions:log
```

If syntax errors are reported, edit the *index.js* file and check for mistakes made when entering the code. Another possibility is that the following error is reported:

```
E imageConverter: Function killed. Error: memory limit exceeded
```

To resolve the memory limit problem, the settings for the function will need to be changed within the Google Cloud Platform console.

55.6 **Increasing Cloud Function Memory**

To increase the memory limit for a cloud function, open a browser window and navigate to the Google Cloud Platform Console at the following URL:

https://console.cloud.google.com

Sign in using the same Google account associated with your Firebase projects and select the Cloud Functions option from the left-hand navigation panel:

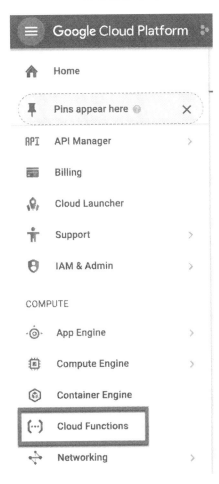

Figure 55-3

If the dialog shown in Figure 55-4 appears, click on the *Enable API* button:

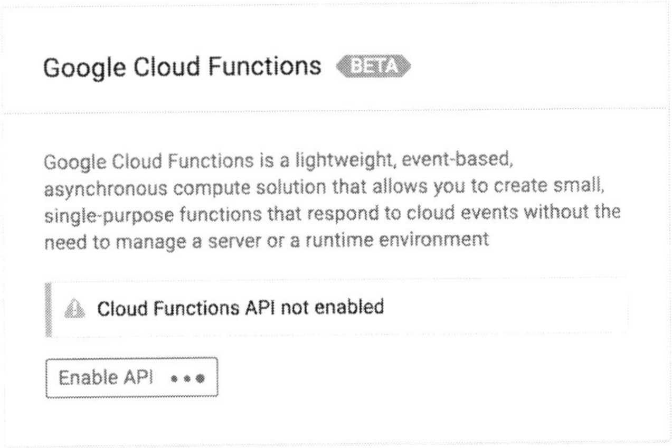

Figure 55-4

A Cloud Functions and Firebase Cloud Storage Example

On the Cloud Functions screen, select the *Firebase Examples* project from the drop down menu at the top of the page (highlighted in Figure 55-5) at which point all of the cloud functions for that project will be listed:

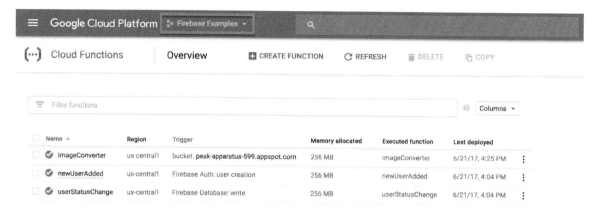

Figure 55-5

Display details for the *imageConverter* function by clicking on the function name in the list. In the details screen, note that *Memory allocation* is currently set to 256 MB. To increase this, click on the Edit button in the toolbar at the top of the page and increase the memory allocation to 512 MB:

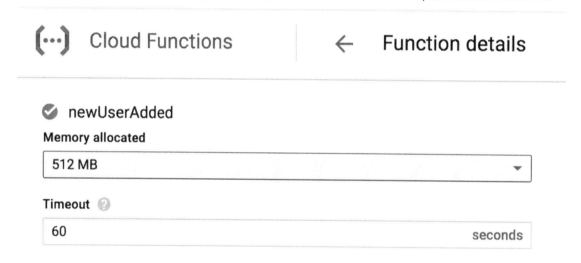

Figure 55-6

Save the new memory allocation setting and then upload the file once again from within the Android app. If the monochrome image file now appears in the cloud storage section of the Firebase console, click the Download button within the app at which point the monochrome version of the image should download and appear in the ImageView.

55.7 **Summary**

This chapter has demonstrated the use of Firebase Cloud Functions to detect when Cloud Storage events occur. The example also covered the downloading, modification and uploading of cloud storage files from within a cloud function, including spawning a process to call the ImageMagick convert tool to transform the image.

The chapter also covered the steps to increase the memory allocated to the virtual machine in which a cloud function runs. If a memory shortage is preventing a function from executing, a message to this effect will be included in the log output for the function.

Index

$

$ Variables · 207

%

%APP_NAME% · 29
%DISPLAY_NAME% · 29
%EMAIL% · 29
%LINK% · 29
%NEW_EMAIL% · 30

A

activateFetched() method · 343
addChildEventListener() method · 215
addListenerForSingleValueEvent() method · 195
addOnFailureListener() method · 92
addValueEventListener() method · 195
Analytics · 359
    active users · 364
    app version · 368
    attribution · 365
    attribution screen · 375
    audience creation · 391
    audiences · 362
    audiences screen · 374
    average revenue · 365
    cohorts screen · 378
    dashboard · 363
    DebugView screen · 379
    demographics · 370
    devices · 369
    enabling debugging modes · 388
    events · 360
    events screen · 373
    funnels screen · 376
    in app purchases · 367
    interests · 370
    location · 369
    overview · 359
    retention cohorts · 365
    screens · 373
    StreamView screen · 378
    tutorial · 385
    user engagement · 367
    user properties · 361
    user properties screen · 382
android.content.Intent · 125
Anonymous Authentication · 165, 166
    performing · 171
App Indexing · 445
    content indexing · 459
    examples · 449
    indexing personal content · 463
    overview · 445
    personal content · 446, 450
    public content · 445, 449
    removing index entries · 453
    service · 451
    testing · 460
    tutorial · 455
    user actions · 446, 452, 458
ARPPU · 365
ARPU · 365
Audience
    creating · 391
AuthCredential class · 8
Authentication
    account linking · 175
    anonymous · 165
    Callbacks and Activity Results · 142
    Completion Listeners · 91
    customization · 25
    email/password · 11, 71
    error handling · 91

Facebook Login · 49, 117
Failure Listener · 92
Firebase SDK · 10
FirebaseUI Auth · 9
Google Sign-In · 37, 101
overview · 7
Password Reset Option · 82
Phone Number · 67, 155
provider classes · 9
results and callbacks · 124
Security Sensitive Actions · 89
testing · 25
Twitter Sign-In · 137
user account management · 85
authentication providers · 7
Authentication State Listener · 78, 107, 170
AuthUI Instance · 8

B

Blaze plan · 5

C

CCS · 288
child() method · 191
Cloud Connection Server · 288
Cloud Functions · 479
    Analytics functions · 481
    Authentication functions · 479
    Cloud Storage example · 501
    Cloud Storage functions · 482
    create a project · 488
    deploying projects · 489
    external operations · 484
    HTTP example · 489
    HTTP functions · 482
    increasing memory · 506
    overview · 479
    Realtime Database functions · 480
    removing functions · 491
    tutorial · 493
Cloud Messaging · 247
    combined messages · 264
    conversion events · 257
    custom data · 253
    data messages · 264
    Destination Registration Token · 263
    device groups · 271
    example app server · 291
    notification handling · 254
    notification messages · 264
    overview · 247
    registration token · 248
    Sender ID · 281
    service account credentials · 262
    topics · 266
    upstream tutorial · 297
    user segments · 256
Cloud Storage · 305
    buckets · 305
    file deletion · 313
    file metadata · 309
    file upload · 307
    memory data upload · 307
    overview · 305
    rule allow keyword · 319
    rules · 317
    rules if statement · 319
    rules match keyword · 319
    rules structure · 318
    storage references · 305
    stream upload · 307
    transfer monitoring · 308
    tutorial · 325
    Upload task snapshot · 308
    user file security · 323
Code Samples
    downloading · 1
collapseKey · 265
Combined Messages · 264
connect() method · 283
contentAvailable · 265
Conversion Events · 257
createSignInIntentBuilder() method · 19, 31
createUserWithEmailAndPassword() method · 80

D

Data Messages · 264
Data Validation Rules · 210
Database Rule Types · 203
Database Rules
    example of · 228
    structuring · 203
DataSnapshot Object · 196
    extracting data · 198
Destination Registration Token · 263
Device Groups · 271
    creating in Andorid apps · 277
    creating with Node.js · 273

managing · 275
removing devices · 285
requirements · 271
sending messages to · 274
dryRun · 265
Dynamic Links · 415
analytics · 438
automatic activity launching · 437
creating in code · 420
Deep Link URL · 434
detecting at launch time · 432
generating · 434
handling · 422
intent filter · 431
link generation example · 429
overview · 415
receiving · 427
sharing · 421, 430
structure of · 415
testing · 427, 435

E

Email Address
changing · 86
Email/Password Authentication
enabling in console · 15
example project · 11
Firebase SDK · 71
FirebaseUI Auth · 11
Errata · 2
ERROR_ACCOUNT_EXISTS_WITH_DIFFERENT_CREDENTI
AL · 95
ERROR_CREDENTIAL_ALREADY_IN_USE · 95
ERROR_EMAIL_ALREADY_IN_USE · 95
ERROR_INVALID_USER_TOKEN · 95
ERROR_USER_DISABLED · 95
ERROR_USER_NOT_FOUND · 95
ERROR_USER_TOKEN_EXPIRED · 95
Espresso
an overview of · 403
Extensible Messaging and Presence Protocol · 288

F

Facebook App ID · 49
Facebook App Secret · 49
Facebook for Developers portal · 49
Facebook Log Out
detecting · 133

Facebook Login
FirebaseUI Auth · 49
FirebaseUI Auth testing · 56
Facebook LoginButton · 122
Facebook SDK
initialization · 123
Facebook SDK Library · 120
facebook_application_id · 119
fetch() method · 342
Firebase
connecting a project to · 11
foreground notification handling · 254
pricing plans · 5
Firebase Admin SDK
initializing · 263
installing · 261
Firebase Analytics · 359
overview · 359
Firebase authentication
overview · 7
Firebase Authentication
error handling · 91
Firebase CLI · 487
installing · 487
logging in · 487
removing functions · 491
Firebase Cloud
upstream messaging · 287
Firebase Cloud Connection Server · 288
Firebase console
authentication user management · 25
cloud storage management · 315
create new project · 4
database rules · 201
dynamic links · 416
Notifications · 251
performance monitoring · 473
sign in · 3
Test Lab · 408
Firebase Projects
overview · 5
Firebase SDK
email/password authentication · 71
Google Sign-In · 101
user account managment · 85
Firebase Tools
installing · 487
FirebaseAnalytics object · 359
firebase-auth
updating · 156
FirebaseAuth
exception types · 93

FirebaseAuth Error Codes · 95
FirebaseAuth Instance · 8
   getting reference to · 77
FirebaseAuthInvalidCredentialsException · 94
FirebaseAuthInvalidUserException · 93, 95
FirebaseAuthRecentLoginRequiredException · 94
FirebaseAuthUserCollisionException · 94, 95
FirebaseAuthWeakPasswordException · 94
FirebaseDatabase class · 189
FirebaseMessagingService · 254
FirebaseRemoteConfig object · 340
FirebaseUI Auth · 9
   adding a logo · 34
   customization · 32
   deleting an account · 23
   dependencies · 14
   email/password sign-in · 11
   Facebook Login · 49
   FirebaseUI Auth · 61
   Google Sign In · 37
   initialization · 17
   Phone authentication · 67
   sign in handling · 21
   signing in with · 18
   signing out · 22
   testing · 25
FirebaseUser class · 8, 21
Flame plan · 5

G

Game Loop Testing · 394
getBucket() method · 306
getBytesTransferred() method · 309
getChildrenCount() method · 198
getConfigSettings() method · 348
getCredential() method · 8, 132, 155
getCurrentUser() method · 8
getCustomMetadataKeys() method · 312
getDownloadUrl() method · 309
getError() method · 309
getExtras() method · 253
getInvitation() method · 424
getKey() method · 199, 213
getLastFetchStatus() method · 347
getMetadata() method · 309
getNotification() method · 255
getParent() method · 306
getProviderData() method · 178
getReason() method · 94
getRef() method · 197

getReference() method · 190
getRoot() method · 306
getStorage() method · 309
getTask() method · 309
getToken() method · 250
getTotalByteCount() method · 309
getUploadSessionUri() method · 309, 314
Google API Client
   initializing · 109
Google Play Authentication Library · 103
Google Sign-in
   profile photo · 43
Google Sign-In
   enabling in Firebase console · 39
   Firebase SDK · 101
   FirebaseUI Auth · 37
   FirebaseUi Auth initialization · 40
   testing · 41
GoogleApiClient · 109, 114
GoogleSignInAccount · 113
GoogleSignInOptions · 109

H

hasChild() method · 198
hasChildren() method · 197, 198

I

incrementCounter() method · 472
Indexing Rules · 211
Instrumentation Testing · 394, 403
   taking screenshots · 409
   tutorial · 403
Invites
   creating · 441
   handling · 443
   sending · 442
   testing · 444
isDeveloperModeEnabled() method · 348
isEmailVerified() method · 89

J

Jabber · 288
JSON
   an overview of · 181

K

keytool command-line tool · 37

L

linkWithCredential() method · 177

M

Material design · 32
Moshi · 292
mutableContent · 265

N

Node.js · 259
    device groups · 273
    initializing and configuring · 260
    installation · 260
    overview · 259
NoSQL database · 181
Notification Handling
    foreground · 254
Notification Messages · 264
Notifications
    receiving · 252
    sending to device · 251
npm tool · 260

O

OAuth Redirect URI · 52
Okio · 292
onChildAdded() callback method · 215
onChildChanged() callback method · 215
onChildMoved() callback method · 215
onChildRemoved() callback method · 215
onCodeAutoRetrievalTimeOut() method · 155
onCodeSent() method · 155
onConnectionFailed() method · 111
onFailure() method · 92
onVerificationCompleted() method · 155
onVerificationFailed() method · 155
openssl tool · 53

P

Password reset email
    modifying · 28
Performance Monitoring · 469
    custom traces · 471
    disabling · 476
    enabling logcat · 472
    overview · 469
Phone Number Authentication
    enabling · 67
    overview · 155
    testing · 68
Phone Number Sign-in · 67
PhoneAuthActivity class · 157
    verification callbacks · 159
PhoneAuthCredential object · 161
PhoneAuthProvider class · 155
Pricing Plans · 5
priority · 265
Promise · 483
push() Method · 213
putBytes() method · 307
putFile() method · 307
putStream() method · 307

Q

queryValueListener · 217

R

Realtime database
    Database Rule Types · 203
Realtime Database · 181
    $ Variables · 207
    adding to project · 186
    child node access · 191
    data storage · 181
    data types · 185
    data validation rules · 210
    database reference · 189
    deep nesting · 184
    deleting data · 193
    detect value changes · 195
    error handling · 194
    handling user data · 183
    Indexing Rules · 211
    Java object storage · 192

list queries · 216
list query example · 233
list tutorial · 233
lists · 213
nesting data · 182
offline handling · 188
overview · 181
predefined variables · 208
querying and indexes · 218
read into Java object · 199
reading data · 195
Rules · 201
securing user data · 206
snapshots · 196
tutorial · 219
write to multiple nodes · 192
writing to · 189, 190
reauthenticate() method · 89
Registration Token
obtaining · 299
Release Key Hash · 53
Remote Config · 339
fetching parameters · 342
in-app parameters · 340
overview · 339
remote parameters · 341
server-side parameters · 341
status information · 347
tutorial · 349
removeValue() method · 193
requestEmail() method · 151
requestIdToken() method · 279
Robo Test
view results · 398
Robo Testing · 393
tutorial · 395
RuleDataSnapShot methods · 208

S

Screenshotter Library · 409
Secure Action Exceptions · 96
Security Sensitive Actions · 89
sendCode() method · 159
sendEmailVerification() method · 88
Sender ID · 281
sendMessage() method · 303
sendPasswordResetEmail() method · 82
sendToDevice() method · 265
sendToDeviceGroup() method · 274
Service Account Credentials · 262

setConfigSettings() method · 343
setCustomMetadata() method · 312
setDefaults() method · 340
setError() method · 80
setIsSmartLockEnabled() method · 31
setLogo() method · 34
setPerformanceCollectionEnabled() method · 476
setTheme() method · 34
setUserProperty() method · 361
setValue() method · 191, 214
SHA-1 Fingerprint
obtaining · 37
SHA-1 Fingerprint Key
entering in Firebase console · 102
signInAnonymously() method · 166, 172
signInWithCredential() method · 132, 155
signInWithEmail() method · 92, 94
signInWithEmailAndPassword() method · 82, 93
signInWithPhoneCredential() method · 161
Smack · 291
Smackx · 291
Smart Lock
enabling · 31
Spark plan · 5
Storage Reference
properties · 306
Storage References · 305
subscribeToTopic() method · 267

T

test dimensions · 393
test execution · 393
Test Lab · 393
overview · 393
test matrix · 393
then() · 483
timeToLive · 265
Topic Conditions · 269
Topics · 266
Twitter access token · 63
Twitter API Keys · 62
Twitter App
creating · 62
Twitter Application Management console · 62
Twitter Library
add dependency · 138
Twitter Login Button · 140
Twitter SDK · 137
Twitter Sign-In · 61
enabling · 61

Enabling Email Address Permission · 151
initialization · 141
library dependecies · 65
Requesting the User's Email Address · 151

U

unlink() method · 178
unsubscribeFromTopic() method · 267
updateChildren() method · 192
updateEmail() method · 86
updateMetadata() method · 313
updatePassword() method · 87
updateProfile() method · 85
UploadTask.Snapshot · 309
Upstream Message
    sending · 289, 303
Upstream Messaging · 287
    architecture · 287
User Account

deleting · 88
User Email
    verifying · 88
User Password
    changing · 87
User Segments · 256
User's Profile Information · 85
UserProfileChangeRequest object · 85

V

val() method · 209
verifyPhoneNumber() method · 155, 159

X

XML Pull · 292
XMPP · 288

Made in the USA
Middletown, DE
12 March 2018